T0312073

SEEMED LIKE A GOOD IDEA

Consumers, public officials, and even managers of health care and insurance are unhappy about care quality, access, and costs. This book shows that is because efforts to do something about these problems often rely on hope or conjecture, not rigorous evidence of effectiveness. In this book, experts in the field separate the speculative from the proven with regard to how care is rendered, how patients can be in control, how providers should be paid, and how disparities can be reduced – and they also identify the issues for which evidence is currently missing. It provides an antidote to frustration and a clear-eyed guide for forward progress, helping health care and insurance innovators make better decisions on deciding whether to go ahead now based on current evidence, to seek and wait for additional evidence, or to move on to different ideas. It will be useful to practitioners in hospital systems, medical groups, and insurance organizations and can also be used in executive and MBA teaching.

MARK PAULY is Bendheim Professor in the Department of Health Care Management at the Wharton School at the University of Pennsylvania.

FLAURA WINSTON is Professor of Pediatrics and Distinguished Chair in the Department of Pediatrics, Perelman School of Medicine, University of Pennsylvania. She is Director of the Innovation Ecosystem and Scientific Co-Director of the Center for Injury Research and Prevention, Children's Hospital of Philadelphia, PA, and is a member of the National Academy of Medicine.

MARY NAYLOR is Marian S. Ware Professor in Gerontology and Director of the NewCourtland Center for Transitions and Health at the University of Pennsylvania School of Nursing.

KEVIN VOLPP is Director of the Center for Health Incentives and Behavioral Economics, Health Policy Division Chief of the Department of Medical Ethics and Health Policy, and the Founders President's Distinguished Professor of Medicine, Medical Ethics and Policy, and Health Care Management, at the Perelman School of Medicine and the Wharton School, all at the University of Pennsylvania.

LAWTON ROBERT BURNS is James Joo-Jin Kim Professor of Health Care Management at the Wharton School and Co-Director of the Roy & Diana Vagelos Program in Life Sciences and Management, all at the University of Pennsylvania.

RALPH MULLER is former Chief Executive Officer (CEO) of the University of Pennsylvania Health System.

DAVID ASCH is John Morgan Professor at the Perelman School of Medicine and the Wharton School and Executive Director of the Center for Health Care Innovation at Penn Medicine.

RACHEL WERNER is the Executive Director of the Leonard Davis Institute of Health Economics, Professor of Medicine at the Perelman School of Medicine, and the Robert D. Eilers Professor of Health Care Management at the Wharton School, all at the University of Pennsylvania.

BIMAL DESAI is Assistant Vice President and Chief Health Informatics Officer at Children's Hospital of Philadelphia and Associate Professor of Clinical Pediatrics, Perelman School of Medicine, University of Pennsylvania.

KRISDA CHAIYACHATI is Assistant Professor, Medicine, at the Perelman School of Medicine and a senior fellow at the Leonard Davis Institute of Health Economics at the University of Pennsylvania as well as Medical Director, Penn Medicine OnDemand Virtual Care (telemedicine).

BENJAMIN CHARTOCK is a doctoral candidate in the Department of Health Care Management at the Wharton School, University of Pennsylvania.

Seemed Like a Good Idea

Alchemy versus Evidence-Based Approaches to Health Care Management Innovation

MARK PAULY

Wharton School of the University of Pennsylvania

FLAURA WINSTON

Children's Hospital of Philadelphia

MARY NAYLOR

University of Pennsylvania School of Nursing

KEVIN VOLPP

University of Pennsylvania Health System

LAWTON ROBERT BURNS

Wharton School of the University of Pennsylvania

RALPH MULLER

University of Pennsylvania Health System

DAVID ASCH

University of Pennsylvania School of Medicine

RACHEL WERNER

University of Pennsylvania School of Medicine

BIMAL DESAI

University of Pennsylvania School of Medicine

KRISDA CHAIYACHATI

University of Pennsylvania School of Medicine

BENJAMIN CHARTOCK

Wharton School of the University of Pennsylvania

CAMBRIDGE
UNIVERSITY PRESS

CAMBRIDGE
UNIVERSITY PRESS

University Printing House, Cambridge CB2 8BS, United Kingdom

One Liberty Plaza, 20th Floor, New York, NY 10006, USA

477 Williamstown Road, Port Melbourne, VIC 3207, Australia

314–321, 3rd Floor, Plot 3, Splendor Forum, Jasola District Centre, New Delhi – 110025, India

103 Penang Road, #05-06/07, Visioncrest Commercial, Singapore 238467

Cambridge University Press is part of the University of Cambridge.

It furthers the University's mission by disseminating knowledge in the pursuit of education, learning, and research at the highest international levels of excellence.

www.cambridge.org
Information on this title: www.cambridge.org/9781316519035
DOI: 10.1017/9781009004534

© Mark Pauly, Kevin Volpp, Ralph Muller, Rachel Werner, Mary Naylor, Flaura Winston, Lawton Robert Burns, Bimal Desai, Krisda Chaiyachati, Benjamin Chartock and David Asch 2022

First published 2022

A catalogue record for this publication is available from the British Library.

Library of Congress Cataloging-in-Publication Data
Names: Pauly, Mark, 1941– author.
Title: Seemed like a good idea : alchemy versus evidence-based approaches to healthcare management innovation / Mark Pauly, Wharton School of the University of Pennsylvania [and 10 others].
Description: New York, NY : Cambridge University Press, [2022] | Includes index.
Identifiers: LCCN 2021060099 (print) | LCCN 2021060100 (ebook) | ISBN 9781316519035 (hardback) | ISBN 9781009001274 (paperback) | ISBN 9781009004534 (epub)
Subjects: LCSH: Evidence-based medicine. | Health services administration. | BISAC: BUSINESS & ECONOMICS / Entrepreneurship
Classification: LCC R723.7 .P38 2022 (print) | LCC R723.7 (ebook) | DDC 610.68–dc23/eng/ 20220216
LC record available at https://lccn.loc.gov/2021060099
LC ebook record available at https://lccn.loc.gov/2021060100

ISBN 978-1-316-51903-5 Hardback
ISBN 978-1-009-00127-4 Paperback

Contents

Figures

Contributors

David Asch, John Morgan Professor at the Perelman School of Medicine and the Wharton School, and Executive Director of the University of Pennsylvania Medicine Center for Health Care Innovation

Lawton Robert Burns, James Joo-Jin Kim Professor of Health Care Management at the Wharton School, and Co-Director of the Roy & Diana Vagelos Program in Life Sciences and Management, all at the University of Pennsylvania

Krisda H. Chaiyachati, Assistant Professor of Medicine at the Perelman School of Medicine and a Senior Fellow at the Leonard Davis Institute of Health Economics at the University of Pennsylvania, as well as Medical Director, Penn Medicine OnDemand Virtual Care (telemedicine)

Benjamin Chartock, Doctoral Student in the Department of Health Care Management at the Wharton School, University of Pennsylvania

Bimal Desai, Assistant Vice President and Chief Health Informatics Officer at Children's Hospital of Philadelphia and Clinical Associate Professor of Pediatrics, Perelman School of Medicine, University of Pennsylvania

Ralph Muller, former Chief Executive Officer (CEO) of the University of Pennsylvania Health System

Mary Naylor, Marian S. Ware Professor in Gerontology and Director of the NewCourtland Center for Transitions and Health at the University of Pennsylvania School of Nursing

Mark Pauly, Bendheim Professor in the Department of Health Care Management at the Wharton School of the University of Pennsylvania

Kevin Volpp, Director of the Center for Health Incentives and Behavioral Economics, Health Policy Division Chief of the Department of Medical Ethics and Health Policy, and the Founder's Presidential Distinguished Professor of Medicine, Medical Ethics and Policy, and Health Care Management at the Perelman School of Medicine and the Wharton School, all at the University of Pennsylvania

Rachel Werner, Executive Director of the Leonard Davis Institute of Health Economics, Professor of Medicine at the University of Pennsylvania Perelman School of Medicine, and the Robert D. Eilers Professor of Health Care Management at the Wharton School

Flaura Winston, Professor of Pediatrics and Distinguished Chair in the Department of Pediatrics, University of Pennsylvania Perelman School of Medicine, Director at Innovation Ecosystem, Scientific Co-Director at the Center for Injury Research and Prevention, Children's Hospital of Philadelphia, and member of the National Academy of Medicine

Preface

This book grew out of conversation among senior faculty and administrators from the University of Pennsylvania (Penn)'s Wharton School, School of Nursing, and Perelman School of Medicine and Health System, as well as the Children's Hospital of Philadelphia, all part of the Leonard Davis Institute of Health Economics at Penn, which transformed into an informal seminar – in person at first and then virtual due to the pandemic. The subject was our disappointment at the relative neglect by real-world decision-makers in health systems and health insurers of our major product – rigorous research findings on the effectiveness (or lack thereof) of managerial and financial interventions in health care. There was also an acute awareness among the group of experts that clinical research results were required for the approval and use of drugs and devices and were disseminated widely, while equally consequential interventions in management – whether published in peer-reviewed journals or developed in the health system's innovation center – were not required and were less well disseminated.

In the course of writing these chapters, we found evidence of innovations for many of the problems identified, but more commonly we found a lack of evidence. We also found, however, reasons why the need for evidence should be less compelling when the production of evidence is costly or time consuming. We hope we have provided a comprehensive picture of what evidence there is on some crucial issues in health care and insurance management, as well as how it is or is not used. Current focus on implementation of effective interventions adds to our hope that this story will matter for the US health care system going forward, as will our own observations on managerial decision-making and the determination of when evidence is enough for good choices.

In this effort we were greatly assisted by many people, and enumerating everyone who helped make this book a reality would be too enormous a task. However, we would like to call out a few individuals who went above and beyond to help turn a few good ideas into a fully-fledged book. Tina Horowitz of the Wharton School Department of Health Care Management provided invaluable guidance, sifted through literally hundreds of references, and looked at drafts at various stages of writing. Chris Tachibana and Peter Stokes provided thoughtful, critical, and timely editorial feedback. University of Pennsylvania students Harriet Jeon, Sasmira Matta, and Brianna Carvalho provided comments as well. Doctoral student Ben Chartock helped to marshal the whole operation, coordinating among many authors and navigating the process of weaving together experts of various backgrounds and areas of knowledge. Finally, we thank Valerie Appleby of Cambridge University Press, without whom this book would not have come into existence.

We hope that readers find enjoyment and insight in the accompanying pages. If we have moved the needle at all, it is only by standing on the shoulders of those who provided the evidence we summarize and whose use we encourage. And the usual caveat applies: all errors are our own.

Baseline Observations

Mark Pauly

INTRODUCTION

Over the last 40 years, spending on both hospital and physician services in the United States has inexorably increased, often faster than gross domestic product (GDP) or any other aggregate measure. In contrast to industries such as computer software, hospitality, sports and recreation – where spending has also grown faster than the economy – health care spending growth is not thought to be matched by increased customer or patient satisfaction or improved outcomes. For some groups, especially those that are socially disadvantaged or lower income, measures of health have remained stubbornly lower relative to the rest of the population. Despite continuous criticism of the status quo and calls for transformation, little has changed. Why has this sector of the economy uniquely resisted changes in products, productivity, and services aimed at improving consumer satisfaction or reducing spending growth?

It is not from a lack of discussion about the need for change, or a shortage of proposals with promising ideas for change. Armies of innovation promoters, often speaking a special language of their own that is foreign to the language of health care, have descended upon the industry. They bring shiny new technologies and services that lack evidence, resulting in little improvement and much misdirection. While these promoters have succeeded in raising the alarm that major changes are coming, so far the transformation they promise has not worked to produce detectable improvements.

The claim and substance of this book is, fundamentally:

Health care in the United States needs help, and evidence can provide that help.

Some of the problems in health care are the result of investments in unsubstantiated – and often costly – innovations. At the same time this practice is rampant, investment in and implementation of evidence-based, effective innovations in the delivery of hospital and medical services appears to have lagged. This situation must change, and this book is a call to action to provide the evidence needed to support that change. Where there is underuse and misuse of evidence, our goal is to find out why that happens and propose ways to change things.

THE PROBLEM

In contrast to our past, and to the rest of the world, US health outcomes are now more resistant to improvement despite health care spending outpacing all measures of national income growth. This unchanging pattern is especially unsettling in light of the striking advancements and discoveries in human biology and clinical medicine. While it is true that in recent decades we have seen cures for diseases that were previously considered incurable, the combination of social and environmental problems that have worsened health and our inability to improve the efficiency of care delivery is distressing. In health care, in both the economic and public health spheres, things were not going well even before the novel coronavirus appeared, and there is little reason to believe that they will improve even after the pandemic is controlled. Attempts to improve the fundamentals of equitable and efficient care delivery through evidence-based care have faltered. There is reason to believe that effective, evidence-based interventions to lower spending growth and improve outcomes exist – and these should guide health care management strategies that, in turn, should promote strategies that prevent or minimize known potential negative effects on equity or cost. At a minimum, we need to see what interventions can do more harm than good. We also need to see if the problem of absence of evidence for the effectiveness of innovations is getting worse. Particularly regarding innovations in health care and insurance management, has the use of evidence eroded in favor of fad, fashion, or a misdirected need to do something, even if it is unproven? This book will provide the answers to such questions.

Thankfully, the management story is not all gloom and doom. There have been bright spots of innovations in care delivery that lower cost and improve outcomes, or at least accomplish one of those tasks without affecting the other. There is considerable interest in implementing programs that generate such innovations. Not only can we make better use of new scientific discoveries with better management, but we can also discover innovative ways to manage the technology we currently have that go beyond the buzzwords of "leadership" and "cultural change" to produce improvements.

However, frustrations still persist. Many of the demonstrated improvements have languished without adoption and dissemination. Instead of investing in programs with strong evidence of effectiveness, managers instead opt for unproven programs backed only by plausible stories, often because they require less investment or are easier to deliver, but sometimes even when they have substantial, known upfront costs. Through both trying to spend less than what is known to be needed and spending more on efforts not known to be effective, resources are wasted. Moreover, the benefits of past programs that worked when piloted on a smaller scale do not yet add up to noteworthy changes in aggregate measures of spending growth and quality improvement. Too often, they get overtaken by the tide of more spending with less improvement, and so poor overall performance rolls on.

THIS BOOK

Our goal with this book is to contribute to understanding and to potentially improve the use of evidence in management decisions about innovative interventions. Before we offer remedies, we first tackle the task of describing the use or nonuse of evidence in decision-making around innovation in health care management by everyone from top-level systems managers, insurers, line managers, and employers buying insurance on behalf of their workers to physicians and other health professionals acting collectively or individually. We then attempt to explain the current trends in evidence use – when evidence is sought, how it is responded to when it appears, and what happens if it is impossible to obtain. We describe how decisions come about with and without evidence and evaluate whether evidence is currently generated and used in the most efficient ways. We take a neutral position, noting that the usefulness of evidence is context dependent, and that at times it does not pay to incur the cost to obtain or consume evidence (though accurate information that falls in your lap by chance is often of value, too). Finally, we address the challenge of deciding whether and when better evidence should be sought and how that evidence should be used. Here again we are neutral and acknowledge that there are multiple ways to generate more useful evidence for managers and methods to ensure it is used properly. As noted above, we pay particular attention to evidence (or its absence) for innovations in health care spanning clinical, managerial, and financial decisions.

We offer as much evidence as we can muster on the big strategy questions: How much gain is possible with better use of evidence in the most important places? Are there areas where gains have already been exhausted? Is the cost-quality relationship in health care as good as it is going to get? We try to be optimistic and offer some innovative ideas that come from our review, along with sage advice about what to do when the only thing you know is that no one knows.

RUNNING DOWN THE COMPETITION

Are there alternatives to the development and use of novel evidence that could lower spending growth and/or improve health care outcomes? A common answer is to change leadership or culture. There is evidence, mostly from the education setting where outcomes are measured by student test scores, that variation in school performance can be attributed to differences in their leadership and/or culture – the principal, the administration, and the morale among the teaching staff.

Indeed, there are similar opinions even in the literature on evidence-based health care that the most important key to progress and improvement is getting the right people to implement the best evidence-based new programs, though that is not always clear.[1] However, while we acknowledge the role of leadership and culture, we plan to resist the temptation to go for these nostrums for two reasons: inability to measure leadership/culture, and a shortage of good leaders. Leadership and culture are often hard to measure objectively, and so are inferred from observations after the fact. Entities with the best performance are almost always identified retrospectively, and the leaders who presided over their performance (and therefore must have led it) are named as heroes. They are given credit for wise leadership and for building a relationship with and among their workers that is happy, satisfying, and productive. A prospective study identifying organizations with good leadership beforehand and then seeing which kinds do better is rare.

The problem is that the production process for leadership and culture is not known and surely constrained. Many people talk about how to develop someone into a leader of the workers who will implement an organization's

---

[1] Kovner, A. R., and D'Aunno, T. A. (2017). *Evidence-Based Management in Healthcare: Principles, Cases, and Perspectives.* Chicago: Health Administration Press.

culture, and yet we are always confronted by a shortage of good leaders. Further, changing culture at all levels in an organization is hard. Often there are limited numbers of potential workers who will fit an organization's culture, and an even smaller number of gifted leaders – it is hard to mold people to an organizational culture when they have divergent or different cultural preconditioning.

The upshot is that this book will focus more on health interventions with documented effectiveness for improving outcomes and the implementation strategies that were necessary for the adoption of evidence. We will talk about the role of leadership and culture in the context of evidence-based programs that change leadership and culture for the better. Prospective efforts to produce great leaders or otherwise alter things for the better are on the same footing with organizational changes in systems or behavioral changes in insurance buyers, patients, and physicians – all of which are also hard to change. These efforts are worth a look – but a skeptical one. What is crucial, however, is sound decision-making by leaders based on evidence (whenever possible) and clear concepts of costs and benefits (and knowledge of who will bear the costs and receive the benefits). Recognizing that there will always be "unknown unknowns," applying the existing evidence base can reduce uncertainty and de-risk new concepts, but judgment will always be needed. In addition, leaders in innovative implementation must recognize the required culture change that starts with clear bidirectional communication that will facilitate buy-in from frontline staff who will be responsible for change, as well as the population of patients who will be affected by it.

AN EXAMPLE OF CHALLENGES IN DETERMINING THE BEST USE OF INFORMATION: MEDICARE'S HOSPITAL READMISSION REDUCTION PROGRAM

In 2012, the Obama Administration and Centers for Medicare and Medicaid Services (CMS) wanted to show that it was possible to simultaneously implement health reform, reduce spending, and improve quality. Efforts to achieve that goal had been strongly encouraged by the Medicare Payment Advisory Committee (MedPAC) to CMS, which proposed reducing hospital readmissions as a way to achieve all three. Both CMS and MedPAC lobbied for the Medicare Hospital Readmission Reduction Program (HRRP) in the Affordable Care Act to financially penalize hospitals with higher than expected readmission rates. It was generally agreed that a high rate of readmissions adjusted for risk was a sign of poor quality in a hospital, other things being equal. Readmission meant that the hospital's first effort to cure or stabilize a patient failed, and another costly attempt was necessary. The conclusion that fewer readmissions would save money was thought to be obvious. The conclusion that fewer readmissions would result in improved health outcomes followed from the definition of quality of care. There was evidence that other extant programs successfully achieved such outcomes; there was no evidence that financial penalties would cause all hospitals to choose to implement those programs.

Many hospitals did have readmission rates above what would have been expected based on their patient risk (though perhaps not based on the social vulnerability of those patients). However, there was little evidence that the hospitals affected by penalties would choose the best or least harmful methods if they did try to respond. Still, Congress proceeded with HRRP legislation, without waiting for evidence of effectiveness or safety from the policy it contained.[2]

The intervention relied on using financial penalties to offset what were viewed as distorted incentives to hospitals. After all, under Medicare's diagnosis-related group (DRG) based payment system, a hospital readmission meant more revenue and potentially more profit if the payment was above the hospital's marginal or opportunity cost. The relatively modest penalty at least reduced the financial reward even if it did not necessarily turn it into a loss. Why some hospitals responded to these incentives while others did not was also unknown. To make hospitals comparable, each admission was adjusted by Medicare's risk score (for higher risk and more costly patients within a DRG).

In all, there were some valid reasons why this policy seemed like a good idea at the time, even if not all analysts were in favor then and many have subsequently become more critical. Given what was known at the time, the policy was not unreasonable on its face – but it was risky. The need to make a good showing on what had been labeled the "Triple Aim"[3] (health care cost, quality, and access) – and the logic behind the financial and clinical arguments – won, and the program was implemented nationwide without a control group.

The initial results following implementation of this new program in October 2012 were striking. Almost immediately, the risk-adjusted

[2] James, J. (2013). Medicare hospital readmissions reduction program. *Health Affairs*, 34(2), 1–5.

[3] Berwick, D. M., Nolan, T. W., and Whittington, J. (2008) The triple aim: Care, health, and cost. *Health Affairs*, 27(3)(May/June), 759–769.

readmission rate fell, and eventually fell by 22 percent.[4] In fact, the rate had begun to fall for several years prior to the initiation of the program (or even the passage of the legislation). In addition, the measured readmission rate fell significantly just after the penalty went into effect, implying that opportunities to respond had been developed, stored away, and were able to be scheduled and implemented quickly.

Subsequent research has raised issues about the effectiveness of HRRP for spending reductions and health outcomes. Cutler et al. (2019)[5] noted that the onset of the penalty coincided with significant changes in the measured risk of hospitals subject to the penalty. These researchers speculate that there may have been no change in readmission behavior in such hospitals, but rather a change in risk that affected readmissions that would account for more as it was instituted, as well as linked improvements in mortality.

Some studies also found suggestive – though far from conclusive – evidence that the 30-day mortality rate may have risen soon after the program took effect at impacted hospitals.[6] These hospitals substituted longer stays in the emergency department ("observation stays") or transfers to post-acute care facilities for readmissions, and researchers inferred that death was more likely in such settings than if the patient had been readmitted as an inpatient. However, the 45-day mortality rate was unaffected, suggesting that any benefit from readmission was a few more days of survival. Thus, there was no rigorous prior evidence on the benefits and risks of HRRP, while subsequent evidence suggests that cost reduction may have been less than initially estimated and some adverse health outcomes may have occurred. In contrast, recent analysis by Gupta finds that the program did account for the bulk of the reduction in readmissions and was associated with some improvements in mortality rates.[7]

Hindsight cannot directly determine what should have been done. However, had this information been available at the outset, would

[4] Zuckerman, R. B., Sheingold, S. H., Orav, E. J. et al. (2016). Readmissions, observation, and the hospital readmissions reduction program. *New England Journal of Medicine*, 374(16), 1543–1551.

[5] Ody, C., Msall, L., Dafny, L. S. et al. (2019). Decreases in readmissions credited to Medicare's program to reduce hospital readmissions have been overstated. *Health Affairs*, 38(1), 36–43.

[6] Krumholz, H. M., Lin, Z., Keenan, P. S. et al. (2013). Relationship between hospital readmission and mortality rates for patients hospitalized with acute myocardial infarction, heart failure, or pneumonia. *JAMA*, 309(6), 587–593.

[7] Gupta, A. (2021). Impacts of performance pay for hospitals: The Readmissions Reduction Program. *American Economic Review*, 111(4), 1241–1283.

Medicare's managerial decision have been different? One question pertains to the perceived likelihood of what actually happened at the time of implementation: How likely was it that the program would have gone off without a hitch? No one knows the answer. There were no prior estimates of cost savings that informed the decision. The threat of worsening mortality rates was discounted based on the observation that low readmission hospitals did not have significantly worse outcomes. The possibility that hospitals differed in managerial skills and styles rather than responsiveness to financial incentives was not considered.

We may be able to provide some information on yet another question: Would recommendations for HRRP have gone ahead if decision-makers knew in advance it might lead to an increase in short-term mortality and only moderate cost savings? Would evidence suggesting this possibility have been enough to influence the decision? This is the larger question at play here – as is the question of whether gathering such information by a prior trial rather than by before-and-after observations with no controls would have been worth the time delay and the research costs.

In this initiative, we do not believe that the answer is obvious because we do not know how decision-makers would value these trade-offs. But this example does show the preventive benefits as well as the need for a study to provide prior evidence in decisions about program initiation.

Would having this information, or better and more reliable information, have changed the decision to implement HRRP? The embarrassment of demonstrating worse health outcomes might have been the deciding factor. How much worse would the outcome had to have been, and how firm would the evidence need to be?

This example illustrates several points that will be further discussed in this book: (1) If good information on the effectiveness of an intervention can be obtained with limited time or resource investment, decisions will be improved; (2) However, information obtained at great cost and time will be of limited value unless unanticipated side effects and outcomes are found that would change substantially the estimated or suspected balance between costs and benefits; (3) Regardless, the importance placed on the costs and benefits will drive decisions. In the case of HRRP, If developments after implementation proxy what would have been found with evidence development, it is not certain that the adoption decision would have been different.

The primary conclusion is that the key factor is an "unknown unknown." What impacts are likely to be turned up by better evidence as compared to current evidence? Some decision-maker has to make an estimate of this factor, but the task will be challenging.

CORONAVIRUS 2020

The onset of the novel coronavirus epidemic has exacerbated the improper and controversial use of evidence in decision-making. This new threat to health has increased ("exponentially," as they say) the number of impending decisions, of which a large share rely on evidence that is either absent or inconclusive. Swift decisions have had to be made without gold standard, randomized controlled trial evidence, given the novelty of the virus. Throughout the health care system, protocols have been overturned, drugs have been redirected, and conjectures about what does or does not seem like a good idea for management or treatment have proliferated.

With the novel coronavirus, the model of obtaining rigorous evidence before decision-making has been seriously and appropriately challenged by the immediacy of making crucial decisions about new drugs, new uses for old drugs, changes in care provision, and the need for staff protection. The decision model we will describe in this book can be used to guide best practices in this or any bad situation – and it will yield the common-sense conclusion that neither waiting for bulletproof evidence nor going on a hunch will be optimal. The case for the strongest model of evidence-based decision-making, such as that used by the US Food and Drug Administration, will need to be modified.

The dust still has to settle on a tumultuous period made worse by partisan criticism. Some innovations will turn out to be mistakes, others that work will have been delayed too long, and much will remain unknown and unresolved. We intend to avoid advocacy and criticism, but inevitably, in a world where politicians assume positions without appropriate facts, the actual rigorous research will dispel some of those positions. Moreover, the subjective nature of decisions when neither facts nor probabilities are known – situations of true (or, in the title of a recent book, "radical")[8] uncertainty mean that differences of opinion that cannot be settled by "science" will necessarily remain. We will use and describe the use of as much evidence as possible to circumscribe the limits on reasonable differences of opinion. After that, readers will have to make their own bets on which sources of evidence and authoritative speculation to trust.

---

[8] Kay, J., and King, M. (2020). *Radical Uncertainty: Decision-Making beyond the Numbers*. New York: W. W. Norton & Company.

OUTLINE OF THE BOOK

The next two chapters provide general observations on the "unknown unknowns" problem. One chapter looks at aggregate data on spending levels, growth, outcome levels, and changes over time. It asks what evidence we currently have for these patterns, and what evidence remains conjectural. It further questions how to relate decisions on specific innovations to the visible, although sometimes misleading, aggregate patterns. Can we relate the trends in total spending to reports on transformations that have lowered spending without harming health care quality – or is there no connection? The next chapter models the managerial problem of when to seek more rigorous information on the likely outcome of an intervention. It then goes on to discuss the subsequent question of how to respond to that information. It concludes with the issue of how to tell after the fact whether better information helped.

The remaining chapters are case studies of particular classes of decisions where information has or has not been available and/or used. In each case, the core question is: Given a set of decisions to be made, would those decisions have been different and/or better had they been made with more (or less) rigorous evidence? The goal here is to draw conclusive statements in each case about "evidence on the role of evidence" in this particular setting, or, if not to provide statements about actual evidence, at least offer a discussion of reasonable expectations about how much benefit there was or would have been from better evidence – and how that compares with the cost of that evidence. We think it is important for leaders in health care management and policy to be convinced that there is a problem with a lack of good evidence for decisions they make on innovations in care delivery and financing. Once they decide no good evidence exists, it is important to identify where that problem is most severe. But in addition to this task, we will offer ideas on what can be done – some based themselves on evidence of interventions that have worked or on efforts that have identified the blockages in obtaining and using evidence. Other ideas are generated based on the logical diagnosis of the malfunction and sensible correctives. There are informed actions that can be taken, and we will tell you what they are.

Evidence and Growth in Aggregate Spending and Changes in Health Outcomes

Where Has the Battleship Been Going, and How Can We Turn It?

Mark Pauly and Benjamin Chartock

INTRODUCTION

A trite, if apt, metaphor for the American health care and insurance system is a battleship that has been sailing in a particular direction for many years, with many of us as free riders in a direction we do not prefer. That direction is characterized by spending growth that outpaces virtually any other sectoral trend in the economy, and by quality and outcome measures that, at best, improve little and, at worst, deteriorate. The battleship takes up 18 percent of gross domestic product (GDP), furnishes employment to nearly 15 percent of the workforce, and consumes a large share of federal and state governmental budgets (Figure 2.1). Even if we could figure out how to cut the power, this dreadnought would continue to coast in the same direction for the foreseeable future. The obvious conclusion is that it has been and will continue to be hard to turn the vessel to go in a different direction. As of this writing, the novel coronavirus pandemic has affected the use of care as well, putting many "normal" services on hold to accommodate sick patients. And while it is too early to conclusively confirm the effect of the pandemic on spending trends, there is likely to be an effect (although even the direction is not known). Once the pandemic stabilizes, consumption of health care services will probably not return exactly to past behaviors, but there will be a strong tendency to slide back. What might help to avoid doing so, and most importantly, what evidence can be currently offered or generated to support efforts to change course?

To understand the causes for the persistent prepandemic health care trends, we need to go behind the total or aggregated numbers. For health spending to grow, either the number of units consumed or the price per

Historical health spending

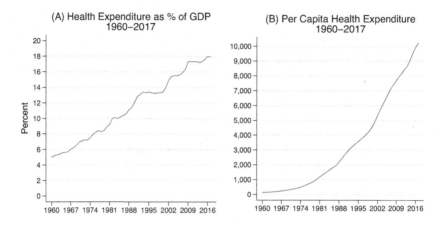

Spending Data from CMS National Health Expenditure Accounts (NHEA) Historical Data, Measured in Current Dollars

Figure 2.1. Historical health spending

unit has to grow. With respect to changes in health outcomes per person, either the types of persons or the outcomes they experience have to change. In this book, we will engage in the accounting exercise of asking which types of care, which prices or costs, and which populations experienced undesirable changes in these factors in recent years. But we must look further for an explanation of what caused each of these components to change – a much more challenging and uncertain enterprise.

INNOVATIONS AND THEIR EFFECTS

Almost all of the changes developed by health care stakeholders to reduce spending growth or improve outcomes have been limited, almost by necessity, by either geography or by scope. For example, reorganizations of medical delivery systems by a single organization such as Geisinger Health System or Intermountain Healthcare can affect provision of care only to the people those systems serve, a tiny fraction of the US population (see Chapter 7). Attempts by a national organization such as the American College of Physicians to reduce or eliminate specific low-value physician services are limited to those services, a tiny fraction of spending on all physician services, which itself is small relative to spending by hospitals. The Transitional Care Model (Chapter 5) produced a net reduction in spending on hospital readmission and post-acute services, but payment for readmissions is a small part of Medicare spending, and the fraction of the population transitioning from hospital to home in a given year is small.

Nevertheless, one might hope that programs like these that do show evidence of success, and the hundreds that to a greater or lesser extent copy them, might add up to enough effort to produce a noticeable change in the aggregate nationwide numbers for total spending and population-wide average outcomes.[1] However, as we will show, that does not appear to have been the case, nor does it seem to be happening yet (understandably) during the pandemic.

What are the possible answers to this puzzling problem of limited impact of innovations? If some things are shown to work and people are doing more of them, why does the overall situation not improve much, as we will demonstrate in later chapters? One conjecture is that individual impacts, even when multiplied many times over, do not repeat the results from the evidence-based studies, which often are randomized controlled trials (RCTs). The failure of RCTs to generalize (display the same results in more general and less controlled or controllable settings) is well known, and should strike all of us with a pang of humility. Somewhat similar, though different, is the difficulty of replicating systemwide change with good results in one environment in other geographic settings with different environments. The most likely cause of a failure to reproduce is that both the leadership and the followership of physician groups vary in their ability to enforce an innovative change, and few effective leaders and willing disciples/physicians are available across the country who can make major practice changes. So even though some good ideas seem to be spreading – in the sense that organizations say they are implementing programs with the same name as an evidence-based intervention – the programs are not scaling up with anything like the expected effectiveness. Real-world delivery settings are caught between the need for fidelity to what has been proven and the need for adaptation to their particular setting, and giving up on the first seems to be the cost of the second.

Another possibility is that the resource savings produced by one intervention may be diverted to another medical use, and therefore not released

---

[1] For example, see Sanger-Katz, M. (2018). How to tame health care spending? Look for one-percent solutions. *The New York Times*, August 27. Available online at: www.nytimes.com/2018/08/27/upshot/rising-health-care-costs-economists-propose-small-solutions.html

from the health care sector. This might improve outcomes but will not lower total medical costs. Given its labor-intensive nature, health care cost reductions must in large part be driven by labor cost reductions. The only way this can occur is if someone is terminated from their health care job (and presumably goes elsewhere in the economy where their labor will be more valuable). But this may not happen. If those other uses of labor are not effective as measured by our usual outcome measures (or are not effective at all), health costs will fall, but outcomes will not improve.

Think of the innovation of emphasizing primary care in a health system that permits less use of specialty care by usually requiring a referral – for example, this is said to be the model through which the Kaiser Permanente health plans have been successful. Their data does show a higher ratio of primary care physicians per member and a much lower ratio of specialist physicians. But suppose a large fraction of an area's population (but not all) moves into Kaiser-type delivery systems. If the number of specialist physicians in the area remains the same, there must be an offsetting increase in the intensity of specialist care for the remainder of the population. Perhaps the price of specialist care will fall, but that does not reduce the real resource costs: it reduces only the excess money income of specialists. Some specialist care, such as Cesarean sections or other kinds of surgery that are thought to exceed the levels at which they are safe and effective, may rise in part of the population (since specialists are not so busy) and offset the gains in the other part. There must be a limit to this process, but it may take a while and a sweeping change to get there.

For another example, think of a hospital that implements a plan to successfully reduce readmissions. The plan will save real resource costs only if the health professionals who formerly treated those patients leave the sector. If instead a hospital with a high occupancy rate uses the freed-up beds for other (more profitable) admissions, there will be no reduction in costs and an increase in spending – unless those new admissions are diverted from other hospitals that in turn reduce staff.

Then there is the possibility of some unknown dark and sinister force that converts spending reductions in one area into spending increases in other areas, or patient behavior that cancels out improvements in health status (for example, buying a motorcycle, with a high propensity for crash injuries, as a reward for stopping smoking).

In this book, we will look hard for these sources of frustration for health care leaders trying to reduce costs and improve outcomes – and we will, unfortunately, find evidence of them. But a serious puzzle still remains concerning care costs and outcomes, requiring a concerted effort to pull ourselves up by our bootstraps to improve matters.

WOULD BETTER EVIDENCE AFFECT SPENDING GROWTH?

Has evidence on drivers of spending growth improved, and has response to that evidence been more effective? To set the stage for answering those questions, Figure 2.2 shows the spending growth patterns in terms of Medicare payments between 1990 and recent times.

Health economists generally agree that a driver of spending growth has been changes to more costly but beneficial technology, such as personalized medicine or robotic surgery. Not all new technology increases spending; some lowers spending, but often while increasing quality or improving outcomes – which in turn spurs more spending. The ideal would be to determine which new technologies are cost-effective for which patients and implement only those. To do so in a way that slows spending growth by rejecting other costly technologies, two things are needed: (1) evidence on which technologies are cost-effective for which populations, and (2) tools to limit the technologies to only those populations. What has been happening with the use of evidence?

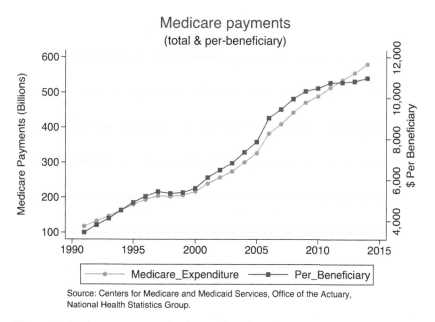

Source: Centers for Medicare and Medicaid Services, Office of the Actuary, National Health Statistics Group.

Figure 2.2. Medicare payments (total & per-beneficiary)

Based on a proliferation of studies, it seems reasonable to conclude that evidence on the cost-effectiveness of innovation in the United States has increased, certainly in volume and perhaps in quality. However, there has been resistance to using this information in insurance coverage or management. Federal law actually forbids use of cost-effectiveness analyses by Medicare, and the specter of "death panels" has so far blocked explicit use in clinical decisions. However, some insurers have been willing to use this kind of analysis to specify formularies for drugs and implement co-payments. However, there is no evidence that this impacted spending.

In contrast, almost all other developed countries use cost-effectiveness analysis for policies on new drugs, so at least this component of spending growth might be better managed in the United States. However, drug spending accounts for only about 15 percent of total US health care spending. There is no evidence that we know of to suggest that other countries use better information to manage how they provide or produce inpatient care, or to evaluate innovations in such care, but they probably do so more consistently. There is also little evidence that such evaluation slows the rate of spending growth appreciably, though it does seem to lower the level of spending. For example, one of previous UK Prime Minister Tony Blair's goals for the National Health Service was to increase access and modernize facilities, and spending grew rapidly in the United Kingdom for a time, despite the presence of a cost-effectiveness advisory board for drugs.[2] Even the process of managing access to new, more costly drugs is not obviously superior in other countries.

In terms of changes over time within the United States, here again we have no reason to think that the use of evidence in management has gotten worse; if anything, the contrary seems to be true. However, as already noted, the gap between what could be done and what is being done is still large. More importantly, the focus has not been on the drivers of growth, but rather on old technologies that have yet to phase out completely, such as standalone electronic medical records.

The other driver of spending growth is unit prices, a somewhat elusive concept since there are no natural measures of the units of medical services. Still, there is no evidence on ways in which management can affect overall price growth – for example, by more aggressive bargaining across the board. Indeed, hospitals often have bargained aggressively for higher reimbursements from insurers, and insurers have not always

[2] For example, see Beecham, L. (2000). Tony Blair launches radical NHS plan for England. *British Medical Journal*, 321(7257), 317.

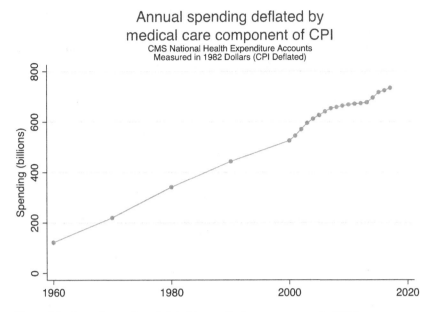

Figure 2.3. Annual spending deflated by medical care component of CPI

returned the gains from lower prices to consumers. See Figure 2.3 for a graph of the annual health spending deflated by the medical care component of the consumer price index (CPI). There is reason to believe that better information on the added health benefits from innovations (whether drugs, procedures, or social programs) can be a component of determining their value and thus the price that would be paid for them. This type of evidence could also result in higher prices for innovations that turn out to be more effective than anticipated, but it can also set a ceiling on the level of prices at which new products are launched. What is less clear is how evidence can be brought to bear on increases in prices after product launch. Greater competition over time can push prices down, but either rising costs of production or rising demand can cause prices to increase, even more so if the innovation is protected by patents or is difficult to copy. Price increases that reward innovations that provide high or increasing health benefits over time can be salutary. Nonetheless, there is little work on the role of evidence in affecting price levels or growth. Advocates of more competition in medical markets believe that greater price transparency will help to reduce prices and their growth, but there is as yet no evidence for programs, either public or private, to achieve that goal.

Price increases for equipment such as face masks and ventilators followed a surge in demand from the novel coronavirus pandemic. In most cases, hospitals paid on a diagnosis-related group (DRG) basis did not have immediate ability to shift those higher prices to insurers, either public or private. Hospitals have since been provided with unearmarked federal government funds to cover higher prices as well as losses from lower volumes of emergency room and other care. Any measure of the effect of the novel coronavirus pandemic on unit prices remains to be determined. But its overall effect on health care spending is likely to be negative.

COMPONENTS OF SPENDING GROWTH

What about individual components of spending growth? We have already discussed drug coverage and how it has been changing, and we have already noted that drug spending seems to be affected by innovation. What is less clear, as noted, is what has happened or could have happened to care management.

The absence of intellectual property protection for novel ways to manage care that are not linked to some essential and patentable technology implies that innovation development may be suboptimal. The offset is that the adoption of good ideas should not be deterred by high prices, but it may be deterred by the absence of incentives for innovators to market their new ideas.

The drug component of spending in particular should be more affected than other contributors by evidence since the introduction of new products is regulated by the US Food and Drug Administration, which requires rigorous evidence on safety and effectiveness. However, it does not require cost-effectiveness information (though this is often furnished by researchers). And the US FDA cannot control either the pattern of drug use after approval or insurance coverage of drugs, though the Affordable Care Act (ACA) does give the government the power to mandate zero cost-sharing for immunizations recommended by federal preventive care advisory bodies (also without necessary evidence on cost-effectiveness).

How has this been working out? Not so well in terms of relative spending growth on drugs versus other types of medical care. If anything, while the growth rate of drug spending is much more volatile and while it is hard to track spending for specialty drugs used in hospitals rather than sold at retail, we cannot find any large effect relative to other categories. How cost-effectiveness information might affect drug pricing or use in the United States has not been established. On the one hand, some insurers and critics have used such cost-effectiveness analysis to argue that some drug launch prices are too high, in the sense that their medical benefits are not large or valuable enough to make purchase at those prices rational. On the other hand, the great majority of interventions[3] subject to cost-effectiveness analysis meet the criteria of health benefits greater than prices or costs. Of course, we do not know what the drug spending growth rates would have been without the FDA, and any effect it had in deterring spending on new, ineffective drugs may have been more than offset by the discovery of effective drugs sold at high prices. Still, it is hard to find hints of the impact of evidence on aggregate drug spending data or its component parts. Offering some new medicines, especially oncology drugs, at lower launch prices might have led to lower spending growth, but the likelihood of greater use and the increasing prevalence of discounts to insurers and discount coupons for consumers mean the net effect is difficult to judge.

TRENDS IN SPENDING AND HEALTH OUTCOMES

The other influence on spending growth in the last decade has been the expansion of coverage under the ACA. Perhaps surprisingly, the evidence we have suggests that the contribution of coverage expansion to improving access to care has been relatively modest.[4] What has been lacking is evidence that the expansion improved health outcomes. Perhaps this is because providers had apparently few evidence-based plans for how they would manage the new business in a way that would maximize health gains.

Research so far suggests that health outcomes improved in states that expanded Medicaid for the working poor, but not because of anything novel about care management. Insurance coverage lessened financial hardship, a phenomenon already well known. There was no evidence of overall cost containment associated with the program.

DRIVERS OF CROSS-NATIONAL SPENDING DIFFERENCES

The United States spends more on health care per capita than other countries with similar levels of GDP per capita. Other countries do place

---

[3] Glick, H., McElligott, S., Pauly, M. et al. (2015). Comparative effectiveness and cost-effectiveness analyses frequently agree on value. *Health Affairs*, 34(5), 805–811.

[4] For example, see Taubman, S., Allen, H., Bernstein, M. et al. (2013). The Oregon experiment – Medicaid's effects on clinical outcomes. *New England Journal of Medicine*, 368(18), 1713–1722.

Life expectancy at 65 in the USA
OECD countries in Gray

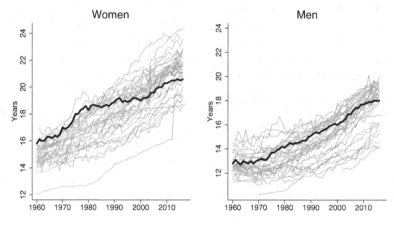

Source: OECD (2019), Life expectancy at 65 (indicator). https://doi.org/10.1787/0e9a3f00-en.

Figure 2.4. Life expectancy at 65 in the USA

more emphasis on primary care and less on specialty care, and shortages of specialty care in those countries are more common. Is this approach evidence-based?

When the United Kingdom put in place a more competitive hospital system or Germany rolled out a DRG-type arrangement, had they already developed rigorous evidence that these changes would reduce expenditure? Probably not. But those innovations did not have a perceptible effect on spending or outcomes in those countries.

What about evidence on health outcomes? The general message from research on outcomes such as life expectancy is that the worse US health outcomes compared to other countries (Figure 2.4) and the worsening outcomes over time come from causes outside the health care system – so-called lifestyle factors and social vulnerabilities.

There is indeed strong evidence that factors other than medical care affect the level and growth of health outcomes. Usually those other factors are given colorful but imprecise labels, such as "lifestyle" or "social deprivation." The idea is that actions individuals take other than seeking medical care – such as choices about diet, exercise, and avoidance of risky behaviors – affect their probability of premature death and their quality of life and functioning. In addition, those actions may be affected by outside influences, such as access to affordable housing, nourishing food, transportation, and information. The problem from an evidential perspective is that the number of potentially important outside influences is enormous and their levels are partially determined by incomes and education; some are difficult (like crime rates) or impossible (like the weather) to manipulate by anyone, much less by health insurers or health professionals. That there are other influences on health does not mean that use of effective care has no influence, but it does mean that health deficits caused by those influences may themselves increase spending on care, thus obscuring or obliterating any measure of positive effect of care use or spending on health outcomes.

The challenge of the decision maker, then, is to find evidence on which changes in medical care use or other potentially alterable influences are the more cost-effective, and undertake those cost-effective actions until the cost-effectiveness ratios are equalized across actions and equal to the value of improved health. This is easier said than done by a health system or health insurer dealing with a population with disadvantages in education, social services, and other influences on health.

There has been recent useful evidence provided on how to best utilize scarce resources from a cross national point of view. Researcher Elizabeth Bradley and colleagues show that spending on social services in other countries is virtually completely offset by spending on medical care, especially with regard to the USA, a low spender on the former and (as noted) a high spender on the latter – though not necessarily with a stronger trend toward medical care.[5] See Figure 2.5. Does this evidence provide the basis for a reasonable conjecture that more spending on social services, even with medical spending held constant, would improve health outcomes in the United States, and if so, are there incentives programs that could be put in place to move in that direction?

How feasible would it be for the United States to move in the direction of more social services, as other countries have done? Let us begin with the Medicare population, for which insurance coverage is near universal. In principle, health insurance could pay for better housing, food, and transportation, but in practice that will be difficult for Medicare insurers. Some Medicare Advantage plans have made small steps in this direction but need to bump up their premiums to cover major changes – something that buyers might be willing to fund if they could be convinced. The government-run original Medicare (covering about 60 percent of

---

[5] Bradley, E. H., Elkins, B. R., Herrin J. et al. (2011). Health and social services expenditures: Associations with health outcomes. *BMJ Quality & Safety*, 20, 826–831.

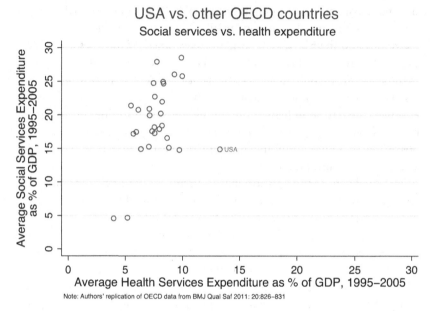

Figure 2.5. USA vs. other OECD countries

age-eligible adults) is experimenting with paying for some social services but is limited by law and budget. Provision of housing or transportation is not a federally financed service in the United States, whereas other countries pay much more of the whole package of services and can therefore coordinate both spending and services better. Capitated delivery systems (such as accountable care organizations) could also provide and pay for social services, though having the local health system be a landlord or run a bus company may be a surprise for many people.

The other major difference across countries is the measured level of medical care spending, either per capita or relative to gross national product. The United States is by far the highest on either measure. There is also strong evidence that the most important reason for the difference is that prices (for drugs) and wages of medical workers are higher – in absolute amounts and relative to average wages – in the United States compared to other countries; other contributors include moderately higher administrative spending in the US system, and greater use of some high-tech imaging and similar services.

Are any of these differences based on different use of evidence? Not on prices and wages – the lower medical spending levels in other countries are the result of the government's power to set lower payments because it controls the insurance and to varying extents the care delivery systems. Lower administrative costs seem to flow primarily from the same cause: there is less individual choice and therefore less product differentiation in insurance and care delivery arrangements (though often more choice of individual doctor) in publicly managed or regulated systems. Finally, the greater use of new technology in the United States may be attributable, as already noted, to the presence of more or less binding cost-effectiveness evidence in other countries, plus higher consumer incomes and more desire for the latest treatment among US patients. Again, it is worth noting that the United States does not have higher growth attributable to new technology compared to most other countries.

LOOKING AT THE DATA

We now turn to detailed data on levels and changes over time in spending and health outcomes measures to see which, if any, might have been or might in the future be affected by changes in evidence-based management. Is there a reason to think that changes in evidence might have accounted for beneficial changes? Or that if changes in evidence had been present, management could have avoided adverse outcomes?

Figure 2.6 shows trends in US life expectancy at birth and at age 65 over time and relative to other comparator Organization for Economic Co-Operation and Development (OECD) countries. As indicated, the US performance falls short of many other countries and has not improved relative to them; the trend for women in particular has failed to keep up.

Figure 2.7 shows the trend in economy-wide inflation-adjusted medical spending growth and growth relative to GDP since 1960. The most obvious pattern in total spending is a continuous upward trend. As might have been expected, as the base level of spending grew, the rate of increase declined modestly, especially since the 2007–2009 Great Recession. The chart shows a stairstep pattern in growth relative to GDP, with upward shifts during each recession (when the denominator, GDP growth, would have slowed). When GDP growth resumed, the growth in medical spending grew at an equal rate. However, for the periods of recession, GDP growth and medical spending growth were similar.

Neither of these patterns is easy to relate to changes in the use of evidence-based health management. The component of heath spending that was most volatile, retail drug spending, grew more rapidly than average but has recently fallen relative to overall spending. Its share has

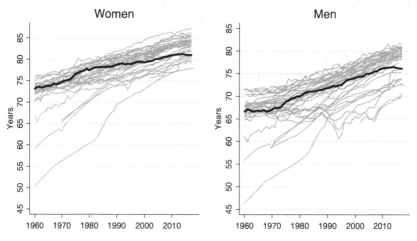

Source: OECD (2019), Life expectancy at birth (indicator). https://doi.org/10.1787/27e0fc9d-en

Figure 2.6. Life expectancy at birth in the USA

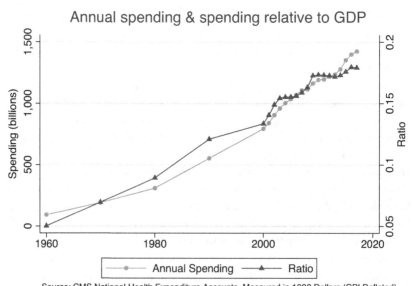

Source: CMS National Health Expenditure Accounts. Measured in 1982 Dollars (CPI Deflated)

Figure 2.7. Annual spending & spending relative to GDP

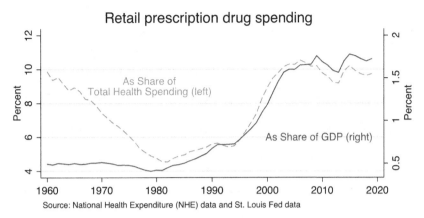

Figure 2.8. Retail prescription drug spending

remained at about 10 percent of GDP in the past decade or so, as shown in Figure 2.8.

Specialty drug spending is included in the physician and hospital spending categories (drugs are inputs for the services for which hospitals and doctors receive payments). So the component that is unmanaged by health care management grew more slowly, while the potentially managed part grew more rapidly than average. Neither of these growth patterns is consistent with the hypothesis of effective evidence-based management. Nursing home spending shows the same below-average spending growth pattern as drugs, while home health spending has been rising more rapidly; the sum of spending growth for specialty drugs, nursing home use, and home health is fairly close to average growth.

Figure 2.9 shows the change over time in the sources of payment for this spending. The share of the public programs has been growing relative to the private share and within private spending, payment out of pocket has stabilized at about 10 percent. These patterns have largely been the result of political choice (the expansion of Medicaid under the ACA) or demographics (driving Medicare spending). The fall in patient cost-sharing has occurred both because public plans now cover more of the formerly uninsured who paid out of pocket, and because private coverage has increased especially for drugs and home health. None of these trends can be tied directly to new evidence on value of care or transformation of financing.

Figure 2.10 shows the time path of the major real input into medical care provision – labor. Employment has grown both absolutely and, to a lesser

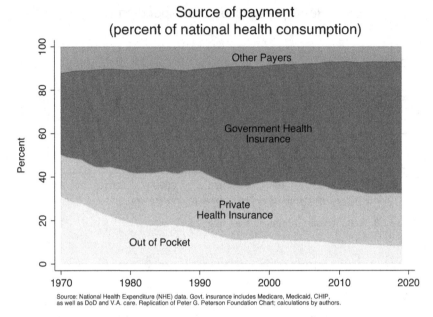

Figure 2.9. Source of payment (percent of national health consumption)

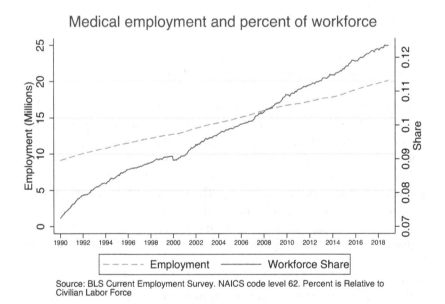

Figure 2.10. Medical employment and percent of workforce

extent, as a share of the labor force over time, with few interruptions. Here again there are few links to evidence.

These patterns will doubtless change after 2020 because of the novel coronavirus pandemic, which shut down large parts of the medical delivery system as it focused on the treatment of patients infected with COVID–19. Preliminary data suggests that aggregate spending may actually fall as the former effect of reducing parts of the system more than offsets the latter effect of treating infected patients. The pattern after the disease is controlled is uncertain.

UPS AND DOWNS IN HEALTH OUTCOME TRENDS

We have already noted the pattern of much slower improvements in health outcomes for all ages and sexes in the United States, relative to past trends or to current trends in other countries. We should also note that this less pleasing pattern coincides with high medical spending growth, but a slowdown in publicly financed growth in social services for vulnerable populations.

It seems to be hard to get ahead. There was major progress in the treatment and prevention of cardiovascular disease and stroke at the end of the last century, reducing their incidence. Some progress was attributable to public policies discouraging smoking (such as higher tobacco taxes) and some to new private innovations, such as statins and blood pressure drugs, and medical procedures, such as stents and heart surgery. These changes produced important declines in death rates from these causes, but paradoxically, they did not appear to have affected the all-cause death rate or the associated trend in life expectancy.[6] Either there were other factors that adversely affected health that offset these gains, or the gains were lost in the statistical noise of random changes in death rates from competing risks.

In contrast, the surge in drug abuse among the younger population appeared immediately as unprecedented surges in age-specific death rates overall.[7] And infant mortality presented a mixed bag with some improvement but continuing disparities based on race. There is as yet no solid

---

[6] See, for example, both the life expectancy figures as well as Cutler, D. M. (2004). *Your Money or Your Life: Strong Medicine for America's Health Care System*. New York: Oxford University Press.

[7] Case, A., and Deaton, A. (2021). *Deaths of Despair and the Future of Capitalism*. Princeton: Princeton University Press.

evidence on what will work to offset either of these problems, so it is not as if evidence is being ignored. Yet it is not being produced at a rapid clip either.

CONCLUSION

There is no smoking-gun evidence on the impact of the presence (or absence) of evidence on effectiveness and value in the national health expenditure or health outcomes data. There is evidence of the opportunities for evidence on better practices if it can be discovered and proven (for example, for challenges such as opioid abuse and cancer treatment), but that only means we have targets that are still out of reach. Use by other countries of evidence on cost-effectiveness may contribute to their lower spending levels, although even that is subject to dispute.[8] And our trends in spending are not much different than other countries. However, more adverse trends in health outcomes may be curable if evidence on the effectiveness of nonmedical social-service-type innovations were to be strengthened – but even there, glitches in the US decision-making structure may get in the way. In the chapters that follow, we will see in specific cases what has worked and what has been ignored. This exploration will be an exercise in humility.

---

[8] For example, see Comanor, W. S., Schweitzer, S. O., Riddle, J. M., et al. (2018). Value based pricing of pharmaceuticals in the US and UK: Does centralized cost-effectiveness analysis matter?. *Review of Industrial Organization*, 52, 589–602. Available online at: https://doi .org/10.1007/s11151-018-9616-1

3

The Benchmark Decision Model, the Value of Evidence, and Alternative Decision Processes

Mark Pauly

INTRODUCTION

It seems so obvious that good decisions on innovations in medical and hospital management – or on anything – should be based on good evidence. Decision-makers are advised by business school professors (and their mothers) that decisions should be based on the best available evidence – and who could argue against that? However, despite the general reverence for evidence in medical practice and drug approval, there is a consensus (discussed later in this chapter) that decision-making on medical delivery or insurance innovations – which also can have effects on health, life, death, and spending – is often not evidence-based, sometimes contradictory to evidence, and surely not as evidence-based as it could be. In this introductory chapter we explore two related questions: (1) what is the value of evidence for these decisions, and (2) where in health care management is evidence not being generated or used as it should be? This chapter will in a sense discuss "evidence on evidence," and ask when and what kind of evidence is needed to improve not only decision-making, but also final outcomes in terms of spending and quality.

WHERE WE ARE NOW

The extent of requirements for evidence, and probably use of evidence, varies substantially across medical care decisions. At one extreme, innovative drugs are forbidden by the US Food and Drug Administration (FDA) from being sold without its approval; that approval depends primarily on the results of randomized controlled trials (RCTs) to establish safety and effectiveness.[1] The standards for approval can be relaxed in cases of need (such as the coronavirus vaccine) to permit emergency use, but in such cases followup is intended with more data analysis to grant permanent approval. Experimental drugs under investigation in clinical trials are sometimes exempt from the prohibition on use. There is also a slow effort to review the safety and effectiveness of older drugs that were grand-fathered in when these regulations were approved in 1962. Medical devices are sometimes subject to similar requirements, depending on their differ-ence from existing approved products and the nature of their mechanism of action. However, once a drug is approved for a given indication, physicians can and do prescribe it for other "off label" indications – so not all actual use is based on the RCT evidence required. Hence the patterns of off-label use of drugs can vary substantially without evidence for their safety and effectiveness for the indications for which they are used. For other services and procedures in medicine, there is both less requirement for and less use of RCT evidence and other types of evidence. For example, the now large number of value-based provider payment and insurance systems and programs put in place in recent years do not have rigorous evidence for safety and effectiveness compared to usual care and usual reimbursement or, for that matter, their value.

An intermediate position is occupied by clinical medicine where there has been a private (nonregulatory) effort to foster (more) evidence-based medicine.[2] Here again the benchmark for proof about a clinical interven-tion is almost always the RCT, but the effort also involves use of evidence of lesser rigor when it is the only evidence available. Moreover, almost all of the critical firepower has been directed at already common clinical practices for which evidence is either lacking or unused, and not specific-ally at these other kinds of innovations.

At the other extreme are the kinds of managerial decisions we will discuss in this book: innovations in when and how care is rendered and managed by different types of personnel for different types of patient populations. While there have been some RCTs of selected managerial innovations, the bulk do not have that type of evidence.

---

[1] US Food and Drug Administration (2020). Real world evidence – From safety to a potential tool for advancing innovative ways to develop new medical therapies. Available online at: www.fda.gov/drugs/news-events-human-drugs/real-world-evidence-safety-potential-tool-advancing-innovative-ways-develop-new-medical-therapies

[2] Haughom, J. (2015). 5 reasons the practice of evidence-based medicine is a hot topic. *Health Catalyst*, October 27. Available online at: www.healthcatalyst.com/5-reasons-prac tice-evidence-based-medicine-is-hot-topic

In terms of innovation in health care management, the warnings about underuse of evidence are many and the description of current practice disquieting. In the most comprehensive book on the subject to date, D'Aunno and Kovner[3] tell us that "good quality decisions should be based on a combination of critical thinking and the best evidence available" but warn that "even practitioners and industry experts with many years of experience are poor at making forecasts and calculating risks when relying on their personal judgment." In his essay in the same book, Eric Branch says,

Most human beings are overconfident. We have to know what the problem is and how to solve the problem. Managers and business leaders with MBAs do this in a split second. The three hardest words in management are 'I don't know'. Taking an evidence-based approach is very counterintuitive to the way human beings make decisions.

And D'Aunno and Kovner add, "Most practitioners pay little attention to scientific evidence, instead placing too much trust in personal experiences, 'best practice,' and the beliefs of leaders."

The evidence on how decisions are made and the role of evidence in making them is itself very limited beyond these kinds of generalizations, as will be shown later in this chapter. Still, it seems safe to conclude that at present many decisions on implementing or rejecting innovations in health care delivery are not based on rigorous evidence – many more decisions than are made about innovative drugs or clinical practices. But is that a problem that we know how to correct in ways that could provide large net benefit by doing much more good than harm? The surprising answer we provide (in contrast to other views) is not necessarily – it all depends.

What Kind of Evidence and What Good Would It Do?

Cass Sunstein, President Obama's regulatory czar, outlined the argument for and the nature of better evidence in his book *The Cost-Benefit Revolution*.[4] He talks about evidence for new governmental regulatory policies, but the same arguments apply to managers thinking about new activities within their delivery or insurance systems. Sunstein notes that "the central goal is not to rely on expert judgment about likely effects but

---

[3] A. Kovner, and T. D'Aunno, eds. (2016). *Evidence-Based Management in Healthcare: Principles, Cases, and Perspectives*, 2nd Ed. Chicago: Health Administration Press.
[4] Sunstein, C. R. (2018). *The Cost-Benefit Revolution*. Cambridge, MA: MIT Press.

instead to compile evidence from the real world – not retrospectively but in advance." While it is unclear what is wrong with retrospective evidence if it is rigorous, presumably the problem is that old evidence will not match new situations – so the advocated strategy is rigorously experimental or demonstration projects of new models and methods. In Sunstein's view, those experiments need to gather two kinds of information: (1) the impacts of a new policy on outcomes (including side effects) and (2) their impact on costs. These measures are then all to be monetized and incorporated into a cost-benefit analysis – add up the beneficial effects as positive and the costs as negative and see if the sum is positive or negative. If the sum is positive, do it or allow it. That was the policy Sunstein followed in government; a policy that, according to Haskins and Margolis,[5] is or was sweeping the federal government. But so far there is a problem: evidence for the effectiveness of policies that require more evidence to be used in a particular setting consists, however, of anecdotes about mistakes avoided. There has not yet been any evidence on size or sign of the differences this approach makes over other management policies from an RCT where one arm followed the evidence gospel and the other made governmental decisions in the usual way.

To sum up: the experts cited here advocate for data from RCTs that both establish evidence of effectiveness and that permit benefit cost analysis, as a necessary condition for making good decisions. They think there is a serious problem now because of the absence of evidence and they have a serious solution: more reliance on evidence. But where to start, and how to get there from here? Our challenge in this book is both to see how better problem-solving might be done in health care management by different use of evidence, and then to determine whether doing so itself passes the cost-benefit test.

WHAT IS EVIDENCE, AND WHAT IS RIGOROUS EVIDENCE?

The proliferation of calls for management decisions worthy of the name to be based on evidence implies that we can know evidence when we see it (e.g., in *Evidence-Based Management,* Jeffrey Pfeffer & Robert Sutton, HBR 2006). Perhaps expectedly, there are a variety of conflicting views here. There is a view that there is a hierarchy of evidence and, if at all possible, decision makers should seek and use the best type. This approach does not

---

[5] Haskins, R., and Margolis, G. (2014). *Show Me the Evidence: Obama's Fight for Rigor and Results in Social Policy.* Washington, DC: Brookings Institution Press.

say much about what to do if the best evidence is not very good. The polar view is that in situations of true uncertainty (to be defined later) there is really no such thing as evidence, and decision makers need to be encouraged to use a much more instinctive process. Then there is an intermediate view that says all evidence should be used, no kind of evidence is intrinsically better than any other, and somehow (in ways not usually specified), decision makers should pick advice about what to do out of a stew of bits and pieces. The benchmark Bayesian decision model described below provides a theory of what to do with evidence of varying quality, and does indeed say that nothing should be wasted.[6] However, in practice, that theory is often nearly useless as an easy-to-interpret guide, so we will consider it after other approaches.

We take the hierarchical view – the one behind Sunstein's claims – first. The one point of agreement among holders of this view is that the RCT constitutes evidence of causation in the setting in which it was performed. All other evidence is regarded as "less rigorous," although there is debate about how to characterize the strength (however defined) of such evidence (for example, is "weak evidence" better than no evidence?). Studies that use large datasets to observe natural variation in care and correlations among variation and selected factors are sometimes ranked next in the evidence hierarchy, with or without statistical efforts to identify control groups. They might apply propensity scores to match individuals when there is concern about interactions between their observed characteristics and the intervention effects or use natural experiments usually based on changes or variations in government actions or rules to increase the likelihood of exogeneity. Small-sample case studies, qualitative evidence, before-and-after experience reports, and other assorted data are in the third rank. The experience and judgement of decision makers, the logical plausibility of the causal argument, and stakeholder impressions bring up the rear.

As we will see in more detail, RCT evidence is specific to the environment of the trial, and sample sizes sometimes reduce power to detect positive effects. Meta-analysis is sometimes used to combine data from multiple trials (but often in different environments and even in different currencies for cost analyses), and research syntheses that require judgments of the quality of included studies abound. Sometimes such summaries are used to score evidence in terms of its quality; while the probability of causation of a given magnitude cannot usually be elicited from study

---

[6] Ma, W. J. (2019). Bayesian decision models: A primer. *Neuron*, 104(1), 164–175.

summaries, adjectives are sometimes used as stand-ins for gradations of confidence. For example, evidence might be classified as highly-, moderately-, or un– reliable.

In actual application, the procedures followed by the US FDA to determine if drugs and some devices "are safe and effective" are based on RCT evidence interpreted by expert panels. For several reasons, some plausible and others not, this benchmark is, as noted in the introduction, rarely used to determine if care management innovations are safe and effective or to forbid the use of such innovations until there is this standard of proof.

Developers and implementers of nonpharmaceutical medical innovations chafe at being restrained to the RCT as a standard of proof, and there remains considerable controversy even among those who accept the hierarchical model about how much evidence is rigorous enough when an RCT has not been done. We first review the inevitable tradeoff between rigor of evidence and generalizability, and then use the movement to foster "real-world evidence" as an example of different views and potential reconciliation.

WHY EVIDENCE IS NOT SOUGHT OR USED

There are some practical reasons why RCT evidence is not brought to bear on management decisions. One is the view, itself supported by evidence, that an innovation can't work in a new setting. As Haskins and Margolis note, "Many programs produce significant effects for the team that developed the program, only to fail when other program operators implement [them]." Either something special about the skill or dedication of the program developers is missing, or the environment in which programs work does not generalize to other settings.

Moreover, priorities in an operational setting are often not ones that emphasize evidence. "Perhaps the most important reason program operators avoid RCTs is that they are so busy trying to run their programs that they have neither the time nor the money to use RCTs."[7] Obviously, some of the issues here are the value that would be created if an intervention was developed that worked, the evidence on the adverse side effects of an intervention that seemed likely to work but flopped, and how the value of getting an innovation exactly right compares with the loss from

[7] Ibid.

interrupting normal business – a tradeoff that surely varies across sites but may itself not always be appreciated or measured by program operators.

What may be helpful here – even to busy managers – is a framework for deciding when information has enough value to justify a search for it or production of it – and the time and money needed to make that search. In a broad but unhelpful sense, information may sometimes not provide benefits that justify its time, trouble, and cost – but sometimes it can. The ideal amount and type of information therefore depends on its net value – when is it worth more than its cost? In the rest of this chapter, we provide such a framework and ask whether there are impediments to its use in real-world settings.

THINKING ABOUT THE VALUE OF EVIDENCE: THE CORE BAYESIAN MODEL AND ALTERNATIVES

Warning: The following discussion is somewhat technical and theoretical. But try to get the gist of it; you will benefit.

Suppose you are a manager trying to decide whether or not to adopt some innovation with a cost of \$C. You know that the evidence you currently have on whether the innovation will succeed and provide a benefit of \$B is incomplete. If it succeeds, you get net benefit (B-C), but if it fails you wasted the cost and so your payoff is –C. Given your current knowledge, you have a subjective estimate of p, the probability of success. You can adopt the innovation without more evidence, decide not to adopt it and gather no more evidence, or decide to obtain more evidence at a price P that will tell you for sure whether p is zero or one. What should you do?

Without evidence, you calculate pB-C; if that is a positive number, setting aside any attitudes toward risk or peace of mind, you will adopt. If the number is negative, you will decide not to adopt. What about gathering more evidence instead before deciding? Evidence will be worth its cost P only if it changes your decision. Suppose that you already know that a potential intervention will do no harm (B cannot be negative). Suppose evidence if you get it is sure to be "fully informative" – to tell you for sure whether the intervention works. Then there are two cases: First, if you would have adopted the innovation, the benefit from evidence is that it might deter you from adopting and incurring the cost –C. So you need to think about the chance that evidence will indicate that p is zero, and how the expected avoided loss compares with P. The second case is if, in the absence of evidence, you probably will not adopt the innovation.

Then the benefit from evidence that shows that the program has a chance of succeeding depends on how the expected net benefit compares with P. The important point here is that evidence has different effects depending on the no-evidence decision. If that decision would have been positive, evidence only saves money. If that decision would have been negative, evidence saves lives but costs money. If evidence is not fully informative but would change p to be closer or further away from one, its value then depends on how large that change would be and what would be the expected gain (in saving money or lives) from greater certainty.

In other words, you would rationally buy evidence (with money, time, or both), as opposed to going ahead based on the evidence you have, when the cost of evidence is less than your expectation of the cost of avoiding failure. You buy evidence, as opposed to not going ahead based on available evidence, if the cost of evidence is less than the expected net benefit you would obtain. In either case, you buy evidence if you expect it will help you avoid mistakes. If p is near one (almost a sure thing) evidence is valuable only if the cost of failure is very high. If p is close to zero (the innovation probably will fail), evidence is valuable if the net benefit from success is a high, meaning the innovation is a long-shot breakthrough.

Evidence is thus more likely to be of value if its cost is low, if it provides accurate information about what is likely to happen if an innovation is implemented, and if either the cost of failure or result of success is high. In many ways, this is an obvious message, but it does suggest modifying a rule that says that innovations should be undertaken only if there is a lot of evidence. Instead, we will try to determine not only what evidence was (or was not) used to support decision on innovations in the chapters that follow, but also whether the evidence was at the "efficient" level based on its cost and potential impact in avoiding losing resources or harm to health. Simply observing that bad outcomes occurred that could, in retrospect, have been avoided by more evidence is not itself evidence that decisions were made inappropriately, and we will try to be appreciative of the fine line between too little evidence before the decision was taken and too much time or resources wasted in waiting for evidence that may never come.

To sum up: if additional evidence were free and available instantly, decisions that used the additional information would on average be better (in terms of some combination of lower spending and better health outcomes) than if the information were not produced and used, just as common sense would suggest. The words "on average" are important since individual decisions might not be changed at all or might be changed in ways associated with worse outcomes – it is the batting average that would be improved. How much it would be improved depends on how often it changes decisions and the consequences of less well informed decisions, factors that might vary across areas of innovation.

If information is costly in terms of resources or time, those costs would need to be compared with the potential benefits just described, so it is not always better on balance to seek more evidence than not; there is an optimal extent of "evidence-based decision-making" for innovations in care delivery or insurance design, just as for any other decision with imperfect information about all future consequences (which is almost every decision). In what follows we will explore what evidence does or could support decisions being made in key areas in management and financing, in order to see whether organizations in practice do what they should in theory.

Deviating from Bayesian Benchmark "Ideal" Behavior

This model is what rational decision makers are supposed to use to arrive at decisions that are best for them or their organization. However, in practice, those decisions may not be ideal from a societal or even an organizational perspective. Why not? One possible answer, to be discussed below and throughout the book, is that this is not the right model, and there is a different and better way to make good decisions. Another, which we will discuss now, is that the decision maker wants to use this model but runs into problems.

One problem that is important in practice is that the benefit to the decision maker is not the same as the benefit to some larger entity, such as the health system or "society." For example, suppose there is some prospective action that would improve the quality of care to a greater extent than it increases the cost of care. However, if the manager or the manager's firm is not, indirectly or directly, going to receive a financial or reputational reward for taking this action, it may well not do so. Avoiding innovations that improve quality but do not bring in more revenue (or even increase financial losses) will be preferred, and initiating innovations that waste money or do harm but still have a positive effect on the bottom line will be favored. Not only that, the decision maker will also be motivated to seek information that helps to achieve these biased objectives: decisions can be evidence-based, but bad. The same thing can happen within organizations if their structure is siloed, so incurring costs or expending effort that benefits the organization as a whole but does not help the decision maker's department or division will not be preferred.

Another potential problem arises if the decision maker's initial information is persuasive but wrong. Most obviously, anyone would be inclined to take actions that other peers are taking, even without a thorough investigation of the evidence for their expected net benefit. Such follow-the-crowd strategies are common in management, especially as fads flow (and eventually ebb, but not until a lot of people have been tempted by bandwagon effects). Indeed, it is not surprising that myths get stronger as everyone starts quoting everyone else, and surprising that evidence finally causes them to dissipate.

Who Cares?

In principle, it would seem that every decision maker in health care ought to care about evidence. In the case of innovations in care management, organization, and financing, however, it is fair to say that insurers, both public and private, have paid more attention to the need for evidence than physicians and hospital managers to date. The reason in part is that insurers must be able to forecast the effect of changes on claims and costs, and they need some basis in evidence for doing so. The other related reason is that if insurers are to pay for innovations, they need to forecast how much they might change premiums and to some extent the effect on quality of care or consumer satisfaction, if only because their annual decisions affecting premiums and quality are often the main focus of public scrutiny. Transparency of medical delivery systems is sometimes high but varies; transparency about the evidence that supports management decisions is not high, especially for physician behavior. As already noted, drug firms, in contrast to insurers and health systems, do have to provide data to get approval to market their products, although they usually do not base either pricing or marketing on explicit evidence that they share or that is taken from the research literature. Public policymakers pay attention to evidence, but often selectively, when it applies to matters of immediate concern or supports their previous political decisions.

THE VALUE OF EVIDENCE: FROM THEORY TO PRACTICE

In ordinary decision-making, the implication of the opinions we reviewed earlier in this chapter is that their authors think health care managers often do not buy evidence when it would have cheaply helped them avoid going ahead with a costly and/or risky project that turns out to be a mistake. Less common, but still prevalent in health management, are decisions to reject or ignore some evidence-based innovation that is still a gamble but probably would be a game changer. Before we conclude that managers are inept, we need to consider two things that are related: (1) Are there considerations in adopting decisions in addition to the ones we have enumerated, and (2) Do rewards to managers from these decisions align with the overall costs and benefits to the organization from program success or failure?

Other Considerations about Risks

Suppose a manager knows about the prospective payoffs from an innovation and how likely they are to take on different values (depending on how other things turn out) but is concerned about risk and how that will impact her. On the one hand, if she goes ahead with the innovation and it fails, she may be blamed for the wasted cost. If she does not go ahead, the failure to obtain benefit may never be noticed – unless others try it and provide an example. Peace of the managerial mind may matter here too. It's likely to be low if the manager proceeds, but not much affected if she does not, as long as no one notices.

We also do not know the stakeholders who obtain the net benefits and would pay the cost of the innovation or of evidence – nor how they feel about risks. In for profit firms the stakeholders would be shareholders; in nonprofit firms they are the donors, board members, and community leaders who direct the organization. If these key decisionmakers are averse to risks, that risk aversion may tip the scales toward paying for information to guarantee a more certain outcome – although the decision to buy information is itself risky. If the stakeholders have a diversified portfolio of interests (stockholders with many investments, donors who support many organizations), they may not care much about the uncertainty of any single one innovation decision or organization. If you would have gone ahead anyway with the innovation but will incur delay and cost to provide evidence that it will work, will you suffer obloquy from wasting time and money? Or if you try and fail at a reasonable but high-stakes gamble, will you be blamed or excused?

These organizational, environmental, and personal characteristics may be important in determining whether information is sought and used. Their roles will be considered in the case study chapters that follow.

A CONTINUUM WITH TRADEOFFS

The standard for actionable evidence in the United States with regard to prescription drugs is that they must be "found" to be safe and effective by the use of an RCT.[8] "Found" here usually means a 95 percent level of statistical confidence or better. Interventions other than drugs can have impacts on patient and provider safety and health improvement, but are subject to standards less strict than those that apply to drugs.

Here we want to consider why this is so, and also whether there is evidence that the strictness of regulatory standards or other standards matters for outcome safety and effectiveness.

Safety and Effectiveness of Drugs versus Devices: What Kinds of Evidence Are Enough?

Drugs are assumed to work in the body in the same way for all members of a population defined in some clinical way. This assumption is clearly incorrect, since effective drugs usually are not equally effective for all who take them, but some variation in effectiveness is often assumed to be random and unknowable (unless there is a companion diagnostic). There is also an assumption that the environment (broadly defined) does not affect the way drugs work in the body. Hence, it is plausible that effectiveness and safety in a trial for a carefully specified population can be generalized to use of the drug in otherwise identical populations. The same kind of easy generalization may not prevail for the effectiveness of other innovations. We therefore consider the role of evidence for devices (much like drugs but with some differences), and then delivery of care and insurance which can be much more variable across different environments.

"Devices" cover a wide range of tangible and intangible items used to provide medical care, from bandages and braces though devices (active or passive) implanted in the body to devices used in diagnosis and testing. The FDA regulates them in several categories, distinguished primarily by novelty and transparency of action. Simple devices or those that are essentially similar in mechanism and purpose to those in common use for a long time or are already approved are permitted to be marketed without further information on their safety and effectiveness. These devices are judged "substantially equivalent" to already approved devices

---

[8] US Food and Drug Administration (2020). Real world evidence – From safety to a potential tool for advancing innovative ways to develop new medical therapies. Available online at: www.fda.gov/drugs/news-events-human-drugs/real-world-evidence-safety-potential-tool-advancing-innovative-ways-develop-new-medical-therapies

(called "predicate devices" in intellectual property law).[9] One aspect of devices that receives heavy regulatory scrutiny is efforts made during development to avoid failures or shutdowns of the device. Rather than use evidence on the frequency of failure in a clinical trial, a firm may substitute data on how it corrected software during the development process. That is, internal information on the logic and design of the intervention subject to the innovator's review and control is shared with the FDA to make the case for approval. The firm's efforts in quality management need to be communicated to the FDA along with its adherence to International Organization for Standards guidelines.

For more complex and novel devices intended to affect the course of treatment or disease, flexible standards are applied, but the default option is to require an RCT for proof of safety and efficacy when they are not obvious from the design of the device. Intermediate outcomes are permitted.

The aspect of device regulation that comes closest to management is the regulation of software and protocols.[10] Devices that intend to furnish information in novel ways for clinical use are increasingly subject to regulation, as regulators around the world declare them to be part of their area of authority. Sometimes such computer programs and similar activities are related to a device (i.e., a probe or implant), but sometimes they only guide clinical decisions (i.e., a program to help implement a treatment protocol). Some electronic activities are not included as devices subject to regulation (i.e., electronic medical records), but some are. At present, the dividing line between what is or is not to be regulated and how evidence for safety and effectiveness (especially) is to be provided is in flux. Software that only retrieves information or organizes data is not a device.

Examples so far of software that has been approved as a device include programs to interpret various kinds of scans and tests, such as magnetic resonance imaging, images for breast cancer screening, or measurements for blood pressure monitoring – where the software interprets the images

[9] Swearingen, A. (2016). Determining Substantial Equivalence for FDA Device Clearance. Austin, TX: Emergo Group. Available Online at: www.emergobyul.com/resources/articles/white-paper-determining-substantial-equivalence-us-fda

[10] US Food and Drug Administration (2020). Guidances with digital health content. Available online at: www.fda.gov/medical-devices/digital-health-center-excellence/guidances-digital-health-content

to provide clinical guidance. Another example is software that supplies information for the use of a linear accelerator to treat cancer.[11]

The definition of artificial intelligence/machine learning software to be subject to regulatory approval is:

Those AI/ML-based software, when intended to treat, diagnose, cure, mitigate, or prevent diseases or other conditions, are medical devices under the FD&C Act, and are called "Software as a Medical Device" (SaMD) by FDA and IMDRF. The intended use of AI/ML-based SaMD, similar to other SaMDs, may exist on a spectrum of impact to patients as categorized by IMDRF.[12]

The regulation of SaMD is based on "significance of information in the health care decision" and whether it drives the clinical management of serious situations. If the software is linked to hardware or drugs, it is not SaMD and is regulated along with the product. Of particular interest are FDA rulings on postmarketing surveillance of the use of SaMD, where methods other than RCTs are used to discover impacts on safety and outcomes – and potential termination of approval.

Hence, the extent to which software affects the treatment of individual patients (rather than groups of patients) and the severity of illness are relevant. The rationale for regulation of devices is much the same as for drugs: They are assumed to work the same way if used in the specified approved environment.

How is this type of regulation potentially linked to care management? The most obvious link at present is the development of phone-based apps that monitor indicators to disease or distress and then recommend clinical actions. Just transmitting results from some kind of cardiac monitor though the use of software is not a device to be regulated, but incorporation of that information into computer-generated prompts to clinicians might well be.

Pragmatic Clinical Trials

An alternative to RCTs that has received some support is the pragmatic clinical trial.[13] This is a trial in which individual patients are not assigned

---

[11] Baker, M. (2007). Medical linear accelerator celebrates 50 years of treating cancer. Stanford University, April 18. Available online at: https://news.stanford.edu/news/2007/april18/med-accelerator-041807.html

[12] US Food and Drug Administration (2019). Proposed regulatory framework for modifications to artificial intelligence/machine learning-based software as a medical device. Available online at: www.fda.gov/files/medical%20devices/published/US-FDA-Artificial-Intelligence-and-Machine-Learning-Discussion-Paper.pdf

[13] Salive, M. (2017). Pragmatic clinical trials: Testing treatments in the real world. National Institute on Aging (NIH). Available online at: www.nia.nih.gov/research/blog/2017/06/pragmatic-clinical-trials-testing-treatments-real-world

randomly to treatment or placebo, but instead patients grouped by hospital, ward, geography, insurance plan, or some other method are assigned to treatment and control roles. The purpose of this approach is not only greater realism, but also an ability to avoid excluding some types of patients. This assignment might or might not be random. Generally, the number of groups is much smaller than the number of individuals in an RCT, which raises issues of how to determine statistical significance if it is reasonable to assume that there might be unmeasured differences across groups (in patient characteristics or treatment management).

Pragmatic trials have two advantages over RCTs – they take place in more of a real-world setting, and they can overcome ethical or practical barriers to double-blinded randomization of patients. The first advantage arises because interventions often display smaller apparent effects when implemented on a large scale or in alternative settings to the highly controlled trial setting. Presumably, the problem is that there are different environmental or management factors at work in such settings compared to what happened in the trial, and the setting for the trial was explicitly or implicitly chosen *a priori* to yield a high estimate of any effect. If pragmatic trials produce generally uniform effects across a relatively large number of groups, that would be evidence that the intervention's effects are not sensitive to any environmental factors that might differ across settings.

So far, pragmatic trials have not been used for initial approval of drugs or devices but have been employed in phase four monitoring or in situations where FDA approval is not required – either the effectiveness of a drug in usual practice, or an intervention that does not require FDA approval.[14]

Off-Label Use of Drugs

For a drug to be sold, US law requires that it be approved by the FDA based on an RCT for a specific condition. However, once a drug is approved for a particular use, physicians can prescribe it without restrictions for other indications (for example, hydroxychloroquine for COVID-19). What evidence governs these off-label decisions? FDA marketing rules forbid drug makers from publicizing any evidence they may have on off-label use of a drug; they must obtain approval for that use before promoting the drug for that indication. Other entities can publish studies for off-label

---

[14] Ford, I., and Norrie, J. (2016). Pragmatic trials. *New England Journal of Medicine*, 375, 454–463. Available online at: www.nejm.org/doi/full/10.1056/NEJMra1510059

use (i.e., injections of Avastin rather than Lucentis for age-related macular degeneration), and sometimes such studies are even paid for by the government. In general, however, there is little systematic evidence on the variety of off-label uses physicians actually pursue.

TRADEOFFS

It is clear that there is a spectrum of the rigor of evidence for different kinds of medical interventions. The high rigor required for evidence for novel drugs and devices might be rationalized if, absent such information, they are likely to do more harm than good than other interventions or be used in situations when they are useless – and if the cost in money and time of obtaining evidence is relatively low. We are not aware of any evidence that this is the case.

There seems to be general consensus that the RCT model is not appropriate for all interventions, but no rigorous rationale exists to explain why or what the alternative is. If interventions supported by RCTs, even if not required, were more attractive to managers than ones that were not supported by rigorous evidence, that would be a useful market test – but so far, the demand for more rigor by actual managers seems weak. Then we are back to the conundrum of whether managers are ill-informed or improperly incentivized, or whether they have made optimal tradeoffs. The absence of evidence on the benefits of more rigorous evidence is a barrier to clear conclusions and a clear path forward.

SUMMARY AND A WAY FORWARD

Is the FDA (or a similar regulatory model) one that will produce the ideal reliance on evidence in affecting adoption of innovation? The model has been subject to the obvious criticism that the requirement for an RCT or an approximation of one entails higher cost and more delay than in an alternative world where an RCT is possible but not required. Physician users might in such a world be expected to seek evidence that a new drug (which, like new procedures, would not be regulated) will be safe and effective, and so drug firms would produce it even if it were not required – so not all of the cost or the benefit of trials would go away if regulation were limited. The cost of trials also creates biases against the introduction of new drugs that require more extensive and expensive trials. An example is vaccines or other preventive measures that provide modest expected benefits to a large population compared to cancer drugs that might provide high expected benefits but to a small number of those at risk. It is an open but researchable question what evidence would be available in the absence of a requirement for evidence before a product could be sold. That system may discourage the introduction of inferior products which, if offered, would be hard for physicians and patients to identify – so the total cost of evaluating evidence could be reduced because products with weak evidence would not need to be investigated (i.e., hydroxychloroquine). Hence, even if the RCT standard is too high (in some sense), its presence may cause savings in avoided costs and reduced errors because of the benefits from filtering out products that are not effective. Those advantages can, however, be offset by less and less timely access to truly effective innovations.

All of this speculation could be cleared away if there was enough "evidence on evidence" to determine what happens when either voluntary or mandatory standards for evidence on safety and efficacy are varied. What would be the differences in overall health outcomes and spending between the two regimes? Here we review such literature as there is on this subject and point to useful paths for future research.

The observations that decisions about different kinds of innovations can be and are subject to different standards of rigor of evidence suggest a way to overcome the conundrum of evaluation described earlier. I discussed the near impossibility of judging whether a single decision was normatively good or better than some standard. In the case of the Medicare Readmission Reduction Program, as discussed in Chapter 1, not only was there difference of opinion on what the outcome actually was, there was even greater uncertainty about how to use that actual outcome to judge the decision process. For example, the program may have been the best policy to follow, given the information available to decision makers at the time the decision was made, and the level of information might also have been ideal – and yet the outcome might have turned out to be undesirable. "Monday morning quarterback" review of a single decision can rarely provide evidence on whether that decision model or process was ideal before the outcome could be known.

We have just discussed a variety of decision models and evidence standards that have been applied to a large number of decisions. Here, it seems worthwhile to look at the mean batting average (to switch sports metaphors) and its variance as a way of judging the welfare properties of the model. Comparing approval of drugs in the US versus Europe, devices versus drugs versus procedures, or management interventions versus other innovations, all yield portfolios of results that can be evaluated in terms of the consumer's surplus (excess of benefits over cost paid) that they yield – at least in principle. As will be discussed later, Peltzman[15] tried to do this with the 1962 drug amendments, and Zuckerman[16] with the 501 process for approving devices. Whether or not you agree with their conclusions, they assemble some "evidence on evidence use" that allow us to judge the benefits and costs of more compared to less rigorous evidence.

REAL-WORLD EVIDENCE

The limitation to generalizability of RCTs has prompted many in both the scientific and policy communities to wish for evidence on effectiveness derived from more realistic or more varied "real-world" settings. Attempts to satisfy this wish have led to the development of methods and firms offering to furnish "real-world evidence" (RWE) for both drugs and other medical interventions.[17] Congress favored RWE in legislation, in the 21st Century Cures Act that was intended to encourage the introduction of beneficial new drugs by reducing some elements of regulation.[18]

RWE clearly requires that an intervention was already introduced into the real world at some sufficiently high number, for potential observations. Hence, it cannot be used to determine the safety, efficacy, or cost effectiveness of some action that is brand new or uncommon – raising issues of generating such evidence when there is, beforehand, a prior risk of harm or waste.

The methods used to generate RWE do not appear to be novel or technical. Some RWE simply provides useful but not per se actionable information on patterns of disease or use of different treatments for different populations. Some RWE is represented by efforts to mimic clinical trials in nonclinical settings in larger or more heterogeneous settings. For example, an intervention might be implemented in randomly selected organizations or geographic markets, with comparisons about subsequent changes in outcomes for treatment versus control groups given

---

[15] Peltzman, S. (1973). An evaluation of consumer protection legislation: The 1962 drug amendments. *Journal of Political Economy*, 81(5), 1049–1091. Available online at: www .journals.uchicago.edu/doi/abs/10.1086/260107

[16] Zuckerman, D., Brown, P., and Das, A. (2014). Lack of publicly available scientific evidence on the safety and effectiveness of implanted medical devices. *JAMA Internal Medicine*, 174(11), 1781–1187.

[17] US Food and Drug Administration (2020). Real world evidence. Available online at: www .fda.gov/science-research/science-and-research-special-topics/real-world-evidence

[18] US Food and Drug Administration (2018). Framework for FDA's real world evidence program. Available online at: www.fda.gov/media/120060/download

a causal interpretation. The problem is that the groups (say, one state compared to another) do not have randomly selected populations or controlled environments. However, these approaches generally are thought to produce reasonably robust evidence; their main problem is the expense and effort to randomize across populations and deal with voluminous population-level data. A more common approach is to use data on individuals who did or did not receive the treatment of interest, and then try to match those who did receive the treatment with others who did not but who have similar characteristics. For example, in addition to matching on demographics and location, individual may be matched on stage of disease or clinical baseline measures. Further, if potential interaction between the effectiveness of the intervention and some observable characteristics is thought likely (or feared), analysts may use "propensity score matching," which attempts to find observable characteristics that predict use or non-use of treatment and further match on the most important predictors if possible.

Alternatives to RCTs

While these methods are unquestionably superior (but often costlier) than simpler comparisons, there still seems to be general agreement that using them to attribute causation is risky. However, the FDA subsequently has been more favorable to RWE, especially for determining if there are postmarketing effects of already approved drugs. RWE-based methods have also gotten more traction and fewer apologies when applied to other innovations of the type we are considering. The problem is that no breakthrough has occurred in changing the tradeoff between rigor and relevance or generalizability. The data require that some people use the intervention while others do not – so we know if there were differences between the groups. Perhaps the choice to use or not use an intervention was random – but without explicit randomization, one never knows.

Another approach (advanced by economists and econometricians but still not widely used) is to find some kind of "identifying variables," defined as predictors of treatment or its absence that are not themselves going to affect the outcome measure. The last phrase is the challenge – how does one know a priori that something will not affect something else? Sometimes identification seems fairly simple and persuasive (i.e., if politicians enact rules or regulations requiring or forbidding a novel intervention in some jurisdictions but not others). Such settings can lend themselves to so-called "difference in differences" methods, in which postintervention trends in one setting (the difference from before) are compared with trends in other similar, nonintervention settings. However, if political choice responds to current levels of bad outcomes, there will be a problem. There can likewise be a problem if the treatment setting is selected based on current, unusually bad levels of the outcome measure, because here randomness (in the form of regression to the mean) can do harm by driving postintervention results closer to those of a control group.

More sophisticated approaches to choosing instrumental variable methods and interpreting their rigor have been developed; these methods primarily help to rule out settings where causation cannot properly be attributed.

These challenges mean that oftentimes, it is simply impossible to tell if an intervention works, even with millions of observations and brilliant analysts. Less than rigorous analysis can sometimes serve to limit the space of uncertainty, though sometimes huge datasets poorly analyzed can lead to more bias and overconfidence. Subjective judgement, otherwise known as guessing, is often hard to avoid.

The unresolved and contentious debate about what is sufficient evidence for government approval of drugs and devices continues, with the use of RWE (however that is defined) being resisted by those who contend that only RCT evidence is evidence. From the viewpoint of our benchmark Bayesian decision model, the conceptual aspects of this debate seem undebatable – evidence is any information that causes decision makers to change their estimates of benefits, costs, and adverse events associated with an innovation. Weak evidence is information that does not change these estimates much; strong evidence is information that does. Decision maker preferences toward risk – how they value benefits compared to adverse events – are always a subjective and disquieting presence.

AUTHORITATIVE EVIDENCE ON METHODS

So how goes the battle on which method is best and when? I do not claim to provide a complete account here but mention some of the recent views. Two opinion pieces that appeared a week apart in the *New England Journal of Medicine* in December 2016 provide, on close reading, conflicting views on the subject. This conflict is all the more surprising because some key opinion leaders appear in the author lists for both papers. Interpretation or reconciliation of the current discussion is that leaders want a less costly and time-consuming way of assembling evidence with many data points from real-world settings, someday.

The first article, "Real-World Evidence – What Is It and What Can It Tell Us?,"[19] is skeptical of RWE, but in a polite way: "It is incorrect to contrast the terms 'real world evidence' with the use of randomization in a manner that implies they are disparate or incompatible concepts." But they are – because observational data is always threatened by confounding, especially if the measured effect of the intervention is small – even if many observables are held constant. And the threat arises for the usual reason – if all observables were held constant and A got the new treatment and B did not, there must have been a reason. Without knowing that reason (e.g., it was based on randomization) we cannot rule out the possibility that A was different from B in some way that is unmeasured so far, and it was that unobserved difference that caused the outcome (along with the decision by someone to treat A and not B). So attributing causation to the treatment could be a fatal flaw.

How does the article say this? It first offers hope – it is possible though tricky to implement RCTs in more realistic settings. But these attempts and other similar ones to use data from real-world variation "do not yet suffice to fully overcome the fundamental issues" of confounding, data quality, and bias. Only RCTs are the genuine article when it comes to evidence.

A subsequent article, "Transforming Evidence Generation to Support Health and Health Care Decisions," takes a different viewpoint.[20] It reviews the same possibility of large data analyzed by really smart people in cooperative ways and then goes on to explain in much more detail how wonderful it would be if the problems (noted previously) could somehow be solved. It is primarily a compilation of problems with RCTs but also with decisions not based on strong evidence. The authors express hopes such as "the use of qualitative data to supplement high quality quantitative data with a more focused approach," or a process in which "decisions about health and health care are supported by continuously updated high quality evidence" and accelerated collaborations to do so. The problem is that the article does not outline a way in which these hopes can be realized.

Indeed, we are back to the point raised earlier – any decision maker confronts a tradeoff between rigorous evidence of causation in a given setting and problems of delay, cost, and generalization. Better evidence

[19] Sherman, R. E., Anderson, S. A., Dal Pan, G. J. et al. (2016). Real-world evidence: What is it and what can it tell us? *New England Journal of Medicine*. Available online at: www .nejm.org/doi/full/10.1056/nejmsb1609216

[20] Califf, R. M., Robb, M. A., Bindman, A. B. et al. (2016). Transforming evidence generation to support health and health care decisions. *New England Journal of Medicine*, 375, 2395–2400. Available online at: www.nejm.org/doi/full/10.1056/NEJMsb1610128

may avoid one kind of error (unintended harm from premature adoption) at the cost of another (delay or omission of an intervention that will work).

This point is made in the most recent contribution to the discussion, a 2020 NEJM article by University of Oxford statisticians and epidemiologists laying down the law that there is no good substitute for a good RCT.[21] They asserted: "Replacement of randomized trials with nonrandomized observational analyses is a false solution to the serious problem of ensuring that patients receive treatment that is both safe and effective." Further, "an RCT of adequate size is needed to ensure that any evidence of benefit or moderate harms of a treatment are assessed reliably enough to guide patient care."

The key but soft word here is "ensure." How much sureness is needed or to be expected when causation can be known only probabilistically no matter what you do? How sure is it if the chance you are wrong is one in 20, the usual accepted level of statistical significance? This view seems overstated even for clinical settings and certainly for innovations in management, large or small. The Bayesian model gives the right story: It is up to the decision maker, not the statisticians, to decide whether odds on the bet are acceptable enough to choose the innovation.

RADICAL UNCERTAINTY FACED HEAD-ON: A NEW VIEW

The model at the beginning of this chapter is the standard economic decision model for dealing with both risk and uncertainty. In this model, decision makers are assumed to assign probabilities in some way to all possible outcomes, no matter how strange or unprecedented, potentially including a small sliver of probability for "outcomes we have not even thought of yet" (or unknown unknowns). Utilities (values, measured by willingness to pay in some fashion, compared to alternatives) are assigned by the subject to outcomes, and the best decision is the one that yields the highest expected utility. If more information becomes available, the decision maker uses Bayes' rule to update probabilities. The value of information is determined using this model under different hypothetical messages from evidence by having the decision maker conjecture how likely those messages are.

[21] Collins, R., Bowman, L., Collins, R. et al. (2020). The magic of randomization versus the myth of real-world evidence. *New England Journal of Medicine*, 382, 674–678. Available online at: www.nejm.org/doi/full/10.1056/NEJMsb1901642

There has recently been a renewal of controversy over whether this model is the best way to think about decision making under "uncertainty" (as opposed to risk) – either in terms of describing what successful managers do or what they should do (John Kay and Mervyn King, *Radical Uncertainty: Decision-Making beyond the Numbers*). Their book is a fun read, chock full of examples of decisions (or indecisions) in history and macroeconomics (King is a former deputy governor of the Bank of England.) The book includes puzzles and inside-economics controversies (though the book actually requires a working knowledge of cricket rules to be fully comprehended). The authors revive the idea that there is a difference between future outcomes that can take on different values but for which the probabilities are known based on either large numbers of experiences or understanding of the situation (which is called "risk") versus situations in which various future outcomes are known to be possible but beyond that, there is no basis in experience or theory to know their frequency ("uncertainty" or "radical uncertainty"). The usual homely example of risk is the toss of a fair die: We know that there are equal odds of a number from one to six dots being on top. We know this either because we have spent several hours tossing the die, recording the numbers, and observing that each occurs just about one-sixth of the time, or because we can use physics and geometry to know that a fair die will behave in this way (and that a die which does not has been whittled or weighted to be unfair). Kay and King, and the famous University of Chicago economist Frank Knight before them, thus make the distinction between situations in which there are known probabilities (risk) with probabilities that are not known with precision (uncertainty) and where the probabilities are not known at all (radical uncertainty). Kay and King use as an example of radical uncertainty President Obama's decision to send Navy SEALs to a compound in Pakistan in 2011 to deal with Osama bin Laden. There is no way he or anyone else could know from past experience how likely bin Laden was to be or not be in the compound. Kay and King say some decisions in US foreign policy (i.e., Bay of Pigs, Vietnam War) were based on assigning numerical probabilities and did not turn out well for the whiz-kid analysts who borrowed this model from economics. They vigorously criticize efforts to turn uncertainty into risk by assuming probabilities. Instead, they argue the best way to make decisions under uncertainty (and the method Obama used) is to ask and determine as fully as possible, "What is going on here?" Based on the answers, one constructs various narratives of different possibilities and finds a good decision maker to pick one. Kay and King offer the bin Laden case and the handling of the Cuban missile crisis by a reeducated President Kennedy as examples of success of this method.

Here (and throughout the Kay and King book), the decisions resulting in failure are all made using the economic model, while all examples of coping with radical uncertainty resulted in success. One might note that there are other examples of efforts to kill or capture tyrants – Saddam Hussein in a "spider hole" in Iraq in 2003, Adolf Hitler in 1944 – some of which found the subject in the right place at the time and some which did not. Kay and King admit that the standard model might work for "small world" decisions but not big world ones, like capture of a tyrant or bailing out an economy. They do not provide quantitative evidence on the historical batting average of the subjective probability model compared to their alternative model dealing with radical uncertainty – but they would probably argue that this approach to evaluating models is itself deficient.

The Kay and King narrative of what is going on here seems closer to what health care managers seem to do than the whiz-kids probability model (Sunstein to the contrary notwithstanding). But it does not seem to come very close to how the FDA makes decisions on new drugs, which fasten on avoiding multiple mistakes, defining the outcome in advance, and using the RCT apparatus to reduce the chance of a harmful or useless drug to below one in twenty.

The Kay and King book is to a great extent an enthusiastic critique of Milton Friedman and the "Chicago School" of economics and finance. The coup de grace for this "subjective probability" approach, in their view, was its failure to predict or prevent the Great Recession of 2008 (no credit is given for the virtually unbroken and unprecedented decades of recession-free years before.) Anecdotes are provided about other mistakes and misstatements (by financial consultants, not researchers), and predictions by many, not just adherents of the Chicago school, that financial down-turns had been banished from economic life – so there is a target to aim at. However, in the end, the book does not make an airtight case for a superior alternative predictive model, either in terms of a formal model or an elaboration of the "what is going on here?" trope. The Kay-King model may be a better way of looking backwards, but lacks evidence that it copes better with the uncertain future.

How to Deal with Radical Uncertainty

The Kay and King book is therefore much more an attack on an alternative view and an argument about how not to make decisions in the face of uncertainty than an operational description of the alternative. We are advised not to mess with quantitative subjective probabilities and not to listen to Milton Friedman, but be willing to admit we don't know rather than pretend to have a false quantification. A decision maker should even turn down most bets. "Rational people will decline to participate in any proposed wager when their information is imperfect and may differ from that held by other people" (80). No betting on the Patriots-Giants game, no matter what the odds.

What are the elements, according to Kay and King, that serious decision makers should consider? Construct a narrative or narratives of "what is going on here." Be prepared for multiple narratives: "There will be different actions which might properly be described as 'rational' for any given set of particular beliefs about the world" (139) and "we can only talk in terms of stories" (40). Be creative, because creativity and coping with uncertainty are linked. Do not be so risk averse as to seek certainty in an uncertain world. Listen to your genes. "Our knowledge of context and our ability to interpret it have been acquired over thousands of years," King and Kay write. "These capabilities are encoded in our genes, are taught to us by parents and teachers, are enshrined in the social norms of our culture" (401). Be entrepreneurial, they advise: "People who challenge conventional approaches are the drivers of entrepreneurship and are in economics a source of practical knowledge" (405). Beyond that, lots of luck.

In the end, what pronouncements do Kay and King offer on decision making? "Humans thrive in conditions of radical uncertainty when creative individuals can draw on collective intelligence, hone their ideas in communication with others, and operate in an environment which permits a stable reference narrative" (432). The authors provide no test of this hypothesis, but probably would not challenge the idea that a necessary condition for making good decisions in the face of uncertainty would be an environment of unlimited creativity and stability. But knowing how to prevent bad decisions is surely not enough to assure good decisions. As an alternative to the Chicago model, the discussion in Kay and King seems fairly thin.

OTHER ATTEMPTS TO BETTER USE EVIDENCE

Evidence-based medicine (EBM). Some years ago, a consensus began to emerge among physician leaders that their colleagues (although not they themselves) often fail to gather or follow evidence already developed that would indicate the best treatment choice in a given situation.[22] This movement began in the 1990s and was widely embraced by movers and shakers in medicine. One major reason for this embrace was the development of data that showed that how physicians treated patients with a given condition often (though not always) varied widely both across and within local areas. Surgery rates, hospital admission decisions, and the mix between medical and invasive treatment varied widely in aggregated data, and for many specific conditions. This kind of data challenged the assumption that medical decisions came from a common understanding of science and its translation into care. If doctors cannot agree on some procedure or other course of action, people were asking, how good could a recommendation be?

The technical definition of EBM is "the conscientious, explicit, and judicious use of current best evidence" in clinical practice.[23] "Conscientious," "judicious," and "current best practice" are not defined – they seem to be subjective matters of opinion rather than evidence-based themselves – so there is room for interpretation. Two alternative methods of implementing EBM have been specified (Eddy):[24] the development and use of guidelines, and evidence-based decision making by individual clinicians. The former does not require the physician treating the patient to know the evidence, but the latter involves both knowledge and judicious or rational use of that evidence. There is surprisingly little data on what fraction of health care spending is potentially affected by new guidelines or what proportion of physicians make what proportion of their decisions based on evidence (compared to what they would have done without evidence). EBM was viewed as a way of achieving the triple aims of improved quality, better population health, and lower spending levels mentioned earlier. In line with our discussion in Chapter 2, there is no obvious evidence in the aggregated data that EBM has, over time, improved measures of these aims, though we have no way to know what would have happened without it.

Much of the target for EBM was not innovative care but entrenched, decades-old situations where some physicians did one thing and others

---

[22] Eddy, D. M. (2011). The origins of evidence-based medicine: A personal perspective. *AMA Journal of Ethics*. Available online at: https://journalofethics.ama-assn.org/article/origins-evidence-based-medicine-personal-perspective/2011-01

[23] Sackett, D. L. (1997). Evidence-based medicine. *Seminars in Perinatology*, 21(3), 3–5. Available online at: https://pubmed.ncbi.nlm.nih.gov/9190027/

[24] Eddy, D. M. (2005). Evidence-based medicine: A unified approach. *Health Affairs*, 24(1), 9–17. Available online at: www.healthaffairs.org/doi/10.1377/hlthaff.24.1.9

another. The first step, then, was to develop the evidence that would show which approach was better, or which was better when. The last step was supposed to be change in provider behavior to get uniform care that the evidence showed was best, and away from care that evidence proved to be ineffective or harmful.

Large-scale embrace of this proposition then followed – who could argue for ignorance? In this case, and in the example that follows in the next section, the primary point of pride among advocates was the development of bandwagon effects. Many more people started talking about evidence, endorsing the idea that more is better in both volume and use, but then what? About 10 years later the positive acceptance of the evidence-based clinical model became the basis for advocacy of evidence-based management across the economy, including but by no means limited to nonclinical health care management. Such a shift obviously skipped at least several stages – evidence that evidence could be developed in a cost-effective way, evidence that actual physician practice responded to new evidence or summaries of evidence, and evidence that such changes actually did result in better outcomes. For each of these stages, it is fair to say that definitive and sweeping conclusions are hard to come by.

Instead, most of the evidence we have is from case studies, understandably because of the variety of medical actions and decisions that might be improved by either guidelines or more provider attention to what is known. Virtually all case studies are self-selected, before-and-after accounts, and many are of plans to use evidence rather than discussions of the effects of its use. In Colla et al.'s survey[25] of efforts to target low-value care, clinical decision supports (which were protocols or second-opinion requirements) were found to be effective sometimes. Included in the category of decision support was "providing information to physicians on evidence-based care" which might have included providing the evidence itself but probably did not.

There have also been strenuous efforts, primarily in the UK and Australia but also in the United States, to develop programs that synthesize the available evidence, grade it using a series of adjectives, and offer it to practitioners. The Cochrane program in the UK,[26] and the Joanna Briggs

---

[25] Colla, C. H. (2014). Swimming against the current – What might work to reduce low-value care? *New England Journal of Medicine*, 371(14). Available online at: www.ncbi.nlm.nih.gov/pmc/articles/PMC4499847/

[26] Cochrane UK. Available online at: https://uk.cochrane.org/

Institute in Australia,[27] are examples. Most of the evidence applies to clinical matters, but a fair amount of it deals with organizational programs and issues.

Each source has been used in specific settings for specific problems, and most large health systems, including our own, now have facilities for generating summaries of evidence in ever more refined, plain language and easy to use form. However, there has been very little research attempting to document an impact. Most attempts at documentation in the USA deal with frequency of access to summaries or stories about particular clinical decisions. Some of the evidence (i.e., on use of a database in Canada) does point to impacts on outcomes. A synthesis of evidence by a Canadian research group on the difference in mortality rates at for-profit versus nonprofit US hospitals persuaded Canada to continue its ban on for-profit hospitals that is still being challenged even today.[28] The synthesis looked at about a dozen observational studies, none of which could control for selection of hospitals by patients or control for hospital locations, so all results (by economics standards) would not be regarded as offering evidence of causation. The synthesis also provided a meta-analysis. A well-done meta-analysis of flawed studies will produce a flawed meta-analysis.

To sum up: EBM is one of a number of quality improvement programs that have been tried in health care over the decades. There is, however, little evidence that it or its siblings have had an impact – on quality or on anything else. Certainly, there has been no trend of an overall improvement in medical care quality in the United States despite rapidly increasing spending and modestly increasing real resources devoted to this effort. Either there is not that much room for improvement, or there are entrenched obstacles to using evidence to make a difference.

Choosing Wisely. In an effort to show that physicians were helping to reduce medical spending, the American Board of Internal Medicine began a campaign to identify low-value procedures. The primary indicator of behavior used was a particular procedure or process (such as a type of scan, surgery, or prescription), but often qualified by a measure of disease type or severity (i.e., back surgery for uncomplicated patients or antibiotics for ear infections).[29] The implication was that any performance of procedures

[27] JBI. Available online at: https://jbi.global/

[28] Devereaux, P. J. Choi, P. T. L., Lacchetti, C. et al. (2002). A systematic review and meta-analysis of studies comparing mortality rates of private for-profit and private not-for-profit hospitals. *Canadian Medical Association Journal*, 166(11), 1399–1406. Available online at: https://pnhp.org/system/assets/uploads/2006/06/devereaux_mortality.pdf

[29] Choosing Wisely. Available online at: www.choosingwisely.org/

in this set was low value. There was no attempt to distinguish between procedures of zero or negative marginal health benefits and those with positive expected health benefits that are very low, but the emphasis and narrative especially points to the former – things that are never expected to help. The list was compiled by consensus among different physician specialty societies. The definition of low-value involved types of care that were "clinically inappropriate, excessively intensive, or are too-frequently used" for given populations of patients. Obviously this definition was replete with value judgments. One estimate claimed that $200 billion (out of $3.4 trillion) in health care spending is spent on such low-value care.

The evidence for clinical recommendations was discussed, but the primary vehicle for communication to physicians was via a Choosing Wisely guideline or protocol that these things should never or rarely be done, based on the "best evidence," with little or no exposure to physicians of the evidence itself (physicians were assumed to be too busy to care and to follow the opinions of key opinion leaders). This "campaign" did not appear to include an attempt to get practicing physicians to review the evidence for procure effectiveness, but rather imagines that they will respond to guideline as individuals or by instituting institutional rules or protocols where they work.

Treatments commonly performed for which evidence, old or new, suggested that such treatments were of low value compared to other treatments (or no treatment) were listed. The program wanted to show that physicians could engage in responsible governance of their own behavior and engage in stewardship of the resources their decisions directed – whether those resources were physicians' own time or other costly resources.

Evidence so far suggests ostensible support for this campaign from physician leaders and anecdotes of before-and-after adoption for specific procedures.[30] However, simply asking doctors to order low-value tests more parsimoniously has had little effect on their behavior. Investigation of trends in low-value procedures has not shown an across-the-board absolute reduction, though there have been no comparisons to prior trends to indicate whether a growth trend might have been slowed significantly.[31] Analysis of supporters of the program finds not surprisingly that they are

---

[30] PerryUndem Research/Communication (2014). Unnecessary tests and procedures in the health care system. Available online at: www.choosingwisely.org/wp-content/uploads/2015/04/Final-Choosing-Wisely-Survey-Report.pdf

[31] Cope, E. L., and Armstong, P. (2020). What is the status of research on low-value care? *Health Affairs*. Available online at: www.healthaffairs.org/do/10.1377/hblog20200106.99070/full/

those unlikely to be engaged in providing low-value services[32] at baseline. There have been no RCTs of adoption programs by a system compared to one that did not adopt a program. Another principle of Choosing Wisely – communicating with patients about why an antibiotic or a test has low value and so should not be ordered – has had little documentation.[33]

Providing information on the prices of recommended services to physicians. Physicians' biggest effect on spending may not come from payments to themselves but from the services or goods they recommend. There have been a series of initiatives to see if providing evidence on prices or additional spending and insurance benefits associated with alternative treatments in a given setting can cause changes in physician behavior. Research shows that, at best, providing information changes behavior only for a while but then behavior returns to the status quo ante.[34] When physicians are not only informed but put at personal financial risk for the cost of expensive recommendations, they do change behavior.

COMPILATIONS OF EVIDENCE

There are several programs that are intended to gather all evidence from the literature, evaluate it in some way, and present it in a distilled or compiled form. Here, we discuss two such examples: the Cochrane and the JBI models.

Cochrane is the best-known and longest running attempt to survey the literature and provide summaries of the evidence, such as it is, on key decisions. It necessarily is limited to a finite number of questions and most of them are clinical (e.g., does aspirin help with a sore throat) but some deal with the evidence on larger-scale interventions, such as programs for high-risk or disadvantaged groups.[35] Cochrane not only provides a

---

[32] Zadro, J. R., Farey, J., Harris, I. A. et al. (2019). Do choosing wisely recommendations about low-value care target income-generating treatments provided by members? A content analysis of 1293 recommendations. *BMC Health Services Research*. Available online at: https://bmchealthservres.biomedcentral.com/articles/10.1186/s12913-019-4576-1

[33] Seervai, S. n.d. Choosing wisely: An international movement toward appropriate medical care. The Commonwealth Fund. Available online at: http://features.commonwealthfund.org/choosing-wisely

[34] Goetz, C., Rotman, S. R., Hartoularos, G. et al. (2015). The effect of charge display on cost of care and physician practice behaviors: A systematic review. *Journal of General Internal Medicine*, 30(6), 835–842. Available online at: www.ncbi.nlm.nih.gov/pmc/articles/PMC4441675/

[35] Cochrane. About us. Available online at: www.cochrane.org/about-us

summary of the evidence in the literature, but also classifies (subjectively) the strength of evidence based on acceptable metrics such as sample size, number of studies, methods, and applicability.

In terms of the economic decision model, this compiled information can be useful, but it suffers both from the challenge of generalizing to a particular environment and accounting for the decision maker's tolerance for risk in the applicability of evidence to a given situation. Often the clinical question answered is irritatingly different in subtle ways from the question a decision maker would ask. More obviously, there is not a rule for how to deal with the adjectives used to characterize the strength or unanimity of evidence; the Chicago School decision maker will have to substitute some probabilities, and the radical uncertainties users will have to do more reading of the actual studies to see what is going on. To our knowledge, there has been no RCT of whether decisions made with the use of Cochrane data have better average outcomes than decisions made in some other way.

The Joanna Briggs Institute model specifies "effectiveness" as one of its four key measures or concepts and so is subject to similar criticism as Cochrane evaluations. It differs in taking the explicit stance that experience can be a substitute for RCTs, but in its scoring of the literature it is close to Cochrane. Decision makers are also explicitly advised that, in addition to personal experience, they should pay attention to feasibility (i.e., are resources available, is the intervention permitted under some cost-effectiveness criterion), appropriateness (to the cultural environment) and meaningfulness (fit with experience and environment).

The same overall comment applies here: the JBI model may provide useful information, but how it is to be used is not specified. Nor has its incremental value compared to some other (perhaps ad hoc) way of summarizing the literature been proved.

EVIDENCE ON EVIDENCE

Is there a way out of this thicket of models, conjectures, platitudes, and uncertainty? One approach is to view a particular model of the decision process itself as a kind of intervention. Then we can, in principle, have a large number of observations on its use that can be evaluated with an RCT, where the control alternative would be some other decision model.

An attempt to apply this approach to the model the FDA used after the requirements for evidence of safety and efficacy were implemented was made by economist Sam Peltzman decades ago.[36] Rather than reverently accept the proposition that there is nothing more important than blocking drugs that might be unsafe or ineffective, Peltzman identified a policy tradeoff between fewer such drugs versus delays and absence of what turn out to be good drugs. His conclusion was that the FDA rules and the procedures used to enforce them have done more to discourage good drugs than avoid harm from dangerous or useless drugs.

This conclusion has, not surprisingly, been very controversial. But most surprising of all is that conclusive evidence on whether the FDA evidence rules do more harm than good (especially compared to something other than no rules at all, but different from current ones) is still absent. Peltzman might have been wrong, but after all these years one would think there would be proof of that; there isn't. Moreover, political leaders have been pushing to get the FDA to loosen up and use less restrictive (and rigorous) methods as specified in the 21st Century Cures Act, again without evidence of what difference various versions of compassionate use and other changes might make. It seems obvious that experiments in which some new drugs are assigned to the FDA model and others to an alternative model (say, one that used intermediate endpoints or certification) would be as valuable as it would be politically impossible without a major change in public policy.

If that change could be made (for the FDA model and the other models discussed above) it would be superior to another way commonly used to evaluate a decision – whether or not it turned out to have a good outcome. The problem with such a "Monday Morning" *ex post* approach is that it does not address the key question – whether the decision picked the best thing to do given both the uncertainty and the incomplete evidence available when it was made. It would seem obvious that evidence that becomes available should lead to better decisions than the absence of such evidence (setting aside any cost of evidence for the moment). "By using rigorous evidence to inform decisions, policymakers can achieve substantially better results by funding and operating public programs that are proven to work," Pew-McArthur concludes.[37] But is it necessarily the case

---

[36] Peltzman, S. (1973) An evaluation of consumer protection legislation: The 1962 drug amendments. *Journal of Political Economy*, 81(5), 1049–1091. Available online at: www .journals.uchicago.edu/doi/abs/10.1086/260107

[37] Dube, S. (2014). Evidence-based policymaking: A guide for effective government. Pew-McArthur Foundation. Available online at: www.pewtrusts.org/en/research-and-analysis/ reports/2014/11/evidence-based-policymaking-a-guide-for-effective-government

that more evidence leads to better decisions, and substantially better decisions? The previous analysis suggests some possible situations in which it might not – if it does not alter decisions, either because it always endorses the "no evidence" decision based on internal logic or decision maker feelings, or because decision makers do not view the evidence as valid to their specific contexts. Initiatives with names like "Results First" may therefore just delay good decisions without affecting what eventually happens. Thus, it is or should be an empirical question when and if evidence matters. As noted, if new evidence is inexpensive and correct, it should in theory improve outcomes. However, so far we do not even know if outcomes are improved before taking the cost and delay of getting evidence into account. That question ideally should be answered with an RCT.

What would that RCT look like? There would be treatment and control groups, some of which get (more) evidence and some of which do not. It would not be possible to blind subjects to the intervention since there is no such thing as placebo evidence, and both random assignment and limits of evidence (a public good generally transmittable to others at near zero) make it hard to keep the two groups totally isolated from each other. Still, in principle, one group of randomly selected decision makers for one set of organizations could be provided with or offered free evidence, and another group could be left to use whatever evidence they had to begin with. Then one could see if there are differences in decisions between the two groups and, if there are, whether the outcomes (in health or cost added) for the treatment group are superior to those achieved by the control group.

It probably goes without saying that this kind of trial is rarely done. Instead, the absence of prior evidence either triggers a call for that evidence or a decision not to undertake a particular action. For example, if doctors cannot agree at the outset on the merits of some treatment, a practical decision maker or a consumer might wonder how good it could be. In what follows, we proceed on two fronts. First, we examine some prominent efforts to produce more evidence or to get decision makers to use existing evidence to see what we know about the impact of this approach, either from formal or informal studies. Second, we talk about efforts in the literature to judge the effectiveness of evidence, from the individual physician-patient dyad on up to managerial choices for large organizations of providers or insurers.

EVIDENCE ON EVIDENCE OF EVIDENCE

Now we turn to studies specifically intended to show that generating or disseminating better evidence actually matters. One such study was done by the British Academy of Medical Royal Colleges, summarizing evidence from the constituent colleges or specialties on the impact of evidence.[38] The cases primarily consisted of specific anecdotes in which developing evidence that one clinical course of treatment worked better than another was associated with an increase in the use of the better treatment. Stool testing before colonoscopy, esophageal Doppler probes during surgery, and the use of intestinal steroids are examples. Other colleges pointed to questions they were currently investigating but had yet to develop evidence for. There was no attempt at all to provide a summary conclusion about whether the better use of evidence mattered for whether the full set of procedures of members of a College changed behavior substantially, changed it for the better, or avoided mistakes or side effects.

There is no rigorous evidence on the effect of rigorous evidence (compared to less rigorous evidence) on outcomes of medical or managerial decisions in health care. Experts assume (and we will follow in assuming) that it will lead to better outcomes. But some skepticism and a lot of humility is called for here. We know neither the incremental benefit from more rigorous evidence nor its incremental cost.

Is There Good News?

This skeptical review of the actual role of and possibility of net benefit from recent practices about evidence in decisions can go too far. Compared to the status quo ex ante, where decisions were based on remembered experience, feelings, judgment, copying of group norms, and so forth, recent developments have probably been salutary (we may never know, however). The main problem is that so far, beyond (a lot of) dialogue, there is not much evidence for an impact and much less evaluation of that impact. In that sense, our subsequent discussion in this book of the presence or absence of evidence in management decisions is by no means catchup, but is on the cutting edge itself.

---

[38] Sense About Science and the Academy of Royal Medical Colleges 2013 Evidence-Based Medicine Matters. Available online at: https://archive.senseaboutscience.org/data/files/resources/124/Evidence-Based-Medicine-Matters.pdf

CONCLUSION

There is very little evidence that the development and use of better evidence has led to better decisions about innovations and has done so in the realm of health care management; it could potentially do so, but we do not know how much it helps, nor whether it is worth the effort. In this book, we will document successes and failures, and offer some thoughts on where evidence could make the biggest improvement and how to generate the kind of information that decision makers will use to change what they do.

4

Care Coordination

Lawton R. Burns and Rachel M. Werner[*]

THE PROBLEM

"Fragmentation" – the breakdown in communication among many providers treating a single patient, such that multiple decision makers make a set of health care decisions that would be made better through unified decision-making[1] – is frequently cited as a major problem in the US health care system.[2] It plagues both the payment system (which has multiple payers) as well as the delivery system (which has siloed providers). This chapter focuses on the latter problem of fragmentation among care providers and calls to correct it via "care coordination." The problem is not just provider fragmentation, however. It is also the lack of clarity regarding what care coordination (the proposed solution) means, what benefits it confers, and how to do it.

Organization theory suggests a number of coordinative mechanisms for any industry that relies on structural solutions.[3] These include: the use of generalists to overcome the specialty-based division of labor; reducing the overuse of services often associated with specialists;

[*] **Acknowledgments:** The authors thank Randall Brown and Jody Hoffer Gittell for their very helpful suggestions and comments on this chapter.

[1] Elhauge, E. (2010). Why we should care about health care fragmentation and how to fix it, in Einer Elhauge (Ed.), *The Fragmentation of US Health Care: Causes and Solutions.* New York: Oxford University Press.

[2] Institute of Medicine. (2001). *Crossing the Quality Chasm: A New Health System for the 21st Century.* Washington, DC: National Academies Press.

[3] Lawrence, P., and Lorsch, J. (1967). *Organization and Environment.* Boston, MA: Harvard Business School; Thompson, J. D. (1967). *Organizations in Action.* New York: McGraw-Hill; Galbraith, J. (1974). Organization design: An information processing view. *Interfaces,* 4(3), 28–36.

the use of lateral devices (integrators, teams); the adoption of vertical information systems; the application of rules and programs; the setting of targets and goals; and the use of formal hierarchical models. These mechanisms anticipate many of the economic and clinical integration devices that developed to promote coordinated health care such as: an emphasis on primary care and patient care teams; the use of behavioral health workers in a clinic; the use of alternative payment models (APMs, such as bundled payment) that include incentives for providers to coordinate care; the adoption of electronic health records (EHRs), also known as electronic medical records (EMRs), and clinical practice guidelines; the employment of physicians; and the rise of integration models such as integrated delivery networks (IDNs) and accountable care organizations (ACOs). Some of these mechanisms are examined here; others are discussed in other chapters in this book.

This chapter reviews evidence to evaluate the mechanisms that have been employed to promote care coordination. We conclude that most mechanisms have not performed well, primarily because they have focused on structural solutions rather than changing the process of interactions among caregivers. The latter approach appears to help solve the problem. However, it is people-intensive, unlikely to scale easily, and perhaps a solution aimed more at quality rather than efficiency.

We begin with a discussion of the fragmentation problem and the mechanisms by which care coordination is theorized to solve it. The chapter then focuses heavily on one such mechanism, primary care, where the responsibility for care coordination is often assigned to primary care providers. We outline the "theory of action" of primary care and why coordination is important for health care outcomes of interest. This discussion also highlights some problematic issues for coordination. We then turn to an analysis of some of the elements of primary care, including patient care teams, care continuity, disease management, patient-centered medical homes (PCMHs), chronic care management (CCM), and coordination of care. We also briefly consider the ability of other mechanisms such as EMRs and APMs to further the goal of coordinated care. Our review concludes that most of these elements still await confirmation of their benefits, and offers several reasons why this might be the case. Finally, we discuss some reasons why it is hard to uncover any evidence for the effects of coordination on both cost and quality of care, and conclude with a discussion of where to look (and not look) for answers for improving coordination.

ROOTS OF THE FRAGMENTATION PROBLEM

Historical Sources of Fragmentation

A seemingly endless cast of characters has taken the stage over time in the US health care system.[4] We started with some apothecaries, physicians, quasi-physicians (e.g., bone setters, herbalists), and quasi-hospitals (almshouses) in the eighteenth century. In the mid-late nineteenth century, we added more professionally trained physicians and nurses, hospitals, pharmacies, and pharmaceutical companies. In the twentieth century, we then added a succession of other players (in roughly chronological order): private insurers, nursing homes, employers offering health insurance benefits, group purchasing organizations, hospital outpatient departments, public insurers (Medicare and Medicaid), long-term care hospitals, emergency rooms, drug wholesalers, pharmacy benefit managers, hospices, medical device firms, ambulatory surgery centers, biotechnology firms, managed care organizations, home health care agencies, information technology firms, and retail clinics. None of the recent entrants has supplanted the older entrants; they have merely enlarged the cast. Nor has there arisen (1) any central casting agency to assign everyone their particular roles as part of a coherent division of labor, or (2) any central director to serve as an "integrator" of the parts.[5]

The proliferation in health care occupations and organizations has thus been going on for over a century.[6] Decades ago, public health and policy researcher Milton Roemer documented the increased ratio of nonphysician health care professionals (e.g., nurses, dentists, technologists) to physicians from 0.58:1 (1900) to 3.35:1 (1950) and then to 12:1 (1973).[7] More recently, David Lawrence, former CEO of Kaiser Foundation Health Plan and Hospitals, noted that the number of categories of health care professionals mushroomed from 10 to 12 in the 1950s to more than 220 by the early 2000s. Similarly, the number of specialties in medicine grew from

---

[4] Burns, L. R.. (2021). *The US Healthcare Ecosystem.* New York: McGraw-Hill.

[5] Berwick, D., Nolan, T., and Whittington, J. (2008). The triple aim: Care, health, and cost. *Health Affairs,* 27(3), 759–769.

[6] See Davis, R. A. (1971). Fresh thoughts on a growing problem: How we could arrest proliferation of allied health professions. *CMA Journal,* 105, 193–194, 213.

[7] Roemer, M. (1981). *Ambulatory Health Services in America.* Rockville, MD: Aspen Systems.

6 to 8 following World War II to more than 100.[8] Such specialization has likely led on balance to improvements in the quality of care provided; unfortunately, there have been few successful efforts to harmonize and direct the efforts of all of these specialists, since professionals all want to "manage" themselves.

The US health care ecosystem features the dual problem of specialized sites of care and a decentralized, geographic sprawl of thousands of small providers – what some label a "cottage industry." This is true both among physician offices as well as post-acute care (PAC) sites. The result is a large number of venues to which patients must travel for their care.

At the same time that the health care ecosystem has expanded and fragmented, the disease burden among the patient population has shifted from acute to chronic illness. There are currently more patients with chronic conditions and more patients with multiple chronic conditions (what some refer to as "polychronics") – both of which lead to more visits to more types of providers. The result is a large number of "coordination relationships" among providers that multiply geometrically as patients visit more than one specialized site and "touch" more providers within a given venue (e.g., doctor, nurse, medical assistant, pharmacist).

Chronic conditions call for a different type of care that integrates a wide range of professional expertise as well as nonprofessional and informal services (e.g., medical care, rehabilitative care, personal assistance).[9] The centrifugal forces inherent in provider fragmentation and the treatment of chronic illness need to be counterbalanced by centripetal forces to assist these patients. Such forces are not likely to be supplied by vertical integration strategies that link up physicians and hospitals. Chapter 6 in this volume shows that economic integration of physicians does not translate into clinical integration among them.[10] This chapter explores the potential of another source of clinical integration that is labeled care coordination.

[8] Lawrence, D. (2005). Bridging the quality chasm, in P. P. Reid, W. D. Compton, J. H. Grossman, and G. Fanjiang, (Eds), *Building a Better Delivery System: A New Engineering/ Health Care Partnership*. Washington, DC: National Academies Press, 99–101.

[9] The Robert Wood Johnson Foundation. (1996). *Chronic Care in America: A 21st Century Challenge*. Princeton, NJ: The Robert Wood Johnson Foundation.

[10] Burns, L. R., Asch, D., and Muller, R. "Physician-Hospital Integration: Three Decades of Futility?"

Historical Calls to Combat Fragmentation

For decades, analysts have made repeated calls for coordinated health care to combat fragmentation. These calls have focused on coordination at different levels of analysis. In the mid-1970s, primary care advocate Barbara Starfield drew attention to coordination – measured in terms of provider continuity across patient visits and the availability of information to help providers recognize the patient's problems and therapies – as a hallmark of primary care and contributor to quality of care.[11] At the same time, the sociologist Edward Lehman drew attention to the need to articulate the linkages among organizations in the community that provide different types of care and services to patients.[12] During the 1990s, major foundations and workgroups called for efforts to improve coordination and communication among providers to combat fragmentation to serve the growing number of patients with chronic conditions.[13] And during the past decade, multiple researchers have advanced models of care coordination to solve this problem.[14]

These observations suggest three important points. First, coordinating care is not a new topic or issue, but has been of interest and concern for some time. Second, coordinating care is likely difficult to achieve, given that researchers have been discussing the topic for nearly 50 years (at least). Third, as outlined below, few interventions have thus far yielded any consistent evidence that they reduce costs and improve quality.

Diverse Perspectives on the Problem of Fragmentation

Achieving coordinated care may be hard because it is difficult just to get a handle on the problem of fragmentation. The literature dealing with care coordination has identified (1) multiple foci and levels of analysis that need

---

[11] Starfield, B., Simborg, D., Horn, S. et al. (1976). Continuity and coordination in primary care: Their achievement and utility. *Medical Care*, 14(7), 625–636.

[12] Lehman, E. (1976). *Coordinating Health Care: Explorations in Interorganizational Relations*. Sage.

[13] The Robert Wood Johnson Foundation. (1996). *Chronic Care in America: A 21st Century Challenge*. Princeton, NJ: The Robert Wood Johnson Foundation; Institute of Medicine. (2001). *Crossing the Quality Chasm: A New Health System for the 21st Century*. Washington, DC: National Academies Press.

[14] Wagner, E., Sandhu, N., Coleman, K., et al. (2014). Improving care coordination in primary care. *Medical Care*, 52(11), S33–S38; NEJM Catalyst. *What Is Care Coordination* (January 1, 2018). Available online at: https://catalyst.nejm.org/doi/full/10.1056/CAT.18.0291. Accessed on November 10, 2020.

to be addressed, (2) multiple provider settings and professional groups that need to be linked together, and (3) multiple ways to conceptualize and interpret the problem. These are reviewed below.

Multiple Foci and Levels of Analysis

Consider first the variability in the foci in the care coordination literature. These include a focus on:

- Specific disease (often referred to as "disease management") *versus* overall health (often referred to as "case management" or "care management")
- Specific setting (e.g., primary care, hospital acute care, PAC) *versus* linkages among sites of care
- Specific caregiver *versus* a group/team of caregivers
- Particular professional group/specialty *versus* multiple groups
- Particular level of analysis (e.g., micro-level teams) *versus* other levels (e.g., organization-level or "meso" activities, macro-level linkages between health and social service agencies)
- One type of coordination (e.g., standardization) *versus* other types (e.g., scheduling, mutual adjustment or relational coordination)
- Specific coordinative mechanism and activity (e.g., communication, information transfer, monitoring and followup, patient transitions) *versus* a constellation or package of such mechanisms, and
- Including *versus* excluding the patient's family (informal caregivers).

The existence of multiple dimensions complicates any effort to summarize research findings and draw any firm conclusions from comparable studies.

Multiple Provider Settings and Professional Groups

Next consider the multiple care sites and professions that need to be coordinated. The proliferation of occupations and care settings has led some analysts to identify several "domains of care coordination" that need attention. These include relationships between:

- Primary care physicians (PCPs) and specialists (e.g., referrals and feedback of information)
- PCPs and emergency department (ED) physicians (e.g., PCP informed of ED treatment, ED physician receives patient history and lab results)
- Physicians and diagnostic testing centers (e.g., physicians have access to test results to avoid ordering duplicate tests)
- PCPs and hospitalists (e.g., after hospital admission and treatment by hospitalist, PCP receives information on discharge plans and medications)

- Physicians and patients and family members (e.g., physician contacts with patients and family post-visit, patient understanding of physician orders given at time of visit)[15]
- Hospital discharge planners and PAC sites[16]
- PCPs and social workers and community health workers who address social determinants of health
- Patients treated in both the general and mental health care systems,[17] and
- PCPs and behavioral health specialists who help patients with mental health conditions and substance abuse disorders.

Multiple Interpretations of the Fragmentation Problem

The proliferation of providers has been interpreted in a variety of ways.[18] Management theorists view this dispassionately as *differentiation* of tasks that calls for a requisite amount of *integration*.[19] Not surprisingly, the literature on integrated health care focuses heavily on coordination. Three other views are not so neutral. First, some view the growing sprawl as evidence of "Taylorism" in health care: an increasing specialization and division of labor that leaves professionals in ever narrow, bureaucratically confined roles. Some extrapolate further and suggest that these professionals have become "proletarianized" and/or burned out. Second, some view fragmentation as the fracturing of patient treatment, where no one professional or organization takes account of the "whole person" in the delivery of health care. Third, some view fragmentation as contests among competing professional groups – "turf battles" – for control over health care work that used to be dominated by physicians. None of these interpretations sounds good. They may all be accurate.

The above discussion of different perspectives suggests that the literature on the fragmentation problem is itself fragmented. We are not off to a fast

[15] Bodenheimer, T. (2008). Coordinating care – A perilous journey through the health care system. *New England Journal of Medicine*, 358(10), 1064–1071.

[16] Wissoker, D., and Garrett, B. (2018). *Characteristics, Costs, and Payments for Stays within a Sequence of Post-Acute Care*. Washington, DC: Medical Payment Advisory Commission.

[17] Burnam, M. A., and Watkins, K. (2006). Substance abuse with mental disorders: Specialized public systems and integrated care. *Health Affairs*, 25(3), 648–658.

[18] See for example: Rastegar, D. (2004). Health care becomes an industry. *Annals of Family Medicine*, 2(1), 79–83; Aiken, L., and Lasater, K. (2017). Commentary on "The Changing Medical Division of Labor." *Journal of Ambulatory Care Management*, 40(3), 176–178.

[19] Lawrence, P., and Lorsch, J. (1967). *Organization and Environment*. Boston, MA: Harvard Business School.

start to solving the problem. But wait, we may get bogged down even further as we consider the solution.

THE PROPOSED SOLUTION: CARE COORDINATION

Coordination in Organization Research

Early management research conceptualized organizations and their need for coordination in terms of managing the demands of "information processing." Different forms of information processing were required in different mechanisms of coordination. Organization theorists March and Simon contrasted "coordination by programming," which is impersonal and bureaucratic in nature, with "coordination by feedback," which involves lateral and vertical communication, as well as scheduled and unscheduled meetings.[20] In a similar vein, James Thompson distinguished three types of coordination: standardization (of processes, outputs, and worker skills), scheduling, and mutual adjustment.[21]

Most health care organizations appear to rely on the first two types, using bureaucratic tools such as supervision, routines, pre-planning, and standardization. Organizations rely less on mutual adjustment since it entails investments (higher costs) in processes of communication and relationship-building. It is also harder to use as firms grow in size due to the increasing number of personnel who are interdependent. However, it may be the most essential form of coordination when conducting complex tasks under difficult circumstances – such as in patient care. As management professor Henry Mintzberg noted:[22]

Consider the organization charged with putting a man on the moon for the first time. Such an activity requires an incredibly elaborate division of labor, with thousands of specialists doing all kinds of specific jobs. But at the outset, no one can be sure exactly what needs to be done. That knowledge develops as the work unfolds. So in the final analysis, despite the use of other coordinating mechanisms, the success of the undertaking depends primarily on the ability of the specialists to adapt to each other along their uncharted route . . . .

The structural approach – exemplified by Thompson's standardization and scheduling modes – was articulated decades ago by other management

---

[20] March, J., and Simon, H. (1958). *Organizations*. New York: Wiley.
[21] Thompson, J. D. (1967). *Organizations in Action*. New York: McGraw-Hill.
[22] Mintzberg, H. (1979). *The Structuring of Organizations*. Prentice Hall, 3.

researchers as the "integration solution" to the "differentiation problem."[23] Organizational theorist Jay Galbraith explicitly tied information processing and coordination directly to integration. He argued that higher levels of task uncertainty required greater amounts of information to be processed among decision-makers during task execution.[24] During task execution, new knowledge was acquired which necessitated changes among these decision-makers in their schedules, prioritization, and resource allocation – thereby explicating what Thompson referred to as mutual adjustment.

Galbraith further argued that firms could seek to improve their information-processing capabilities through the use of "integrating mechanisms" that permit coordinated action. These mechanisms included the use of generalists rather than specialists, the use of rules and programs, the use of targets and goals, the replacement of ad hoc decision-making by hierarchies, the use of vertical information systems, and the use of lateral devices (integrators, teams). These mechanisms seem to anticipate many of the economic and clinical integration devices developed to promote integrated health care. These efforts and their ability to solve the coordination problem are reviewed below.

Coordination in Health Care

Care coordination is like quality of care: it is an umbrella concept that subsumes a LOT of topics and means a LOT of different things to a LOT of different stakeholders. The main point here is that there is likely no "one best way" to define care coordination and, thus, perhaps no best approach to performing it.

One systematic review of the field found more than 40 definitions of care coordination.[25] One working definition in use in the twenty-first century is:

... the deliberate organization of patient care activities between two or more participants (including the patient) involved in a patient's care to facilitate the appropriate delivery of health care services. Organizing care involves the

---

[23] Lawrence, P., and Lorsch, J. (1967). *Organization and Environment.* New York: McGraw-Hill; Galbraith, J. (1973). *Designing Complex Organizations.* Reading, MA: Addison-Wesley.

[24] Galbraith, J. (1974). Organization design: An information processing view. *Interfaces,* 4 (3), 28–36.

[25] McDonald, K., Sundaram, V., Bravata, D. et al. (2007). *Closing the Quality Gap: A Critical Analysis of Quality Improvement Strategies.* Technical Review 9. AHRQ Publication No. 04(07)-0051-7. Rockville, MD: Agency for Healthcare Research and Quality; Ovretveit, J. (2011). *Does Clinical Coordination Improve Quality and Save Money?* London, UK: The Health Foundation.

marshalling of personnel and other resources needed to carry out all required patient care activities and is often managed by the exchange of information among participants responsible for different aspects of care.[26]

Care coordination is also linked to many other related concepts. It is often associated with *primary care* efforts, such as patient-centered care, "appropriateness" of care, collaborative care, continuity of care, and teamwork (among others) – all intended to combat fragmentation of care across siloed providers. For example, some analysts view care continuity as the opposite of care fragmentation, and suggest that coordination is rarely needed in the presence of continuity and that care coordination is virtually impossible without a strong primary care foundation.[27] Others disagree, arguing that (1) continuity is compatible with visits to many physicians provided there is sufficient information exchange among them, and (2) specialists (e.g., a pulmonologist) can effectively serve as the primary physician for patients with particular conditions (e.g., congestive heart failure).[28]

Care coordination is also associated with *institutional* efforts that link specialists, hospitals, and PAC providers. Such efforts at vertical integration – including IDNs and ACOs – as well as patient care transitions are dealt with in greater detail in Chapters 5 and 6 in this volume. The subject of care coordination overlaps lots of related terms and fields such as care management, case management, disease management, medication management, integrated care, and care navigation.[29] Researchers who focus on their own piece of the care coordination puzzle may not recognize the overall picture.

Solution to Specific Problems

Care coordination is frequently proposed as a solution to fragmentation and its attendant waste (e.g., duplication of tests, delays in service, conflicting recommendations from different specialists). The problems to be solved are sometimes identified in patient surveys.[30] One survey suggests

[26] Bynum, J., and Ross, J. (2013). A measure of care coordination? *Journal of General Internal Medicine*, 28(3), 336–338.

[27] Bodenheimer, T. (2008). Coordinating care – A perilous journey through the health care system. *New England Journal of Medicine*, 358(10), 1064–1071.

[28] Randall Brown. Personal communication.

[29] McDonald, K., Sundaram, V., Bravata, D. et al. (2007). *Closing the Quality Gap: A Critical Analysis of Quality Improvement Strategies*. Technical Review 9. AHRQ Publication No. 04(07)-0051-7. Rockville, MD: Agency for Healthcare Research and Quality.

[30] Osborn, R., Moulds, D., Squires, D. et al. (2014). International survey of older adults finds shortcoming in access, coordination, and patient-centered care. *Health Affairs*, 33(12), 2247–2255.

that fragmentation subsumes lots of specific problems to be solved. For example, US patients are more likely than their counterparts in 10 other industrialized countries to report any coordination problem or to report particular coordination problems such as (1) test results/records not available at the appointment or duplicate tests ordered, and (2) receipt of conflicting information from different physicians. Conversely, compared to their global counterparts, US patients are more likely to (1) discuss health-promoting behaviors with a clinician, (2) have a chronic care plan tailored to their daily life, and (3) engage in end-of-life care planning. Finally, US patients report comparable experiences to patients in other countries on a third set of coordination issues such as (1) PCPs and specialists lacking information on the care provided by each other, with slightly better experiences with (2) professionals reviewing prescriptions during the prior year, (3) closing gaps in hospital discharge planning in the past two years, and (4) PCPs being informed about 'hospital care after discharge during the past two years.

Nevertheless, a slightly higher percentage (9.8 percent) of US patients experienced "poor primary care coordination" (defined as three or more of the self-reported gaps in care cited above) compared to patients in other countries (5 percent overall). These gaps are associated with the absence of positive, established relationships with a PCP. Such gaps are also associated with higher odds of being hospitalized and use of the ED for both urgent and nonurgent care. The likelihood of experiencing poor care coordination appears to be unrelated to the patient's insurance status, health status, and household income, but may be due to systemic reasons such as the ease of self-referral to a specialist. This problem is not just a US problem, but is also found in France, Germany, and Switzerland.[31]

When PCPs are asked about care coordination issues, on the one hand, US physicians are less likely to report coordination with social services and community providers than their counterparts in other countries. On the other hand, they are as likely or more likely to report coordination between themselves and specialists or home care providers, and notification of patient discharge from hospitals.[32]

[31] Penm, J., MacKinnon, N., Strakowski, S. et al. (2017). Minding the gap: factors associated with primary care coordination of adults in 11 countries. *Annals of Family Medicine*, 15 (2), 113–119.

[32] Osborn, R., Moulds, D., Schneider, E. et al. (2015). Primary care physicians in 10 countries report challenges caring for patients with complex health needs. *Health Affairs* 34(12), 2104–2112.

Solution to Broader Problems

Care coordination is viewed by payers as a specific mechanism to reduce costs, such as inappropriate hospitalization and use of the hospital ED. Policy analysts argue that such reductions are good for both the patient (improved quality of care and patient experience) and the payer (lower cost); the only loser under fee-for-service is the hospital. For such instances, care coordination solves tangible problems.

However, for many other stakeholders, care coordination constitutes the solution *du jour* to many broad, societal goals including "the iron triangle" (lower cost, higher quality, improved access) as well as "the triple aim" (lower per capita cost, improved patient experience of care, improved health status) – partially through enhanced communication with providers. More generally, care coordination is believed to aid the pursuit of a wide range of goals, including bridging gaps along the patient's care pathway, optimizing hospital inpatient capacity, and reducing adverse outcomes of poor transfers.

Most recently, care coordination has become viewed as the "silver bullet" (or at least the leading strategy) to reap savings under APMs, such as the Medicare's ACO and bundled payment programs, as well as new models of health care delivery, such as the PCMH. While APMs, ACOs, and PCMHs offer the potential to reduce spending through a variety of mechanisms, the Centers for Medicare and Medicaid Services (CMS) defines them in terms focused almost exclusively on care coordination.[33]

Summarizing the evidence on care coordination is akin to summarizing the evidence on quality of care. There are numerous definitions, conceptual frameworks, objectives and goals, empirical measures, and research studies. Some researchers have likened the quality literature to the Tower of Babel (read: babble, different languages).[34] The same may be said of care coordination; just read any of the lengthy literature reviews.[35] The next three sections examine (1) primary care, (2) some of the constituent elements of primary care, and (3) other mechanisms such as EMRs and

---

[33] McWilliams, J. M. (2016). Cost containment and the tale of care coordination. *New England Journal of Medicine*, 375(23), 2218–2220.

[34] Teisberg, E., and Wallace, S. (2015).The quality tower of Babel. *Health Affairs Blog.*

[35] McDonald, K., Sundaram, V., Bravata, D., et al. (2007). *Closing the Quality Gap: A Critical Analysis of Quality Improvement Strategies.* Technical Review 9. AHRQ Publication No. 04(07)-0051-7. Rockville, MD: Agency for Healthcare Research and Quality.

APMs as solutions to care coordination. After being weighed in the balance, the evidence is found wanting.

PRIMARY CARE AND COORDINATION

For decades, researchers have argued that the solution to fragmentation resides in primary care. Some go further to suggest that care coordination is "a defining characteristic of primary care" – hearkening back to the Marcus Welby model.[36] These arguments are explicated below.

Theory of Action

Barbara Starfield has been preeminent among researchers in advancing the mechanisms through which primary care influences health care outcomes – what some call its "theory of action."[37] Starfield identified six such mechanisms: (1) greater access to needed services (e.g., by providing a first point of contact with health services for disadvantaged populations); (2) attention to broader, generic (i.e., nondisease-specific) outcomes by addressing multiple aspects of health; (3) attention to preventive health care and early detection of disease; (4) early management of health problems before they become serious; (5) focus on the person rather than the disease; and (6) reduction in use of unnecessary or inappropriate specialty care. Starfield also identified "four pillars" of primary care practice: (1) first-contact care, (2) continuity of care, (3) comprehensive care, and (4) coordination of care (also known as the "four Cs"). According to Starfield, coordination (defined as the availability of information about prior problems and services and the recognition of that information at the time of current treatment) is essential for the attainment of the other three pillars (Figure 4.1).[38]

Elements of Primary Care

In the current era of ACOs, researchers have now distilled five elements of primary care that, when collectively present, distinguish it from specialty-oriented care: (1) first-contact accessibility, (2) continuity, (3)

[36] Wagner, E., Sandhu, N., Coleman, K. et al. (2014). Improving care coordination in primary care. *Medical Care*, 52(11), S33–S38.

[37] Starfield, B. (1998). *Primary Care: Balancing Health Needs, Services, and Technology*. New York: Oxford University Press; Starfield, B., Shi, L., and Macinko, J. (2005). Contribution of primary care to health systems and health. *Milbank Quarterly*, 83(3), 457–502.

[38] Starfield, B. (1998). *Primary Care: Balancing Health Needs, Services, and Technology*. New York: Oxford University Press, 213.

Starfield's model of primary care

Figure 4.1. Starfield's model of primary care

Figure 4.2
Elements of primary care

1. **Accessible first-contact care**
   Primary care clinicians make their services available and easily accessible to patients with new medical needs or ongoing health concerns. This includes shorter waiting times for urgent needs, enhanced in-person hours, around-the-clock telephone or electronic access to a member of the care team who has access to the patient's medical record, and alternative methods of communication including patient portals. This also includes providers who speak the language of the population served.

2. **Continuous care**
   Primary care clinicians have a personal and uninterrupted caring relationship with their patients, with continuous exchange of relevant information about health care and health needs.

3. **Comprehensiveness of care**
   Primary care clinicians, working with the interprofessional primary care team, meet the large majority of each patient's physical and mental health care needs, including prevention and wellness, acute care, chronic and comorbid care, to include discussing end-of-life care.

4. **Coordinated care**
   Primary care practices coordinate care across all elements of the broader health care system, including specialty care, hospitals, home health care, and community services and support.

5. **Accountable whole-person care**
   Primary care clinician/team is knowledgeable about and oriented toward the whole person, understanding and respecting each patient's unique needs, culture, values, and preferences in the context of their family and community. "Accountability" refers to caring for the whole person, not just an isolated body system.

Figure 4.2 Elements of primary care

comprehensiveness, (4) coordination, and (5) whole-person accountability.[39] These five elements represent an amalgam of Starfield's six mechanisms and four pillars identified above. The definitions for these five elements are presented in Figure 4.2.

There is a widely-held belief (assumption) that primary care serves as the cornerstone of any health care system and exerts a positive impact on important patient outcomes. This belief is buttressed by some literature

---

[39] O'Malley, A., Rich, E., Maccarone, A. et al. (2015). Disentangling the linkage of primary care features to patient outcomes: A review of current literature, data sources, and measurement needs. *Journal of General Internal Medicine*, 30 (Supplement 3), S576–S585.

reviews,[40] which suggest that the five elements of primary care have the following effects: (1) *accessibility* impacts hospitalization rates, ED visits, and patient satisfaction; (2) *continuity* impacts hospitalization rates, complication rates, ED visits, total costs, and adherence to provider recommendations; (3) *comprehensiveness* impacts hospitalization rates, better health outcomes at lower cost, and self-reported health outcomes; (4) *coordination* reduces duplication of services and improves patient outcomes and satisfaction; and (5) *accountability* impacts patient self-management for chronic conditions and adherence to provider recommendations.

Issues with Primary Care

Primary care has, thus, long been viewed as essential to controlling per-capita costs, improving the patient's experience of care, and maintaining and promoting the health status of the population (i.e., the triple aim). Historically, it has also been viewed as critical to lowering the cost of care, improving quality of care, and improving access to care (i.e., the iron triangle).[41] Finally, analysts suggest that primary care benefits both population and personal health by increasing use of preventive services, reducing disease and death rates, and reducing the negative health effects of income inequality on health and mortality, especially in areas where income inequality is greatest.[42] In other words, primary care constitutes a big picture solution to big picture goals.

Two recent studies published in the medical literature lend credence to these claims. They indicate that the availability of primary care is associated with higher health status (as measured by patient mortality), higher quality of care (as measured by clinical process measures), and higher patient experience measures.

One study using an epidemiological approach found a positive association of primary care physician supply (i.e., number of PCPs per 100,000 individuals in a region) with changes in life expectancy between 2005 and 2015. Every additional 10 PCPs was linked to an increased life expectancy of 51.5 days, as well as reduced rates of mortality from cardiovascular,

---

[40] Shi, L. (2012). The impact of primary care: A focused review. *Scientifica*. Available online at: www.ncbi.nlm.nih.gov/pmc/articles/PMC3820521/pdf/SCIENTIFICA2012-432892.pdf. Accessed on November 15, 2020.

[41] Starfield, B., Shi, L., and Macinko, J. (2005). Contribution of primary care to health systems and health. *Milbank Quarterly*, 83(3), 457–502.

[42] Petterson, S., McNellis, R., Klink, K. et al. (2018). *The State of Primary Care in the United States*. Washington, DC: Robert Graham Center.

respiratory, and cancer conditions. By contrast, the supply of specialist physicians had weaker, but still positive associations with the same outcomes.[43] The study did not demonstrate causality, however; nor did it address whether a greater supply of PCPs reduced patient difficulties in getting appointments.

The other study used a national population survey approach and found that adults with a "usual source of primary care" (defined as a physician) were more likely to fill their prescriptions, have preventive office visits, and have higher-value (and often underused) care, such as cancer screening, counseling, and recommended diagnostic and preventive testing. However, they had the same levels of inpatient, outpatient, and emergency room utilization, and similar levels of low-value care; indeed, those with a usual source of primary care were slightly more likely to report more low-value care for some conditions. Those with a usual source of primary care also reported higher patient access and experience scores as well.[44] Note that these summarized benefits of PCP supply are not always or directly tied to care coordination benefits. The variables that intervene between PCP supply and health status are likely to be manifold.

There are, nevertheless, important caveats and some disquieting findings in these (and other recent) studies that may pose questions about care coordination benefits accruing to PCPs. First, while the number of PCPs has increased over time, it has not kept up with population growth. From 2005 to 2015, the ratio of PCPs per 100,000 fell from 46.6 to 41.4. This is due not only to a larger population, but also physician migration, loss of physician supply in certain (i.e., rural) areas, and medical student choice of specialty over primary care residencies. In 2017, the USA had an estimated 223,125 office-based PCPs. Among these, the three biggest specialties were family practitioners (39.5%), general internal medicine (34.5%), and general pediatricians (21.3%). The number of physician graduates from primary care residency programs peaked in the late 1990s and (through 2014) had not risen above that level.

Second, Americans' use of primary care appears to be both low and falling. At the aggregate level, the percentage of health care spending

[43] Basu, S., Berkowitz, S., Phillips, R. et al. (2019). Association of primary care physician supply with population mortality in the United States, 2005–2015. *JAMA Internal Medicine*, 179(4), 506–514.

[44] Levine, D., Landon, B., and Linder, J. (2019). Quality and experience of outpatient care in the United States for adults with or without primary care. *JAMA Internal Medicine*, 179 (3), 363–372.

devoted to primary care fell from 6.5% in 2002 to 5.4% by 2016.[45] Research indicates that roughly one quarter of the adult population lacks a usual source of primary care (i.e., a PCP) – despite the fact that two-thirds have health insurance coverage. This may reflect geographic access issues (i.e., low supply in some areas), or it may reflect a lower perceived need for primary care, as has been reported recently among the millennial population born between 1981 and 1996. Empirical research also shows declining use of PCPs between 2008–2016: the proportion of adults with no medical visits rose from 26.1% to 32.5%, and the percentage with no PCP visits rose from 38.1% to 46.4%.[46] By contrast, visits to specialists did not change. Declines were greatest for younger, healthier adults, those with lower-acuity conditions, and those in low-income communities. These patterns may thus reflect several dynamics at work: preference for convenience care among millennials, a decline in unnecessary visits, growing financial barriers to care, a shift within PCP practices to offering preventive services, and/or substitution of PCP visits by specialist visits.

Regardless of the cause, the decline in PCP use may lead to fewer medical school graduates going into primary care specialties, leading to a vicious cycle that fosters even greater medical specialization and perhaps lower care continuity. Of course, the opposite may be true: greater medical specialization may foster a decline in PCP use.

Third, the beneficial effects of primary care availability are not across-the-board. It does not appear to affect utilization of expensive services (e.g., hospital admissions, emergency room use) or to lower all forms of low-value (unnecessary) care. These are benefits often felt to be addressable by care coordination.

In most studies, the measured association between primary care utilization and spending is static (rather than dynamic) and often based on observational studies (e.g., studies that describe where spending is high or low).[47] There is some question as to whether increasing the amount of primary care spending by a county or state would bend the trend in health care spending over time. Rhode Island passed a statute that required commercial insurers to increase the percentage of spending on primary

[45] Martin, S., Phillips, R., Petterson, S. et al. (2020). Primary care spending in the United States, 2002–2016. *Journal of the American Medical Association*, 180(7), 1019–1020.

[46] Ganguli, I., Shi, Z., Orav, J. et al. (2020). Declining use of primary care among commercially insured adults in the United States, 2008–2016. *Annals of Internal Medicine*, 172(4), 240–247.

[47] Friedberg, M., Hussey, P., and Schneider, E. (2010). Primary care: A critical review of the evidence on quality and costs of health care. *Health Affairs*, 29(5), 766–772.

care by one percent, raising spending on primary care statewide from $47 million to $74 million over seven years. The underlying "theory of action" is that such spending will be devoted to prevention and care coordination, which can lead to healthier lives and lower need for acute care utilization. Overall, the thesis is that primary care can substitute for secondary and tertiary care. Unfortunately, the evidence supporting this theory is scant (see below). Some economists would argue instead that increasing the number of physicians would foster induced demand for their services and lead to increased (and sometimes unnecessary) utilization.

Fourth, empirical evidence is mixed on whether primary care and specialty care are substitutes or complements for each other (or both).[48] There are three reasons why they might be substitutes: (1) prevention and detection in the PCP setting may avoid need for specialty care, (2) PCP management of chronic illness may prevent or delay the need for specialty care, and (3) PCP gatekeeping may reduce specialist referrals. There are three reasons why they might be complements: (1) PCPs may order specialty diagnostic tests as followup care, (2) PCPs may detect illness that cannot be treated in that office, and (3) PCPs may identify acute episodes that need specialty treatment. If primary and specialty care are substitutes, then building primary care capacity may promote continuity and coordination of care; if they are complements, then a greater burden is imposed on coordination. That is because there will be more visits to more physicians in more sites of care that need to be linked and coordinated.

Fifth, efforts by the Patient Protection and Affordable Care Act (ACA) to foster two new delivery models in primary care have had only limited success. The Comprehensive Primary Care (CPC) and CPC Plus (CPC+) initiatives embedded care managers in PCP offices to enhance their management of chronic conditions, linked patients to a single PCP to promote continuity and post-hospitalization followup, and included integration with behavioral health care. However, practices found it difficult to find the time and resources to implement these changes fully (e.g., hire and integrate staff) as well as make the necessary changes in their care processes. This suggests a major problem with relying on PCPs for care coordination. Moreover, the models left the volume-based, fee-for-service incentives largely intact, and did not give the practices a large bump in reimbursement to make changes. Needless to say, the practices exerted

---

[48] Fortney, J., Steffick, D., Burgess, J. et al. (2005). Are primary care services a substitute or complement for specialty and inpatient services? *Health Services Research*, 40(5), 1422–1442.

little impact on cost, quality, and utilization of either hospitals or EDs.[49] Overall, the "care management fees" paid to providers far outweighed any savings on utilization. It may be that more primary care improves health status (although that was not supported by evidence from CPC), but it may also cost more and will not bend the cost curve.[50]

Sixth, the presence of PCPs may not be the same as the provision of primary care. Researchers suggest that the constellation of all five elements of primary care (Figure 4.2) are needed. Initiatives that focus on workforce levels and other *structural* interventions neglect the *process* dimensions of the care that is delivered. PCP practices likely vary in their capabilities regarding these five elements, and their patients will vary in terms of their need for all of these elements.

Seventh, it is unclear just how much value other providers such as specialists and hospitals place on the coordination benefits that accrue from interaction with PCPs. Starfield herself wrote that PCPs have not enjoyed a history of "centrality in patient care," and that specialists assigned lower values to receiving information from PCPs than PCPs did in sending it.[51] Indeed, analysts believe that some specialists have little respect for PCPs, who are near the bottom of the income and prestige scale among physicians. More recently, researchers have found that health systems' spending on primary care for beneficiaries attributed to them ranges from only 2 to 5 percent (depending on the definition of primary care) and that such spending is not associated with any of seven measures of clinical quality.[52] Primary care spending is thus dwarfed by spending on secondary and tertiary care services.

Eighth, according to one ethnographic study, PCPs are under siege.[53] Since the 1970s, most PCPs transitioned from a traditional professional role to a primarily business role, where they now see themselves as performing a job rather than fulfilling a vocation. This transition reflects the dictates of maximizing patient volume and productivity targets in the

---

[49] Peikes, D., Taylor, E., O'Malley, A. et al. (2020). The changing landscape of primary care: Effects of the ACA and other efforts over the past decade. *Health Affairs*, 39(3), 421–428.

[50] Song, Z., and Gondi, S. (2019). Will increasing primary care spending alone save money? *JAMA*, 322(14), 1349–1350.

[51] Starfield, B. (1998). *Primary Care: Balancing Health Needs, Services, and Technology*. New York: Oxford University Press, 220.

[52] Reid, R., Kofner, A., Friedberg, M. et al. (2020). "Variation in health system primary care spending and association with quality measure performance," Paper presented at Fifth Annual CHSP Grantee Workshop.

[53] Hoff, T. (2010). *Practice under Pressure: Primary Care Physicians and Their Medicine in the Twenty-First Century*. New Brunswick, NJ: Rutgers University Press.

face of constrained reimbursement. Moreover, PCPs have undergone a "deskilling" and narrowing of their scope of work whereby they delegate all facility-based visits to hospitalists and cede responsibility for procedures to subspecialists (sometimes due to concerns over malpractice). PCPs have thus lost technical skills and medical knowledge as a consequence of not following their patients across office and hospital settings, as well as become isolated from other specialties.

Ninth, as discussed in other chapters in this book, primary care physicians need to be more thoughtful than at present about what other services they will order and how they will refer patients. Incentives or processes to get them to do that are not well identified.

Why are these nine observations important? Asking PCPs to deliver on the "four pillars" (or four Cs) of primary care conflicts with the reality of the "hamster on a treadmill" state of primary care. Researchers have portrayed the daily work of PCPs as a series of nonstop, 10–20 minute, one-on-one interactions with a stream of patients, with little or no interaction with others on the care team. The only interaction consists of a quick patient handoff of instructions for followup tests or next appointment visits; there is no collaboration.[54] The office practice team operates in separate social silos, isolating physicians not only from one another, but also from the rest of the practice. Office practice structures are primarily focused on supporting the physician's hectic routine, leaving physician-physician, physician-nursing, and physician-patient fissures. The problems of stagnant incomes and productivity-based (relative value unit, or RVU) payment, compounded by growing PCP shortages, may make coordination increasingly difficult. And yet society has come to expect PCPs to (1) provide acute, chronic, and preventive care to patients, (2) develop positive patient experiences and build strong patient relationships that foster trust, (3) manage multiple diagnoses (often for chronic conditions) if present, and also (4) adhere to practice guidelines.[55]

Some suggest the answer lies in greater investments in "extensivists:" that is, physicians who handle both inpatient and outpatient care for the small portion of a clinic's patient panel with multiple chronic conditions. These physicians are supported by a cadre of nurse care managers. Such an approach was pioneered by CareMore, an integrated health plan and care

[54] Chesluk, B., and Holmboe, E. (2010). How teams work – or don't – in primary care: A field study on internal medicine practices. *Health Affairs*, 29(5), 874–879.

[55] Bodenheimer, T. (2007). *Building Teams in Primary Care: Lessons Learned*. Oakland, CA: California HealthCare Foundation.

system for patients with Medicare or Medicaid, in its early days in Southern California that has been emulated elsewhere. Early data from CareMore suggested better outcomes at lower costs (e.g., 42 percent fewer hospital admissions than the national average).[56]

Others suggest the answer lies in greater investments in nursing and pharmacists. One needs to be cautious here. The growing use of non-PCPs as a first point of contact multiplies the number of providers and patient contacts that require care coordination. Greater investments in nonphysician PCPs and virtual care delivery models (aided by telemedicine) may also replace the "one-to-one" patient-physician relationship with a "one-to-many" relationship.[57] The impacts of such a shift will also need to be closely monitored, particularly on coordination, continuity, followup, and patient trust.[58] One of the studies performed supplementary analyses that included nurse practitioners and physician assistants in its measure of primary care supply. Greater supply was positively associated with increased life expectancy, but the results were not statistically significant.[59]

THE ELEMENTS OF PRIMARY CARE AND COORDINATION: HOW SHAKY A FOUNDATION

The issues raised above regarding the supply of PCPs, their utilization by patients, and the performance of new PCP-based models of delivery suggest that relying on PCPs alone to coordinate care may be misguided.

---

[56] Sinsky, C., and Sinsky, T. (2015). Lessons from CareMore: A stepping stone to stronger primary care of frail elderly patients. *American Journal of Accountable Care*, 3(2), 45–48.

[57] Nundy, S., Kvedar, J., and Cella, G. (2020). From one-to-one to one-to many: Rethinking the health care relationships in the digital age. *Health Affairs Blog.*

[58] As a cautionary note, PCPs are not generally positive about the impact of using nurse practitioners (NPs) and physician assistants (PAs) on their own ability to provide quality of care. Survey data gathered by the Commonwealth Fund reveal that only 29% are positive about the quality impact of NPs and PAs; 41% are negative, while 18% report no impact and 12% are unsure. PCPs are more likely to be satisfied if they have an NP or PA in their office. While the vast majority (81%) of PCPs are satisfied with their collaboration with NPs and PAs, more are somewhat satisfied (46%) than very satisfied (35%). Of greater concern is that PCPs are less satisfied with this collaboration than are the NPs and PAs (89%). These are not necessarily research findings, but rather survey comments from a nonrandom sample of practitioners. Commonwealth Fund. *Primary Care Providers' Views of Recent Trends in Health Care Delivery and Payment.* August 2015 Issue Brief. Available online at: www.issuelab.org/resources/25044/25044.pdf. Accessed on March 6, 2020.

[59] Basu, S., Berkowitz, S., Phillips, R. et al. (2019). Association of primary care physician supply with population mortality in the United States, 2005–2015. *JAMA Internal Medicine*, 179(4), 506–514.

Even if valid, these approaches may be insufficient. Most researchers acknowledge that the elements of primary care identified above – e.g., teams, continuity of care, chronic care management, PCMHs, care coordination – must also be present. Teams serve the purposes of comprehensiveness, coordination, and collaboration; chronic care management likewise serves the purpose of comprehensiveness and continuity; and PCMHs serve the purposes of first-contact care and patient-centered care. The presence of such features is often what researchers mean when they use the phrase "well-functioning" or "high-performing" primary care.[60] However, the research base documenting the benefits bestowed by these elements is shaky.

Patient Care Teams

Advocates of health care reform have long been interested in the formation of *teams* of practitioners – within and across the disciplinary boundaries of medicine and nursing – to combat growing specialization and to offer more coordinated, comprehensive care. There are a large number of definitions of teams. One widely used definition is "a collection of individuals who are interdependent in their tasks, who share responsibility for outcomes, who see themselves and who are seen by others as an intact social entity embedded in one or more larger social systems ... and who manage their relationships across organizational boundaries."[61] This definition highlights a number of variables likely at play in determining some of the patient outcomes of teamwork.

Some have also espoused teams as vehicles to reduce status hierarchies among the different professions. A review of the history of health care teams – as seen by the fields of medicine and nursing – suggests the team concept may have had much less to do with coordinated care than previously thought. The team concept has been a long time in the making (perhaps without commensurate improvements), and has not yet leveled

---

[60] Primary care teams would follow in the late 1940s and 1950s. Cf.: Bodenheimer, T. (2007). *Building Teams in Primary Care: Lessons Learned*. Oakland, CA: California HealthCare Foundation; Levine, D., Landon, B. and Linder, J. (2019). Quality and experience of outpatient care in the United States for adults with or without primary care. *JAMA Internal Medicine*, 179(3), 363–372.

[61] Cohen, S. G., and Bailey, D. R. (1997). What makes teams work: Group effectiveness research from the shop floor to the executive suite. *Journal of Management*, 23(4), 238–290.

the status hierarchies separating the different professions. This argument is explored below.

The Physician View of Teams

In the era following release of *Medical Education in the United States and Canada*, a 1910 review and set of recommendations for medical schools that is also called the Flexner report, teams of physicians, health educators, and social workers were developed in some hospital outpatient departments.[62] Michael Davis, one of the pioneer investigators of medical care, advocated for efficiency improvements to bolster the efforts of scientifically trained specialists who were replacing the primary care, solo-practice physician (who had worked as a "lone ranger"). Specialized physicians would work cooperatively in an early form of "pooled interdependence,"[63] sharing space and equipment and drawing upon a common pool of nursing and other ancillary personnel (e.g., social workers) – referred to at the time as "subsidiary personnel" – in a hierarchical division of labor.

The Committee on the Costs of Medical Care (CCMC), of which Davis was a member, advocated for something more radical: prepaid, multi-disciplinary group practices to treat defined patient populations. These relied more on "reciprocal interdependence" in which specialists worked more interactively and collaboratively with PCPs, other specialists, and nonmedical personnel – often in multidisciplinary groups. However, Morris Fishbein, Editor of the *Journal of the American Medical Association (JAMA)* from 1924 to 1950, labeled the CCMC Report an "incitement to revolution," "socialist," and "communist." Shortly thereafter, *JAMA* published an article on the tenets of medical practice, emphasizing the primacy of solo practice and fee-for-service payment.[64]

Historians of this early "team approach" argue that it served the ideological purposes of the medical profession more than practical purposes. Team language and rhetoric were used extensively to describe the cooperation of scientifically specialized physicians with socially and behaviorally oriented nonphysicians. This was part of a conscious effort to compensate for the weak social considerations then given by physicians in medical care,

---

[62] Bodenheimer, T. (2007). *Building Teams in Primary Care: Lessons Learned*. Oakland, CA: California HealthCare Foundation.

[63] Thompson, J. D. (1967). *Organizations in Action*. New York: McGraw-Hill.

[64] For background on Fishbein's comments, see Gore, T. (2013). *Baylor University Medical Center Proceedings*, 26(2), 142–143.

and to dump onto other personnel the functions with which physicians no longer felt comfortable.[65]

Nevertheless, the physician team approach did take root at the periphery of the medical profession during subsequent decades in the form of prepaid group practices – as Davis and the CMMC had envisioned. Later known as health maintenance organizations (HMOs), these models included both generalist and specialist physicians caring for defined populations of enrolled patients – functioning much in the manner of Donald Berwick's "integrator" (i.e., an entity that accepts responsibility for the triple aim).[66] The HMO movement received federal imprimatur and financial support (through planning grants) in the 1973 HMO Act and initial Medicare support as a demonstration in the early 1980s. Employer support in the late 1980s and early 1990s was part of a private sector effort to control rising health care premiums. Economist Alain Enthoven's model of "managed competition" was based on rival HMO plans accepting capitated risk (paying per patient rather than per procedure, such as the Kaiser Permanente model) on a wide geographic basis.[67] Enthoven's model theorized that capitated, risk-bearing plans would be more effective at care management and cost containment by reversing the incentives of fee-for-service.[68]

The group/staff employment model HMOs that Davis and Enthoven envisioned achieved roughly one third of the share of the employer market by 1996, but then saw that share diminish rapidly over time. One reason was consumer backlash against the narrow networks and utilization review practices of such managed care plans during the late 1990s. A second reason was physician preference for the American Medical Association's tenets of fee-for-service, solo practice. Physicians manifested this

---

[65] Brown, T. (1982). An historical view of health care teams, in G. Agich (Ed.), *Responsibility in Health Care*. Dordrecht, Holland: D. Reidel Publishing, 3–21.

[66] Berwick, D., Nolan, T., and Whittington, J. (2008). The triple aim: Care, health, and cost. *Health Affairs*, 27(3), 759–769.

[67] Enthoven, A. (1993). The history and principles of managed competition. *Health Affairs*, 24–48, Supplement; Enthoven, A., and Singer, S. (1996). Managed competition and California's health care economy. *Health Affairs*, 15(1), 39–57.

[68] Whereas fee-for-service (FFS) promotes overuse, capitation promotes efficiency and maybe even errs on the side of underuse. The big question at the time was whether capitation led to skimping on care and poorer quality. Research suggested not: Medicare HMO patients were moderately less satisfied with the care they got than were Medicare FFS patients, but experienced no difference in quality. However, unlike in the commercial population, researchers found no discernible effects of HMOs on hospitalizations. HMOs ended up costing Medicare money. Insights courtesy of Randall Brown.

preference by forming their own HMOs – "independent practitioner associations" (IPAs) – in the 1970s and 1980s as a competitive reaction to the group/staff models. Consumers then manifested their own preference for the IPA model by migrating to such open-network models in the late 1990s and early 2000s. Nevertheless, policy advocates recognized the continuing importance of the group/staff HMO model for their "integration that encourages teamwork and coordination" and their cost containment and quality improvement capabilities.[69]

Despite these developments, the team model today may still reflect more policy aspiration than market reality. Research suggests that primary care practices remain fragmented and hierarchical rather than coordinated and collaborative.[70] Physicians may feel they do not have the time to collaborate with a team. Other research suggests that the replacement of hierarchies by teams may depend on idiosyncratic factors such as the physician's network centrality (e.g., enjoys the respect of others) and personality (e.g., orientation to being a team player).[71]

The Nursing View of Teams

Like physicians, nurses also employed team language after the Flexner Report, but for a different purpose: to minimize the hierarchy in the relationships between physicians and nonphysicians and to promote more egalitarian modes of organization and decision-making.[72] This was part of an effort to elevate the stature of nursing as a profession. This professionalization movement was pursued in terms of moving nurse training from hospital diploma programs to university-based bachelors' degree programs – a process that began in the 1920s and accelerated after the 1930s, and is nearly complete at present. Similar to the Flexner Report in medicine, the Goldmark Report of 1923 (*Nursing and Nurse Education in the United States*) called for strengthening the link between nurse education and

[69] Minott, J., Helms, D., Luft, H. et al. (2010). *The Group Employed Model as a Foundation for Health Care Delivery Reform*. New York: Commonwealth Fund.

[70] Chesluk, B., and Holmboe, E. (2010). How teams work – or don't – in primary care: A field study on internal medicine practices. *Health Affairs*, 29(5), 874–879.

[71] Riley, W., Wholey, D., Wilson, A. et al. "Informal Consultation in Medical Clinics: Intra- and Inter-Professional Talk," Paper presented at Organization Theory in Health Care Association Annual Meeting (Boston University, June 8, 2004).

[72] Brown, T. (1982). An historical view of health care teams, in G. Agich (Ed.), *Responsibility in Health Care*. Dordrecht, Holland: D. Reidel Publishing, 3–21.

university affiliations for schools of nursing.[73] Over time, many nonaffiliated schools closed while those with university affiliations increased.

The nursing profession also focused on team nursing. The concept of nursing teams developed in the 1950s to respond to shortages dating back to World War II and to changes in nursing skill mix by pairing nurses who worked together as a team to deliver patient care, thereby using the diversity of skills, education, and qualification level of the entire staff.[74] Instead of assigning hospital nurses as individuals to care for patients (hence, "private duty"), nurses were grouped together and overseen collectively by the nursing staff. This latter arrangement was labeled "team nursing" and allowed for greater nursing solidarity and enhanced status in the hospital. This movement also had its own hierarchic dimensions, however. Registered nurses returned home from World War II to find a host of nonnursing personnel (e.g., lesser-trained nurse aides and auxiliaries) who had replaced their depleted wartime numbers and were retained as hospitals underwent massive postwar expansion. The nursing profession responded by asserting the notion of teamwork but housing it under the leadership and authority of graduate-level nurses.

Earlier Literature on Teams
This historical chronicle suggests that team functioning was "challenged" from the beginning. Physicians did not view nurses as peers or valued colleagues, but rather as staff to do their bidding; nurses may have viewed nonnursing personnel the same way. Both physicians and nurses were quite territorial, and reluctant to share their knowledge and authority with others.[75] Medical sociologists writing in the 1970s acknowledged that the so-called teams that had been espoused by both physicians and nurses "did not function as they had been envisioned. The participants were too diverse and too unfamiliar to each other for the teams to function ideally. The peer relationship sought never emerged."[76] That is, the rhetoric of teams vastly outstripped reality. Others reached a similar conclusion.

[73] Goldmark, J. (1923). "Nursing and Nursing Education in the United States: Report of the Committee for the Study of Nursing Education and a Report of a Survey." New York: Macmillan.

[74] Fernandez, R., Johnson, M., Tran, D. T. et al. (2012). Models of care in nursing: A systematic review. *International Journal of Evidence-Based Healthcare*, 10(4), 324–337.

[75] Bodenheimer, T. (2007). *Building Teams in Primary Care: Lessons Learned*. Oakland, CA: California HealthCare Foundation.

[76] Banta, D., and Fox, R. (1972). Role strains of a health care team in a poverty community. *Social Science and Medicine*, (6), 697–722.

"Few interdisciplinary teams now practice in . . . [an] ideal way. Such teams are hard to form and even more difficult to maintain."[77]

During the 1980s, health care researchers began to examine delivery models that emphasized integrated, patient-centered care, often based on concepts taken from total quality management and W. Edwards Deming, an engineer and statistician.[78] Researchers at Dartmouth Medical School borrowed ideas from their colleagues at Dartmouth's business school. Paul Batalden (physician and researcher) and his colleagues recognized the potential benefit from applying such an approach to health care delivery in various patient units, including the spine center and intensive care nursery. Batalden, applying the work of Deming, emphasized the need to focus on the patient, the staff, and the leadership of the unit in *first-generation* "clinically-integrated microsystems" that cared for patients along their journey. These microsystems represented a new type of patient care team.[79]

Over time, a patient would move into and out of an assortment of clinical microsystems, such as a family practitioner's office, an emergency department, an intensive care unit, a surgical suite, an inpatient care unit, a cardiologist's office, a cardiac rehabilitation program, a nutritionist's office, and home-based nursing care from a visiting nurse. This assortment of clinical microsystems – combined with the patient's own actions to improve or maintain health – was viewed as the patient's unique health system. This patient-centric view of a health system became the foundation of *second-generation* clinical microsystems. There is no evidence that clinical micro-systems have widely diffused, perhaps because the evidence base for clinical microsystems has not been whopping. One study suggests that smaller scale projects are more successful than organization-wide changes, and that efforts are more often directed at administrative processes than clinical outputs.[80]

[77] Given, B., and Simmons, S. (1977). The interdisciplinary health team: Fact or fiction? *Nursing Forum*, (16), 165–184.

[78] Gerteis, M., Levitan, S. E., Daley, J. et al. (1993). *Through the Patient's Eyes: Understanding and Promoting Patient-Centered Care*. San Francisco: Jossey-Bass; Berwick, D., Godfrey, A. B., and Roessner, J. (1990). *Curing Health Care: New Strategies for Quality Improvement*. San Francisco, CA: John Wiley.

[79] Mohr, J. J., Batalden, P., and Barach, P. (2004). Integrating patient safety into the clinical microsystem. *Quality and Safety in Health Care*, (13), ii34–ii38; Nelson, E. C., Godfrey, M. M., Batalden, P. B. et al. (2008). Clinical microsystems, Part 1: The building blocks of health systems. *The Joint Commission Journal on Quality and Patient Safety*, 34(7), 367–378.

[80] Abrahamson, V., Jaswal, S., and Wilson, P. (2020). An evaluation of the clinical micro-systems approach in general practice quality improvement. *Primary Health Care Research & Development*, 21. https://doi.org/10.1017/S1463423620000158.

More Recent Literature on Teams

The word "team" in health care came into vogue as an umbrella concept and catch-all term for many different types of care delivery units, such as surgical teams, primary care clinics, and (later on) PCMHs, covered below. (It is also now in use in many other service businesses, as in your Starbucks team.) As an illustration, some researchers distinguish teams that emphasize the coordination of (1) care between nurses and other ancillary personnel on the front line of patient care; (2) the work of physicians with other physician specialties, subspecialties and the hospitals in which they work; and (3) clinical support services with diagnostic and therapeutic services.[81] They are all oriented to solving the problem of coordinating care for patients in a seamless fashion that meets the needs of individuals.

Other researchers distinguish care provider teams, patient clinics, and care management teams – and their implications for coordination.[82] *Care provider teams* consist of *all* the providers and caregivers who deliver care and support for a patient during the patient's trajectory (e.g., oncology care) through the health care system. Team members are unlikely to be colocated within the same organizational unit or even organization, but rather form a virtual network spanning multiple organizations. By contrast, *clinics* are usually functional teams located in one organization that are organized around a particular type of care (e.g., primary care, specialty) that focuses on providing a set of similar services to multiple patients. Less frequently, clinics can be multifunctional teams that encompass both primary and specialty care in the same building, but perhaps not colocated inside. Although the gains from organizing and colocating professionals by functional areas can be valuable (e.g., enhancing expertise in that area), the losses involve the difficulty in coordinating and integrating actions across clinics. *Care management teams* offer a third approach. Such teams provide services tailored to patients' circumstances and coordinated with multiprofessional team members. Examples include chronic care teams and PCMHs for individuals with multimorbidity. One advantage of the care management team is its ability to provide patients with a relational home, an expert adviser in navigating the care provider network, and immediate access to a range of needed expertise.

---

[81] Gerteis, M., Levitan, S. E., Daley, J. et al. (1993). *Through the Patient's Eyes: Understanding and Promoting Patient-Centered Care*. San Francisco: Jossey-Bass.

[82] Wholey, D. R., Zhu, X., Knoke, D. et al. (2012). Managing to care: Design and implementation of patient-centered care management teams, in D. Goldberg and S. Mick (Eds.), *Advances in Health Care Organization Theory*, 2nd Edition. San Francisco: Jossey-Bass.

Research Evidence on Teams

Given the diversity of teams (and team typologies) that have been developed, it is likely impossible to accumulate sufficient evidence on the impacts of any given team on patient outcomes and cost of care. Earlier research examined team structures and composition; similar to the quality literature, such structural measures were easy to collect but not powerful in explaining outcomes. More recently, researchers have sought to document the impact of "teamwork." This has led them to focus on antecedents (knowledge, skills, and attitudes) and team processes such as learning, psychological safety (perceived freedom to speak up), and changing on the fly (executing core tasks while learning and synthesizing new information).[83]

One review of the literature published between 1990 and 2008 summarized evidence around a causal model of team inputs (e.g., structure, organizational context), team process (e.g., leadership, communication, decision-making), and team outputs (e.g., clinical outcomes, cost effectiveness, quality).[84] As hinted at above, the review concludes that the types of teams studied are often not taken into account. Moreover, the outcomes analyzed are often too heterogeneous to draw comparisons and conclusions across studies. Finally, the causal mechanisms behind any observed team effects are rarely articulated since team characteristics are seldom measured, leaving the team intervention as "a black box." The handful of findings reported indicate that enhancing team expertise (e.g., by adding another clinician) may improve team process (e.g., adherence to clinical guidelines, care coordination, needs assessment) but with mixed impact on patient outcomes, utilization, and costs. Adding team members with responsibility for coordination (e.g., hospitalist, clinical nurse specialist) and other structural measures to improve communication has some positive effects on patient outcomes, but not on utilization or costs. There is no evidence for additive effects of enhancing expertise and adding members with coordinative responsibility.

Another literature review of studies conducted in England and published between 2001 and 2012 similarly used an input/process/outcome

[83] Rosen, M., Diaz-Granados, D., Dietz, A. et al. (2018). Teamwork in health care: Key discoveries enabling safer, high-quality care. *American Psychologist*, 73(4), 433–450.

[84] Bosch, M., Faber, M., Cruijsberg, J. et al. (2009). Effectiveness of patient care teams and the role of clinical expertise and coordination: A literature review. *Medical Care Research and Review*, 66(6), 5S–35S.

model to summarize findings on the performance of teams.[85] The review found that studies focus on several team processes, such as leadership, coordination, communication, teamwork, and nontechnical skills. Studies typically use different research approaches (e.g., observational studies, surveys) and different measures. The 28 studies reviewed use 41 different measures of team clinical performance (typically care errors and guideline adherence), and rarely conduct multivariate analyses. A third review highlights the pervasive nature of communication and coordination risks in teamwork.[86] For example, observational studies indicate that roughly 30 percent of team interactions in surgical services include a communication failure, and that such failures can result in preventable patient deaths.

Some Research Conclusions about Teams

The literature on the performance of care management teams offers several important conclusions.[87] First, teams may function better in specialized sites where the scope of work is narrow, faces less variation in patient conditions, and is more easily standardized. Such might be the case for teams in dental offices and medical specialists. By contrast, teams may not work as well in primary care sites and other clinics treating a wide diversity of patient conditions that resist standardization and routinization of work.[88]

Second, teamwork is a complex process that involves multiple disciplines and their sharing of knowledge, expertise, and skills in an iterative and reciprocal fashion. On the one hand, the addition of providers with unique expertise should provide quality advantages. On the other hand, their addition increases transaction costs – such as patient handoffs, time expended in them, and their potential communication lapses and

[85] Schmutz, J., and Manser, T. (2013). Do team processes really have an effect on clinical performance? A systematic literature review. *British Journal of Anaesthesia*, 110 (4), 529–544.

[86] Rosen, M., Diaz-Granados, D., Dietz, A. et al. (2018). Teamwork in health care: Key discoveries enabling safer, high-quality care. *American Psychologist*, 73(4), 433–450.

[87] Schmutz, J, Meier, L., and Manser, T. (2019). How effective is teamwork really? The relationship between teamwork and performance in health care teams: A systematic review and meta-analysis. *BMJ Open* (9); Lemieux-Charles, L., and McGuire, W. (2006). What do we know about health care team effectiveness? A review of the literature. *Medical Care Research and Review*, 63(3), 263–300; Rosen, M., Diaz-Granados, D., Dietz, A. et al. (2018). Teamwork in health care: Key discoveries enabling safer, high-quality care. *American Psychologist*, 73(4), 433–450.

[88] Bodenheimer, T. (2007). *Building Teams in Primary Care: Lessons Learned*. Oakland, CA: California Health Care Foundation.

errors – that increase the information flow and communication burden, and may harm team performance. Starfield herself acknowledged that primary care teams may have an optimal size of six people.[89]

Third, the team literature suggests the importance of processes believed to help foster organizational learning, human resource development, resource utilization, reduction of unnecessary costs, improved quality of work, and (finally) patient outcomes.[90] Many also highlight the need for good team leadership, a clearly defined division of labor, training of team members in nontechnical skills (e.g., team functioning), and the adoption of team rules regarding decision-making and communication. The team performance advantage may also rest on important but difficult changes in physician behavior, attitudes towards other non-physician professionals, and physician leadership, as well as supportive conditions in the organizational climate such as "psychological safety" and strategic implementation of team-based change efforts. As a result, there may be substantial infrastructure and process requirements for high-performing teams.

Fourth, "sharing" and "learning" are processes that are hard to develop and scale across an organization. As alluded to above, status differences within and across professional disciplines, communication difficulties, and task complexity serve as barriers to team performance.

Overall, the literature suggests a mixed track record on the relationship between teamwork and clinical performance – with several contextual variables impacting the teamwork effect (e.g., team size, composition, types and diversity of expertise, task characteristics, clinical setting, leadership). Moreover, we should note that some researchers have noted the faddish nature of these interdisciplinary care management teams and the tendency to view them as "the silver bullet" in health care.[91] Management research suggests that innovation adoption for faddish reasons may limit improvements in organizational performance.

---

[89] Starfield, B. (1998). *Primary Care: Balancing Health Needs, Services, and Technology*. New York: Oxford University Press.

[90] Marsilio, M., Torbica, A., and Villa, S. (2016). Health care multidisciplinary teams: The sociotechnical approach for an integrated system-wide perspective. *Health Care Management Review*, 42(4).

[91] Johnson, J. D. (2017). Interprofessional care teams: The perils of fad and fashions. *International Journal of Healthcare Management*, 19(2), 127–134; Grace, S., Rich, J., Chin, W. et al. (2016). Implementing interdisciplinary teams does not necessarily improve primary care practice climate. *American Journal of Medical Quality*, 31(1), 5–11.

Research has also demonstrated that it is not just the existence of a team, but rather its design and process (e.g., interactions) that are important. One study examined the performance of mental health teams in affecting hospitalizations.[92] Utilization was associated with two main factors in the team's design: expertise redundancy and transactive memory accuracy. Expertise redundancy is measured by the extent to which team members possess highly overlapping knowledge, which muddies the division of labor, reduces role clarity, and complicates its knowledge structure. Transactive memory accuracy is the extent to which team members accurately recognize experts in relevant knowledge domains, which allows team members to quickly access needed expertise and improves decision-making, task performance, and care.

Such collaborative models, although increasingly in the news, nevertheless face incredible headwinds.[93] There is a joint lack of a comprehensive theory on teams as well as little evidence base for the ability of several of these models to reduce cost and improve quality of care.[94] Not surprisingly, surveys reveal that clinicians express mixed views about the ability of such structures to improve the quality of care they deliver to patients.[95] Physicians may feel they do not have time for team meetings and collaboration. If care coordination is designed in a way to economize on the physician's time (i.e., saves rather than increases the time demands), then it has a chance of working. Otherwise, the intervention is not likely to get physician buy-in. Physicians are less sanguine about team prospects than nurse practitioners and physician assistants.[96] Such divergent opinions may make professional collaboration and thus organizational success more difficult to achieve.

---

[92] Zhu, X., and Wholey, D. (2018). Expertise redundancy, transactive memory, and team performance in interdisciplinary care teams. *Health Services Research*, 53(6), 4921–4942.

[93] Nordegraaf, M, and Burns, L. R. (2016). The paradoxes of leading and managing health care professionals: Toward the integration of health care services, in T. Hoff, K. Sutcliffe, and G. Young (Eds.), *The Healthcare Professional Work Force: New Directions in Theory and Practice.* Oxford, UK: Oxford University Press.

[94] Hoff, T., Prout, K., and Carabetta, S. (2020). How teams impact patient satisfaction: A review of the empirical literature. *Health Care Management Review*, 46(1), 75–85.

[95] Ryan, J., Doty, M. M., Hamel, L. et al. (2015). *Primary Care Providers' Views of Recent Trends in Health Care Delivery and Payment.* Washington, DC: The Commonwealth Fund, Available online at: www.commonwealthfund.org/publications/issue-briefs/2015/aug/primary-care-pro viders-views-recent-trends-health-care-delivery. Accessed September 29, 2020.

[96] Burns, L. R., and Pauly, M. V. (2018). Transformation of the health care industry: Curb your enthusiasm? *Milbank Quarterly*, 96(1), 57–109.

Care Management Practices

Similar to care management teams, there is a parallel literature on *care management practices* (CMPs) that are typically performed in teams. CMPs have perhaps been most extensively studied in the various waves of the National Survey of Physician Organizations. The CMPs include practice guidelines, carepaths and protocols, case management, disease management, demand management, patient registries, physician reminders, use of health risk appraisals, patient reminders, practice feedback to physicians, nurse care managers, and deployment of PCMH components (including use of EMRs, primary care teams, and electronic data interchange with hospitals and specialists).

Summarizing this literature is not easy; it is covered more fully in Chapter 6 in this volume. There are a large number of studies; the studies were conducted over nearly two decades; the types of CMPs studied are both large and changing (e.g., case management, performance feedback, disease registries, practice guidelines); and the outcome variables of interest are also both large and changing. Three general points are worth mentioning. First, CMPs are not widely practiced across physician organizations (medical groups, IPAs). Second, group performance is hard to improve over time. Third, research has examined the use of CMPs, but not whether they impact the cost and quality of care.

Care Continuity

Care continuity is one of Starfield's four pillars of primary care. Given that continuity is often considered the opposite of fragmentation, we briefly summarize some of the research on this element. Continuity has been studied in several different ways. Using a Herfindahl-Hirschman Index (HHI), some researchers examine continuity in terms of the concentration of patient visits with a particular provider. Others use a measure of network density to define continuity in terms of the cross-referrals of patients among a defined set of practitioners in a clinic or organization. The latter approach lends itself to efforts to promote continuity (and comprehensiveness) of care within closed network models of delivery like Kaiser Permanente. Still others use an HHI-like measure to assess the degree of dispersion or sharing of patients across hospitals in a network.

Regardless of the approach, studies find similar results. One set of researchers examined the cost, utilization, and complications among Medicare patients with chronic conditions seen for outpatient evaluation and management visits. The more these visits were concentrated in a single or small number of providers, the fewer the number of ED visits, the lower the risk of patient complications, and the lower their episode-of-care costs.[97] A similar study conducted among the Medicaid population in one state found that continuity was associated with a lower likelihood of hospitalization.[98] A third study established that the beneficial effects of provider continuity (in terms of fewer ED visits, fewer hospitalizations, lower costs) extended not only to PCPs but also to specialists.[99] Two other studies reported that continuity of care was also associated with substantial reductions in long-term mortality and lower rates of cardiovascular events.[100] Other studies report that continuity is correlated with fewer departures from best clinical practice, a reduction in preventable hospitalizations from ambulatory-sensitive conditions, and lower total cost of care.[101] Finally, studies report that higher levels of "sharing" (concentrating rather than dispersing) patients among a network of hospitals is associated with lower levels of Medicare spending per beneficiary and lower readmission rates.[102]

These studies are important because they rest on a similar underlying concept: concentration of patient visits over time with a similar set of providers. This parallels Berwick's notion of a provider organization serving as an integrator to assume accountability and financial risk for a defined population and its health and arrange a closed practitioner network (e.g., Kaiser Permanente) that can monitor and coordinate patient visits.[103] Unfortunately, such risk-based, closed network models are low in prevalence, as is the spread of capitation that undergirds the Kaiser

[97] Hussey, P., Schneider, E., Rudin, R. et al. (2014). Continuity and the costs of care for chronic disease. *JAMA Internal Medicine*, 174(5), 742–748.

[98] Gill, J., and Mainous III, A. (1998). The role of provider continuity in preventing hospitalizations. *Archives of Family Medicine* 7, 352–357.

[99] Romaire, M., Haber, S., Wensky, S. et al. (2014). Primary care and specialty providers: An assessment of continuity of care, utilization, and expenditures. *Medical Care*, 52(12), 1042–1049.

[100] Wolinsky, F., Bentler, S., Geweke, J. et al. (2010). Continuity of care with a primary care physician and mortality in older adults. *Journal of Gerontology*, 65A(4), 421–428; Shin, D. W., Cho, J., Yang, H. K. et al. (2014). Impact of continuity of care on mortality and health care costs: A nationwide cohort study in Korea. *Annals of Family Medicine*, 12(6), 534–541.

[101] Frandsen, B., Joynt, K., Rebitzer, J., et al. (2015). Care fragmentation, quality, and costs among chronically ill patients. *The American Journal of Managed Care*, 21(5), 355–362.

[102] Everson, J., Adler-Milstein, J., Hollingsworth, J. et al. (2020). Dispersion in the hospital network of shared patients is associated with less efficient care. *Health Care Management Review*. 08 Dec 2020, DOI: 10.1097/hmr.0000000000000295 PMID: 33298805.

[103] Berwick, D., Nolan, T., and Whittington, J. (2008). The triple aim: Care, health, and cost. *Health Affairs*, 27(3), 759–769.

Permanente model (see Chapter 6 in this volume on "Vertical Integration"). By contrast, the United States is dominated by fee-for-service payment models and open access networks that allow patients free provider choice and (oftentimes) self-referral without need of a PCP gatekeeper. Of course, it is important to try to determine the causal direction behind the associations reported in such studies. Perhaps what researchers have found reflects the possibility that patients who take better care of themselves have fewer needs and/or see fewer physicians.

Disease Management

Historically, providers that took on capitated risk (e.g., Kaiser Permanente) developed two models to care for the chronically ill population that they serve: disease management and chronic care management.[104] Disease management is more condition-specific; chronic care management reflects the growing reality of patients with multiple chronic conditions that need to be managed simultaneously. In one sense, chronic care management involves the coordination of multiple, condition-specific disease management programs. Both programs were developed for the primary care setting (e.g., to manage patients with diabetes) and share many of the same elements. Chronic care management programs are discussed in the section on care coordination below.

Providers have long experimented with disease management programs that identify patients with chronic conditions, monitor and educate those patients to better manage their conditions, and thereby pursue the goals of comprehensiveness, continuity, and coordination. Despite two decades of efforts, net program benefits – in terms of health status or spending – have remained elusive. The Congressional Budget Office found insufficient evidence that disease management programs for Medicare can even pay for themselves, concluding that any reduction in the cost of care is tempered by implementation costs.[105] Such programs sometimes improve patients' functional status but do not save money.[106] One nagging problem

---

[104] Wallace, P. (2005). Physician involvement in disease management as part of the CCM. *Health Care Financing Review*, 27(1), 19–31; Leeman, J., and Mark, B. (2006). The chronic care model versus disease management programs: A transaction cost analysis approach. *Health Care Management Review*, 31(1), 18–25.

[105] Congressional Budget Office. (2004). *An Analysis of the Literature on Disease Management Programs*. Washington, DC: CBO.

[106] Galbreath, A. D., Krasuski, R. A., and Smith, B. (2004). Long-term health care and cost outcomes of disease management in a large, randomized, community-based population with heart failure. *Circulation*, 110, 3518–3526.

has been patient disenrollment from health plans that curtails the latter's incentive to invest in such programs. Another related problem has been the long-term payout from disease management, whereby pediatric disease management efforts (e.g., to address type 2 diabetes or pre-diabetes) may yield benefits later on in adulthood – that are perhaps not detected by researchers.

Researchers summarized the experience of nine demonstration projects, many of them disease management demonstration programs funded since 1999 by CMS and its predecessor agency. There was a net increase in costs in most programs, no widespread evidence of improved compliance with evidence-based care, and no evidence of behavioral change by patients. One likely problem with these programs is their reliance on telephonic interventions by nurses in a call center (often in another state) who do not know the patient or the physician. CMS concluded that how a program is implemented and its willingness to undergo continual refinement are critical to overcoming operating problems in these programs.[107]

Such programs may improve quality but have no (or, at best, mixed) impact on cost and utilization. Supporters of disease management argue that the results of good programs are not published in scholarly journals. Major insurers continue to experiment and believe that they have achieved success. Often, however, patient sample sizes in their experiments are too small or the research designs are too informal to qualify as publishable evidence. Other studies suggest that disease management can sometimes control spending for beneficiaries who fully participate over long periods of time.[108] These findings, however, do not fully account for program costs and selection effects.

Lackluster results from disease management programs continue to be reported. A diabetes disease management program for Medicaid beneficiaries implemented in three states between 2000 and 2008 failed to impact inpatient costs and ED admissions.[109] A study of Medicaid disease

[107] Bott, D. M., Kapp, M. C., Johnson, L. B. et al. (2009). Disease management for chronically ill beneficiaries in traditional Medicare. *Health Affairs (Millwood)*, 28(1), 86–98.

[108] Atherly, A., and Thorpe, K. E. (2011). Analysis of the treatment effect of Healthways' Medicare health support Phase 1 pilot on Medicare costs. *Population Health Management*, 14(Supplement 1), S23–S28; Rula, E. Y., Pope, J. E., and Stone, R. E. (2011). A review of Healthways' Medicare health support program and final results for two cohorts. *Population Health Management*, 14(Supplement 1), S3–S10.

[109] Conti, M. (2013). Effect of Medicaid disease management programs on emergency department admissions and inpatient costs. *Health Services Research*, 48(4), 1359–1374.

management implementation in Georgia reported savings in the higher-risk patient groups that were not sufficient to offset program costs.[110] More recently, a team of researchers examined variation in patient responses to a disease management program that used community health workers, and found that over one third of those receiving the intervention experienced worse chronic disease control. The study illustrated that such programs do not work in general, and that the health behavior changes called for in such programs are challenging to many, leading to failure.[111]

Patient-Centered Medical Homes

To address the issue of coordination in disease management, Medicare and other insurers have implemented models to support and financially reimburse providers for care coordination. One prominent example is the PCMH, in which a team provides comprehensive patient services and is financially accountable for the care both inside and outside of the office. PCMHs embellish the PCP's office with a nurse practitioner, EMR, and linkages to help coordinate care with other practitioners. According to advocates, the PCMH works best when treating patients who have high-risk chronic conditions and when using face-to-face interactions among patients, physicians, and care coordinators. According to critics, the PCMH movement has assumed that these homes have the four pillars of primary care (the four Cs identified by Starfield), despite evidence to the contrary.[112]

Evidence suggests that PCMHs (1) improve certain aspects of quality, such as prevention and chronic disease management; (2) improve the

---

[110] Kranker, K. (2016). Effects of Medicaid disease management programs on medical expenditures: Evidence from a natural experiment in Georgia. *Journal of Health Economics*, (46), 52–69.

[111] Edlind, M., Mitra, N., Grande, D. et al. (2018). Why effective interventions do not work for all patients: Exploring variation in response to a chronic disease management intervention. *Medical Care*, Aug, 56(8), 719–726. By contrast, one promising (but unpublished) study suggests that disease management can greatly benefit patients if they are not receiving recommended testing at baseline and, thus, are not included in the programs. Such programs may yield substantial cost savings and improved health outcomes in the short term. The key to these programs is correct targeting of patients who have not been assessed in terms of their health status and can benefit from treatment. Simcoe, T., Catillon, M., and Gertler, P. (2017). Who Benefits Most in Disease Management Programs: Improving Target Efficiency. (Unpublished manuscript).

[112] Berenson, R., and Burton, R. (2016). How solid is the primary care foundation of the medical home? *Health Affairs Blog*, https://www.healthaffairs.org/do/10.1377/forefront.20160325.054144/full/.

patient's experience; and (3) reduce ED utilization.[113] By achieving these results, the homes bend the cost trend for a while and address the triple aim, including improving care for individuals and populations. Much of this evidence comes from dominant, well-established care networks.[114] Evidence from Seattle-based Group Health (now Kaiser Permanente Washington), for instance, indicates that realizing these improvements may require large staffs, strong institutional management, and the capacity to manage change.[115] Other evidence suggests that PCMHs have exhibited a decreasing commitment to three of the four Cs by virtue of focusing solely on care coordination.[116] More generally, demonstration projects suggest that any improvements rest on a multiyear commitment to change, long-term practice transformation, an internal capability for organizational learning, and development by physicians of a willingness to collaborate and function as a part of a care team. Most interventions to redesign physician practices do not meet such expectations.[117]

PCPs are also not entirely positive about the impact of PCMHs. Only 33% of PCPs believe the PCMH helps to improve the quality of care they provide; 14% report it has a negative impact; 26% report no impact, and 27% are unsure. Similarly, only 14% of PCPs report that accountable care organizations (ACOs) have a positive impact on the quality of care they provide to their patients; 26% report that ACOs exert a negative impact; 21% report no impact, while 38% are unsure. Finally, only 22% of PCPs

---

[113] Cooley, W. C., McAllister, J. W., Sherrieb, K. et al. (2009). Improved outcomes associated with medical home implementation in pediatric primary care. *Pediatrics*, 124(1), 358–364; Grumbach, K., Bodeheimer, T., and Grundy, P. (2010). *Outcomes of Implementing Patient Centered Medical Home Interventions: A Review of the Evidence from Prospective Evaluation Studies in the United States.* Washington, DC: Patient-Centered Primary Care Collaborative.

[114] Grumbach, K., Bodenheimer, T., and Grundy, P. (2010). *Outcomes of Implementing Patient-Centered Medical Home Interventions: A Review of the Evidence from Prospective Evaluation Studies in the United States.* Washington, DC: Patient-Centered Primary Care Collaborative.

[115] Reid, R. J., Coleman, K., Johnson, E. A. et al. (2010). The group health medical home at year two: Cost savings, higher patient satisfaction, and less burnout for providers. *Health Affairs (Millwood)*, 29(5), 835–843.

[116] Berenson, R., and Burton, R. (2016). How solid is the primary care foundation of the medical home? *Health Affairs Blog*, https://www.healthaffairs.org/do/10.1377/forefront.20160325.054144/full/.

[117] Crabtree, B. F., Chase, S. M., Wise, C. G. et al. (2011). Evaluation of patient-centered medical home practice transformation initiatives. *Medical Care* 49(1), 10–16; Nutting, P. A., Crabtree, B. F., Miller, W. M. et al. (2011). Transforming physician practices to patient-centered medical homes: Lessons from the national demonstration project. *Health Affairs*, 30(3), 439–446.

believe that the use of quality metrics as a vehicle to assess their performance has a positive impact on the quality of care they provide; 50% believe
these metrics have a negative impact![118]

Chronic Care Management

CCM possesses many of the same features as care coordination programs,
making them difficult to distinguish. For example, CCM is one suggested
way to reduce care fragmentation and improve coordination for
patients.[119] CCM attempts to directly address care coordination by emphasizing specific activities that improve coordination, such as the use of care
managers to support remote patient monitoring, referral coordination, and
self-care management plans.[120] Such activities can increase integration of
patient care activities, and, hopefully, improve outcomes through more
frequent patient contact, better communication, and closer followup.[121]

CCM success may rely on work that occurs outside of traditional, in-
person care models. For instance, longitudinal monitoring of care across
and between in-person provider visits takes significant time and resources.
As a result, CCM activities can be hard to integrate into traditional care
delivery models. Compounding this is the fact that CCM activities have
historically been excluded from fee-for-service reimbursement systems,
giving providers little incentive for providers to adopt these approaches.

---

[118] Burns, L. R., and Pauly, M. V. (2018). Transformation of the health care industry: Curb
your enthusiasm? *Milbank Quarterly*, 96(1), 57–109.

[119] Hong, C. S., Siegel, A. L., and Ferris, T. G. (2014). Caring for high-need, high-cost
patients: What makes for a successful care management program? *Commonwealth Fund*
(Available online at: www.commonwealthfund.org/publications/issue-briefs/2014/aug/
caring-high-need-high-cost-patients-what-makes-successful-care. Accessed September
29, 2020);
Hong, C. S., Abrams, M.K., and Ferris, T. G. (2014). Toward increased adoption of
complex care management. *New England Journal of Medicine*, 371(6), 491–493.

[120] McDonald, K. M., Sundaram, V., Bravata, D. M. et al. (2007). *Closing the Quality Gap:
A Critical Analysis of Quality Improvement Strategies*, Volume 7 – Care Coordination.
Rockville, MD: Agency for Healthcare Research and Quality, US Department of Health
and Human Services.

[121] Dalzell, M. D. (2015). Chronic care management payments: Another step away from fee-
for-service. *Management Care*, 24(2), 33–35; O'Malley, A. S., Sarwar, R., Keith, R. et al.
(2017); Provider experiences with chronic care management (CCM) services and fees:
A qualitative research study, *Journal of General Internal Medicine*, 32(12), 1294–1300;
Wilson, C., O'Malley, A. S., Bozzolo, C. et al. (2019). Patient experiences with chronic
care management services and fees: A qualitative study. *Journal of General Internal
Medicine*, 34(2), 250–255.

Care Coordination Programs

Like CCM, care coordination attempts to manage patients with multiple chronic conditions.[122] Health care delivery is typically organized around organ systems or medical conditions, making coordination across physicians difficult.[123] Care is often dispersed across multiple providers, settings, and health systems, with patients visiting multiple PCPs and specialists annually.

For example, Medicare fee-for-service beneficiaries see an average of two primary care providers and five specialists across four sites of care annually.[124] A physician treating 257 Medicare patients would be linked through patients with up to 229 other physicians practicing in 117 care sites.[125] The coordination burden rises with chronicity of illness. Medicare beneficiaries with seven or more chronic conditions see an average of eight specialists working in seven different sites.[126] In one case of oncological care, the cancer patient and their PCP were joined by 11 other providers (e.g., surgeon, hematologist, interventional radiologist, pathologist, social worker) – involving 11 office visits and 5 procedures – in the first 80 days after diagnosis. The PCP alone had 52 communications with other providers and the patient during this interval as part of the effort to coordinate care.[127] The coordination burden may be even greater: over 30 percent of Medicare patients who are "high utilizers" use multiple hospitals within two years.[128]

---

[122] Bodenheimer, T. and Berry-Millett, R. (2009). *Care Management of Patients with Complex Health Care Needs*. Princeton, NJ: Robert Wood Johnson Foundation, Research Synthesis Report No. 19.

[123] Bodenheimer, T. (2008). Coordinating care – A perilous journey through the health care system. *New England Journal of Medicine*, 358(10), 1064.

[124] Pham, H. H., Schrag, D., O'Malley, A. S. et al. (2007). Care patterns in Medicare and their implications for pay for performance. *New England Journal of Medicine*, 356(11), 1130–1139s.

[125] Pham, H. H., O'Malley, A. S., Bach, P. B. et al. (2009). Primary care physicians' links to other physicians through Medicare patients: The scope of care coordination. *Annals of Internal Medicine*, 150(4), 236–242.

[126] Pham, H. H., O'Malley, A. S., Bach, P. B. et al. (2009). Primary care physicians' links to other physicians through Medicare patients: The scope of care coordination. *Annals of Internal Medicine*, 150(4), 236–242.

[127] Press, M. J. (2014). Instant replay: A quarterback's view of care coordination. *New England Journal of Medicine*, 371, 489–491.

[128] Pham, H. H., Schrag, D., O'Malley, A. S. et al. (2007). Care patterns in Medicare and their implications for pay for performance. *New England Journal of Medicine*, 356(11), 1130–1139; Hempstead, K., Delia, D., Cantor, J. C. et al. (2014). The fragmentation of hospital use among a cohort of high utilizers: Implications for emerging care coordination strategies for patients with multiple chronic conditions. *Medical Care*, 52 (Supplement 3), S67–S74.

Care is thus dispersed across multiple practitioners in multiple specialties practicing in multiple sites. That is a lot of care coordination to perform. To paraphrase the saying popularized by Hillary Clinton, "it takes a village" to coordinate care. However, it may not be easy to coordinate such a large village.

Patients with multiple chronic conditions use an even larger number of providers and have lower percentages of visits to their assigned PCPs than other patients do. By definition, providers thus face challenges in ensuring continuity of care (concentration of visits in one office). Physicians will be challenged to coordinate care for such patients unless ACOs and IDNs can drastically reduce the number of providers patients can choose among. This will be hard, because traditional fee-for-service Medicare does not mandate narrow networks and most patients do not prefer them. It will remain a difficult task even in narrower networks, however: PCPs likely do not have the expertise or time to address the multiple needs of their chronically ill patients. But this continuity may be important to pursue because, at any one time, a relatively small proportion of Medicare patients account for most of Medicare's spending.[129]

Research Evidence on Care Coordination

The evidence base for care coordination has never been strong, despite the fact that researchers have been examining the issue for nearly half a century. Starfield herself acknowledged that the benefits of coordination are less well documented than the other pillars of primary care.

While care coordination among multiple providers has long remained a target, it has also remained an elusive goal. CMS funded 15 demonstrations of care coordination between 2002 and 2006 for Medicare populations under the Medicare Coordinated Care Demonstration. None of the 15 programs generated net savings for the full population; most failed to reduce hospitalizations.[130] Only three sites reduced patient costs and admissions; and even in those sites, there were no net savings to Medicare after factoring in care coordination fees. The most favorable conclusion was that the demonstration's mixed findings were more positive than the negative results of

---

[129] Anderson, G., and Horvath, J. (2004). Chronic conditions: Making the case for ongoing care. Baltimore: Partnership for Solutions, September 1.

[130] Peikes, D., Chen, A., Schore, J. et al. (2009). Effects of care coordination on hospitalization, quality of care, and health care expenditures among Medicare beneficiaries. *Journal of the American Medical Association*, 301(6), 603–618.

two prior care coordination efforts undertaken by CMS that had similar goals and patient populations: the Medicare Health Support program and the Medicare Disease Management Demonstration. Evaluators concluded that care coordination alone "holds little promise of reducing total Medicare expenditures for beneficiaries with chronic illness." Researchers studying another multicenter trial of care coordination similarly found little impact on utilization.[131]

Two of the three sites that reduced gross spending subsequently shut down after six years in the demonstration; only one site – Health Quality Partners (HQP) – continued to operate under the demonstration to be evaluated by CMS. The researchers singled out HQP for its promise to improve patients' health status. It too, was then closed down.[132] Followup research by one of the chapter authors uncovered some additional features of the HQP site that may have supported its success. These included the fact that the program was a spinoff operation of Doylestown Hospital, which is located in a geographic market with a good payer mix and relatively few minority, poor, or Medicaid-insured patients.[133] Moreover, at the time of the study, Doylestown Hospital had operated a physician-hospital organization, had its CEO in place for more than 20 years, and had stable medical staff leadership over that same period. Such characteristics have been found in prior research to foster strong physician-hospital relationships and collaboration.[134] Finally, HQP had three idiosyncratic features: (1) a web-based and data-driven approach to patient management used by physicians and care managers to routinely generate reports; (2) group

---

[131] Boult, C., Reider, L., Leff, B. et al. (2011). The effect of guided care teams on the use of health services: Results from a cluster-randomized controlled trial. *Archives of Internal Medicine*, 171(5), 460–466. Boult, C., Leff, B., Boyd, C. M. et al. (2013). A matched-pair cluster-randomized trial of guided care for high-risk older patients. *Journal of General Internal Medicine*, 28(5), 612–621.

[132] When queried why it closed down the one quasi-successful program, CMS officials responded, "It was a demonstration site and we demonstrated that it could work." According to Randall Brown, the story is a bit more complicated than that. "What happened was that CMS commissioned Mathematica to prepare a detailed operational protocol for HQPs program, so that other organizations could implement it too. Unfortunately, after having favorable results for the high-risk subset of its patients for six years and expanding to nearby areas to serve such patients, the program was no longer found to be effective. So the operational protocol was not distributed."

[133] Nevertheless, the Washington University program had a lot of minority and poor Medicaid patients; it was quite successful (even more than HQP, actually, with bigger impacts on a much larger sample).

[134] Prospective Payment Assessment Commission (ProPAC). (1992). *Winners and Losers under the Medicare Program*. Washington, DC: ProPAC.

education on fall prevention and weight loss; and (3) protocols to ensure that interventions were implemented consistently as the program grew.

The sophistication and comprehensiveness of its approach enabled HQP to achieve higher success with high-risk enrollees (e.g., patients with congestive heart failure, coronary artery disease, congestive obstructive pulmonary disease) compared to the control group, including 34 percent fewer hospitalizations, 22 percent lower Medicare costs, and improved outcomes on several measures.

The Coordinated Care Demonstration nevertheless offered several lessons. First, the programs demonstrated positive but modest impacts only for Medicare beneficiaries with multiple treatable chronic conditions and very serious illness; they were not effective for the broader, lower-risk Medicare population with chronic illnesses. Thus, programs need to be "targeted" at patients with substantial but easily identified risk for repeated hospitalization. Four of the programs had statistically significant reductions in hospitalizations for this high-risk subgroup over a six-year period. As evidence, one of the 15 sites that was initially unsuccessful in reducing hospitalizations or spending ultimately achieved some success when it abandoned care management for most patients and focused instead on those at greatest risk for hospitalization.[135]

Second, the four successful sites shared certain characteristics that most of the unsuccessful ones did not have, including: (1) nurse coordinators who were specially trained care managers with low caseloads that serve as the communication hub; (2) explicit transitional care models (e.g., coordinators contacted patients during hospital stays, requested copies of patient discharge instructions, and used protocols for patient transitions); (3) timely information for coordinators on acute episodes (hospital admissions, ED visits); (4) patient self-management education using proven behavioral change techniques (e.g., taking medications properly); (5) in-person contact with the nurse care coordinator; (6) presence of informal caregivers; (7) multidisciplinary teams that included physicians who were in close proximity to care coordinators; and (8) substantial and intensive interactions among patients and care coordinators – but not requiring substantial time from the PCP.[136]

[135] Peikes, D., Peterson, G., Brown, R. et al. (2012). How changes in Washington University's Medicare coordinated care demonstration pilot ultimately achieved savings. *Health Affairs*, 31(6), 1216–1226.

[136] Brown, R. (2009). *The Promise of Care Coordination: Models that Decrease Hospitalizations and Improve Outcomes for Medicare Beneficiaries with Chronic Illnesses.* (National Commission on Care Coordination (N3C); Brown, R. (2013).

This is a constellation of many features that may need to be present. Such discussions of constellations are quite frequent in the literature on care coordination. They are also embedded in descriptions of "comprehensive care models" that serve the high-cost, chronically ill population.[137] Unfortunately, it is difficult to test models with a constellation of features and know which features are most important; it may not even be a sensible or realistic approach.[138] Evaluation researchers refer to this as "multi-treatment interference" which serves as a threat to internal validity. It is also difficult to fully replicate such empirical evaluations.

The four sites in the Medicare Coordinated Care Demonstration developed four different care coordination programs that reduced hospitalizations over a six-year period. This was not just a one-off finding: the sites proved it was possible to do so. However, the reductions were not enough to offset the cost of the total program. This suggests that program costs need to be kept low to make such programs feasible. The results also call into question whether massive, large-scale programs can achieve the success observed in the four local sites.

Care Coordination Networks Involving Multiple Organizations

A complement to care coordination models focused on primary care practices is interorganizational models of care to facilitate transitions in cancer care, mental health, PAC, and palliative care. Network coordination

"Lessons for ACOs and Medical Homes on Care Coordination for High-Need Beneficiaries." Presentation to AcademyHealth Annual Meeting; Brown, R., Peikes, D., Peterson, G. et al. (2012). Six features of Medicare coordinated care demonstration programs that cut hospital admissions of high-risk patients. *Health Affairs*, 31(6), 1156–1166.

[137] McCarthy, D., Ryan, J., and Klein, S. (2015). *Models of Care for High-Need, High-Cost Patients: An Evidence Synthesis.* New York: Commonwealth Fund.

[138] Different features will "be important" for different patients and different programs/providers. Moreover, how well the component is implemented will influence whether it turns out to be effective. According to Randall Brown, "We aren't looking for the nonexistent silver bullet. We are looking for a set of features that have been found to be associated with success. Individual programs/payors/providers will have to see what is feasible in their system. Doing a few of the things well may matter more than doing them all poorly. More importantly, the nurse care coordinators need to figure out what each patient needs to overcome the problems that lead to their hospitalizations. The point is that small programs that have certain features can actually reduce hospitalizations by about 15 percent. That's consistent with about a 10 percent reduction in Medicare costs. That may not produce much or any net savings, but even if it breaks even, it's an improvement, since beneficiaries are much better off for not having to be in the hospital as often."

can be accomplished by developing tools to help organizations share information by establishing boundary-spanning roles, developing care plans, and standardizing provider roles and care pathways across organizations. Accomplishing coordination in interorganizational networks is likely to require significant investment in information technology as well as the willingness of providers and organizations to adapt their practices to network standards. Justifying this investment requires a high number of clients shared across network providers in order to achieve scale economies.

Such coordination also runs the risk of eliminating the "exceptionalism" of some types of care (e.g., treatment for substance abuse disorders) when it is rolled under the administrative hierarchy of other types of care (e.g., mental health), resulting in the erosion of distinctive treatment approaches and priorities.[139] This suggests that not all that is specialized should be integrated, or that it should be done so with caution. There may be more of a dialectic between the two that cautions against structural efforts to coordinate them. To effectively coordinate such care, efforts must make clear who takes the lead responsibility – e.g., a behavioral health coordinator or a nursing care coordinator – for the patient who is both severely mentally and chronically ill.

Research on the interplay of other organizations in promoting higher quality and/or cost-effective patient care has emerged slowly and sporadically. Lehman explored the need for organizations involved in societal health to coordinate their efforts.[140] Researchers also analyzed community-based, multidisciplinary treatment teams that began in the 1970s. Such teams evolved into community treatment networks in the early 2000s, such as the National Cancer Institute Community Cancer Centers Program.[141]

Community Care Networks

During the early 1990s, a vision took shape in a movement paralleling the movement towards IDNs. Researchers, professional associations, and foundations came together to sponsor and study interagency collaborations known as "community care networks" (CCNs), a demonstration

[139] Burnam, M. A., and Watkins, K. (2006). Substance abuse with mental disorders: Specialized public systems and integrated care. *Health Affairs*, 25(3), 648–658.

[140] Lehman, E. (1975). *Coordinating Health Care: Exploration of Interorganizational Relations*. Beverly Hills, CA: Sage.

[141] Clausner, S., Johnson, M., O'Brien, D. et al. (2009). Improving clinical research and cancer care delivery in community settings: Evaluating the NCI community cancer centers program. *Implementation Science*, 4.

running from 1994 to 1997. Partnerships developed between hospitals, community health centers, public agencies, community and advocacy groups, insurers, and educational institutions. Specific components of the CCN vision were community accountability, community health focus, creation of a seamless service continuum, and management under limited resources. Researchers concluded there were at least five primary attributes and activities of CCN partnerships that contributed to the value and sustainability of such collaborative capacity: outcomes-based advocacy, vision-focus balance, systems orientation, infrastructure development, and community linkages.[142] Nevertheless, while the partnering organizations willingly collaborated in identifying community health needs, coordinating services, and reporting to the community, they showed less alacrity in joining forces to reduce redundancy and increase efficiency.[143] Moreover, like other touted demonstration projects, the CCN funding was terminated.

Post-Acute Care Networks

During the past decade, some researchers have begun to focus their attention on PAC providers, such as home health agencies, skilled nursing facilities (SNFs), intermediate rehabilitation facilities (IRFs), and long-term care hospitals. This focus has been driven by several factors.

- First, a slowly rising percentage (roughly 40–42 percent) of Medicare beneficiaries with an episode of acute care hospitalization are discharged to PAC sites of care (versus to home).
- Second, research suggests that perhaps the greatest source of Medicare spending variation is not found among acute care hospitals, but rather among PAC providers.[144]
- Third, hospitals have developed vertical and virtual relationships with some PAC providers in building their IDN and ACO networks.[145]

[142] Alexander, J., Weiner, B., Metzger, M. et al. (2003). Sustainability of collaborative capacity in community health partnerships. *Medical Care Research and Review*, 60(4).

[143] Bazzoli, G., Stein, R., Alexander, J., et al. (2001). Public–private collaboration in health and human service delivery: Evidence from community partnerships. *Milbank Quarterly*, 75(4), 533–561.

[144] Newhouse, J., and Garber, A. (2013). Geographic variation in Medicare services. *New England Journal of Medicine*, 368, 1465–1468; Banerjee, M., Chen, L., Norton, E. et al. (2017). Surgical post-acute care spending driven by choice of post-acute care setting rather than intensity of services. *Health Affairs*, 36(1), 83–90.

[145] Konetzka, R. T., Stuart, E., and Werner, R. (2018). The effect of integration of hospitals and post-acute care providers on Medicare payment and patient outcomes. *Journal of Health Economics*, 61, 244–258.

- Fourth, CMS sponsorship of value-based payment models (e.g., Hospital Readmissions Reduction Program, ACOs) places a premium on using more cost-effective sites of care, including PAC sites.
- Fifth, the Medicare Payment Advisory Commission has examined how to identify higher-quality PAC providers and encourage Medicare beneficiaries to utilize them.[146]
- Sixth, like IDNs and ACOs, Medicare Advantage (MA) plans have developed networks of providers (including PAC sites) that are more narrow than those available to the Medicare fee-for-service population in an effort to channel patients to lower-cost sites of care, reduce utilization of higher-cost sites (e.g., SNFs), and achieve higher MA "Star Ratings" of quality.[147] Other plans serving the Medicaid population and individuals enrolled on the state health insurance exchanges encouraged by the ACA have similarly developed narrow network plans. As noted above, narrow networks may promote continuity of care.

There has been a long-standing focus on using interorganizational networks of providers to coordinate a patient's care across sites and increase "value" (defined as the quotient of quality over cost). Following the Inpatient Prospective Payment System, hospitals focused on discharging patients to certain PAC sites (nursing homes) to reduce hospital stays (not to improve quality but to lower the hospital's cost). More recently, hospitals have shifted emphasis to reducing use of more expensive PAC sites (like nursing homes) to using less expensive PAC sites (e.g., home health care). This focus has been driven in part by bundled payments as well as evidence that much of the variation in cost rests in PAC services.

Just having linkages to PAC sites (whether via vertical integration or a contractual relationship) does not impact readmissions and intensity of care in the Medicare population, however.[148] Research on the Medicare population shows that the major driver of variation in PAC spending after hospital discharge is the choice of the particular PAC site (i.e., IRF versus

---

[146] Medicare Payment Advisory Commission. (2018). Encouraging Medicare Beneficiaries to Use Higher Quality Post-Acute Care Providers, *Report to the Congress: Medicare and the Health Care Delivery System*. Washington, DC: MedPAC. Chapter 5.

[147] Skopec, L., Berenson, R., and Feder, J. (2018). *Why Do Medicare Advantage Plans Have Narrow Networks?* Washington, DC: The Urban Institute.

[148] Konetzka, R. T., Stuart, E., and Werner, R. (2018). The effect of integration of hospitals and post-acute care providers on Medicare payment and patient outcomes. *Journal of Health Economics*, 61, 244–258.

SNF), which suggests that an important form of coordination is facility selection at time of discharge.[149] There is some evidence that concentration of PAC for MA enrollees in a smaller number of PAC provider sites (i.e., concentration of care – similar to care continuity) may help to facilitate a reduction in both hospital readmissions and intensity of PAC utilization compared to the Medicare fee-for-service population.[150] Indeed, some research suggests that it is not so much that narrow networks foster more cost-effective care, but rather that hospitals, particularly those operating their own risk plan (e.g., MA) or operating within an ACO, contract with a narrow subset of PAC providers with more cost-effective care with whom they have established relationships.[151]

Nevertheless, there may be some natural limits to using the narrow network and concentration strategy to promote coordinated care. First, physicians have to play two crucial roles in PAC, which can inform the treatment options chosen by patients and their families: (1) ensure the seamless delivery of care and (2) advocate/facilitate better decision-making. They need to know enough to make proper referrals; this, in turn, requires collaboration with discharge planners and patients.[152] Second, efforts to promote "regionalization" of care in a smaller number of advanced sites (now referred to as centers of excellence) have suffered fits and starts since the 1960s – suggesting it is an attractive idea that is nevertheless difficult to implement. Third, there is no strong evidence base for the sustained savings from such centers of excellence. Fourth, the use of narrow networks in defined populations may itself be limited. According to the Urban Institute, one third of Medicare enrollees have enrolled in MA plans; among them, only one third are enrolled in narrow network plans.[153] Fifth, despite some recent traction in the MA, ACO, and

---

[149] Chen, L., Norton, E., Banerjee, M. et al. (2017). Surgical post-acute care spending driven by choice of post-acute care setting rather than intensity of services. *Health Affairs*, 36 (1), 83–90; Werner, R. M., Coe, N. B., Qi, M., et al. (2019). Patient outcomes after hospital discharge to home with home health care vs to a skilled nursing facility. *JAMA Internal Medicine*, 179, 617–623. https://doi.org/10.1001/jamainternmed.2018.7998.

[150] Huckfeldt, P., Escarce, J., Rabideau, B. et al. (2017). Less intense post-acute care, better outcomes for enrollees in Medicare advantage than those in fee-for-service. *Health Affairs*, 36(1).

[151] Skopec, L., Berenson, R., and Feder, J. (2018). *Why Do Medicare Advantage Plans Have Narrow Networks?* Washington, DC: The Urban Institute.

[152] Kane, R. (2011). Finding the right level of posthospital care. *Journal of the American Medical Association*, 305(3), 284–293.

[153] Skopec, L., Berenson, R., and Feder, J. (2018). *Why Do Medicare Advantage Plans Have Narrow Networks?* Washington, DC: The Urban Institute.

ObamaCare health insurance exchange markets, employers and the bulk of the privately insured commercial market have not moved in that direction. Part of this is due to the historical contraction in the HMO model among employer insurance offerings; part of this is due to employers' and employees' preference for broader access networks. Kaiser Family Foundation data indicate that only 8 percent of firms offering health benefits had narrow networks in 2017; by contrast, employers are more likely to offer high-deductible health plans that may or may not restrict network access.[154] There are also potential downsides of such narrow networks, at least for some clinical conditions. Finally, research shows that narrow networks on the health insurance exchanges may also exclude high-quality providers of cancer care, such as National Cancer Institute-Designated Cancer Centers.[155]

OTHER MECHANISMS TO PROMOTE COORDINATION

The EMR System as the Solution

There is a widespread belief that care coordination is promoted by the presence of an EMR, separate from its integration into care delivery models such as the PCMH. Some may actually believe that the EMR is care coordination. This belief should not be surprising. For decades, researchers have similarly equated the mere presence of an EMR with "clinical integration." Chapter 6 suggests that may not be true. As we explicate below, EMRs may be more a tool that can be used well or poorly than a powerful solution.

Promise of the EMR

EMRs may help to collate and organize patient information for providers and improve the easy distribution of this information across all providers caring for a patient. Such distribution of information could decrease fragmentation, decrease duplicate test ordering, reduce medical errors, and alert providers of new health issues or events (e.g., hospitalization), all of which could facilitate care coordination. This may be particularly helpful for patients who see multiple specialists, when patients have an acute hospitalization or emergency room visit, or transition across care

---

[154] Claxton, G., Rae, M., Long, M. et al. (2017). Employer health benefits survey. Kaiser Family Foundation and Health Research & Educational Trust.

[155] Yasaitis, L., Bekelman, J., Polsky, D. (2017). Relation between narrow networks and providers of cancer care. *Journal of Clinical Oncology*, 35(27), 3131–3136.

settings. With well-developed EMRs, every provider can have access to the same accurate and up-to-date information about a patient.

Inherent Limits to this Promise

EMRs do indeed contain valuable information to support care coordination, such as: lab test results, image scans, medication lists, and physician progress notes. In this manner, EMRs can facilitate *within-office* care coordination, mainly by providing real-time access to data during the patient encounter when it can be used in decision-making with patients, and through electronic messaging with office staff. EMRs serve as a digital version of the patient's paper-based medical chart, which constitutes a single record and source of access to the patient's medical history and updates that history via new provider entries at the time of new patient visits. Indeed, in one study of small- and medium-sized physician practices, physicians and staff reported that EMR systems helped them coordinate patient care within their practice.

The utility of EMRs for *across-office* coordination – i.e., visits by patients to different providers in different sites of care – is more debatable. EMRs potentially allow different providers to track the patient's condition at sporadic moments (tied to new patient visits) and "communicate" with one another asynchronously via updated, written notes rather than synchronous conversations. There are obviously several limits here: no real-time interaction among providers, no synchronous coordination, and no care coordination in the absence of interoperable EMRs.

EMRs were never designed to serve the purpose of care coordination across the continuum of care – e.g., to manage clinical conditions (interactive decision-making, setting care plans) as part of a dynamic process involving multiple, distributed practitioners.[156] Rather, they were designed to capture diagnostic codes for purposes of billing and point-in-time documentation in a patient visit. EMRs also lack the ability and functionality to engage physicians, patients, and/or their families in care coordination.

A Harris Poll conducted on behalf of Stanford Medicine found that physicians discount the value of EMRs as a clinical tool, and see them instead as data storage devices. Only 13% of office-based and 23% of hospital-based physicians stated that the EMR's primary value was care

---

[156] O'Malley, A., Grossman, J., Cohen, G. et al. (2009). Are electronic medical records helpful for care coordination? Experiences of physician practices. *Journal of General Internal Medicine*, 25(3), 177–185.

coordination; by contrast, 47% of office-based and 31% of hospital-based physicians saw its primary value as digital storage of information they could access. More germane to this chapter, while 94% of PCPs recognize the importance of the EMR's capabilities to coordinate care for patients with complex conditions, only 56% were satisfied with the EMR's performance.[157]

Indeed, the presence of EMRs may detract from care coordination. Physician surveys reveal that EMRs lead to an increase in time devoted to documentation, including keystrokes and gazing at a computer screen. There is less patient involvement and increased patient silence – both of which retard communication, exchange of psychosocial information, and shared decision-making.[158] Part of this increase reflects the increased number of "clinical items" that need to be addressed during the patient visit (diagnosis codes, medication lists, diagnostic tests, counseling, and physical therapy), which increased from 5.4 in 1997 to 7.1 in 2005. Even though physicians spent more time with patients during the 1997–2005 interval (rising from 18 to nearly 21 minutes), they spent less time on each item – thus requiring them to manage clinical conditions at a faster pace.[159] Part of the physician's time management problem also reflects the increase in clerical and administrative tasks, including documentation, order entry, refills and results management, coding, billing, system security, letter generation, and patient demand for non-face-to-face care, such as communication via patient portals. In one study, such tasks consumed a combined 241 minutes of the day, compared with 114 minutes spent on patient care.[160] Research suggests that channeling team interactions among clinic team members through an EMR distracts the team from higher quality verbal communication, and leads to lower efficiency and quality of care.

---

[157] The Harris Poll and Stanford Medicine. *How Doctors Feel About Electronic Health Records* (June 2018). Available online at: https://med.stanford.edu/content/dam/sm/ehr/documents/EHR-Poll-Presentation.pdf. Accessed on November 25, 2020.

[158] Street, R., Liu, L., Farber, N. et al. (2017). Keystrokes, mouse clicks, and gazing at the computer: How physician interaction with the EHR affects patient participation. *Journal of General Internal Medicine*, 33(4), 423–428.

[159] Abbo, E., Zhang, Q., Zelder, M. et al. (2008). The increasing number of clinical items addressed during the time of adult primary care visits. *Journal of General Internal Medicine*, 23(12), 2058–2065.

[160] Arndt, B., Beasley, J., Watkinson, M. et al. (2017). Tethered to the EHR: Primary care physician workload assessment using HER event log data and time-motion observation. *Annals of Family Medicine*, 15(5), 419–426.

More recent surveys reveal a reduction in the amount of physician time spent with the patient, and a negative impact on their patient interactions and relationships.[161] Nearly 70 percent of those surveyed (1) agreed that the EMR took time away from their patients, and (2) disagreed that the EMR strengthened their patient relationships. Overall, for each patient seen, physicians are spending more time with the EMR (8 minutes during the visit, 11 minutes more outside of the visit) than with the patient (12 minutes)![162]

Empirical Research on EMR Impact on Care Coordination
The effect of EMR adoption on care coordination is mixed. First, there is inconsistent evidence that EMR adoption facilitates physician efforts to engage in clinical integration, chronic care management, and population health management.[163] A major field investigation of physician groups found that the number of health care information technology (HCIT) components used was not associated with the use of care management practices.[164] That is, care management was not dependent on information technology. Another found that EMR capabilities were not associated with diabetes management, asthma maintenance, or other processes of care (preventive services).[165] A third study found that changes in EMR capability were not associated with changes in a medical group's index of care management activity.[166]

[161] Pelland, K., Baier, R., and Gardner, R. (2017). 'It is like texting at the dinner table;' A qualitative analysis of the impact of electronic health records on patient-physician interaction in hospitals. *Journal of Innovation in Health Informatics*, 24(2), 216–223.

[162] The Harris Poll and Stanford Medicine. *How Doctors Feel About Electronic Health Records* (June 2018). Available online at: https://med.stanford.edu/content/dam/sm/ehr/documents/EHR-Poll-Presentation.pdf. Accessed on November 25, 2020.

[163] Graetz, I., Reed, M., Shortell, S. et al. (2014). The association between EHRs and care coordination varies by team cohesion. *Health Services Research* 49(1) Part II, 438–452; Graetz, I., Reed, M., Shortell, S. et al. (2014). The next step towards making use meaningful: Electronic information exchange and care coordination across clinicians and delivery sites. *Medical Care*, 52(12), 1037–1041.

[164] Rittenhouse, D., Shortell, S., Gillies, R. et al. (2010). Improving chronic illness care: Findings from a national study of care management processes in large physician practices. *Medical Care Research and Review*, 67(3), 301–320.

[165] Damberg, C., Shortell, S., Raube, K. et al. (2010). Relationship between quality improvement processes and clinical performance. *The American Journal of Managed Care*, 16(8), 601–606.

[166] Shortell, S., Gillies, R., Siddique, J. et al. (2009). Improving chronic illness care: A longitudinal cohort analysis of large physician organizations. *Medical Care*, 47(9), 932–939.

Second, studies report that HCIT usage is not associated with care coordination.[167] One study reported that EMR usage did not improve care coordination across sites of care, such as inpatient, outpatient, and emergency department areas.[168] What explains these surprising findings? Physicians require several pieces of patient information to coordinate care, including: results from patient referrals for consultation, the patient's history and reasons for referral, and hospital discharge information. They do not always get this information. Data suggest that only 16 percent of clinicians reported they sent a summary of care record for the majority of their patient transitions and referrals. There are also barriers posed by some specialty clinicians' failure to provide hospital admission or patient discharge summaries to PCPs in a timely fashion which may be needed at the point of care. Nurses likewise require several types of information to prepare for and conduct patient handover at shift changes. EMRs have proved cumbersome and limiting in assisting nurses with such transitions.[169]

Moreover, there are only small differences in the receipt of information to coordinate care when comparing physicians not using HCIT with those using HCIT. Researchers conclude that EMR adoption and electronic sharing of patient data among physicians may not be enough to ensure care coordination.[170] There are several barriers to achieving this promise.

Barrier #1: Interoperability. There are hundreds of EMR vendors, little standardization of EMR code and data elements, and thus major issues of interoperability among them. Information transmission is also likely impeded by the decentralized configuration of hospital systems (and the health care ecosystem in general) which limits standardization of EMR platforms, operating processes, and the cultural importance of timely

---

[167] O'Malley, A., Tynan, A., Cohen, G. et al. (2009). *Coordination of Care by Primary Care Practices: Strategies, Lessons and Implications.* Research Brief No. 12. Washington, DC: Center for Studying Health System Change; Kellerman, A., and Jones, S. (2013). What it will take to achieve the as-yet-unfulfilled promises of health information technology. *Health Affairs,* 32(1), 63–68.

[168] Graetz, I., Reed, M., Shortell, S. et al. (2014). The association between EHRs and care coordination varies by team cohesion. *Health Services Research* 49(1) Part II, 438–452; Graetz, I., Reed, M., Shortell, S. et al. (2014). The next step towards making use meaningful: Electronic information exchange and care coordination across clinicians and delivery sites. *Medical Care,* 52(12), 1037–1041.

[169] Ghosh, K., Dohan, M., Curl, E. et al. (2020). Information tools for care coordination in patient handover: Is an electronic medical record enough to support nurses? *Health Care Management Review.*

[170] Hsiao, C.-J., King, J., Hing, E. et al. (2015). The role of health information technology in care coordination in the United States. *Medical Care,* 53(2), 184–190.

communication exchange among physicians. EMRs are thus less able to support coordination across practices and care settings.[171] More chronic illness means more PCP and specialty visits to more sites of care. That means there are more "dots" to connect. But one first has to "collect the dots" before one can "connect the dots." Problems of interoperability limit this capacity.

Barrier #2: Financial Incentives. The initial lack of reimbursement for EMR usage inhibited the adoption of systems. Without financial incentives for coordination among providers, practices had little incentive to adopt EMR systems to help with coordination, and EMR system developers had little incentive to prioritize functionality to support coordination. The Health Information Technology for Economic and Clinical Health (HITECH) Act of 2009 was an ambitious policy effort to address this by providing financial incentives to adopt EMRs. Whether it has achieved its primary goal is debatable. Existing incentive programs to promote meaningful use of HCIT have resulted in only limited adoption of optional care coordination objectives.[172] While there is evidence that the HITECH Act accelerated EMR adoption in hospitals,[173] basic EMR adoption in the ambulatory care setting was not significantly altered by HITECH incentives, according to one study.[174] Whether adoption in hospitals translated into coordination improvements for hospitalized patients is less well described.

Barrier #3: Alternative Payment and Delivery Models. More recently, APMs and new provider organizations, such as ACOs, have provided indirect financial incentives to adopt EMRs by encouraging care coordination across providers and care settings. One investigation found that ACOs that used a single EMR system across providers within the ACO reported being able to share data, thus improving their ability to coordinate care. However, a number of ACOs do not have a single EMR system, due to more decentralized hospital systems and multiple types of provider

[171] O'Malley, J. M., Grossman, G. R., Cohen, N. M. et al. (2010). Are electronic medical records helpful for care coordination? Experiences of physician practices. *Journal of General Internal Medicine*, 25(3), 177–185.

[172] Morton, S., Shih, S., Winther, C. et al. (2015). Health IT-enabled care coordination: A national survey of patient-centered medical home clinicians. *Annals of Family Medicine*, 13(3), 250–256.

[173] Adler-Milstein, J., and Jha, A. K. (2017). HITECH Act drove large gains in hospital electronic health record adoption. *Health Affairs*, 36(8), 1416–1422.

[174] Mennemeyer, S. T., Menachemi, N., Rahurkar, S., Ford, E. W. et al. (2016). Impact of the HITECH Act on physicians' adoption of electronic health records. *Journal of the American Medical Informatics Association*, 23, 375–379.

members – all of which limit data sharing abilities across providers. There have also been ongoing concerns about the burden of EMRs, and whether this burden contributes to physician burnout.[175]

EMRs are also used to produce reports that respond to value-based payment program incentives offered to practices to collect data on clinical quality. It is not so clear that such data gathering has supported quality improvement initiatives or led to improvements in quality.[176] Indeed, there is some evidence that the collection of the data that go into the EMR can complicate the clinical doctor-patient encounter. Some liken the EMR's introduction to a change from a duet into a *menage-a-trois*, making it an additional participant in the exam room.[177]

Barrier #4: Concomitant Changes Required. In general, research shows that HCIT is infrequently used to coordinate care.[178] Barriers to such use include the need for interpersonal sharing of information to coordinate care, the need to reengineer internal workflows in tandem with installations of HCIT, and the lack of customization.

For example, care coordination means different things in different patient settings, patients, and treatments. As a result, different features and data may be required for care coordination in outpatient specialty areas that treat patients with chronic care needs. In contrast to patients seen by PCPs, patients seen by specialists may be more likely to see multiple providers in multiple sites for longer periods of time. For example, oncology care coordinators and nurse navigators must handle tasks that span risk screening, genetic counseling, clinical trial enrollment, and participation in support groups. Different protocols and procedures may be guided by complex algorithms that are tailored to different types of tumors and their genetic makeup.[179] Thus, one size of EMR may not fit all needs of care coordination.

[175] Levinson, D. R. (2019). Using Health IT for Care Coordination: Insights From Six Medicare Accountable Care Organizations. US Department of Health and Human Services Office of the Inspector General OEI-01-16-00180.

[176] Cohen, D., Dorr, D., Knierim, K. et al. (2018). Primary care practices' abilities and challenges in using electronic health record data for quality improvement. *Health Affairs*, 37(4), 635–643.

[177] Ofri, D. (2019). The EMR has changed the doctor-patient duet into a ménage-a-trois. *Stat* https://www.statnews.com/2019/10/31/emr-changed-doctor-patient-duet-into-menage-a-trois/.

[178] Furukawa, M., King, J., Patel, V. et al. (2014). Despite substantial progress in EHR adoption, health information exchange and patient engagement remain low in office settings. *Health Affairs*, 33(9), 1672–1679.

[179] Winzenread, G. (2016). 7 things to know about EMRs and care coordination. *Becker's Hospital Review*. https://www.beckershospitalreview.com/healthcare-information-technology/7-things-to-know-about-emrs-and-care-coordination.html.

EMR adoption may also require other factors to be present to coordinate care, including the presence of a cohesive provider team and use of a care coordinator who acts as a communications hub between the care team providers and patient.[180] Some experts suggest that a cultural shift among physicians may be needed to increase the perceived importance of timely communication and information transmission. We, by contrast, think that physicians would be happy to have timely information if they could access it easily and spend less time entering it.

Alternative Payment Models As the Stimulus to Coordination

A major strategy supporting the rollout of care coordination networks is the expansion of APMs that hold providers financially accountable for both the quality and the costs of care across a continuum of services. CMS has implemented and scaled up two types of APMs to reform fee-for-service Medicare payments: population-based and episode-based models. Population-based payment models emphasize accountability for the total costs of care and quality outcomes for defined patient populations, thereby encouraging providers to reduce unwarranted care overall without compromising quality. In comparison, episode-based payment models are triggered by health care utilization (often a procedure or a hospitalization) and hold providers accountable for quality and costs across the discrete episode of care that follows (including PAC), encouraging providers to address spending on acute care and PAC and improving coordination between these two settings.

To date, Medicare's hallmark approaches to population-based payment have been ACOs.[181] Available evidence suggests that ACOs have contributed to modest reductions in Medicare spending, which some have interpreted as evidence of improved care coordination (or just decreased

---

[180] Morton, S., Shih, S., Winther, C. et al. (2015). Health IT-enabled care coordination: A national survey of patient-centered medical home clinicians. *Annals of Family Medicine,* 13(3), 250–256; Brown, R. (2013). Lessons for ACOs and Medical Homes on Care Coordination for High-Need Beneficiaries. Presentation to AcademyHealth Annual Research Meeting. Baltimore, MD; Congressional Budget Office. (2012). *Lessons from Medicare's Demonstration Projects on Disease Management, Care Coordination, and Value-Based Payment* Washington, DC: CBO.

[181] Center for Medicare and Medicaid Services (CMS). Accountable Care Organizations (ACOs). Available online at: www.cms.gov/Medicare/Medicare-Fee-for-Service-Payment/ACO/. Accessed September 29, 2020.

utilization),[182] but the evidence on the success of ACOs is mixed.[183] Moreover, recent analyses suggest that CMS' estimates of savings are grossly overstated.[184]

Analogous to the position of ACOs within population-based payment reforms, bundled payments represent Medicare's cornerstone approach to implementing episode-based payment reforms. Episode-based models have had more success at coordinating care after hospital discharge, particularly in the PAC setting where savings have largely been driven by reduction in use of institutional PAC.[185] But this payment model addresses only the coordination within the context of an episode, not the patient's ongoing risk for future hospitalization. Other, more narrowly-focused APMs have not proven successful.[186]

A major problem for APMs is that any associated payment risk rests with the organization and not with the clinician. As noted elsewhere, many hospitals and physician groups are loathe to pass economic risk down to their individual providers.[187] Instead, the providers are heavily incentivized by productivity measures, such as RVUs. Incentives for care coordination are either absent or minimal. In one large medical group we have seen, 85% of the physician's compensation was based on RVUs, 10% was based on leadership and mentorship activities, and only 5% targeted behaviors such as care coordination. Even then, the desired behaviors focused on reducing hospital admissions, reconciling medications at time of hospital discharge, and addressing the patient's chronic conditions.

[182] Agarwal, D., and Werner, R. M. Effect of hospital and post-acute care provider participation in accountable care organizations on patient outcomes and Medicare spending. *Health Services Research*, 53 (2018), 5035–5056.

[183] Liao, J. M., Navathe, A. S., and Werner, R. M. (2020). The impact of Medicare's alternative payment models on the value of care. *Annual Review of Public Health*, 41 (1), 551–565.

[184] McWilliams, J. M., and Chen, A. (2020). Understanding the latest ACO 'savings': Curb your enthusiasm and sharpen your pencils – Part I. *Health Affairs Blog*. https://www.healthaffairs.org/do/10.1377/forefront.20201106.719550/.

[185] Liao, J. M., Navathe, A. S., and Werner, R. M. (2020). The impact of Medicare's alternative payment models on the value of care. *Annual Review of Public Health*, 41 (1), 551–565; Barnett, M., Maddix, K. J., Orav, E. J. et al. (2020). Association of skilled nursing facility participation in a bundled payment model with institutional spending for joint replacement surgery. *Journal of the American Medical Association*, 324(18), 1869–1877.

[186] Gaus, C., and Pittman, D. (2020). Evaluation of Medicare alternative payment models: What the data show. *Health Affairs Blog*. https://www.healthaffairs.org/do/10.1377/forefront.20201106.971990/full/

[187] Burns, L. R., and Pauly, M. V. (2018). Transformation of the health care industry: Curb your enthusiasm? *Milbank Quarterly*, 96(1), 57–109.

CONCLUSION: CHALLENGES FACING CARE COORDINATION

Care coordination efforts face multiple challenges to deliver "value." We decompose these challenges below into those dealing with the denominator (cost) and the numerator (quality). We also highlight the role of contextual factors and results based on best practices. We conclude with a discussion of more (and less) hopeful avenues to consider.

Efforts to Reduce Costs

The biggest challenge facing the ability of care coordination to reduce cost is the prevalence of fee-for-service payment (compared to capitation or bundled payment). In this environment, no one has the direct incentive (or resources) to coordinate care. The payer is the entity with the incentive. HMOs have their own methods for care coordination, using PCP gate-keepers, narrow networks, and co-managing medical and pharmacy bene-fits (among other strategies). The Medicare program is still looking for effective ways to inspire and pay for care coordination in a mostly fee-for-service world where traditional Medicare patients prefer to go to any provider they want and there is no funding for managing a patient. It remains to be seen if MA plans can do a better job than traditional Medicare. As noted above, much of this may rest with how much risk individual providers bear and what types of behaviors are incentivized.

A second challenge facing care coordination efforts is that they involve increased access to health care providers and services, often in an effort to address underutilization of care. Such improved access almost necessarily increases spending, even if it is cost effective; patients experience more physician visits and physician interventions (e.g., prescriptions, tests). Care coordination often encompasses overly broad (rather than targeted) popu-lations of patients, all of whom do not benefit from the program but are expensive to treat. Care coordination programs also require much person-nel and infrastructure that is expensive. Many of the care coordination demonstration programs have failed to recoup these investments.[188] Policy advocates fail to recognize that economies of scale tend to accompany technological investments rather than human resource investment; thus, it is hard to efficiently scale up a coordination program that is people-intensive.

---

[188] McWilliams, J. M. (2016). Cost containment and the tale of care coordination. *New England Journal of Medicine*, 375(23), 2218–2220.

A third challenge involves treating chronic illness. Evidence shows that patients with the most dispersed care (e.g., fragmented across multiple providers, low continuity with one provider) are much more likely to have two or more chronic conditions and to have more PCP and specialist visits, and see a wider number of different specialists across different specialties.[189] The most costly patients to treat – the "polychronic" patients with five or more chronic conditions – tend to use multiple hospitals (up to nine!) and multiple physicians. They are allowed to do so under both Medicare fee-for-service and Medicare ACO payments, which allow free choice of provider. Such use may not be clinically inappropriate, but certainly complicates any effort to track (let alone coordinate) their care.[190] In fee-for-service Medicare, no one is even trying to coordinate the patients' care across providers; they aren't getting paid to do it and they don't have the tools to do so. All providers are their own silo.

A fourth challenge to care coordination is balancing provider collaboration with the need to retain some competition in the private sector.[191] Multiple hospital admissions are more likely to contribute to fragmentation when the care is emergent (e.g., due to injury) rather than planned, and when the admission is for the same or related condition (such that provider sharing of patient information and continuity in the provider seen may be more crucial). IDNs and ACOs may be unable to address this problem unless they encompass a large swath of facilities in the local market. This can have the undesirable effect of reducing competition and driving up prices charged to commercial insurers.

A final issue deals with causality: Do narrow networks foster better patient outcomes, or does having hospitals and plans form narrow networks with PAC providers lead to better outcomes? The available evidence suggests that both are likely true and that selection effects are important. Similarly, it is likely the case that (1) low care coordination leads to higher costs and (2) higher-cost patients tend to utilize more providers and thus "look more fragmented."

Given these limitations, some observers have argued that cost containment is not the appropriate goal for care coordination programs to target. Instead, such programs should be viewed as part of the effort to reduce use

---

[189] Frandsen, B., Joynt, K., Rebitzer, J. et al. (2015). Care fragmentation, quality, and costs among chronically ill patients. *The American Journal of Managed Care*, 21(5), 355–362.

[190] Hempstead, K., DeLia, D., Cantor, J. et al. (2014). The fragmentation of hospital use among a cohort of high utilizers. *Medical Care*, 52(3)(Supplement 2), S67–S74.

[191] Baicker, K., and Levy, H. (2013). Coordination versus competition in health care reform. *New England Journal of Medicine*, 369(9), 789–791.

of "low-value" care and increase use of more efficient and/or higher-quality providers within a network.[192] This effort may reflect the fact that while poor coordination is associated with higher cost, we do not really understand why. One possible explanation – not often discussed – is that the culprit may be specialists who are generally quicker to hospitalize a patient. Thus, if a PCP quickly refers their patient to see a specialist, the odds of that patient getting expensive services like hospitalization, PAC, and diagnostic tests rises. This is not always because those services were necessary or cost-effective ways to treat the patient, but rather were more financially rewarding to the specialist than just providing the patient a disappointing consultation. Unfortunately, progress on reducing low-value care has been decidedly slow.[193]

Efforts to Improve Quality

The need to address the care needs of patients with polychronic conditions complicates care coordination efforts to improve quality. By definition, such patients are likely on multiple medications. Drugs prescribed for one condition may be contraindicated for another; alternatively, several drugs may be needed to adequately treat a single condition. The aging of this patient group further complicates treatment by virtue of additional chronic conditions, the changing nature of their diseases, and growing severity of illness.

The care experience of this group is also affected by nonmedical or social determinants of health – e.g., poverty, the presence/absence of informal family caregivers, the degree of stress upon family members – that affect health status and patient outcomes, but may not be explicitly taken into account in care coordination programs. There is considerable controversy regarding the role that physicians can play in ameliorating these conditions.[194] Care coordination requires greater complexity and dynamism, rather than a static single-condition orientation. Such an approach is beginning to be addressed by more robust chronic disease models.[195]

---

[192] McWilliams, J. M. (2016). Cost containment and the tale of care coordination. *New England Journal of Medicine*, 375(23), 2218–2220.

[193] Available online at: https://altarum.org/news/new-research-shows-more-work-needed-shift-health-care-spending-low-value-high-value-care. Accessed on September 30, 2020.

[194] Maani, N., and Galea, S. (2020). The role of physicians in addressing social determinants of health. *Journal of the American Medical Association*, 323(16), 1551–1552.

[195] Grembowski, D., Schaefer, J., Johnson, D. et al. (2014). A conceptual model of complexity in the care of patients with multiple chronic conditions. *Medical Care*, 52(3) (Supplement 2), S7–S14.

Beware of Best Practices?

Oftentimes, analysts develop a subjective list of the "best practices" of "successful care management programs." They suggest a host of elements that may resist empirical testing as well as emulation by other providers due to their tacit nature. These practices include: building trusting relationships with patients, building trusting relationships between care coordinators and PCPs, matching care team composition (e.g., community health workers, social workers) and interventions to patient needs, providing specialized training for care team members, applying a mix of quantitative and qualitative methods to target patients, using information technology and strategic use of data, using care coordination agreements that allocate responsibility across team members, and leadership.[196]

These practices are important to note, since 12 reported best practices of so-called "best-practice organizations" – not randomized controlled trials – underlie the Care Coordination Model used to improve primary care delivery in 61 sites funded by The Commonwealth Fund to accelerate PCMH transformation. Empirical research on this model's implementation indicates that some of the 12 practices are positively correlated with some of the 5 elements of PCMH coordination, but not with others. Indeed, among the 60 correlations computed, only 7 were statistically significant.[197]

These tepid empirical results are paralleled by manifold other problems with such "best practices." The best practices movement began in earnest with consultants who promulgated the belief that emulation of practices of successful companies will make you successful.[198] This has shown up in health care with everyone suggesting that hospitals strive to be like Kaiser Permanente, Mayo Clinic, and Cleveland Clinic. In 2009, President Obama

[196] Hong, C., Siegel, A., and Ferris, T. (2014). *Caring for High-Need, High-Cost Patients: What Makes for a Successful Care Management Program?* New York: Commonwealth Fund; Anderson, G., Ballreich, J., Bleich, S. et al. (2015). Attributes common to programs that successfully treat high-need, high-cost individuals. *The American Journal of Managed Care,* 21(11), e597–e600; Carrier, E., Dowling, M., and Pham, H. (2012). Care coordination agreements: Barriers, facilitators, and lessons learned. *The American Journal of Managed Care,* 18(11), e398–e404.

[197] Wagner, E., Sandhu, N., Coleman, K. et al. (2014). Improving care coordination in primary care. *Medical Care,* 52(11)(Supplement 4), S33–S38.

[198] Peters, T., and Waterman, R. (1982). *In Search of Excellence: Lessons from America's Best-Run Companies.* New York: HarperCollins.

encouraged hospitals to emulate Cleveland Clinic and Mayo Clinic.[199] Of course, no one bothered to ask whether the success of these organizations was due to local circumstances (i.e., the *terroir* effect),[200] whether it could be bottled, and whether anyone else really had the chops to do it. They did not ask whether the apparent success extended to all the goals that matter; Kaiser Permanente has experienced the same growth rate in spending as the rest of the medical sector. Nor did they ask whether any observed success (compared to the rest of health care) by Kaiser, Mayo, or Cleveland was sustainable or transferable to other geographic locales, even by these same exemplary organizations – which apparently is not always the case.

Challenges Posed by Contextual Factors

The complicated US health care ecosystem will likely hamper most efforts to improve coordination and achieve its desired results. The top-down goal (and ideology) of "coordination" – which is baked into several public policy efforts – does not fit well with a pluralistic payment system and a chaotic, decentralized delivery system. The US health care system is characterized by multiple payers and delivery organizations, and multiple and independent professions that have conflicting goals and constraints. What works for one payer or one provider may not work as well for others. Moreover, hierarchies and professional status differences still exist and will continue to hinder the progress of top-down policies like team-based, coordinated care. In the absence of a robust evidence base on its benefits as well as effective implementation, coordination will remain difficult. If that were not enough, due to trends in use of telehealth, care coordination may need to be increasingly pursued in "distributed teams" – separated in geographic space if not also in time – rather than "co-located teams." We are not sure if this trend is underway or what the evidence base is for this.

Calls for care coordination of patient care have coincided with calls for integration among health care providers and between the providers and the payers. Two decades ago, the Institute of Medicine (now called the National Academy of Medicine) noted that providers and health plans have vigorously pursued horizontal and vertical integration strategies to

---

[199] Tribble, S. J. (2009). "Cleveland Clinic praised by President Barack Obama for efficiency, control of costs," *The Plain Dealer*. Available online at www.cleveland.com/medical/2009/06/cleveland_clinic_praised_by_pr.html.

[200] Goldsmith, J., and Burns, L. R. (2016). Fail to scale: Why great ideas in health care don't thrive everywhere https://www.healthaffairs.org/do/10.1377/forefront.20160929.056856/full/.

deal with competitive and payment pressures. And yet, "all this organizational turmoil has resulted in little change in the way health care is delivered. Some of the new arrangements have failed following disappointing results."[201] It may be the case that coordination has come in a distant second place behind vertical integration and structural linkages among the players in the industry. Indeed, it may be the case that the success of HMOs rested more on favorable patient selection (at least initially) and on negotiating good prices with good provider networks (again via self-selection, as well as the promise of more patients) than on paying for care coordination and actually making health care more efficient.

Light at the End of the Tunnel?

As noted above, most efforts to achieve care coordination have adopted *structural solutions*. By contrast, Thompson's "coordination by mutual adjustment"[202] focuses on *processual solutions*, such as patterned interactions, joint decision-making, sharing of resources, interactive communication, and reformulating tasks and priorities as new knowledge emerges and is shared. Health care research suggests that structural solutions to integrated health care are not associated with processual solutions and are insufficient to generate them.[203]

Management research has argued that knowledge-intensive firms (which have concomitant needs for high information processing and professional autonomy) resist structural methods of control and must instead rely on strong normative cultures built around collaboration and fluid modes of work.[204] Recent health care research on one of the proposed structural solutions, the EMR, may actually point us in a more promising direction. One study reports that the operation of social networks in primary care clinics may be more important than the presence and use of an EMR for promoting quality of care and lowering both cost and

[201] Institute of Medicine. (2001). *Crossing the Quality Chasm: A New Health System for the 21st Century*. Washington, DC: National Academies Press, 3.

[202] Thompson, J. D. (1967). *Organizations in Action*. New York: McGraw-Hill.

[203] Kim, K. D., Funk, R., Zaheer, A. et al. (2019). Better off friends? Network bounding and the performance implications of formalization. *Academy of Management Proceedings*. https://doi.org/10.5465/AMBPP.2018.231; Kim, D., Funk, R.J., Yan, P. et al. (2019). Informal clinical integration in Medicare accountable care organizations and mortality following coronary artery bypass graft surgery. *Medical Care*, 57(3), 194–201.

[204] Robertson, M., and Swan, J. (2003). 'Control – What control?' Culture and ambiguity within a knowledge intensive firm. *Journal of Management Studies*, 40(4), 831–858.

utilization of services. The study conducted interviews with clinicians and staff in six PCP clinics and found that density of face-to-face interactions (i.e., the interpersonal connectedness of the care team) reduced costs and utilization (urgent care, emergency visits, hospital days) and improved the management of the patient's chronic disease (cholesterol levels). This finding is consistent with the Medicare Care Coordination Demonstration that found that programs having ongoing personal relationships/contacts between the care coordinator and the PCP were more likely to have reductions in hospitalizations. By contrast, in the absence of such personal ties, the density of EMR-based interactions was associated with increased costs, utilization, and less effective management of cholesterol levels. Moreover, the degree of network decentralization (i.e., interactions dispersed rather than organized around a single or small group of individuals) was also associated with lower cost and utilization. Finally, interpersonal networks appeared to foster specific team climates (e.g., shared vision) that promote cost and quality outcomes.

The researchers concluded that "neither individual professional excellence nor electronic health records solutions alone could produce desired improvements in quality of care."[205] Instead, health care teams should be viewed as complex, adaptive systems that are interconnected in nonlinear ways that require relational connectedness to manage patient care effectively. Their research suggests the importance of processual solutions rather than structural solutions to the problem of coordination.

One articulation of the process approach is known as "relational coordination." This encompasses seven dimensions, including communication that is frequent, timely, accurate, and problem-solving in nature, as well as the sharing of goals, knowledge, and respect.[206] Research suggests that the process of interactive communication among physicians (e.g., between PCPs and specialists) that entails improved information exchange can improve patient outcomes, quality of care, patient safety, patient engagement, and efficiency.[207] Additional research that examines the antecedents

[205] Mundt, M., Gilchrist, V., Fleming, M. et al. (2015). Effects of primary care team social networks on quality of care and costs for patients with cardiovascular disease. *Annals of Family Medicine*, 13(2), 139–148.

[206] Gittell, J. H., and Ali, H. N. (2021). *Relational Analytics: Guidelines for Analysis and Action*. Routledge.

[207] Foy, R., Hempel, S., Rubenstein, L. et al. (2010). Meta-analysis: Effect of interactive communication between collaborating primary care physicians and specialists. *Annals of Internal Medicine*, 152, 247–258; Gittell, J. H. (2016). *Transforming Relationships for High Performance: The Power of Relational Coordination*. Palo Alto, CA: Stanford

to interactive communication highlights the importance of psychological safety (perceived freedom to speak up), team leadership (motivate input from those below, minimize status differences), and a supportive managerial environment (e.g., provide resources and rewards, promote team stability).[208] One of the advantages of this type of solution is that it doesn't necessarily require a lot more time from the physician or other team members (e.g., more meetings, forms to complete). Showing respect and sharing goals can be ingrained in the workings of a clinic or office without adding time burdens to an already stressed network of providers; it just requires attitude adjustment and leadership that insists on and promotes it.

Relational coordination is similar to what other researchers call "collaborative capacity." Collaborative capacity is defined as the routines and work processes – often embedded in work cultures, decision-making styles, shared commitments, and team dynamics – that foster coordinated behavior among professionals and other stakeholders. Such capacity is promoted by patient-centered values and supportive contexts but constrained by the division of labor and status hierarchy among the health care professions.[209] Such collaborative capacity may be related to team dynamics of quality information exchange, mutual trust, and role clarity – which have been found to impact patient outcomes.[210] Our understanding of collaborative capacity is constrained by the focus of most research on the *structures* rather than the *processes* of collaboration.[211]

University Press; Bolton, R., Logan, C., and Gittell, J. H. (2012). Revisiting relational coordination: A systematic review. *Journal of Applied Behavioral Science*, 57(3). https://doi.org/10.1177/0021886321991597.

[208] Edmondson, A. (2003). Speaking up in the operating room: How team leaders promote learning in interdisciplinary action teams. *Journal of Management Studies*, 40(6), 1419–1452.

[209] Weinberg, D. B., Cooney-Miner, D., Perloff, J. N. et al. (2011). Building collaborative capacity: Promoting interdisciplinary teamwork in the absence of formal teams. *Medical Care*, 49(8), 716–723.

[210] Gittell, J. H., Fairfield, K., Bierbaum, B. et al. (2000). Impact of relational coordination on quality of care, postoperative pain and functioning, and length of stay: A nine hospital study of surgical patients. *Medical Care*, 38(8), 807–819.

[211] Song, H., Ryan, M., Tendulkar, S. et al. (2015). Team dynamics, clinical work satisfaction, and care coordination between primary care providers: A mixed methods study. *Health Care Management Review*, 42(1), 28–41; Valentijn, P. P., Ruwaard, D., Vrijhoef, H. J. M. et al. (2015). Collaboration processes and perceived effectiveness of integrated care projects in primary care: A longitudinal mixed-methods study. *BMC Health Services Research*, 15, 463.

Summation and Final Thoughts

The challenges to coordination are at least three-fold: (1) the growing diversity of occupations and specialties; (2) the growing number, size, and diversity of delivery organizations in which these occupational and specialty groupings work; and (3) the growing chronicity of illness. All of these developments fragment health care delivery. The rise of chronic illness and growing number of polychronic patients mean that sicker patients have more "ports of call" that need to be involved and thus linked together. This calls for coordination – and calls for it have been made since at least the 1970s and likely decades earlier.

This chapter has reviewed the diverse approaches taken to address the coordination problem. One *leitmotif* of this chapter is that care coordination requires communication, information availability and exchange, joint problem solving by multiple decision-makers (including feedback between them), and exerting of influence both from above (e.g., leadership) and below (speaking up). Such processes can begin to address the specific problems identified in care coordination surveys, such as: unavailability of test results; no discussion of health promoting behaviors with the clinician; PCPs uninformed about hospital care; physicians who fail to review prescriptions; and physicians who fail to encourage participation of nonphysicians in decision-making. The solution to these specific problems speak to the heart of Starfield's model of care coordination. They may be the prerequisite to solving the broader problems of the iron triangle and triple aim.

Such "process work" is hard work. It is also time-consuming and, thus, expensive. Busy professionals in health care settings – many of whom are trained to take the initiative and/or leader roles in patient care – may not place a high value on such work. This may explain why it does not always occur, even in an information exchange as basic as patient referrals. Data show that the purpose of the referral is not always communicated from the PCP to the specialist, just as the findings from the specialist are not always fed back to the referring PCP.[212] Such exchanges are further hampered by differing perceptions as to who should play the principal role, as well as the persistence of hierarchy in health care. There is also evidence that relational coordination work is perceived as incompatible with the other tasks PCPs are called on to perform, and may even be perceived as fragmenting

---

[212] Chen, A., and Yee, H. (2009). Improving the primary care – specialty care interface. *Archives of Internal Medicine*, 169(11), 1024–1026.

the PCP's numerous tasks and already busy schedule.[213] Finally, the evidence for its impact on patient outcomes is modest. There are thus no easy answers here, and certainly no quick fixes.

Such process work goes beyond the mere existence of teams. What happens within and across teams is much more relevant. As noted above, most studies of health care teams utilize a model of "Structure – Process – Outcome." Reviews of the team literature comment on the large number of factors that impact team effectiveness, many of which involve behavioral science processes of leadership, communication, speaking up, influence, decision-making, and learning.[214] Such processes are not amenable to empirical analysis and, thus, are not easily summarized in terms of "what we know that works."

Process work, however difficult to do and study, may be our best path forward. The National Academy of Medicine's report on *Crossing the Quality Chasm* long ago identified the core problem as one of information and its communication among all of the providers involved in the patient's care:

The fact that more than 40 percent of people with chronic conditions have more than one such condition argues strongly for more sophisticated mechanisms to communicate and coordinate care . . . Yet physician groups, hospitals, and other health care organizations operate as silos, often providing care without the benefit of complete information about the patient's condition, medical history, services provided in other settings, or medications prescribed by other clinicians.[215]

The focus of coordination efforts should perhaps shift to interactive communication as the antecedent to what we seek – care coordination – as depicted in Figure 4.3. Each box in this figure masks a lot of detail in the activities to be performed, which is a huge challenge.

Emphasis should shift from structural mechanisms to relational coordination, collaborative capacity, and the need for quality information exchange – which involves both information and communication. These

[213] Nembhard, I. and Lee, Y. (2019). Creative Strategies to Improve Patient Care Experience. Presentation to Agency for Health care Research and Quality. Available online at: www .ahrq.gov/cahps/news-and-events/events/webinar-041819.html.

[214] Fried, B., Topping, S., and Edmondson, A. (2012). Teams and team effectiveness in health services organizations, in E. Bradley, L. R. Burns, and B. Weiner (Eds.), *Shortell & Kaluzny's Health Care Management: Organization Design and Behavior*. Sixth Ed. Delmar Cengage Learning, 121–162.

[215] Institute of Medicine. (2001). *Crossing the Quality Chasm: A New Health System for the 21st Century*. Washington, DC: National Academies Press, 3.

Theory of care coordination

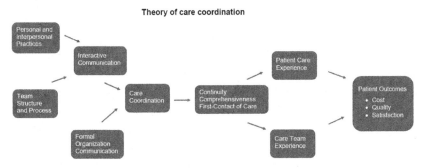

Figure 4.3. Theory of care coordination

appear to be two key ingredients to care coordination. Efforts might also focus on the interrelationships among all four elements of Starfield's original model, as recently suggested by researchers.[216] To paraphrase the famous line from the old Paul Newman movie, *Cool Hand Luke,* "What we have here . . . is failure to communicate and coordinate."

---

[216] Nembhard, I. and Lee, Y. (2019). Creative Strategies to Improve Patient Care Experience. Presentation to Agency for Health care Research and Quality. Available online at: www .ahrq.gov/cahps/news-and-events/events/webinar-041819.html.

5

Evidence-Based Programs to Improve Transitional Care of Older Adults

Mary Naylor and Rachel M. Werner[*]

Care of the rapidly growing segment of older adults living longer with complex health and social needs remains fragmented, costly, and, at times, harmful. A high proportion of the total health care dollars consumed by this group is the result of preventable breakdowns in care experienced during frequent episodes of acute illness. Major changes in health and social systems are urgently needed to improve the quality of care delivered to these patients and control growth in health care spending. Widespread implementation of evidence-based transitional care interventions represents an immediate opportunity to better align care with older adults' preferences and needs, enhance their health and quality of life, and reduce their use of high-cost services. Transitional care encompasses a time-limited, broad range of services to support patients at high risk for poor outcomes, and their families as they move between levels and settings of care.[1]

Despite the availability of solutions proven to promote continuity of care for this population and improve both health and economic outcomes, few have been implemented in health care systems. The goals of this chapter are to explore reasons behind the limited uptake of evidence-based transitional care interventions for older adults and suggest a pathway for change that has implications for a wide range of patient populations. To set the stage, we describe the importance of transitional care for older adults at risk for poor outcomes (hereafter referred to as "high risk"). This section is followed by a review of the evidence on common characteristics of effective

[*] **Acknowledgments:** We thank Drs. Eleanor Rivera, Kristin Levoy, and Karen Hirschman for their literature search, and Lucinda Bertsinger for manuscript preparation.
[1] Naylor, M., and Keating, S. A. (2008). Transitional care. *American Journal of Nursing*, 108, 58–63; Boult, C., and Coleman, E. A. (2003). Improving the quality of transitional care for persons with complex care needs. *Journal of the American Geriatrics Society*, 51, 556–557.

solutions. Next, to establish the current state of the evidence, we describe the current status of health systems' use of proven solutions and hypothesize why many health care decision makers elect alternative options. Finally, we offer recommendations to accelerate the uptake and spread of evidence-based transitional care innovations.

IMPORTANCE OF TRANSITIONAL CARE

Many older adults in the United States are coping with multiple health and social needs. For example, 39 percent have four or more chronic conditions.[2] Due to frequent episodes of acute illness, this group experiences significantly higher rates of physician and emergency department (ED) visits and hospitalizations.[3] Numerous studies reveal that poor management of the complex needs of hospitalized older adults is the norm, often with devastating human and economic consequences.[4] Many health services researchers have described high rates of rehospitalizations or ED visits within 30 days of hospital discharge as evidence that care transitions are poorly managed.[5] These scholars acknowledge that early return of some patients for acute care services is appropriate; an estimated 10 percent

[2] Centers for Medicare & Medicaid Services (2017). Percentage of Medicare FFS Beneficiaries with the 21 Selected Chronic Conditions: (Figures 5–8). Available online at www.cms.gov/Research-Statistics-Data-and-Systems/Statistics-Trends-and-Reports/Chronic-Conditions/Chartbook_Charts (accessed April 1, 2020).

[3] Pham, H. H., O'Malley, A. S., Bach, P. B. et al. (2009). Primary care physicians' links to other physicians through Medicare patients: The scope of care coordination. *Annals of Internal Medicine*, 150, 236–242; Anderson, G. (2010). Chronic care: Making the case for ongoing care. Robert Wood Johnson Foundation. Available online at www.rwjf.org/en/library/research/2010/01/chronic-care.html.

[4] Beach, S. R., Schulz, R., Friedman, E. M. et al. (2018). Adverse consequences of unmet needs for care in high-need/high-cost older adults. *The Journals of Gerontology: Series B*, 75, 459–470; Casado, B. L., van Vulpen, K. S., and Davis, S. L. (2011). Unmet needs for home and community-based services among frail older Americans and their caregivers. *Journal of Aging and Health*, 23, 529–553; Krumholz, H. M. (2013). Post-hospital syndrome – An acquired, transient condition of generalized risk. *New England Journal of Medicine*, 368, 100–102; Naylor, M. D., Aiken, L. H., Kurtzman, E. T. et al. (2011). The care span: The importance of transitional care in achieving health reform. *Health Affairs (Millwood)*, 30, 746–754; Kansagara, D. Englander, H., Salanitro, A. et al. (2011). Risk prediction models for hospital readmission: A systematic review. *Journal of the American Medical Association*, 306, 1688–1698; Lloren, A., Liu, S., Herrin, J. et al. (2019). Measuring hospital-specific disparities by dual eligibility and race to reduce health inequities. *Health Services Research*, 54, 243–254.

[5] Pham, H. H., O'Malley, A. S., Bach, P. B. et al. (2009). Primary care physicians' links to other physicians through Medicare patients: The scope of care coordination. *Annals of Internal Medicine*, 150, 236–242; Anderson, G. (2010). Chronic Care: Making the case for

of rehospitalizations within 30 days has been identified as consistent with medical plans.[6] However, excessive rates of unplanned readmissions are thought to reflect ineffective implementation of transitional care services. Approximately 16 percent of Medicare patients discharged from a hospital are readmitted within 30 days.[7] This has significant financial consequences that more effective transitional care management can address. Medicare pays an estimated $24 billion for hospital readmissions of adults age 65 and older.[8]

Ineffective care transitions have been identified as one of the top causes of preventable readmissions among older adults.[9] Five overlapping categories of modifiable system issues have been associated with preventable rehospitalizations: lack of patient or family caregiver engagement; inadequate preparation of patients and family caregivers to manage complex clinical symptoms and therapies; limited collaboration between and among acute, post-acute and primary care clinicians; poor continuity of care; and serious gaps in the coordination of health and community-based services.[10]

ongoing care. Robert Wood Johnson Foundation. Available online at www.rwjf.org/en/library/research/2010/01/chronic-care.html.

[6] Jencks, S. F., Williams, M. V., and Coleman, E. A. (2009). Rehospitalizations among patients in the Medicare fee-for-service program. *New England Journal of Medicine*, 360, 1418–1428.

[7] Medicare Payment Advisory Commission 2018 Report to the Congress: Medicare Payment Policy. Hospital inpatient and outpatient services (Chapter 3). Washington, DC: Medicare Payment Advisory Commission. Available online at www.medpac.gov/docs/default-source/reports/mar18_medpac_ch3_sec.pdf?sfvrsn=0.

[8] Hines, A.L., Barrett, M. L., Jian, J. et al. (2014). Conditions with the largest number of adult hospital readmissions by payer, 2011. Agency for Healthcare Research and Quality, Statistical Brief #172. Available online at www.hcup-us.ahrq.gov/reports/statbriefs/sb172-Conditions-Readmissions-Payer.pdf

[9] Goldfield, N. I., McCullough, E. C., Hughes, J. S. et al. (2008). Identifying potentially preventable readmissions. *Health Care Financing Review*, 30, 75–91; Medicare Payment Advisory Commission 2018 Report to the Congress: Medicare and the Health Care Delivery System. The effects of the Hospital Readmissions Reduction Program (Chapter 1). Washington, DC: Medicare Payment Advisory Commission. Available online at www.medpac.gov/docs/default-source/reports/jun18_ch1_medpacreport_sec.pdf

[10] Ahsberg, E. (2019). Discharge from hospital – A national survey of transition to outpatient care. *Scandinavian Journal of Caring Sciences*, 33, 329–335; Clibbens, N., Berzins, K., and Baker, J. (2019). Caregivers' experiences of service transitions in adult mental health: An integrative qualitative synthesis. *Health and Social Care in the Community*, 27, e535–e548; Atzema, C. L., and Maclagan, L. C. (2017). The transition of care between emergency department and primary care: A scoping study. *Academic Emergency Medicine*, 24, 201–215; Bryant, J., Mansfield, E., Boyes, A. W. et al. (2016). Involvement of informal caregivers in supporting patients with COPD: A review of intervention studies. *International Journal of Chronic Obstructive Pulmonary Disease*, 11, 1587–1596; Davidson, P. M., and DiGiacomo, M. (2015). Family caregiving: Benefits

In response to these challenges, innovations in transitional care – a range of time-limited services designed to prevent avoidable and costly break-downs, promote continuity across settings and among providers, and enable high risk patients to achieve optimal health and quality of life – have been the focus of rigorous studies for more than three decades.[11]

Societal concern about the quality of transitional care is evident in the number of federal and state policies focused on addressing modifiable barriers to, and stemming the rise in, associated costs. Indeed, many provisions of the Affordable Care Act (ACA) passed in 2010 focused on this health care priority. One such provision, designed specifically to influence outcomes by changing decision-making related to transitional care of older adults, is Medicare's Hospital Readmission Reduction Program (HRRP). With the inception of HRRP's final rule in 2012, the Centers for Medicare and Medicaid Services (CMS) introduced reimbursement penalties imposed on hospitals for excess hospital readmissions within 30 days for certain high-volume conditions, initially including heart failure, acute myocardial infarction, and pneumonia. CMS caps penalties at three percent of a hospital's Medicare inpatient payment (a total of $564 million in 2017).[12] The hope was that management of affected hospitals, faced with penalties, would find some way of changing decisions made about the course of care that would result in fewer readmissions and lower penalties.

and burdens. *Circulation: Cardiovascular Quality and Outcomes*, 8, 133–134; Yancy, C. W., Jessup, M., Bozkurt, B. et al. (2013). AACF/AHA guideline for the management of heart failure: A report of the American college of cardiology foundation/American heart association task force on practice guidelines. *Journal of the American College of Cardiology*, 62, e147–e239; Agency for Healthcare Research and Quality 2012 coordinating care for adults with complex care needs in the patient-centered medical home: Challenges and solutions. Rockville, MD: AHRQ Publication No. 12-0010; Fromer, L. (2011). Implementing chronic care for COPD: Planned visits, care coordination, and patient empowerment for improved outcomes. *International Journal of Chronic Obstructive Pulmonary Disease*, 6, 605–614; Ortiz, G., and Fromer, L. (2011). Patient-centered medical home in chronic obstructive pulmonary disease. *Journal of Multidisciplinary Healthcare*, 4, 357–365; Bowles, K. H., Pham, J., O'Connor, M. et al. (2010). Information deficits in home care: A barrier to evidence based disease management. *Home Health Care Management & Practice*, 22, 278–285.

[11] Naylor, M. D., Shaid, E. C., Carpenter, D. et al. (2017). Components of comprehensive and effective transitional care. *Journal of the American Geriatrics Society*, 65, 1119–1125.

[12] Fontana, E., and Hawes, K. (2018). Map: See the 2,599 hospitals that will face readmissions penalties this year. Advisory Board: The Daily Briefing. Available online at www .advisory.com/daily-briefing/2018/09/27/readmissions#:~:text=Penalty%20burden% 20moves%20away%20from%20safety%2Dnet%20hospitals%20in%202019&text=The% 20average%20penalty%20moved%20from,%24564%20estimate%20for%20FY%202018

Findings regarding the impact of HRRP are either mixed or too limited to draw conclusions. Some studies suggest that rehospitalizations declined after introduction of HRRP. For example, Medicare fee-for-service patients at hospitals subject to penalties under the HRRP were found to have greater reductions in readmission rates compared with those at nonpenalized hospitals.[13] Other scholars suggest that readmission reductions were likely the result of a multi-pronged strategy. Ryan and colleagues[14] found that most hospitals were also participating in voluntary value-based reforms such as Accountable Care Organizations and the Bundled Payments for Care Improvement initiative during the period that HRRP was implemented. Still other researchers suggest that HRRP achieved only modest gains in rehospitalization reductions and that some of these gains might have been achieved by diverting patients from inpatient hospital admissions to observation stays.[15] Unique challenges of specific patient subgroups may account for the observed differential impact of HRRP. Wasfy and colleagues[16] found that the highest penalized hospitals served socially disadvantaged older adults and, due to constrained finances, that these facilities were especially challenged to improve performance. Finally, some researchers found that changes in diagnostic coding for hospital admissions changed HRRP's risk adjustment. Analyses that accounted for these changes resulted in the HRRP policy either having no effect on readmissions or substantially less effect than suggested by CMS and other researchers.[17]

[13] Desai, S., Hatfield, L. A., Hicks, A. L. et al. (2016). Association between availability of a price transparency tool and outpatient spending. *Journal of the American Medical Association*, 315, 1874–1881; Wasfy, J. H., Zigler, C. M., Choirat, C. et al. (2017). Readmission rates after passage of the hospital readmissions reduction program: A pre-post analysis. *Annals of Internal Medicine*, 166, 324–331; Hoffman, G. J., and Yakusheva, O. (2020). Association between financial incentives in Medicare's hospital readmissions reduction program and hospital readmission performance. *JAMA Network Open*, 3, e202044.

[14] Ryan, A. M., Krinsky, S., Adler-Milstein, J. et al. (2017). Association between hospitals' engagement in value-based reforms and readmission reduction in the hospital readmission reduction program. *JAMA Internal Medicine*, 177, 862–868.

[15] Gupta, A. and Fonarow, G. C. (2018). The hospital readmissions reduction program-learning from failure of a healthcare policy. *European Journal of Heart Failure*, 20, 1169–1174.

[16] Wasfy, J. H., Bhambhani, V., Healy, E. W. et al. (2019). Relative effects of the hospital readmissions reduction program on hospitals that serve poorer patients. *Medical Care*, 57, 968–976.

[17] Ody, C., Msall, L., Dafny, L. S. et al. (2019). Decreases in readmissions credited to Medicare's program to reduce hospital readmissions have been overstated. *Health Affairs (Millwood)*, 38, 36–43.

Another attempt to promote the use of transitional care was Medicare's introduction of transitional care management payment codes in 2013. These codes reimburse health care professionals or practices for specified telehealth or in-person care management services that target moderately to highly complex patients discharged from hospitals and are provided within 2–14 days after hospital discharge. The adoption of transitional care payment codes was low initially, but has increased over time.[18] One study of the effects of these billing codes demonstrated a positive association between the implementation of these codes and reduced mortality rates and total Medicare costs in the month after services were provided.[19] These researchers hypothesized that many clinicians who billed for these services were already providing them, an assumption that needs further testing. Additionally, billing is concentrated in a few practices and disproportionately among clinicians in Accountable Care Organizations who have a much broader set of incentives to reduce health care costs than the limited reimbursement provided via these codes. Overall, use of these codes has not achieved expectations, primarily because there is inadequate incentive for this effort and the billing process remains cumbersome.

A REVIEW OF TRANSITIONAL CARE EVIDENCE

The Early Years

The scientific basis in support of transitional care emerged in the 1990s and continued to grow in the first decade of this century. During this period, 21 studies were identified in a systematic review of reported randomized controlled trials (RCTs) that tested interventions targeting adults transitioning from hospital to home.[20] This evidence was generated by testing distinct transitional care models, primarily the Transitional Care

---

[18] Agarwal, S. D., Barnett, M. L., Souza, J. et al. (2018). Adoption of Medicare's transitional care management and chronic care management codes in primary care. *Journal of the American Medical Association*, 320, 2596–2597; Marcotte, L. M., Reddy, A., Zhou, L. et al. (2020). Trends in utilization of transitional care management in the United States. *JAMA Network Open*, 3(1), e1919571.

[19] Bindman, A. B., and Cox, D. F. (2018). Changes in health care costs and mortality associated with transitional care management services after a discharge among Medicare beneficiaries. *JAMA Internal Medicine*, 178, 1165–1171.

[20] Naylor, M. D., Aiken, L. H., Kurtzman, E. T. et al. (2011). The care span: The importance of transitional care in achieving health reform. *Health Affairs (Millwood)*, 30, 746–754.

Model,[21] the Care Transitions Intervention,[22] and Project RED (Re-Engineered Discharge planning).[23] Table 5.1 describes key characteristics of each of these models.

In common, these models shared a focus on chronically ill hospitalized adults at risk for poor outcomes with interventions implemented by nurses that included both discharge planning and post-discharge followup. However, the models varied in terms of their nature (ranging from a set of specified strategies to a broader focus on meeting holistic needs guided by patients' and families' goals); intensity (from one hospital visit plus one telephone call following hospital discharge to multiple contacts during hospitalization and following patients' return home); and duration (from one to two weeks to two months following hospital discharge). Not surprisingly, interventions that were shorter in duration and of lesser intensity reported shorter-term reductions in rehospitalizations rates,[24] while more comprehensive interventions demonstrated more robust quality outcomes and both shorter-term as well as longer-term decreases in rehospitalization rates, with one demonstrating reductions in total costs of care at one year following index hospital discharge.[25]

Models' Return on Investment (ROI). In 2014, Avalere Health, a national health care consulting firm, conducted an analysis of the ROI achieved by transitional care interventions, including the three models identified above.[26] This ROI calculation accounted for the costs of the intervention as well as changes in Medicare fee-for-service beneficiaries' use of inpatient

[21] Naylor, M. D., Brooten, D. A., Campbell, R. L. et al. (2004). Transitional care of older adults hospitalized with heart failure: A randomized, controlled trial. *Journal of the American Geriatrics Society*, 52, 675–684.

[22] Coleman, E. A., Parry, C., Chalmers, S. (2006). The care transitions intervention: Results of a randomized controlled trial. *Archives of Internal Medicine*, 166, 1822–1828.

[23] Jack, B. W., Chetty, V. K., Anthony, D. et al. (2009). A reengineered hospital discharge program to decrease rehospitalization: A randomized trial. *Annals of Internal Medicine*, 150, 178–187.

[24] Coleman, E. A., Parry, C., Chalmers, S., et al. (2006). The care transitions intervention: Results of a randomized controlled trial. *Archives of Internal Medicine*, 166, 1822–1828; Anthony, D., Chetty, V. K., Forsythe, S. R. et al. (2009). A reengineered hospital discharge program to decrease rehospitalization: A randomized trial. *Annals of Internal Medicine*, 150, 178–187.

[25] Naylor, M. D., Brooten, D. A., Campbell, R. L. et al. (2004). Transitional care of older adults hospitalized with heart failure: A randomized, controlled trial. *Journal of the American Geriatrics Society*, 52, 675–684.

[26] Rodriguez, S., Munevar, D., Delaney, C. et al. (2014). Effective management of high-risk Medicare populations. Avalere Health LLC. Available online at: https://avalere.com/insights/avalere-issues-white-paper-on-the-management-of-high-risk-medicare-popula tions-in-partnership-with-the-scan-foundation.

Table 5.1. *Comparison of Early Transitional (Hospital to Home) Models' Program Features and Outcomes*

Transitional Care Program Elements	Transitional Care Model[1]	Care Transitions Intervention[2]	Project RED[3]
Timing and length of intervention	Starts within 24 hours of hospital admission to 60 days post hospital discharge	Starts prior to hospital discharge to 30 days post hospital discharge	Starts within 24 hours of hospital admission to 2–4 days post hospital discharge
Interventionist	Same APRN throughout intervention	APRN	Nurse discharge advocate and pharmacist
Contact pattern	• Daily hospital visits (first visit within 24 hours of admission) • Average of 7 home visits (within 24 hours of discharge, at least weekly in month 1, then every other week) • Attends first followup visit with physician • 7 day/week access	• 1 hospital visit (prior to discharge) • 1 home visit (within 48 hours of discharge) • 3 telephone calls over	• At least 1 hospital visit (within 24 hours of admission) • No home visits • 1 telephone call
Focus of intervention	• Risk assessment • Patient/family caregiver goal identification • Patient-centered discharge plan • Education/teach back • Symptom management • Collaboration with all team members • Coordination of health and social services	• Medication self-management • Patient-centered record • Followup visits (scheduling appointments) • Review of "Red Flags" (assessment of symptoms and education)	• Diagnosis related education • Scheduling appointments • Review of labs/tests • Medication review • Organize outpatient or community services • Review emergency plan • Hand off discharge plan to patient, clinicians, and service providers

(continued)

Table 5.1. (*continued*)

Transitional Care Program Elements	Transitional Care Model[1]	Care Transitions Intervention[2]	Project RED[3]
Length of outcome assessment	12 months	3 months	1 month
Outcomes	• Fewer readmissions (all cause) (12 months) • Longer time to first rehospitalization (12 months) • Lower rehospitalization costs (6 months) • Lower total health care* costs (12 months) • Improvements in quality of life ratings and physical function (3 months) • Higher ratings of satisfaction with care experience (6 weeks)	• Fewer readmissions (all cause) (3 months) • Lower rehospitalization costs (6 months)	• Fewer hospital utilizations (readmissions and ED visits combined) (1 month) • Longer time to first rehospitalization (1 month) • Lower total health care utilization and outpatient care costs (1 month) • Higher ratings of satisfaction with care experience (1 month)

TCM = Transitional Care Model; CTI = Care Transitions Intervention; RED = Reengineered Discharge planning; APRN = advanced practice registered nurse; ED = emergency department

* Total health care costs included hospitalization costs, physician visits, ED visits and home health care.

[1] Brooten, D. A., Campbell, R. L., Maislin, G. et al. (2004). Transitional care of older adults hospitalized with heart failure: A randomized, controlled trial. *Journal of the American Geriatrics Society*, 52, 675–684.

[2] Chalmers, S., Coleman, E. A., Min, S-J. et al. (2006). The care transitions intervention: Results of a randomized controlled trial. *Archives of Internal Medicine*, 166, 1822–1828.

[3] Anthony, D., Chetty, V. K., Forsythe, S. R. et al. (2009). A reengineered hospital discharge program to decrease rehospitalization: A randomized trial. *Annals of Internal Medicine*, 150, 178–187.

Table 5.2. *ROI Estimates for Three Transitional Care Models Targeting High Risk Medicare Beneficiaries*[1]

Model	Annual Cost Per Beneficiary	Annual Savings Per Member	ROI Per Year	PMPM Savings
Transitional Care Model	$1492	$5,334	257.48%	$320.14
Care Transitions Intervention	$999	$2,311	131.3%	$109.34
Project RED	$373	$493	32.37%	$10.05

ROI = return on investment; PMPM = per member per month; RED = Reengineered Discharge planning
[1] Ibid.

and outpatient covered services. An efficacy assumption of 75 percent was used since the target population in reported studies was similar but not identical to Avalere's definition of high-risk beneficiaries. Analysts based program costs on data reported in studies of the interventions. The 2012 5 percent Standard Analytic Files (Medicare claims) were used to obtain medical and payment information related to health care services provided to Medicare beneficiaries. Table 5.2 summarizes the findings from their analysis.

Current Status

Building on the systematic appraisal of transitional care interventions reported in 2011,[27] we reviewed RCTs conducted in the United States and published in peer-reviewed journals from January 2010 through October 2019. Our review was completed in 2020. Using the PubMed, CINAHL and PsycInfo databases, we identified a total of 28 peer-reviewed articles that reported findings from RCTs of innovations designed to improve transitions for older adults from EDs or hospitals to patients' homes or skilled nursing facilities (SNFs). Most of these studies built upon the seminal work of the transitional care models described in Table 5.1. Using the same publication databases, an additional 15 systematic reviews or meta-analyses of reported studies, inclusive of RCTs, and conducted by

[27] Naylor, M. D., Aiken, L. H., Hirschman, K. H. et al. (2011). The care span: The importance of transitional care in achieving health reform. *Health Affairs (Millwood)*, 30, 746–754.

scholars throughout the globe were also reviewed. Compared to earlier studies, more recent studies have expanded to include other high-risk patient populations (e.g., socially disadvantaged, trauma survivors)[28] and extended the use of team members beyond nurses to implement these interventions (e.g., social workers, pharmacists, community health workers [CHW], health coaches).[29] Overall, this updated review reveals program characteristics that are commonly used in effective transitional care models. We summarize this review and highlight findings from a few examples of inconsistent findings.

Common Characteristics of Effective Solutions

Targets "high-risk" older adults. Consistently, study findings reveal the importance of identifying hospitalized older adults at increased risk for poor outcomes, including preventable rehospitalizations as the target population for transitional care services. Older adults with multiple chronic conditions, especially if complicated by functional, cognitive, and emotional deficits or risks are commonly defined as high risk.[30] Specific subgroups including those with serious, progressive health problems, such as heart failure[31] and chronic obstructiv pulmonary disease (COPD),[32] or

[28] Englander, H., Michaels, L., Chan, B. et al. (2014). The care transitions innovation (C-TRAIN) for socioeconomically disadvantaged adults: Results of a cluster randomized controlled trial. *Journal of General Internal Medicine*, 29, 1460–1467; Zatzick, D., Russo, J., Thomas, P. et al. (2018). Patient-centered care transitions after injury hospitalization: A comparative effectiveness trial. *Psychiatry*, 81, 141–157.

[29] Benzo, R., Vickers, K., Novotny, P. J. et al. (2015). Health coaching and chronic obstructive pulmonary disease rehospitalization: A randomized study. *American Journal of Respiratory and Critical Care Medicine*, 194, 672–680; Balaban, R. B., Zhang, F., Vialle-Valentin, C. E. et al. (2017). Impact of a patient navigator program on hospital-based and outpatient utilization over 180 days in a safety-net health system. *Journal of General Internal Medicine*, 32, 981–989; Kangovi, S., Mitra, N., Norton, L. et al. (2018). Effect of community health worker support on clinical outcomes of low-income patients across primary care facilities: A randomized clinical trial. *JAMA Internal Medicine*, 178, 1635–1643; Zatzick, D., Russo, J., Thomas, P. et al. (2018). Patient-centered care transitions after injury hospitalization: A comparative effectiveness trial. *Psychiatry*, 81, 141–157.

[30] Brock, J., Callicoatte, B., Carpenter, D. et al. (2017). Components of comprehensive and effective transitional care. *Journal of the American Geriatrics Society*, 65, 1119–1125.

[31] Arvanitis, M., Cene, C. W., Coker-Schwimmer, E. J. L. et al. (2014). Transitional care interventions to prevent readmissions for persons with heart failure: A systematic review and meta-analysis. *Annals of Internal Medicine*, 160, 774–784.

[32] Hadi, H,, Ridwan, E. S., Tsai, P. S. et al. (2019). Effects of transitional care on hospital readmission and mortality rate in subjects with COPD: A systematic review and

who are socially disadvantaged[33] also have been identified as those most likely to experience poor outcomes. Available evidence reinforces that these individuals and subgroups also are most likely to benefit from effective transitional care.[34]

Employs multiple strategies tailored to patients' goals and needs. Multidimensional interventions, customized to patients' priority needs (physical, functional, emotional, cognitive, and social) and goals, have generally been demonstrated to improve transitional care outcomes.[35] Strategies commonly employed are designed to enhance the following care processes: patient and family caregiver engagement, communication with patients and family caregivers, collaboration among team members, symptom management, patient or caregiver education to promote self-care, and continuity of care.[36] Such a multifaceted approach is used in Transitional Care Model interventions and has consistently demonstrated improved health and economic outcomes with a range of high-risk older adults.[37] Other comprehensive interventions have been found to positively impact some outcomes, but not others. For example, Zatzick and colleagues[38] tested a social worker-led, patient-centered strategy that included care management, in-person visits in the hospital, coordination of services, telephone access (24/7) and "stepped up" care (e.g., access to motivational

meta-analysis. *Respiratory Care*, 64, 1146–1156. Available online at: https://doi.org/10.4187/respcare.06959.

[33] Englander, H., Michaels, L., Chan, B. et al. (2014). The care transitions innovation (C-TRAIN) for socioeconomically disadvantaged adults: Results of a cluster randomized controlled trial. *Journal of General Internal Medicine*, 29, 1460–1467.

[34] Rodriguez, S., Munevar, D., Delaney, C. et al. (2014). Effective management of high-risk Medicare populations. Avalere Health LLC. Available online at https://avalere.com/insights/avalere-issues-white-paper-on-the-management-of-high-risk-medicare-populations-in-partnership-with-the-scan-foundation.

[35] Laugaland, K., Aase, K., and Barach, P. (2012). Interventions to improve patient safety in transitional care – A review of the evidence. *Work*, 41, 2915–2924; Feil Weber, L. A., Dias da Silva Lima, M. A., Marques Acosta, A. et al. (2017). Care transition from hospital to home: Integrative review. *Cogitare Enfermagen*, 22, 6–15; Kansagara, D., Chiovaro, J. C., Kagen, D. et al. (2016). So many options, where do we start? An overview of the care transitions literature. *Journal of Hospital Medicine*, 11, 221–230.

[36] Hirschman, K. B., Shaid, E, McCauley, K., et al. (2015). Continuity of care: The transitional care model. *OJIN: The Online Journal of Issues in Nursing*, 20, Manuscript 1; Deek, H., Hamilton, S., Brown, N. et al. (2016). Family-centred approaches to healthcare interventions in chronic diseases in adults: A quantitative systematic review. *Journal of Advanced Nursing*, 72, 968–979.

[37] Naylor, M. D., Hirschman, K. B., Toles, M. P., et al. (2018). Adaptations of the evidence-based Transitional Care Model in the US. *Social Science & Medicine*, 213, 28–36.

[38] Zatzick, D., Russo, J., Thomas, P. et al. (2018). Patient-centered care transitions after injury hospitalization: A comparative effectiveness trial. *Psychiatry*, 81, 141–157.

interviewing, cognitive behavioral therapy, and psychiatric services) as needed. The researchers found that a comprehensive intervention targeting acutely injured trauma survivors was associated with significant reductions in the percentage of severe post-injury concerns as well as short-term reductions in ED visits, but had no impact on patients' symptoms or functional status.[39] Alternatively, some studies of multidimensional approaches have demonstrated little positive impact. For example, Englander and colleagues[40] tested a multi-component intervention targeting socially disadvantaged adults. The coaching and education intervention was delivered by nurses (in the hospital and, post discharge, through telephone calls and home visits for the highest risk patients) and pharmacists (during hospitalization) with linkages to primary care providers. Results revealed improvements in patients' ratings of their experience with care, but the intervention was not effective in reducing rehospitalizations.

Spans hospital to home and includes in-person visits. Most transitional care innovations demonstrating improved outcomes begin in the hospital and extend well beyond discharge.[41] Consistent with earlier findings, longer periods of post-discharge followup appear to be associated with longer-lasting impact. Specifically, transitional care interventions with followup 1–2 weeks after hospital discharge have generally demonstrated up to 30 day reductions in rehospitalizations,[42] while those extending to 1–2 months have demonstrated positive impact through 6–12 months following the index hospital discharge.[43] Notably, effective interventions

[39] Ibid.

[40] Englander, H., Michaels, L., Chan, B., et al. (2014). The care transitions innovation (C-TRAIN) for socioeconomically disadvantaged adults: Results of a cluster randomized controlled trial. *Journal of General Internal Medicine*, 29, 1460–1467.

[41] Feltner, C., Jones, C. D., Cene, C. W. et al. (2014). Transitional care interventions to prevent readmissions for persons with heart failure: A systematic review and meta-analysis. *Annals of Internal Medicine*, 160, 774–784; Le Berre, M., Maimon, G., Sourial, N. et al. (2017). Impact of transitional care services for chronically ill older patients: A systematic evidence review. *Journal of the American Geriatrics Society*, 65, 1597–1608.

[42] Weeks, L. E., Macdonald, M., Martin-Misener, R. et al. (2018). The impact of transitional care programs on health services utilization in community-dwelling older adults: A systematic review. *JBI Database of Systematic Reviews and Implementation Reports*, 16, 345–384; McKay, C., Park, C., Chang, J. et al. (2019). Systematic review and meta-analysis of pharmacist-led transitions of care services on the 30-day all-cause readmission rate of patients with congestive heart failure. *Clinical Drug Investigation*, 39, 703–712.

[43] Verhaeh, K. J., MacNeil-Vroomen, J. L., Eslami, S. et al. (2014). Transitional care interventions prevent hospital readmissions for adults with chronic illnesses. *Health Affairs (Millwood)*, 33, 1531–1539.

consistently rely on a combination of in-person visits by team members with patients in hospitals, in SNFs, patients' homes, or transitional care clinics augmented by a wide range of telehealth services. For example, Velligan and colleagues[44] demonstrated that a transitional care clinic serving patients with serious mental illness for 90 days following discharge from hospitals or EDs and offering in-person and telephone contacts resulted in improved quality of life and enhanced communication. It is important to stress that it is not just the number of visits or length of intervention that account for differences in outcomes. Central to successful outcomes is what takes place in these contacts. Longer interventions, for example, enable the establishment of trusting relationships foundational to engaging older adults and their family caregivers in implementing individualized plans of care that focus on current challenges and anticipate future needs.

Relies on team approach with designated "point person". Effective solutions rely on team members from a variety of backgrounds but share a reliance on one specified member to coordinate the team's efforts and, importantly, align the team with older adults and family caregivers' goal and assure continuity of care. Nurses, typically advanced practice registered nurses (APRNs),[45] pharmacists,[46] social

[44] Velligan, D. I., Fredrick, M. M., Sierra, C. et al. (2017). Engagement-focused care during transitions from inpatient and emergency psychiatric facilities. *Patient Preference and Adherence*, 11, 919–928.

[45] Bryant-Lukosius, D., Carter, N., Reid, K. et al. The clinical effectiveness and cost-effectiveness of clinical nurse specialist-led hospital to home transitional care: A systematic review. *Journal of Evaluation in Clinical Practice*, 21, 763–781; Donald, F., Kilpatrick, K., Reid, K. et al. (2015). Hospital to community transitional care by nurse practitioners: A systematic review of cost-effectiveness. *International Journal of Nursing Studies*, 52, 436–451; Naylor, M. D., Hirschman, K. B., Hanlon, A. L. (2014). Comparison of evidence-based interventions on outcomes of hospitalized, cognitively impaired older adults. *Journal of Comparative Effectiveness Research*, 3, 245–257; Stauffer, B. D., Fullerton, C., Fleming, N. et al. (2011). Effectiveness and cost of a transitional care program for heart failure. *Archives of Internal Medicine*, 171, 1238–1243.

[46] De Oliveira Jr, G. S., Castro-Alves, L. J., Kendall, M. C. et al. (2017). Effectiveness of pharmacist intervention to reduce medication errors and health care resources utilization after transitions of care: A meta-analysis of randomized controlled trials. *Journal of Patient Safety* June 30, 2017 – Volume Publish Ahead of Print – Issue – Available online at: https://doi.org/10.1097/PTS.0000000000000283; Fredrickson, B-A., and Burkett, E. (2019). Interventions to improve the continuity of medication management upon discharge of patients from hospital to residential aged care facilities. *Journal of Pharmacy Practice and Research*, 49, 162–170; Kitts, N. K., Reeve, A. R., and Tsu, L. (2014). Care transitions in elderly heart failure patients: Current practices and the pharmacist's role. *The Consultant Pharmacist: The Journal of the American Society of Consultant Pharmacists*, 29, 179–190; McKay, C., Park, C., Chang, J. et al. (2019). Systematic review

workers,[47] and CHWs[48,49] have been demonstrated to be effective in coordinating and implementing transitional care services.

Common Characteristics of Ineffective Solutions

Use hospital-based services only. Hospital-based transitional care interventions, including those in which staff call patients within a few days of their discharge, are typically found to be ineffective at improving post-discharge outcomes for high-risk groups. Chan and colleagues[50] tested an intervention consisting of an inpatient visit and post-discharge phone calls to older, multilingual adults from a registered nurse who spoke the same language as the patient to provide disease specific education, coordinate post-discharge services, and reinforce the care plan. The researchers found this intervention did not improve patient experience. These researchers concluded that such patients likely require more intensive post-discharge services. Similarly, a comprehensive hospital-based intervention tested by Linden and Butterworth[51] targeting patients with heart failure and COPD that included predischarge care plan coordination and transitional and post-discharge telephone followup, but no in-home post-discharge followup, had no impact on rehospitalization or ED visit rates. Authors concluded that better collaboration between hospitals and

---

and meta-analysis of pharmacist-led transitions of care services on the 30-day all-cause readmission rate of patients with congestive heart failure. *Clinical Drug Investigation*, 39, 703–712; Rodrigues, C. R., Harrington, A. R., Murdock, N. et al. (2017). Effect of pharmacy-supported transition-of-care interventions on 30-day readmissions: A systematic review and meta-analysis. *The Annals of Pharmacotherapy*, 51, 866–889.

[47] Reevs, M. J., Fritz, M. C., Woodard, A. T. et al. (2019). Michigan stroke transitions trial: A clinical trial to improve stroke transitions. *Circulation: Cardiovascular Quality and Outcomes*, 12, e005493.

[48] Kangovi, S., Mitra, N., Norton, L. et al. (2018). Effect of community health worker support on clinical outcomes of low-income patients across primary care facilities: A randomized clinical trial. *JAMA Internal Medicine*, 178, 1635–1643.

[49] Balaban, R. B., Zhang, F., Vialle-Valentin, C. E. et al. (2017). Impact of a patient navigator program on hospital-based and outpatient utilization over 180 days in a safety-net health system. *Journal of General Internal Medicine*, 32, 981–989.

[50] Chan, B., Goldman, L. E., Sarkar, U. et al. (2015). The effect of a care transition intervention on the patient experience of older multi-lingual adults in the safety net: Results of a randomized controlled trial. *Journal of General Internal Medicine*, 30, 1788–1794.

[51] Linden, A., and Butterworth, S. W. (2014). A comprehensive hospital-based intervention to reduce readmissions for chronically ill patients: A randomized controlled trial. *American Journal of Managed Care*, 20, 783–792.

community-based providers is needed to achieve positive outcomes. Indeed, among older adults hospitalized for COPD, 70 percent of the problems reported (such as medication management, access, and coordination of post-acute and community services) that would benefit from transitional care services did not emerge until after hospital discharge.[52] The conclusion that hospital-only interventions are ineffective was challenged by Joo and Liu[53] who demonstrated that hospital case management services yielded improved outcomes, including reductions in 30 day rehospitalizations.

Employs few targeted strategies. As noted earlier, findings from most studies suggest that multi-component transitional care interventions tailored to address the complex health and social needs of high-risk older adults are essential to influence outcomes. This conclusion is reinforced by the lack of positive impact among interventions that use few specific strategies either in hospitals or during the post-discharge period. For example, Finn and colleagues[54] found that embedding nurse practitioners in medical teams improved communication related to patients' discharges but had no impact on rehospitalization rates. Farris and colleagues[55] revealed that pharmacist case management services alone did not affect medication use following discharge. Similarly, a predischarge bundle intervention did not affect readmissions rates for adults hospitalized with COPD.[56] Post-discharge, an electronic health record-based intervention that alerted primary care physicians of patients' hospital discharges failed to affect either the timeliness of followup visits to these clinicians or rehospitalization rates.[57]

[52] Altfeld, S. J., Rooney, M., Johnson, T. J. et al. (2013). Effects of an enhanced discharge planning intervention for hospitalized older adults: A randomized trial. *The Gerontologist*, 53, 430–440.

[53] Joo, J. Y., and Liu, M. F. (2017). Case management effectiveness in reducing hospital use: A systematic review. *International Nursing Review*, 64, 296–308.

[54] Chang, Y. Bazari, H., Hunt, D. et al. (2011). Improving the discharge process by embedding a discharge facilitator in a resident team. *Journal of Hospital Medicine*, 6, 494–500.

[55] Carter, B. L., Dawson, J. D., Shelsky, C. et al. (2014). Effect of a care transition intervention by pharmacists: An RCT. *BMC Health Services Research*, 14, 406.

[56] Jennings, J. H., Thavarajah, K., Mendez, M.P. et al. (2015). Predischarge bundle for patients with acute exacerbations of COPD to reduce readmissions and ED visits: A randomized controlled trial. *CHEST*, 147, 1227–1234.

[57] Gurwitz, J. H., Field, T. S., Ogarek, J., et al. (2014). An electronic health record-based intervention to increase follow-up office visits and decrease rehospitalization in older adults. *Journal of the American Geriatrics Society*, 62, 865–871.

Relies exclusively on telephone contact. Transitional care interventions delivered only via telephone also have generally been found to be ineffective.[58] Pekmezaris and colleagues[59] found that remote monitoring following hospital discharge did not affect ED visits or rehospitalization rates among older adults with heart failure. There are, however, some exceptions. For example, Melton and colleagues[60] demonstrated that a telephonic case management intervention delivered within 24 hours of discharge and targeting the highest risk patients was associated with reduced readmissions through 60 days following hospital discharge.

There are areas of research related to transitions of high-risk older adults that warrant increased attention. Scholars have specifically emphasized the need for the design and testing of interventions to enhance hospital-to-home transitions of members of ethnic and racial minorities and socially disadvantaged groups,[61] patients with behavioral health issues,[62] or those requiring palliative care.[63] Others have stressed the importance of examining innovative approaches to enhance transitions from other care settings, such as from long-term care facilities to home.[64] Toles and

---

[58] Altfeld, S. J., Shier, G. E., Rooney, M. et al. (2013). Effects of an enhanced discharge planning intervention for hospitalized older adults: A randomized trial. *The Gerontologist*, 53, 430–440; Jayakody, A., Bryant, J., Carey, M. et al. (2016). Effectiveness of interventions utilising telephone follow-up in reducing hospital readmission within 30 days for individuals with chronic disease: A systematic review. *BMC Health Services Research*, 16, 403; Kamermayer, A. K., Leasure, and A. R., Anderson, L. (2017). The effectiveness of transitions-of-care interventions in reducing hospital readmissions and mortality: A systematic review. *Dimensions of Critical Care Nursing*, 36, 311–316; Biese, K. J., Busby-Whitehead, J., Cai, J. et al. (2018). Telephone follow-up for older adults discharged to home from the emergency department: A pragmatic randomized controlled trial. *Journal of the American Geriatrics Society*, 66, 452–458.

[59] Pekmezaris, R. , Mitzner, I., Pecinka, K. R. et al. (2012). The impact of remote patient monitoring (telehealth) upon Medicare beneficiaries with heart failure. *Telemedicine and e-Health*, 18, 101–108.

[60] Melton, L. D., Foreman, C., Scott, E. et al. (2012). Prioritized post-discharge telephonic outreach reduces hospital readmissions for select high-risk patients. *American Journal of Managed Care*, 18, 838–844.

[61] Kim, H., and Thyer, B. A. (2015). Does transitional care prevent older adults from rehospitalization? A review. *Journal of Evidence-Informed Social Work*, 12, 261–271.

[62] Holzinger, F., Fahrenkrog, S., Roll, S. et al. (2017). Discharge management strategies and post-discharge care interventions for depression. *Journal of Affective Disorders*, 223, 82–94.

[63] Saunders, S., Killackey, T., Kurahashi, A. et al. (2019). Palliative care transitions from acute care to community-based care: A systematic review. *Journal of Pain and Symptom Management*, 58, 721–734.e1.

[64] Freeman, S., Bishop, K., Spirgiene, L. et al. (2017). Factors affecting residents transition from long term care facilities to the community: A scoping review. *BMC Health Services Research*, 17, 689.

colleagues,[65] for example, are currently conducting a study funded by the National Institutes of Health (NIH) testing an intervention designed to improve transitions from SNFs to home. Additional studies focused on enhanced integration of digital tools to facilitate communication and collaboration between the "point person" coordinating transitional care services and patients, families, and other team members also are needed.

In summary, this review reveals substantial opportunity for evidence-based transitional care interventions to improve the health and quality of life of high-risk older adults while reducing total health care costs. Note that this general conclusion is tempered by the failure of a few studies of seemingly similar interventions to demonstrate positive outcomes. Similarly, a few studies with negative findings challenged those that showed improvements for high-risk older adults. While most reviewed studies were RCTs (although the systematic reviews included other designs), the heterogeneity of study samples and sites, limited specificity about the interventions tested and level of fidelity to their implementation, and the lack of standard outcome measures makes it difficult to hypothesize why findings were not consistent. Importantly, our review also describes characteristics of ineffective solutions, studies of which share similar methodological challenges as those demonstrating benefits. Despite acknowledged limitations, the body of transitional care evidence describes effective characteristics and offers well-supported solutions that, if widely adopted by health systems, could benefit a substantial segment of especially vulnerable older adults and make much better use of increasingly finite resources.

HEALTH SYSTEMS' USE OF PROVEN SOLUTIONS

While there is substantial evidence on the positive impact of rigorously tested transitional care solutions, data regarding health systems' actual use of these proven solutions is much more limited. Some scholars have cast a wide net to assess the implementation of evidence-based solutions that target similar patient groups and focus on care management. For example, the Center for Health Care Strategies, a nonprofit health policy resource center dedicated to improving health care access and quality, has tracked the national spread of such initiatives. Promising programs identified by

---

[65] National Institutes of Health. Connect-Home: Testing the efficacy of transitional care of patients and caregivers during transitions from skilled nursing facilities to home, 5R01NR017636-03 (2018–2022), Toles MP (Principal Investigator).

the Center are described in *The Better Care Playbook* (www
.bettercareplaybook.org), an initiative sponsored by seven leading health
care foundations. Two examples of evidence-based transitional care programs featured in the playbook are CHW interventions and the
Transitional Care Model. CHWs are individuals from diverse backgrounds
who are prepared to serve as bridges between patients and health systems.
Findings from four studies[66] funded by the Patient-Centered Outcomes
Research Institute demonstrate the benefits of CHWs, especially among
racial and ethnic minorities and socially disadvantaged groups. For
example, patients randomized to an IMPaCT (Individualized
Management for Patient-Centered Targets) intervention, in which CHWs
provided tailored navigation, coaching and social support, reported better
quality of care and had fewer rehospitalizations compared to those who
received usual care.[67] The Bureau of Labor Statistics estimates that
approximately 59,000 CHWs were employed in the United States in
2019, with approximately 11,000 working in health systems.[68]

As noted earlier, the Transitional Care Model is an APRN-coordinated,
team-based approach to transitional care. Multiple NIH-funded RCTs
have consistently demonstrated the effectiveness of this model in improving health care quality and reducing total health care costs for diverse

---

[66] Ell, K., Aranda, M. P., Wu, S. et al. (2018). Working with bilingual community health
worker promotoras to improve depression and self-care among Latino patients with long-
term health problems. Washington, DC: Patient-Centered Outcomes Research Institute
(PCORI). Available online at www.pcori.org/sites/default/files/Ell045-Final-Research-
Report.pdf; Brekke, J., Kelly, E., Duan, L., et al. (2019). Can people who have experience
with serious mental illness help peers manage their health care? Washington, DC:
Patient-Centered Outcomes Research Institute (PCORI). Available online at: www
.pcori.org/sites/default/files/Brekke067-Final-Research-Report.pdf; Jones, M., Gassaway,
J., and Sweatman, R. (2019). Using one-on-one mentors to help patients with a spinal
cord injury transition from rehabilitation to home. Washington, DC: Patient-Centered
Outcomes Research Institute (PCORI). Available online at: www.pcori.org/sites/default/
files/Jones169-Final-Research-Report.pdf; Long, J., Kangovi, S., Mitra, N. et al. (2019).
Collaborative goal setting with or without community health worker support for patients
with multiple chronic conditions. Washington, DC: Patient-Centered Outcomes
Research Institute (PCORI). Available online at: www.pcori.org/sites/default/files/
Long170-Final-Research-Report.pdf.

[67] Kangovi, S., Mitra, N., Grande, D. et al. (2020). Evidence-based community health worker
program addresses unmet social needs and generates positive return on investment.
Health Affairs (Millwood), 39, 207–213.

[68] US Bureau of Labor Statistics (2020). Occupational Employment and Wages, May 2019:
21-1094 Community Health Workers. Available online at: www.bls.gov/oes/current/
oes211094.htm#top

groups of high-risk older adults.[69] In one such study, APRNs coordinated plans of care for heart failure patients while they were hospitalized, and the same nurses implemented these care plans following discharge (substituting for traditional home care services). Intervention group patients demonstrated significant improvement in their care experience and functional status and reductions in all-cause rehospitalizations at one year with an estimated per-patient savings of $5000 (after accounting for the intervention's costs).[70] As of August 2020, the Center for Health Care Strategies identified a total of 342 US health care systems[71] that are implementing the Transitional Care Model.

Despite the solutions identified in *The Better Care Playbook*, available findings suggest very limited use of proven transitional care solutions. For example, in a national survey conducted in 2015, 342 clinician respondents (59 percent of total responses) reported implementing the Transitional Care Model at their organization and only 134 were hospitals.[72] Of the nearly 3000 acute care hospitals serving Medicare beneficiaries in the United States,[73] it is likely all would report the use of transitional care services, but available findings suggest that few would have implemented evidence-based models. The phenomenon of limited use of transitional care evidence is consistent with findings regarding lack of adoption of a much broader suite of evidence-based interventions by health care systems.[74] Notably, findings regarding sparse uptake of evidence-based transitional care interventions persist, despite multiple, multi-pronged

[69] Naylor, M., Brooten, D., Jones, R. et al. (1994). Comprehensive discharge planning for the hospitalized elderly: A randomized clinical trial. *Annals of Internal Medicine*, 120, 999–1006; Naylor, M. D. Brooten, D., Campbell, R. et al. (1999). Comprehensive discharge planning and home follow-up of hospitalized elders: A randomized clinical trial. *Journal of the American Medical Association*, 281, 613–620; Naylor, M. D., Brooten, D. A., Campbell, R. L., et al. (2004). Transitional care of older adults hospitalized with heart failure: A randomized, controlled trial. *Journal of the American Geriatrics Society*, 52, 675–684.

[70] Ibid.

[71] Naylor, M. D., Hirschman, K. B., Toles, M. P. et al. (2018). Adaptations of the evidence-based Transitional Care Model in the US. *Social Science & Medicine*, 213, 28–36.

[72] Naylor, M. D., Hirschman, K. B., Toles, M. P. et al. (2018). Adaptations of the evidence-based Transitional Care Model in the US. *Social Science & Medicine*, 213, 28–36.

[73] Centers for Medicare & Medicaid Services 2020 Hospital General Information. Data. Medicare.gov. Available online at: https://data.medicare.gov/Hospital-Compare/ Hospital-General-Information/xubh-q36u/data

[74] Morris, Z. S., Wooding, S., and Grant, J. (2011). The answer is 17 years, what is the question: Understanding time lags in translational research. *Journal of the Royal Society of Medicine*, 104, 510–520; Pennock, M. J., Yu, Z., Hirschman, K. B. et al. (2018). Developing a policy flight simulator to facilitate the adoption of an evidence-based

efforts to promote widespread use. In the section below, we examine factors influencing decision-making that contribute to such limited use of this evidence.

DECISION-MAKING REGARDING IMPLEMENTATION OF PROVEN SOLUTIONS

In this section, we explore decision-making regarding implementation of evidence-based transitional care by focusing on two central problems – *uptake* of these innovations and *successful replicability and spread* of these solutions. We begin by providing a summary of available evidence regarding each problem, then suggest broad categories of decisions related to each problem that health care leaders or managers might make regarding evidence-based transitional care interventions and offer potential rationale for these choices.

The Uptake Problem

Available Evidence. The uptake of new ideas has been the focus of implementation research since Everett Rogers' seminal book, *Diffusion of Innovations*, was published in 1962.[75] Since then, many scholars have explored what affects their adoption. Some studies have identified attributes of innovations associated with their uptake: having a clear, unambiguous advantage in effectiveness or cost-effectiveness; being compatible with the decision makers' needs and values; and being perceived as simple to use. Others have described characteristics of adopters, including their perceptions of personal risks[76] or beliefs that the innovation will improve their own performance.[77]

However, adoption of simple innovations by one decision maker may not apply to complex process-based innovations, which are often adopted

---

intervention. *IEEE Journal of Translational Engineering in Health and Medicine*, 6,4800112.

[75] Rogers, E. M. (1962). *Diffusion of Innovations*. Free Press of Glencoe.

[76] Meyer, M., Johnson, D., Ethington, C. (1997). Contrasting attributes of preventive health innovations. *Journal of Communication*, 47, 112–131.

[77] Dobbins, M., Cockerill, R., and Barnsley, J. (2001). Factors affecting the utilization of systematic reviews. *International Journal of Technology Assessment in Health Care*, 17, 203–214; Sharma, R., Southon, G., and Yetton, P. (1999). Successful is innovation: The contingent contributions of innovation characteristics and implementation process. *Journal of Information Technology*, 14, 53–68.

by teams, departments, or organizations. Greenhalgh and colleagues[78] completed a systematic review of factors influencing decision-making regarding health service innovations. In addition to fit and alignment with an organization and its goals, innovations developed by independent sources (e.g., research centers) are more likely to be considered for adoption. This is especially the case if the decision makers have had the opportunity to influence the conceptualization and design of the innovation.

Influencers, such as expert opinion leaders, have a major impact on decision-making regarding innovations, both positive and negative.[79] Adoption is more likely if key individuals both within the organization and external networks are willing to support the change.[80] In addition, innovations are more easily assimilated in organizations that are mature and functionally differentiated, employ decentralized decision-making, have a capacity to identify and link new evidence to organizational needs, and have leadership and climate that are receptive to change.[81]

Hypotheses Re: Limited Uptake of Evidence-Based Transitional Care. Guided by available evidence, we suggest two categories of decision-making regarding *uptake* of evidence-based transitional care interventions. Both assume decision makers are aware of these solutions.

(1)   Decision makers are aware of the evidence and decide to adopt.
(2)   Decision makers are aware of the evidence *but*:
        (i) elect to retain status quo or make only nominal changes in services,
        (ii) choose to try out conceptually plausible ideas,
        (iii) adopt solutions not supported by evidence.

As noted earlier, relatively few decision makers have decided to adopt evidence-based transitional care solutions. To help us better understand the reasoning behind decision makers who are aware of the evidence but choose different options, we draw upon findings from a Robert Wood Johnson Foundation-funded project that developed a simulator designed

[78] Greenhalgh, T., Macfarlane, F., Bate, P. et al. (2004). Diffusion of innovations in service organizations: Systematic review and recommendations. *Milbank Quarterly*, 82, 581–629.
[79] Locock, L., Dopson, S., Chambers, D., et al. (2001). Understanding the role of opinion leaders in improving clinical effectiveness. *Social Science & Medicine*, 53, 745–757.
[80] Backer, T. E., and Rogers, E. M. (1998). Diffusion of innovations theory and work-site AIDS programs. *Journal of Health Communication*, 3, 17–28.
[81] Greenhalgh, T., Robert, G., Macfarlane, F. et al. (2004). Diffusion of innovations in service organizations: Systematic review and recommendations. *Milbank Quarterly*, 82, 581–629.

to facilitate decision-making regarding the adoption of the Transitional Care Model.[82] To guide the design of this simulator, the research team engaged leaders from the payer, provider, purchaser and policy-making sectors. A series of structured interviews (individual and group) were conducted over time to understand the concerns of these key stakeholders related to evidence-based interventions in general and the Transitional Care Model in particular. Data were generated both related to the uptake (discussed below) and successful replicability and spread problems (described later) and coded using conventional content analysis techniques.

Findings from analyses of these interviews suggest that decision makers who are aware of available evidence will choose to retain the status quo if incentives to adopt interventions do not align with their system's priorities or with payment systems, or do not provide an adequate ROI. Transitional care is only one of many challenges health care systems are confronting. Even when improving care transitions is identified as a system priority, decision makers still focus on the trade-off between health and economic outcomes. Most insurers do not directly pay for the evidence-based solutions discussed earlier. Rather, these payers provide incentives to hospitals to reduce costly rehospitalizations. In turn, these incentives may or may not result in investments in transitional care. For example, Medicare's HRRP financially penalizes some hospitals with higher-than-expected 30-day readmission rates. The financial incentives of this program directly align with the goals of transitional care programs and thus may promote health system investment in such interventions. However, many hospital administrators are concerned that the reductions in revenue from fewer hospital readmissions, when combined with the costs of investing in strategies to prevent rehospitalizations, will be more costly than the penalties imposed by Medicare's HRRP. Recent evidence suggests that may not be the case. For example, Yakusheva and Hoffman[83] found that for an average hospital, avoiding one excess readmission would result in reimbursement gains of $10,000–$58,000 for Medicare discharges. Additionally, as noted earlier, some transitional care interventions have demonstrated a positive ROI at a societal level, although that does not necessarily translate to direct financial benefits for participating hospitals.

[82] Pennock, M. J., Yu, Z., Hirschman, K. B., et al. (2018). Developing a policy flight simulator to facilitate the adoption of an evidence-based intervention. *IEEE Journal of Translational Engineering in Health and Medicine*, 6, 4800112.

[83] Hoffman, G. J., and Yakusheva, O. (2020). Does a reduction in readmissions result in net savings for most hospitals? An examination of Medicare's hospital readmissions reduction program. *Medical Care Research and Review*, 77, 334–344.

Typically, these interventions require an upfront investment for which hospitals may derive some benefit (in the form of enhanced patient ratings of the care experience and reductions in 30-day readmission rates) but benefits also will accrue to downstream providers (e.g., primary care and post-acute care) who often have not contributed to initial costs and may not have any affiliation with the hospitals. One factor that bears considerable influence in assessments of "quality and cost trade-offs" is the decision by peers, especially local competitors, to adopt an innovation.

Decision makers who are aware of the evidence but choose other options often do so for one or more of the following reasons: they are skeptical that the interventions proven in RCTs will be replicated in their systems with their patient populations (which they believe to be unique in some way); they have had negative experiences after investing in other "evidence-based" solutions; or they prefer simpler, less disruptive and less costly solutions, even when they have much smaller benefits. Some of these decision makers will test out conceptually plausible but not proven solutions, relying on credible champions within their own organizations. Still others elect options demonstrated to be ineffective. Beyond the literature on the effects of influencers and context, there is little evidence to explain such choices.

Strategies to Enhance Uptake. There are multiple paths to accelerate uptake (adoption or adaptation) of complex and dynamic interventions. In general, fostering evidence-based innovation requires investment in the identification of potential solutions and the deliberate integration of these interventions within distinct organizational contexts. Tailoring paths for each context is essential. Specific strategies to promote uptake recommended by Horton and colleagues[84] and reinforced by multiple other scholars include the following:

- developing innovative tools to reach decision makers, such as simulations that allow decision makers to estimate both investment and ROI;
- grounding the selection of the intervention in an understanding of the health and social characteristics of the overall population and subgroups to be served, and the organization's current practices and services;

---

[84] Horton, T., Illingworth, J., and Warburton, W. (2018). The spread challenge: How to support the successful uptake of innovations and improvements in health care. London: The Health Foundation.

- fostering and supporting partnerships between innovators and adopters;
- robustly describing standardized solutions (using playbooks and other tools) to enable end-users to successfully reproduce the intervention in diverse contexts;
- pilot testing and revising interventions in diverse contexts early in the innovation cycle;
- utilizing standardized measures to assess success or failure; and,
- insuring mechanisms are in place for continual sharing and new learning.

The Replicability and Spread Problem

Available Evidence. While considerable attention has been paid to the challenge of getting decision makers to adopt a new intervention, much less has focused on their role in making sure that solutions are positioned to work in new environments. Likely, failure to do so has contributed to the limited success of interventions proven in rigorous studies to replicate similar positive outcomes in "real world" contexts. Some might argue that the fault lies with the architects of innovations who do not adequately describe interventions in research papers. Indeed, Hoffmann and colleagues analyzed reports from a large sample of RCTs of nondrug interventions and found that 61 percent were insufficiently detailed to enable replication.[85]

Horton, Illingworth, and Warburton[86] suggest that the issue is much more complex. These scholars argue that the success of implementing a complex intervention "... depend[s] heavily on context: the underlying systems, culture and circumstances of the environment in which it is implemented" (p. 4). As noted earlier, effective transitional care interventions are multicomponent and, as such, have multiple, interacting causal pathways. Thus, decision makers' knowledge of both the critical elements of the intervention and how it can be operationalized is essential. But a robust playbook alone will not achieve successful replication. When introduced to the real world of health care delivery, these multidimensional

---

[85] Hoffmann, T. C., Erueti, C., and Glasziou, P. P. (2013). Poor description of non-pharmacological interventions: Analysis of consecutive sample of randomised trials. *BMJ*, 347, f3755.

[86] Horton, T., Illingworth, J., and Warburton, W. (2018). The spread challenge: How to support the successful uptake of innovations and improvements in health care. London: The Health Foundation.

interventions must be successfully embedded in diverse and dynamic social systems. Decision makers must attempt to conceptualize what it will take for the innovation to work in their specific contexts. What motivation, behaviors, skills, capabilities, and incentives are required to get the innovation successfully launched? Are the support systems in place to enable interventions to be implemented with fidelity? Are there plans in place to support the spread of intervention across the organization? What mechanisms will be used to generate "buy-in" from others in the organization who are essential to the spread of successfully replicated interventions? Do these mechanisms capture ongoing learning from efforts to tackle implementation challenges? What support is critical to reproduce pilot or single-site programs at an organization-wide scale? Even if an intervention succeeds on average, are there mechanisms in place to support (rather than blame) organizations where it fails?

Hypotheses and Supporting Rationale Re: Challenges in Successful Replicability and Scalability. The role of health care leaders and managers does not end with the decision to adopt an evidence-based transitional care solution. If implementation is to be successful in achieving desired outcomes, these decision makers must also consider the critical issues of replication and spread. Guided by available evidence, we suggest two categories of decision-making regarding *successful replication and spread* of evidence-based transitional care interventions. Once again, we assume that decision makers are aware of implementation challenges.

(1)   Decision makers create the conditions for successful replication and spread within their organization.

(2)   Decision makers do not perceive a role in creating conditions for successful replication and spread and leave implementation to others.

Currently, data regarding what it takes to successfully replicate and spread innovations are limited to studies that have benefitted from the investment of foundations. Information about how decision makers perceive their role in creating the conditions for success is quite limited. As part of their efforts to better understand the replicability and spread challenge, for example, Horton, Illingworth, and Warburton[87] conducted a survey of innovators and adopters of The Health Foundation's "spread challenge"

---

[87]   Horton, T., Illingworth, J., and Warburton, W. (2018). The spread challenge: How to support the successful uptake of innovations and improvements in health care. London: The Health Foundation.

programs (a total of 44 projects). Among the changes that adopters believed would have made the biggest difference in helping them to replicate and spread the intervention were allowing for more time to implement and opportunities to share learning and doing more to support readiness (e.g., providing more training and support). However, no data were reported regarding the role of decision makers in creating the environment for success. Qualitative data from an ongoing RCT of the implementation of the Transitional Care Model in multiple health systems funded by Arnold Ventures suggest that decision makers recognize their central role in creating conditions for successful replication.[88] However, this work is early in the implementation phase.

In contrast, a considerable body of literature suggests that leaders at many health care organizations decide to implement evidence-based interventions, including those focused on transitional care, with limited attention to replication and spread. For example, of the 342 health care organizations that reported implementing the Transitional Care Model in the 2015 national survey described above, many of these organizations were in the early phase of implementation. Only 4% of the group reporting implementation of this model used its 10 core components; the remaining 96% reported a wide range of adaptations (40% 1–3; 43% 4–6; and 17% 7–9).[89] Thus, a major study finding, consistent with others describing modifications to evidence-based interventions,[90] is that adaptations of this transitional care intervention are ubiquitous. While findings do not specify that decision makers were not invested in implementation of the model as intended, they do suggest that many of the leaders and managers did not create or were unsuccessful in creating the conditions for successful replication. Notably, a key finding of this study is that organizations reporting

---

[88] Crossett, E. (2020). Promising program expands to address more complex care patients. Arnold Ventures. Available online at: www.arnoldventures.org/stories/promising-program-expands-to-address-more-complex-care-patients

[89] Naylor, M. D., Hirschman, K. B., Toles, M. P. et al. (2018). Adaptations of the evidence-based Transitional Care Model in the US. *Social Science & Medicine*, 213, 28–36.

[90] Aarons, G. A., Sklar, M., Mustanski, B. et al. (2017). "Scaling-out" evidence-based interventions to new populations or new health care delivery systems. *Implementation Science*, 12, 111; Chambers, D. A., and Norton, W. E. (2016). The Adaptome: Advancing the science of intervention adaptation. *American Journal of Preventive Medicine*, 51, S124–S131; Miller, C. J., Stirman, S. W., Toder, K., and Calloway, A. (2013) Development of a framework and coding system for modifications and adaptations of evidence-based interventions. *Implementation Science*, 8, 65.

implementing higher numbers of Transitional Care Model core components also reported better outcomes.[91]

Strategies to Promote and Accelerate Spread. Similar to uptake, there are
multiple paths to successfully replicate and spread interventions. In general, such efforts require investing in infrastructure to support implementation of the intervention and securing alignment of payments with
sustained use of solutions. Specific strategies recommended by Horton
and colleagues[92] and supported by multiple other scholars include the
following:

- developing easily exportable and standardized models of care that can
  be scaled, including detail steps for implementation and measuring
  progress;
- identifying plans for spread early in the model development process
  and continually refining these plans;
- designing spread programs in ways that build upon adopters' commitment to implementation of proposed solutions;
- organizing spread of solutions in ways that adequately support
  adopters' efforts to reproduce them (e.g., assistance with analytics,
  messaging, metrics);
- using spread opportunities to generate fresh insights about essential
  components that allow innovators to continually revise their descriptions and, in some situations, refine the intervention; and
- maximizing the use of technology.

CONCLUSION

Transitional care is among a relatively few care delivery innovations
targeting high-risk older adults for which there is a rigorous body of
research consistently demonstrating that selected interventions can
improve quality and reduce health care costs. Thus far, however, there is
little evidence of uptake of proven interventions. A key barrier to widespread use of effective transitional care is that implementation requires an
investment in system redesign. Hospitals, post-acute care and primary care
providers, and community service organizations need to collaborate to

[91] Naylor, M. D., Hirschman, K. B., Toles, M. P., et al. (2018). Adaptations of the evidence-based Transitional Care Model in the US. *Social Science & Medicine*, 213, 28–36.

[92] Horton, T., Illingworth, J., and Warburton, W. (2018). The spread challenge: How to support the successful uptake of innovations and improvements in health care. London: The Health Foundation.

assure that the needs of older adults are addressed throughout episodes of illness that span hospital to home. The care provided by clinicians and staff in each of these settings requires a "point person" to provide the continuity of care. Thus far, economic incentives are not aligned with such a care delivery strategy. Lessons from multiple attempts to influence changes in reimbursement policies suggest that no amount of appeal to improve the quality of patient care while simultaneously addressing a societal priority to stem rising health care costs will be effective until insurers put money on the table. Given the projected growth in the need for effective transitional care among high-risk older adults, efforts to promote policy changes need to be accelerated. In the short term, decision makers in hospitals and other settings could advance this agenda by promoting the uptake of evidence-based interventions in their respective organizations and creating the conditions for their successful replication. Findings from such efforts could then be used to strengthen the case for the economic incentives essential for the spread and sustainability of these proven solutions.

6

Vertical Integration of Physicians and Hospitals

Three Decades of Futile Building upon a Shaky Foundation

Lawton R. Burns, David Asch, and Ralph Muller[*]

EXECUTIVE SUMMARY AND OVERVIEW

There has been growing interest in the vertical integration of physicians and hospitals during the past decade, as evidenced by multiple literature reviews and research investigations.[1] Historically, physicians operated small firms that provided "physicians' services" to patients who sometimes used facilities provided by separate hospital firms at which many physicians would have "privileges." This interest in combining the two types of organizations culminated in a December 2020 issue of *Health Services Research* devoted to the topic that expressed surprise (and disappointment) that integration is not "a miracle cure".[2] Just months earlier, two of the major proponents of vertical integration published a study in the August issue of *Health Affairs* that came to a similar, "startling" conclusion: the financial integration of physicians and hospitals (e.g., via employment) had no impact on their clinical integration (and perhaps none on quality).

In reality, these conclusions were neither new nor startling; regulators and a handful of observers had suspected the problem of provider integration for several decades. We can give the academic community "a pass" here: an informed assessment of physician-hospital integration (PHI, for

[*] **Acknowledgments**: The authors wish to thank Bob Berenson, Larry Casalino, Mark Pauly, and (especially) Jeff Goldsmith for their very helpful comments on an earlier draft of this chapter.
[1] Post, B., Buchmueller, T., and Ryan, A. M. (2017). Vertical integration of hospitals and physicians: Economic theory and empirical evidence on spending and quality. *Medical Care Research & Review*, 75(4), 399–433; Machta, R., Maurer, K., Jones, D. et al. (2019). A systematic review of vertical integration and quality of care, efficiency, and patient-centered outcomes. *Health Care Management Review*, 44(2), 159–173.
[2] Blumenthal, D. (2020). Making integration work. *Health Services Research*, 55(6), Part II, 1031–1032.

short) requires considerable contextual understanding of the forerunners and theoretical foundations of vertical integration – although that too was evident by the early 2000s.[3] Perhaps we need to bone up on our history.

This context includes the origins of the integration movement, which extends back to Paul Ellwood's advocacy of health maintenance organizations (HMOs), which both motivated and then gave way to PHI efforts in the 1990s. HMOs and PHI are best viewed as *two* intertwined forms of vertical integration. The integration movement *first* started with efforts to vertically integrate financing and delivery in one organization (the prepaid group practice, or HMO) during the 1970s–1990s. These integrated financing/delivery models were initially advocated to address specific issues with accessible health care, and then later on to control costs. They also served ideological and political agendas that eventually ran out of steam.

The HMO movement spawned the *second* form of integration (PHI) during the 1990s–2010s. These integrated models were purportedly developed to increase collaboration between the two different sets of providers, reorganize their joint operations, jointly improve patient outcomes, and allow their combination to either operate their own HMOs, receive risk contracts from HMOs, or deal with HMOs' pressures for price discounts. Such coordination efforts lacked a strong, supporting theoretical foundation and failed to follow the evidence base from industrial firms on what could be achieved and how to achieve it. As a result, vertical integration to bring the physician and hospital businesses together has failed to deliver on most of its presumed benefits. Other observers suspect that these integrated models served other, less noble purposes – such as growth, larger market share and market power, and control over primary care physicians – to prevent large physician-run medical groups and independent practitioner associations (IPAs) from being able to garner risk contracts from health plans that would turn hospitals into large cost centers and vie with them for prestige.[4]

This chapter focuses primarily on the latter form of integration. A major problem with the PHI literature has been the lack of clarity regarding what "integration" is and what its components are. A detailed analysis of three decades of PHI research (and regulatory investigation of PHI efforts) identifies two core dimensions that are variously labeled as (1) financial/

---

[3] Burns, L. R., Walston, S., Alexander, J. et al. (2001). Just how integrated are integrated delivery systems? Results from a national study. *Health Care Management Review*, 26(1), 20–39.

[4] We thank Larry Casalino for this latter observation.

economic integration (often focusing on physician employment, as well as provider risk contracting with payers) and (2) clinical integration (often focused on care management practices and quality improvement efforts). Regulators and some researchers discovered early on that providers had only weakly developed these two types of integration. Researchers nevertheless looked for their beneficial effects, following a basic model with an implicit (and sometimes explicit) causal logic, summarized as follows:

Financial Integration → *Clinical Integration* → *Cost and Quality Outcomes*

An analysis of the literature shows that the evidence base for this causal model has been severely and consistently lacking. Moreover, the major conceptual dimensions of integration are not strongly correlated with one another – that is, are not themselves integrated. Integration is thus a house divided. If anything, vertical integration and PHI have increased health care costs, contrary to theory, and reduced market competition (which, in turn, may raise prices and costs and reduce quality). Hence, the 2020 studies referenced above were no surprise at all, but rather more confirmation that PHI, and (more generally) vertical integration in health care, may have been a futile "nowhere road" that perhaps should not have been travelled.

Travelling down this road has provided a lengthy list of mistakes to avoid in future efforts to coordinate the actions of physicians and hospitals. These include overcoming the cultural divide between the two parties, solving logistical issues of coordinating providers operating on totally different geographic and spatial scales, abstaining from past failed solutions that get blindly applied to new problems, dealing with the level of risk-bearing in provider organizations, focusing on the wrong targets, avoiding the emulation of Kaiser, and failing to develop mechanisms of "operational integration" that fit with the work of physicians.

Organization of Chapter

This is a long chapter, co-written by three individuals with very different perspectives (health care management researcher, clinician/researcher, and hospital executive). We believe that this multidisciplinary perspective helps to elucidate the issues with vertical integration and PHI. We nevertheless beg the reader's forbearance.

To assist the reader, we offer this roadmap. Section II considers what physician-hospital integration (PHI) actually means. The chapter then charts the historical path undertaken to foster two major forms of integration over the last several decades: Section III deals with the vertical integration of financing and delivery (HMOs), while Section IV deals with vertical integration of physicians and hospitals (PHI). Section V provides a detailed account of integration and PHI efforts from 1960 to 2000; Section VI continues the account from 2000 to 2020. Section VII reviews (1) the growing (and confusing) number of typologies of integration and their component dimensions, and (2) the research evidence on PHI and the surprisingly low degree of support for this model. Section VIII includes a lengthy discussion of the problems that confront efforts to integrate physicians and hospitals and the thorny issues that researchers should address. Section IX concludes the chapter with some considerations for a new perspective on integration.

WHAT IS INTEGRATION?

Integration has never been clearly and consistently defined over time. As illustrated above, it has taken on different meanings and forms (e.g., HMO, PHI) that many mistakenly confuse. In the political arena, integration has often been tied to the policy agendas of various presidents and presidential candidates. In the health care management literature, integration has often been used interchangeably with 'coordination' and 'collaboration'. These terms are usually employed to describe the extent and quality of the relationships among various players in the health care system, including:

- referral and consulting patterns (primary care physicians with specialist physicians, hospitalists with community practitioners, physicians and diagnostic test sites),
- patient care teams (physicians with nurses and other professions, magnet nursing programs),
- care teams with patients and their families,
- professionals and bureaucracies (physicians with hospitals, pharmacists with pharmacies), and
- patient care transitions (clinicians, discharge planners, and alternate sites of care).

Many of these relationships are designed to counter the organizational and behavioral fragmentation of providers in the health care delivery system – or, in management terms, integrate what has been differentiated.[5] Coordination is designed to tackle the issue of fragmentation, which most

[5] Lawrence, P., and Lorsch, J. (1967). *Organization and Environment*. Boston, MA: Harvard Business School.

people assume is a key problem with the market-based health care system. As Chapter 4 on care coordination in this volume demonstrates, the health care system has thrown a host of structures, protocols, information systems, and other mechanisms at this issue of fragmentation. The main point is that coordination through vertically integrated arrangements has been accorded "most favored nation" status by researchers and analysts. Many policy-makers and researchers give it the benefit of the doubt when it comes to evaluating its prospects or performance.

With regard to PHI, one set of researchers distinguished (1) "coordination," which seeks to adjust the parts of health care to facilitate their intersection, from (2) "integration," which seeks to combine them into a unified, synergistic whole, from (3) "collaboration," which serves as one vehicle to achieve integration.[6] In their typology, PHI can be viewed structurally (i.e., the existence of a formal tie or linkage), functionally (i.e., the existence of policies or protocols), culturally (i.e., the existence of shared norms and beliefs), interpersonally (i.e., the existence of collaboration or teamwork), and ritually (i.e., the existence of patterned activities). Multiply their effort across several other research teams over time and you have multiple typologies and dimensions of integration. In our view, the literature is approaching a so-called Tower of Babel (read "babble"). The absence of an agreed-upon and precise definition makes it hard to interpret or compare the evidence on PHI.

INTEGRATING FINANCING AND DELIVERY

Current US health care policy focuses partly on reforming financing (e.g., pay-for-performance, shared savings, bundled payments) and partly on delivery (e.g., structural models like accountable care organizations). To be successful, most of these reforms rely on vertical integration linkages between and among the various players in the health care ecosystem – particularly payers and providers – to coordinate care and deliver it efficiently within budgetary limits. Accountable care organizations (ACOs) and provider-sponsored health plans are but two of the latest versions.

This approach is not new. Efforts to reform health care by integrating financing and delivery are nearly 100 years old, usually spurred by local efforts to solve problems with patient financial access to care. Some early

---

[6] Singer, S., Kerrissey, M., Friedberg, M. et al. (2018). A comprehensive theory of integration. *Medical Care Research & Review*, 77(2), 196–207.

prepaid group practice models, such as Kaiser Permanente, formed on the West Coast starting in the 1930s by combining financing and delivery in areas lacking medical services (whether due to rural work sites or wartime physician shortages). Others, like the Group Health Cooperative (GHC, which formed in 1947 in Puget Sound) and the Group Health Plan (which formed in 1957 in Minneapolis), were consumer cooperatives organized by community groups (farmers, labor) to solve their members' problems with financial and geographic access to providers.

Efforts to combine financing and delivery accelerated during the 1970s, not so much to address access issues, but rather to advance the ideological convictions of their sponsors. The Kaiser model of prepaid, multispecialty group practice served as the template for many of the proposals – whether to promote HMO in the 1970s, "managed competition" in the late 1970s through the early 1990s, or "integrated service networks" (ISNs) that combined physicians, hospitals, and (often) health plans under one roof. Much of this activity took place in Minnesota. These are briefly described below:

In 1971, President Nixon needed a health plan to counter Senator Ted Kennedy's proposal for national health insurance that would use taxes to pay for care produced largely in the conventional delivery system. Nixon latched onto integration of both financing and production of care as his private sector alternative. Nixon's 1973 HMO Act built upon the work of Paul Ellwood's study group on HMOs. Ellwood had grown up in Oakland near Kaiser's ship-building operations, and had moved to Minnesota, which featured not only the Mayo Clinic (the first multispecialty group) but also the Group Health Plan (one of the earliest prepaid health plans) – both of which he supported and tried to propagate. According to the Federal Government, the major purpose of the HMO Act was to offer an alternative delivery system to the expensive fee-for-service (FFS) system and "stimulate interest by consumers and providers in the HMO concept and to make health care delivery under this form available and accessible in the health care market."[7]

In the late 1970s, President Carter was also challenged by Ted Kennedy. Kennedy favored national health insurance, while Carter wanted a more fiscally conservative plan. Carter advanced several models, first his own model for universal health insurance, and then a catastrophic plan. The former built upon Stanford economist Alain Enthoven's proposal, the Consumer Choice Health Plan, which was based on managed competition in the private sector and the existence of integrated HMOs like Kaiser and GHC. After Carter's initiative failed, Enthoven marketed the advantages of managed competition between such plans, hoping it would attract the support of private-sector employers who were complaining their health

---

[7] www.ssa.gov/policy/docs/ssb/v37n3/v37n3p35.pdf.

expenditures were running out of control. Enthoven developed this model in tandem with the Jackson Hole Group, which met at Paul Ellwood's home in Wyoming, to spur formation of health insurance purchasing cooperatives (HIPCs), groupings of employers who would select among competing health plans (e.g., HMOs).

In 1992, candidate Bill Clinton needed a health plan to counter his rivals – Senators Paul Tsongas and Robert Kerrey – each of which had their own proposal. Clinton latched onto portions of the managed competition model advocated by Enthoven. It included HIPCs as organized employer purchaser groups and "regional health alliances," which were competing supplier networks of providers and health plans.

In 1993, the states of Washington and Minnesota enacted similar reforms that paralleled what the Clinton plan sought to achieve on the supply side. Washington State's Health Services Act (1993) and MinnesotaCare (1993) sought to implement Enthoven's managed competition between rival accountable health plans – this time containing hospitals, physicians, and (often) health plans.[8] Minnesota stakeholders viewed ISNs as a natural evolution from and the next generation of the Kaiser HMO. These were to be horizontally and vertically integrated care systems providing a continuum of care, where providers bore financial risk (e.g., capitation) and focused on populations of patients, their outcomes, and their health maintenance.[9] Moreover, MinnesotaCare was designed to ensure not only access to care, but also "contain health care costs and improve quality."[10]

During the first half of the 1990s, it appeared that Enthoven's model might materialize. After the demise of the Clinton plan, employers desperate for cost control shifted their workers into HMOs: between 1993 and 1996, national HMO market share accelerated from 21% to 31%, a more rapid shift than the growth from 16% to 21% during 1988–1993.

As the 1990s wound down, the managed competition movement lost steam.[11] The employers' quick ramp-up in HMO enrollment laid the seeds for the "managed care backlash" among employees which would shortly undermine the closed-network HMOs. Enrollee dissatisfaction with health plans was strongly associated with reduced provider choice, a hallmark of

---

[8] Conant, R., Dowd, B, and Christenson, R. (1995). *MinnesotaCare: A Law That Lost its Way* (Center of the American Experiment) Available online at: www .americanexperiment.org/article/minnesotacare-a-law-that-lost-its-way/.

[9] Kralewski, J., de Vries, A., Dowd, B. et al. (1995). The development of integrated service networks in Minnesota. *Health Care Management Review*, 20(4), 42–56.

[10] Minnesota Health Care Commission. (1994). *Minnesota Health Reform Master Plan*. Minneapolis, MN: Minnesota Health Care Commission.

[11] Alain Enthoven attributes the demise of managed competition to employers and enrollees. It is unclear and perhaps unlikely that hospitals participated in the effort to kill this movement; they were likely not crazy about it.

the Kaiser model.[12] Health plans found employers reluctant to accept closed panel models that relied only on a subset of providers in a given local market. The economic expansion of the late 1990s created a demand for labor; employers did not want to hamper hiring efforts with unpopular closed-panel plans. Employees, for their part, did not want to be forced to switch physicians or hospitals because their employers chose a different health plan, even when doing so would save them money on their insurance premiums. Broad-based health plans, such as preferred provider organizations (PPOs) and point of service (POS) plans, triumphed over closed panel HMO plans. Market share for HMOs dropped from 31% to 24% between 1996–2001, while the PPO share rose from 28% to 46%.[13]

This marked a widespread employer migration away from "delivery system HMOs" (Enthoven's term for narrow-network, Kaiser-like models) to "carrier HMOs" (broad provider network, often using IPA-models). This meant that employers could offer a single, large scale, geographically-spread health plan; the Kaiser model was difficult to emulate anyway, having grown out of particular historical and environmental circumstances (covered below). This concession to worker preferences eliminated the buyer-supplier competition (multiple plans, competing provider networks) that Enthoven sought. The inclusion of more community providers lessened the health plan's bargaining power, thereby dooming managed competition.

Moving the Goalposts on Integration

The early Kaiser plans were designed to guarantee financing for and thus access to needed physician services during the Depression and World War II for unionized, blue-collar workers.[14] These plans offered more comprehensive benefits and more coordinated care programs than were offered by the Blue Cross/Blue Shield plans of the time.[15] Nationally, the 1970s' interest in HMOs was, to be sure, motivated by the rise in provider prices and health care expenditures under the FFS system. However locally, like

---

[12] Enthoven, A. (2005). The US experience with managed care and managed competition. *Conference Series Proceedings*. Boston: Federal Reserve Bank of Boston, 97–117.

[13] Enthoven, A. (2005). The US experience with managed care and managed competition. *Conference Series Proceedings*. Boston: Federal Reserve Bank of Boston, 97–117.

[14] Kochan, T., Eaton, A., McKersie, R. et al. (2009). *Healing Together: The Labor-Management Partnership at Kaiser Permanente*. Ithaca, NY: Cornell University.

[15] Garber, K. M. (2011). *Paul Ellwood, Jr., M.D. in First Person: An Oral History*. Chicago, IL: American Hospital Association,

the Kaiser model, HMOs were created primarily to design a "rational structure" that combined the various players (e.g., providers, management) under one roof with a budget and a known population to serve. Saving money was said to be "an incidental objective".[16] The 1970s–1990s chronicle also suggests that "integration" served the political agendas of successive presidents who could claim to have a new plan; such plans were finally realized in state-level legislation in 1993. By the 1990s, vertical integration was officially endorsed as serving cost and quality goals as well as patient access.

Lack of a Firm Evidence Base to Support These Initiatives

The evidence to support the ability of HMOs to deliver on these cost and quality goals was more speculative than real. The HMO Act of 1973 was not based on rigorous large scale empirical evidence for the superior performance of HMOs; indeed, at the time, HMOs were viewed skeptically by the medical profession as a threat to quality, if not their incomes. It took a randomized controlled trial – the RAND Health Insurance Experiment (HIE) of the 1970s – to demonstrate that the HMO model (GHC) that participated in the trial did not harm (nor help) quality of care. It did, however, feature the lowest cost per capita of care among those who enrolled compared to the mostly fee-for-service care models and sites studied. That was evidence enough.

Researchers faced serious methodological problems in drawing conclusions about the meaning of performance of Kaiser-like HMOs. First, there were few staff model HMOs in the country that paid capitated or salaried fees to multispecialty physician groups; the latter were in rather short supply. Second, the consumers who voluntarily chose those plans obviously had different preferences about their care (especially about the low use of inpatient care) than those who chose other types of coverage.

Third, HMOs were not all the same. Kaiser-like models consisted of staff model HMOs where the physicians were salaried members of a group. But the HMO Act allowed different HMO models, including the IPA model, the group model (which could be salaried or capitated), and the network model, which incorporated multiple groups and independent physicians into the HMO network. Subsequent research showed that staff and group model HMOs outperformed on some dimensions (quality, preventive

---

[16] Anderson, O., Herold, T., Butler, B. et al. (1985). *HMO Development: Patterns and Prospects*. Chicago, IL: Pluribus Press.

services) while IPA models outperformed on others (access and patient satisfaction).[17] Another study suggested that the network model was superior to all of the others.[18]

Fourth, there were really no other systems comparable to Kaiser's three-fold structure of health plans, multispecialty medical groups, and hospitals. Instead, researchers compared patients treated in HMOs with those treated in the FFS system. Hal Luft showed that HMOs saved money compared to fee-for-service (FFS) medicine by (primarily) reducing hospitalizations and (secondarily) shortening hospital lengths of stay.[19] But these cost savings came at a different cost: reduced patient choice of provider and longer waiting times to see physicians (i.e., reduced access).

One study attempted to disentangle the effects of two of the most important elements of Kaiser-like HMOs: prepayment and multispecialty group practice. The Medical Outcomes Study examined different systems of care, including group/staff HMOs, IPA HMOs, multispecialty FFS, and solo practice. There were no significant differences in the technical performance of PCPs across practice settings.[20] However, HMO settings performed relatively poorly in terms of organizational access,[21] patients' ratings of office visits,[22] physical health improvements among elderly patients, and the stability of elderly patients' health.[23]

Enthoven claimed that his managed competition proposal was based on "the evident marketplace success of Kaiser Permanente" (in the early 1990s) and the lower costs observed at GHC. Unfortunately, the research evidence above questions the ability to draw such global conclusions. Moreover, the market share for the Kaiser-like plans, and for HMOs in

[17] Burns, L. R., and Wholey, D. R. (1991). Differences in access and quality of care across HMO types. *Health Services Management Research*, 4(1), 32–45.

[18] Wholey, D. R, and Burns, L. R. (1993). Organizational transitions: Form changes by health maintenance organizations. In *Research in the Sociology of Organizations*, S. Bacharach (Ed.) Greenwich, CT: JAI Press, 257–293.

[19] Luft, H. (1981). *Health Maintenance Organizations: Dimensions of Performance*. New York: John Wiley & Sons.

[20] Safran, D. et al. (1994). Primary care performance in fee-for-service and prepaid health care systems: Results from the medical outcomes study. *Journal of the American Medical Association*, 271(20), 1579–1586.

[21] Safran, D. et al. (1994). Primary care performance in fee-for-service and prepaid health care systems: Results from the medical outcomes study. *Journal of the American Medical Association*, 271(20), 1579–1586.

[22] Rubin, H., et al. (1993). Patients' ratings of outpatient visits in different practice settings: Results from the medical outcomes study. *Journal of the American Medical Association*, 270(7), 835–840.

[23] Ware, J. et al. (1996). Differences in 4-year health outcomes for elderly and poor, chronically ill patients treated in HMO and fee-for-service systems: Results from the medical outcomes study. *Journal of the American Medical Association*, 276(13), 1039–1047.

general, dwindled starting in the late 1990s. Among HMOs, the group/staff model exemplified by Kaiser ceded the stage to IPAs and networks, both in terms of numbers and enrollment.[24] Among health plans, HMOs ceded the stage to PPOs (as noted above). If Kaiser was a superior model, the health care industry did not get the news: the Kaiser-like staff model HMO did not multiply and dominate the HMO sector. To be sure, Kaiser faced a "chicken-and-egg" problem in trying to enter new markets: how could it simultaneously (a) support a large number of physicians and hospitals who only see Kaiser Health Plan enrollees, and (b) attract a large number of enrollees who wanted a closed provider network?

Summary

The 1970s–1990s period was the heyday of HMOs and managed competition. The Kaiser-like HMOs enjoyed a meteoric rise in the first half of the 1990s, followed by a meteoric fall in the second half of the decade, losing a reported $250 million as early as 1995.[25] Their staff models were soon to be replaced by the less restrictive but also less integrated independent practice association (IPA) model HMOs and PPO preferred by consumers. Any performance advantages were more speculative than documented. Nevertheless, ideological support for the Kaiser model took hold (and still remains strong until this day). A new integration model, already in place, would gain ascendance: physician-hospital integration (PHI) now took the stage.

INTEGRATING PHYSICIANS AND HOSPITALS
(AND MAYBE HEALTH PLANS, TOO)

Kaiser-like HMO models were not the only solution advanced. The Integrated Service Networks (ISNs) developed by health care delivery systems in Minnesota during the early-mid 1990s had spread nationally. Some referred to them as "integrated health organizations" (IHOs).[26] More commonly, the vast majority of PHI innovators did not create their own in-house health plans, but rather formed entities to contract with external insurers (and obtain capitated or some other form of risk-based contracts).

---

[24] Data courtesy of Douglas Wholey.
[25] Kochan, Eaton, McKersie, et al (2009). Healing together: *The Labor-Management Partnership at Kaiser Permanente*. Ithaca, NY: Cornell University Press.
[26] Burns, L. R., and Thorpe, D. P. (1993). Trends and models in physician-hospital organization. *Health Care Management Review*, 18(4), 7–20; Burns, L. R., Gimm, G., and Nicholson, S. (2005). The financial performance of Integrated Health Organizations (IHOs). *Journal of Healthcare Management*, 50(3), 191–213.

They became known as integrated delivery networks (IDNs).[27] Control shifted from a single entity providing both care and insurance to a supplier of care contracting with multiple insurers. The return of fragmentation had begun.

Why the switch in strategy? The prepaid Kaiser model did not gain widespread acceptance and market take-up, in part due to professional opposition (e.g., the American Medical Association), in part due to weak employer support for managed competition, in part due to consumer opposition to closed panel networks, in part due to the national shortage of large multispecialty groups, and in part due to limited incentives to transition to such plans. It did not help that some hospital systems (e.g., Hospital Corporation of America, Humana) had previously sought to integrate their hospital operations with health plans during the 1980s, but had floundered due to an inability to develop sufficient health plan enrollment to fill up their existing hospital beds.

Starting especially during the 1990s, providers shifted their focus from tight payer-provider linkages (the Kaiser model) to looser linkages between hospitals and their medical staffs – what we call *physician-hospital integration* (PHI) – and maybe health plans too. Such linkages could be vertical or virtual; the latter were based on strategic alliances among providers and risk-based contracts with plans. The loosely-linked arrangements were needed at the time since most physicians were not salaried hospital employees, but rather members of the quasi-autonomous hospital medical staff (who exerted authority over the hospital's employees and clinical operations).

Early PHI efforts focused on integration vehicles that came with their own TLAs (three-letter acronyms): physician hospital organizations (PHOs), management services organizations (MSOs), and integrated salary models (ISMs), among others.[28] Such vehicles were viewed as (1) ways to combine forces to jointly deal with competitive pressures from managed care organizations (MCOs, such as the HMOs) for price discounts, (2) ways to prepare for new reimbursement methods, such as capitation in California and prospective payment in Medicare, and (3) vehicles to contract with HMOs and other managed care payers to get risk contracts. All of these focused on managing costs. These were all "structures" to house the players under one administrative and contracting roof – even if their daily practice behaviors were not impacted.

---

[27] Burns, L. R., and Pauly, M. V. (2002). Integrated Delivery Networks (IDNs): A detour on the road to integrated health care? *Health Affairs*, 21(4), 128–143.
[28] Burns, L. R., and Thorpe, D. P. (1993). Trends and models in physician-hospital organization. *Health Care Management Review*, 18(4), 7–20.

PHI interested researchers as a possible critical ingredient to hospitals' economic success. Case study research from the early 1990s suggested that the quality of interactions with physicians affects hospitals' ability to contain costs and improve their bottom line.[29] Why might this be so? Physicians enjoy power in several major decision areas: the decision to admit patients to the hospital (from the community or the emergency room), the decision to order diagnostic tests and perform procedures, and the decision to prescribe drugs and specify which ones. In many supply areas, physicians (who were not hospital employees but who belonged to an organizationally separate medical staff) exerted great influence over which products and services hospitals were to use for their patients and from which vendors to order them. They were sometimes offered "incentives" – what some consider to be thinly disguised bribes – by vendors to use their specific products. As a result of this decision-making authority, physicians exerted control (directly or indirectly) over 87 percent of all personal health spending.[30]

The hypothesis (assumption) emerged that if physicians make these decisions in conjunction with the hospital's executives (rather than with product vendors or merely in their own self-interest), such collaboration might bestow a lower-cost advantage. The causal theory of action here was never fully articulated; indeed, it was called into question before the end of the millennium.[31] Many observers at the time felt that all hospitals needed to do was demonstrate their economic interest in the health and welfare of the medical staff, and to make available (on a joint venture basis) their technical and financial resources to targeted physicians with admitting privileges to further their private practices or help develop new forms of care delivery.[32] Researchers and executives also touted the new PHI efforts as possible drivers of quality improvement as well – although the causal mechanisms were again never clearly stated.

---

[29] Prospective Payment Assessment Commission (ProPAC). (1992). *Winners and Losers under the Medicare Program.* Washington, DC; Cromwell, J., Dayhoff, D., McCall, N. et al. (1998). *Medicare Participating Heart Bypass Center Demonstration. Vol. 1, Final Report.* Waltham, MA.: Health Economics Research; Shortell, S. (1991). *Effective Hospital-Physician Relationships.* Ann Arbor, MI: Health Administration Press.

[30] Sager, A., and Socolar, D. (2005). *Health Costs Absorb One Quarter of Economic Growth, 2000-2005.* Boston: Boston University School of Public Health.

[31] Robinson, J. C. (1997). Physician-hospital integration and the economic theory of the firm. *Medical Care Research and Review,* 54(1), 3–24.

[32] Goldsmith, J. C. (1981). *Can Hospitals Survive?* Homewood, IL: Dow-Jones Irwin, 178–181.

THE HISTORICAL PATH TO PHI: 1960–2000

The Rise of Hospital Systems in the 1960s and 1970s

During the 1960s, hospitals responded to the growth opportunities presented by the newly-enacted Medicare program.[33] New corporate forms such as the investor-owned hospital chains took advantage of Medicare's favorable inpatient reimbursement and consolidated small (largely physician-owned) facilities. The historical record documents how these chains pioneered horizontal consolidation of facilities, sought scale economies through more centralized management, and raised capital through the equity markets. Nonprofit hospitals, threatened by the growth of investor-owned hospitals, responded in the early 1970s by developing their own regional chains, such as the Lutheran Hospital Society of Southern California, Samaritan Health Service, and InterMountain. Multi-hospital systems were born.

Hospital systems developed complex corporate structures in which holding companies oversaw a diversified array of businesses, some not even focused on health care. Systems began to develop joint ventures and strategic alliances with one another (for example, through shared services), with their physicians, and sometimes with insurers. They also began to access tax-exempt bond markets to finance these expansions. Their growing size and complex capital structures placed more power and responsibility with system executives, but that power did not necessarily come at the expense of the physicians treating patients in the hospitals within their systems. While there were titular hospital administrators, sometimes drawn from nursing, the hospitals were still largely run by their medical staffs.

The Initial Push for Integration in the 1980s: Cost Containment Pressures

Health care cost containment motivated the early development of PHI. Much of this effort in the 1980s focused on capping institutional payments to hospitals and capitating payments to both health maintenance

---

[33] This section draws on a prior analysis by: Burns, L. R., Goldsmith, J. C., and Muller, R. (2010). History of hospital/physician relationships: Obstacles, opportunities, and issues, in J. Crosson and L. Tollen (Eds.), *Partners in Health*, Oakland, CA: Kaiser Permanente Institute for Health Policy.

organizations (HMOs) and networks of primary care physicians (PCPs), because it was more efficient to target and motivate larger organizations than individual professionals. This effort likely had the effect of motivating hospital administrators to get some control over physicians in order to limit the institution's financial risk under these new reimbursement methods.

The push for modern management escalated in 1983 with the passage of the Medicare Prospective Payment System (PPS), which used diagnosis-related groups (DRGs) that set fixed payments for inpatient episodes of care. The focus of DRGs was to standardize hospital patterns of treatment. This forced hospitals to analyze and then manage care patterns and resource utilization during a hospital stay to avoid losses. Some hospitals also sought to abandon service lines that were unprofitable and discharge patients more quickly (e.g., to post-acute care facilities or just dumping them on families) to save money. This was impossible without the active decision-making by the medical staff.

PPS affected only Medicare Part A payments to the hospital. In 1987, Medicare tried to incorporate fees paid to hospital-based (and often hospital employed) physicians (e.g., radiologists, pathologists, and emergency room) into the DRGs to effectively cap payments for these specialties and bundle them with inpatient care, which would also give the hospital explicit control over these income streams. This proposal was enormously threatening to the *de facto* independent status and incomes of these powerful specialists; it engendered sufficient political controversy and was abandoned after widespread congressional opposition. Thus, Part B payments to physicians were left untouched, potentially creating opposing incentives for inpatient spending and perhaps length of stay. However, now armed with new management strategies and structures, and facing new financing and regulatory requirements, hospital executives became more of a force, but were challenged by the recognition that under DRGs they weren't aligned with their doctors. DRGs placed hospitals at financial risk for physician decision-making they did not control. Their toolbox to deal with this was limited: reasoned discourse, threats, and/or begging. Maybe there were new tools to make physicians more pliant.

System executives now approached physicians for the first time for their help in operating within an admission-based budget constraint (the DRG payment) – a very stressful moment for both parties. Physicians were not accustomed to and, thus, not quite ready for such conversations. They realized they could no longer run the hospital exclusively as their workshop if they wanted it to survive financially. However, the two parties had somewhat separate goals and interests. Still, some physicians became aware that their contribution to excessive hospital spending and poorly coordinated care left hospital executives with fewer resources they could direct to helping the practices of physicians on the medical staff.

Acceleration of Integration Efforts in the 1990s

These 1980s' trends accelerated during the 1990s due to several environmental forces. As noted above, the managed care movement reached its zenith in the mid-1990s, when HMOs penetrated one third of the large, commercially-insured market (although much of the HMO penetration was regional rather than national). DRG payment pressures for Medicare patients were now reinforced by hospital contracting with the burgeoning private sector of HMOs and other MCOs (e.g., PPOs), which likewise required hospitals to ask their physicians to work within fiscal limits. Hospitals were not crazy about taking on such financial risk; many tried to avoid it, while others embraced it under the (mistaken) belief that California-style capitated contracting was inevitable. Private insurers replaced open-ended, after-the-fact payment for hospital services based on what the hospital charged with negotiated rates, fixed rates, or discounted charges determined in many cases on a per diem, per case, or occasionally even per-person (capitated) basis.

Federal pressures intensified this push towards "risk-sharing" – that is, sharing with the hospital-physician dyad the financial risk that patient care might cost more than the reimbursement – with the drafting of the Health Security Act (aka, the Clinton Health Plan) in 1993. The Clinton plan called for regional HIPCs to negotiate with regional health alliances composed of integrated payer and provider networks in local markets.[34] The latter could be exclusive, narrow networks such as the Kaiser model, but, more often would operate on a wide geographic basis through IPAs organized by physician communities outside of the hospital.[35] Enthoven's model theorized that capitated, risk-bearing plans would be more effective at care management and cost containment.

The rise of HMOs and the threat posed by the Clinton plan forced the conversion of much of the provider market into "risk-bearing" entities, and

---

[34] Burns, L. R., and Sechrest, L. (1994). Key challenges posed by the Clinton health care reform proposal, in *Health Care Management: US Healthcare in Transition*. H. Jolt (Ed.) Philadelphia, PA: Hanley & Belfus, 81–90.

[35] Enthoven, A. (1993). The history and principles of managed competition. *Health Affairs*, 12(supplement 1), 24–48; Enthoven, A., and Singer, S. (1996). Managed competition and California's health care economy. *Health Affairs*, 15(1), 39–57.

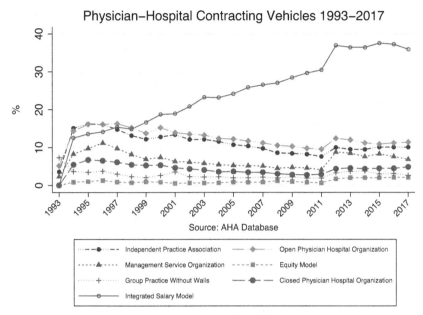

Figure 6.1. Physician-hospital contracting vehicles 1993–2017

induced individual hospitals and their affiliated physicians to form a variety of IDNs (see Figure 6.1). These were perhaps better labeled as entities purportedly capable of bearing risk, since the rhetoric of risk-bearing far exceeded the reality as well as the capability to do so.[36] Figure 6.1 reveals that the period of greatest growth of IDNs (1993–1996) coincided with the period of rapid growth in HMOs. These IDNs were not promoted based on superior performance, but rather as protection against new regulations and legislation. A speedy response to the proposed 1993 Clinton health plan became paramount in hospital executives' minds; evidence would have to wait. Apparently, evidence of passage of the Clinton plan would have to wait too: the provider sector acted as if it had already happened. In fact, the Clinton plan was declared "dead on arrival" in Congress in the spring of 1994; nevertheless, 1994 was

---

[36] Some medical groups and IPAs in California were able to rapidly expand by accepting such risk. This posed a great threat to hospitals, since (1) the savings came from reducing hospital admissions and inpatient days, and (2) the savings accrued to the physicians and the health plans they contracted with. Hospitals would eventually respond by buying up the medical groups. We thank Larry Casalino for his "on-the-ground" insight here.

the modal year for hospitals to develop horizontal systems of hospitals, vertically integrated networks of hospitals and physicians (e.g., PHOs, physician employment models), and formation of their own health plans.[37]

IDNs represented a collaborative effort by hospitals and physicians to confront the mutual threat of managed care and develop contracting vehicles for joint bargaining. Hospitals and physicians decided "the enemy of my enemy is my friend," aligning with one another to deal with the same foe.[38] Hospital consolidation and physician practice acquisition often was explicitly directed at limiting large health plan bargaining power over providers. Health plans had already begun consolidating in the 1980s, and now the race was on to see who could consolidate further and faster (e.g., "lead on speed"). IDNs also represented a generic provider response to an uncertain future whose underlying assumptions included an expected eastward spread of Kaiser-like models and managed competition: closed panel networks, global capitation, and downsizing of provider capacity (number of hospitals, beds, specialists, and so on). While some of these predictions (shrinking hospital bed capacity) did come to pass, many others (e.g., capitation, closed networks, Kaiser takeover) proved to be in error.

Performance Challenges Facing PHIs in the 1990s

The PHI "scorecard" that emerged by the start of the new millennium was not encouraging.[39] Physician practice acquisition and employment strategies did not reduce costs or improve quality. They may have helped to build hospital revenues by building market share and/or reducing the degree to which some physicians split their admissions across competing hospitals, raising insurance premiums. Practice acquisitions cost money that had to be paid annually in the form of guaranteed salaries, whereas the revenue increase was a one-time gain; as a result, the return on investment in physician acquisitions declined over time. These efforts also failed to improve physician-hospital relationships. The large systems and IDNs that developed included more levels of bureaucracy, corporate offices separated

---

[37] Burns, L. R., Gimm, G., and Nicholson, S. (2005). The financial performance of Integrated Health Organizations (IHOs). *Journal of Healthcare Management*, 50(3), 191–213.

[38] Burns, L. R., Nash, D., and Wholey, D. (2007). The evolving role of third parties in the hospital-physician relationship. *American Journal of Medical Quality*, 22(6), 402–409.

[39] Burns, L. R., and Pauly, M. V. (2002). Integrated Delivery Networks (IDNs): A detour on the road to integrated health care? *Health Affairs* 21(4), 128–143.

from the facilities that treated patients, highly-paid system executives, greater dependence on expensive external consultants, slower decision-making, an emphasis on the front-office mentality over the frontline mentality (i.e., C-Suite versus clinicians on the patient floor),[40] and little effort to make system changes meaningful to frontline staff. Indeed, many IDN executives felt they did not have the time to "bring the medical staff along;" time was of the essence – but time caught up with the executives faster than it did with the physicians.

Though some larger systems retained their physician and hospital provider networks, the late 1990s were characterized by dissolution of many systems and physician-hospital contracts. As a result of the failed 1990s experience with global capitation, fewer providers (except for isolated IPAs and some group practices) wanted to assume risk. Those hospitals who wanted to assume risk had difficulty finding insurers who wanted to extend it – whether to keep any profits in-house or to avoid provider bankruptcies like the Allegheny Health, Education and Research Foundation (AHERF) system in 1998.[41] The diffusion of IDNs slowed by the end of the decade due to the diminishing number of hospitals yet to be aligned with systems, financial pressures from the Balanced Budget Act of 1997, and the managed care backlash.

Other headwinds began to confront the IDNs. The threat of the proposed Clinton plan did not lead to managed competition, but led instead to hospital and PHI combinations as a countervailing force. Hospital consolidation resulted in many metropolitan areas being dominated by a handful of hospital systems that also owned extensive salaried physician practices and related health services. These systems eventually achieved significant bargaining leverage over health plans in the early 2000s, reducing competition and increasing prices and premiums – essentially turning the tables on HMOs after what they had done to hospitals a decade earlier.[42]

---

[40] One reviewer relayed this anecdote to us: "When an academic medical center bought a medium-sized physician primary care practice (PCP) during the mid-90s, they brought in a young MD-MBA who had never practiced, was cold as ice, and visited every once in a while to give the PCPs their orders. When these experienced physicians questioned the reasoning behind the orders, his basic reply was, 'Because I said so.'"

[41] Burns, L. R., Cacciamani, J., Clement, J. et al. (2000). The fall of the house of AHERF: The Allegheny bankruptcy. *Health Affairs*, 19(1), 7–41.

[42] Town, R.. J., Wholey, D., Feldman, R. et al. (2007). Revisiting the relationship between managed care and hospital consolidation. *Health Services Research*, 42(1), 219–238; Town, R., Wholey, D., Feldman, R. et al (2007). Hospital consolidation and racial/income disparities in health insurance coverage. *Health Affairs*, 26(4), 1170–1180.

In partial response, the Department of Justice (DOJ) and the Federal Trade Commission (FTC) developed antitrust guidelines for provider combinations to ensure they would be pro-competitive. These guidelines included the types of financial or clinical integration that must be present in physician-hospital collaborations and physician networks in order for provider groups legally to engage in collective contracting with managed care organizations (covered below). The latter half of the 1990s and the early years of the 2000s saw the DOJ and FTC prosecute several provider networks for their failure to adhere to these guidelines. Government agencies prevailed in nearly all of the early prosecutions: PHOs and IPAs were found to have engaged in price fixing without offering any compensatory financial or clinical integration that might lower costs or improve quality.[43] However, the consolidation of hospitals and physician practices using employment models continued (see Figure 6.1) despite these courtroom wins.

The basis of interdependence between physicians and hospitals also underwent a seismic shift. In the past, physician-hospital relationships were characterized by symbiotic interdependence, in which the two parties had compatible incentives to increase the volume of care using the latest technology.[44] Community-based physicians used the hospital, its staff, and its technology as their workshop in exchange for donating their time to taking call in the emergency room and sitting on hospital committees.[45] PPS, DRGs, and HMOs fostered divergent financial incentives, and sometimes growing tensions. At the same time, advances in technology (outpatient surgery), the accompanying shift to ambulatory care, and the rise of consumerism led hospitals and physicians to poach on one another's turf: hospitals competed for patients in outpatient settings, which traditionally were physicians' reserves, while physicians opened their own ambulatory surgery centers and imaging facilities that took such work out of the hospital. These developments altered PHI relationships from symbiotic to competitive interdependence.

The shift to ambulatory care fueled a withdrawal from the hospital of an increasing number of practitioners across the specialty spectrum. PCPs no longer wished to spend time rounding or treating patients in the hospital

---

[43] There are no empirical studies to support this claim. Rather, it rests on the expert testimony of the lead author who worked on several of these cases.

[44] Hawley, A. (1950). *Human Ecology: A Theory of Community Structure.* New York: Ronald Press.

[45] Pauly, M., and Redisch, M. (1973). The not-for-profit hospital as a physicians' cooperative. *American Economic Review*, 63(1), 87–99.

and now focused their attention on office-based, ambulatory practice where they could do procedures and avoid the time, travel, and peer scrutiny of hospital practice.[46] Many surgical specialists, such as ophthalmologists, urologists, plastic surgeons, radiation oncologists, and gastroenterologists, developed completely hospital-independent practices, using freestanding surgical facilities for their practices. Hospitals found it even harder to integrate, even informally, with physicians who were no longer on the premises and were now actively competing with them. These developments directly threatened the core profitability of hospitals, which was increasingly reliant on elective outpatient care. McKinsey estimated that a remarkable 75 percent of hospital profits in 2008 came from elective outpatient care, and only 12 percent from inpatient hospitalization.

Another development of the 1990s (continuing into the 2000s) further distanced the physician and hospital markets. Specialists in a given community began to aggregate into large single-specialty medical groups to gain bargaining leverage with MCOs. This strategy was particularly popular with technology-dependent specialists, such as radiologists, urologists, cardiologists, and gastroenterologists, who could not only leverage their bargaining power with health plans, but also acquire their own imaging equipment under the in-office ancillary service exemption to the Stark laws concerning self-referral. The development of large single-specialty groups ran against the grain of the integrated, multidisciplinary clinics such as Kaiser Permanente and Mayo, which were held out by Ellwood and Enthoven as exemplars of how physicians ought to consolidate.

Single-specialty groups constituted the single largest block of group practices. Their formation did not solve many problems faced in physician-hospital relationships, but rather served as a vehicle for stripping away ancillary services that contributed significant hospital profits. These groups also leveraged their bargaining power to demand explicit subsidies from the hospital for performing hospital–related services, such as covering emergency room call.

Summary of Twentieth Century Efforts

Integration and PHI in the prior millennium were prompted in part by new public and private sector payment systems (DRGs, capitation), by

---

[46] American Medical Association data show that the average number of physician visits on hospital rounds fell by 50 percent between 1982–2001 from 32 visits/week to 16 visits/week.

competitive pressures exerted by HMOs and MCOs, and by competitive rivalry between physicians and hospitals for the growing ambulatory care market. It was all about money, and it was mostly carried out in the private sector. Integration was not about improving quality or access to care. It was a competitive and largely defensive response by providers to what payers were doing and, in the private sector, to seek countervailing power. The track record showed no impact of PHI and IDNs on quality or cost.

THE NEW HISTORICAL PATH TO PHI: 2000–2020

Reinvigoration of Integration in the New Millennium

Several remarkable changes occurred early in the new millennium that reenergized PHI efforts. The earlier withdrawal of physicians from the hospital to render care in nonhospital settings left fewer physicians inside. To compensate for the losses, hospitals partnered with a growing number of physicians as either salaried employees of, or contractors to, the hospital. Hospitals employed specialists required to cover the hospital's 24/7 services (such as cardiology, orthopedics, emergency), or rented them through paid, call coverage arrangements. They also employed hospitalists, intensivists, and laborists to serve the patients of community-based physicians who no longer wanted to come. Thus, at the same time as a diminishing percentage of the physicians in a community needed to use the hospital, an increasing percentage of the remainder received a hefty percentage of their incomes from the hospital.

Second, the 2008 recession decimated the 401(k) plans of baby-boomer physicians, led to falling or stagnant professional incomes, and delayed their plans for retirement. Other physicians sought hospital employment as a buffer from market competition, an avenue to cope with declining skills, and (for some) a financial float until retirement. Newly-minted physicians entered the market burdened with $250–400K in student debt they could not pay off by entering private practice. Hospitals were not seeking dominance over physician practice or health plan negotiating leverage in this new wave of practice consolidation. Rather, they responded (in a largely defensive manner) to spreading economic distress in their physician communities, to fleeting opportunities to grab market share from competitors, and to the emerging efforts of health plans to grow their own physician networks. They responded to physician demands for protection from an increasingly complex and financially uncertain environment. Some physicians who had departed the hospital setting returned; others like ophthalmology, dermatology, and plastic surgery did not and further distanced themselves from hospital systems.

The employment packages developed during the 2000s avoided some of the common mistakes committed during the 1990s, with fewer practice buyouts, less generous compensation packages, shorter income guarantees, and more attention to the satisfaction of their patients. Nevertheless, they were overwhelmingly based on RVU productivity as hospitals sought to avoid the productivity declines (measured by volume of billable services) that accompanied hospital employment of physicians in the 1990s. This would not portend well for future hospital success under ACOs. Moreover, there was no solid evidence that hospitals had yet learned how to make physician employment contribute to profits. Hospital managers did not display competence in managing physicians or the separate markets for physician services. In the absence of a financing vehicle (such as 340B oncology payment, covered below), hospitals *reportedly*[47] lost $200,000 or

---

[47] There is some controversy regarding the accuracy of these reported losses. To be sure, the losses continue to be reported. According to the Voluntary Hospitals of America (VHA), "hospital systems can lose as much as $150,000 to $250,000 per year over the first three years of employing a new physician. But that doesn't necessarily mean the acquisition was a bad deal, says Don Hicks, vice president, VHA Physician Strategies and Services. That's true for a number of reasons, with these three being the primary ones:

- *Ancillary services.* One of the first things hospital systems do after acquiring a physician practice is strip out ancillary services (e.g., imaging, lab, infusion therapy, etc.) and incorporate them into the hospital's ambulatory operations. The dollars may still be flowing, but the revenues are no longer attributed to the physician practice.
- *Employee benefits.* Hospital systems are typically more generous than physician practices in terms of the benefits packages they offer employees. So, in one fell swoop, the benefits packages for the staff of acquired practices go up, making the practice's profitability go down.
- *Electronic medical records.* IDNs often switch newly acquired physician practices to the electronic medical records system being used by their existing practices. "Any major change like that creates an immediate hiccup in terms of productivity," notes Hicks.

There are other reasons physician practices can quickly lose some of their profitability after being acquired by a hospital system, including:

- The IDN overpays for the practice, often for "goodwill." (This happened much more frequently in the 1990s – that is, during the last wave of hospital acquisitions of physician practices – than it does today, says Hicks.)
- Physicians' productivity historically drops when they become employees. That's true unless the IDN can construct ways to keep them as productive as they were prior to the acquisition.
- Productivity of older physicians wanes. Without a strong recruitment program, there may be slippage in terms of the revenue of acquired practices.

more per year per physician (mostly specialists) in the new millennium, compared to losing only $100,000 per physician (mostly primary care) during the 1990s.[48] The change in specialty mix among employed physicians was likely responsible.

Data from the period 1993 2017 (see Figure 6 1) shows the decline in most models of PHI (e.g., PHOs and IPAs) used to contract with health plans in the 1990s, and the growing percentage of hospitals offering physician employment models (ISMs). Compatible with the hospital-level data in Figure 6.1, physician-level data show that physician employment grew from the late 1980s to the early-to-mid-1990s, then tailed off until 2003, after which it resumed. Despite the use of the term "integrated," the fact is that most physicians working under the ISM were still working fee-for-service in productivity contracts. Their salaries depended on their productivity. The degree of risk-sharing was low, and financial rewards for quality were mostly window-dressing. As in the earlier period, there was still little evidence that new physician hospital arrangements had an effect on quality or cost.

Public Sector Involvement and Reinforcement of PHI

Nascent government efforts at payment reform also promoted PHI. These included the creation of payment differentials, bundled payment, and gain sharing. None of them served to improve quality; some helped to reduce costs, mostly by improved collaboration among physicians and hospitals to jointly extract savings from product vendors (a variant of the common enemy approach).

Payment Differentials
Several legislative changes in original Medicare increased the financial reward for the physician's time in the hospital setting above the value of

---

- The hospital/IDN bureaucracy is inherently bigger than that of most physician practices, adding costs to the equation. Source: Physician practice acquisition: A good deal or not? *The Journal of Healthcare Contracting* (June 2, 2020). www.jhconline.com/physician-practice-acquisition-a-good-deal-or-not.html. Accessed on February 18, 2021.

[48] Burns, L. R., Goldsmith, J., and Sen, A. (2013). Horizontal and vertical integration of physicians: A tale of two tails. *Annual Review of Health Care Management: Revisiting the Evolution of Health Systems Organization. Advances in Health Care Management*, Volume 15, 39–117. Emerald Group.

time in the private office setting. This set up opportunities for high-yield physicians to get paid more by converting to hospital employment. This created a physician compensation bubble, which encouraged more physicians to seek employment (and likewise spurred the entry of private equity firms to exploit the asymmetry). At the same time, becoming employees and relying on hospital income increased the physician's dependence on the hospital. These changes included:

The Medicare Outpatient Prospective Payment System (OPPS), developed as part of the 1997 Balanced Budget Act, created a differential in payment for physician services rendered in hospital outpatient department settings ("site of service" = 22) versus community offices ("site of service" = 11). Physician practices owned by a hospital that met certain requirements could bill Medicare (and other payers) as a hospital outpatient department and receive both professional and facility fee payments. This allowed hospitals to get paid more for a physician's services if rendered under the hospital's auspices. This gave hospitals a vehicle to finance physician employment and gave physicians incentives to reorganize their practices under hospital auspices;

The Deficit Reduction Act (2005) sharply cut imaging technical payments to freestanding imaging providers and physician offices. A further downward revision of imaging technical fees in 2010 continued the pressure. These reductions triggered a collapse of private practice cardiology and a rush to hospital employment;

In 2005, the Medicare Modernization Act reduced payments to community-based oncologists for Part B drugs, a major source of their practice revenues. Such reductions did not apply to those employed by hospitals. The PPACA (2010) expanded eligibility to participate in the 340B Drug Discount Program to new classes of hospitals. The Program allowed hospitals to buy drugs at a 20–50 percent discount, thereby increasing the margins hospitals earned from insurers' reimbursements; this, in turn, provided a financing mechanism to offer more services and employ more oncologists. Oncologists could now earn much more money from hospital income guarantees than remaining in private practice; hospitals used the 340B payments as subsidy flows. Hospitals expanded their outpatient cancer centers, chemotherapy services, and employed physicians. Between 2010 and 2015, the number of community oncologists who vertically integrated with hospitals doubled from 30 percent to 60 percent.[49]

None of these changes were based on evidence that they would improve patient outcomes or lower overall costs; instead, they were primarily short-term, opportunistic responses to technicalities in the Medicare and Medicaid payment systems.

---

[49] Alpert, A., Hsi, H., and Jacobson, M. (2017). Evaluating the role of payment policy in driving vertical integration in the oncology market. *Health Affairs*, 36(4), 680–688.

Bundled Payment[50]

The federal government has championed bundled payment as an alternative payment model (APM) through the Medicare Participating Heart Bypass Center Demonstration (1991–1996),[51] the Acute Care Episode (ACE) demonstration (2009 2012), the Comprehensive Care for Joint Replacement Model or CCJR, and a new mandatory demonstration, the Bundled Payments for Care Improvement (BPCI) program. Over time, the government has targeted a broader range of conditions (cardiac surgery and then orthopedics). Overall, the program has achieved modest reductions in spending (<10 percent) and utilization (5–15 percent) but no improvement in either process or outcome measures of quality. Sometimes, as in the ACE program, the savings were offset by increased spending on post-acute (PAC) services; sometimes the savings were generated by joint hospital-physician negotiations with the product vendors of the surgical implants, equipment, and materials used in both orthopedic and cardiovascular DRGs; and sometimes the savings were achieved in judicious use of PAC and lower prices negotiated with product vendors. The results from other demonstration programs are mixed (e.g., inconsistent, small impacts on quality).[52]

Gainsharing

In September 2006, CMS solicited proposals for two separate programs involving "gain-sharing" – that is, incentive programs that would allow physicians and hospitals to share remuneration for implementing and coordinating improvements in efficiency and quality: The Physician-Hospital Collaboration Demonstration and the Medicare Hospital Gainsharing Demonstration.

The first examined whether gain sharing could assist in reducing hospital resource utilization and improving quality. Evaluators concluded that

---

[50] The topic of bundled payment is covered in another chapter in this volume. Here we offer a short historical chronicle and whether or not PHI contributed to any observed benefits.

[51] The Bypass Demonstration program paid a capitated, bundled payment of Part A facility fees and Part B professional fees to hospitals and four physician specialties treating episodes of coronary artery bypass graft (CABG) surgery. Hospitals responded with a set of internal arrangements reflecting *financial integration* (e.g., gain sharing with physicians for lowering ancillary and supply costs) and *clinical integration* (e.g., information exchange and collaborative decision-making with physicians, changes in physician practice behaviors, profiles of physician resource utilization, critical care pathways).

[52] Congressional Budget Office. (2012). *Lessons from Medicare's Demonstration Projects on Disease Management, Care Coordination, and Value-Based Payment.* Issue Brief. Washington, DC: CBO.

physician engagement was difficult to achieve and found little evidence that physicians had changed their practice patterns and behaviors as a result of the gainsharing incentives. Only a small minority of participating physicians understood the gainsharing performance metrics against which they were judged. As a result, Medicare Part B payments did not decrease. There were also no changes in patient length of stay or quality of care.[53]

The second similarly found that demonstration sites were challenged to fully educate participating physicians on the gainsharing reporting metrics, their underlying data, and the overall purpose of the intervention. It also found no evidence of changes in physician practice behaviors, savings to the Medicare program, savings on episodes of care, or improvements of quality of care. The demonstration did succeed in generating internal cost savings for the participating hospitals to pay physician incentives.[54]

Accountable Care Organizations (ACOs)

In 2008, candidate Barack Obama wanted a health plan to counter President Bush's emphasis on private sector insurers and their Medicare Advantage plans, which Obama felt were grossly overpaid. Obama's 2010 legislative package, the Patient Protection and Affordable Care Act (PPACA), cut the payments to these plans. PPACA also rested on ACOs, which relied on the "extended hospital medical staff" model developed by Elliott Fisher, and which used prior structural models of PHI (such as IPAs and PHOs) as their chassis.

What is often ignored is that the ACO model enjoyed little supporting evidence of performance advantages. Research on the ACO's precursor, the Medicare Physician Group Practice Demonstration, suggested advantage was lacking. That demonstration employed a shared savings model built on P4P whereby groups would enjoy savings if they lowered cost relative to local controls and scored well on 32 quality metrics. Results across the 10 demonstration sites showed improvement on quality but mixed results on cost. A small number of sites achieved most of the savings; their efficiencies were counterbalanced by a lack of savings at the other sites. Most of the savings were concentrated among dual-eligible

---

[53] Greenwald, L., Adamache, W., Cole-Beebe, M. et al. (2014). *Evaluation of the Medicare Physician Hospital Collaboration Demonstration – Final Report*. Waltham, MA: RTI International.

[54] *CMS Report to Congress. Medicare Gainsharing Demonstration: Final Report to Congress.* (June 3, 2014). Available online at: https://innovation.cms.gov/files/reports/medicaregainsharingrtc.pdf. Accessed on January 16, 2021.

beneficiaries – suggesting the possible need to target such initiatives to narrow population segments.

Despite the lack of success, CMS officials declared the program a success and moved to expand upon it using ACOs. The ACOs represented CMS's "big bet" to improve the cost-effective delivery of care to Medicare beneficiaries; they have since dominated much of the current drive towards PHI. How well did the ACOs fare? Among the early (Pioneer ACO) models, 23 of 32 had dropped out of the program by the time of its "sunset" in 2016. Program year 2015 data showed an average savings of $2.7 million among the remaining 12 participants; however, of the $34 million earned, one ACO accounted for 72 percent of the savings.[55] Between 2012–2014, many showed improvement on the 30+ quality metrics, but less than 30 percent sufficiently reduced costs to earn shared savings.

Research on the broader ACO program (Medicare Shared Savings Plans, or MSSP) suggested that medical group participation failed to change use of either high-value or low-value specialty care.[56] Additional research suggests little or no impact on hospital readmission rates.[57] Roughly half of the ACOs reduced spending. The percentage of ACOs achieving savings was correlated with earlier start years and higher benchmark spending levels per beneficiary – suggesting that some of the savings may have reflected regression-to-the-mean. ACOs led by physicians achieved a higher savings rate compared to hospital-led ACOs; smaller ACOs (with a mean number of beneficiaries less than 10,000) achieved greater net savings per beneficiary than larger ACOs. The relatively small size of ACOs, and thus the relatively low percentage of providers' patients who have been attributed to the ACO, provided only weak incentives to pursue hospital-wide strategies to reduce costs which might spill over to non-ACO patients.

Among those ACOs that reduced costs, the biggest reductions were in inpatient care and post-acute care (hospice, SNF), largely driven by declines in volumes rather than cost per admission.[58] Recent research

---

[55] Muhlestein, D., Saunders, R., and McClellan, M. (2017). Growth of ACOs and alternative payment models in 2017. *Health Affairs Blog.* Available online at: www.healthaffairs.org/do/10.1377/hblog20170628.060719/full. Accessed November 27, 2017.

[56] Hollingsworth, J. M., Nallmothu, B. K., Yan, P. et al. (2018). Medicare accountable care organizations are not associated with reductions in the use of low-value coronary revascularization. *Circulation: Cardiovascular Quality and Outcomes,* 11(6).

[57] Duggal, R., Zhang, Y., and Diana, M. L. (2018). The association between hospital ACO participation and readmission rates. *Journal of Healthcare Management,* 63(5).

[58] Schulz, J., DeCamp, M., and Berkowitz, S. A. (2018). Spending patterns among Medicare ACOs that have reduced costs. *Journal of Healthcare Management,* 63(6), 374–381.

suggests that ACOs achieve savings in nonhospital, nonphysician care. In one study, hospitals affiliated with ACOs achieved lower re-admissions from skilled nursing facilities than non-ACO affiliated hospitals.[59] In another study, ACOs reduced admissions and stays to post-acute sites without harming quality.[60] There were no changes in hospital readmissions or mortality. These results suggest the ACOs' incentives rest on reducing services used outside rather than inside the hospital. This is a critical difference between the incentives of hospital-led and physician-led ACOs: the former do not reduce hospital costs while the latter do. Overall, however, ACOs do not appear to have substantially or significantly reduced spending on end-of-life care.[61]

Summary: Integration and PHI in the New Millennium as Challenged Ideas

In contrast to the 1970s–1990s period, PHI during the last two decades has been spurred (and even encouraged) by several legislative changes and CMS demonstrations. PHI is more of a public sector than private sector phenomenon. It is no longer driven by private HMOs and managed care pressures, nor even by private Medicare Advantage plans, but by original Medicare. Integration is also no longer designed to address consumer distress over access; instead, PHI is designed to address physician distress over stagnant incomes and government desires to lower Medicare spending. There is thus a lot riding on PHI: integration has a lot of freight to carry. Perhaps it is too much to expect. The earlier vertical integration efforts never attempted to carry such freight.

But to an even greater extent than earlier – where Kaiser-type HMOs that integrated physicians, hospitals, and insurance had been shown to produce a modest (though one time) saving – the evidence that the new arrangements are having good effects on cost or quality is weak. The accumulating evidence questions whether PHI can help improve access to care, reduce the rate of increase in the costs of this care, and raise quality – what some have referred to as solving the "iron triangle" or the

---

[59] Winblad, U., Mor, V., McHugh, J. P. et al. (2017). ACO-affiliated hospitals reduced rehospitalizations from skilled nursing facilities faster than other hospitals. *Health Affairs*, 36(1), 67–73.

[60] McWilliams, J. M., Gilstrap, L. G., Stevenson, D. G. et al. (2017). Changes in postacute care in the Medicare shared savings program. *JAMA Internal Medicine*, 177(4), 518–526.

[61] Gilstrap, L. G., Huskamp, H. A., Stevenson, D. G. et al. (2018). Changes in end-of-life care in the Medicare shared savings program. *Health Affairs*, 37(10), 1693–1700.

"triple aim."[62] On the contrary, PHI and IDN efforts were often developed to counterbalance managed care organizations and their market power. It is not clear whether IDNs made any real efforts to reduce costs or improve quality. It is likely the case that they did not know how to run these new organizations, let alone figure out how to make them high-performers; they may also have faced difficulty in getting physician buy-in or involvement. It may also be the case that they thought that realizable savings were not to be had, at least in the short-term.

Instead, executives may have focused on more straightforward, measurable, and more easily attained goals: growth, market share, and revenues – goals that were not emphasized by Kaiser and the integrated staff model HMOs. To be fair to the IDNs, they might argue that they require capital to develop the infrastructure to meet the financial and clinical integration dictates posed by regulators and health plans. The route taken to acquire this capital, however, has been larger system size and greater leverage over those commercial health plans, which leads to higher payment rates, higher insurance premiums, and higher out-of-pocket costs to enrollees (particular those in the increasingly popular high-deductible health plans). In other words, the size they have sought may be larger than the size optimal for improving quality and controlling costs – resulting in increased administrative and coordination costs of no benefit.

Shaky Theoretical Foundation and Applicability of Industry Vertical Integration

There were three basic problems with the foundation underlying all of the PHI efforts described above. First, the theoretical rationale for vertical integration rested on several tenets, including reducing transaction costs, pooling complementary assets to improve the organization's value, allowing firms to efficiently exchange intangible assets, and avoiding hold-ups to ensure access to needed supplies (among others).[63] Advocates of PHI have not always made the case (at least convincingly) that these

---

[62] Berwick, D., Nolan, T., and Whittington, J. (2008). The triple aim: Care, health, cost. *Health Affairs*, 27(3), 759–769; Kissick, W. (1994). *Medicine's Dilemmas*. New Haven, CT: Yale University Press.

[63] Besanko, D., Dranove, D., and Shanley, M. (2013). *The Economics of Strategy*. New York: John Wiley, Sixth Edition.

rationales apply to the relationships between physicians and hospitals. For example, the first tenet, transaction costs, emphasizes the costs of searching for trading partners, bargaining and negotiation, detecting partner misrepresentation, monitoring partner opportunism and holdups, writing and enforcing contracts, and litigation. It is unclear how and why the costs of physicians seeking medical staff appointments and exercising their professional judgment inside the hospital mandate vertical integration via employment. Indeed, some economists suggest that efforts to do so necessitate significant expenses to develop governance structures and coordinate the joint activities of the two parties – expenses that outweigh the gains of integrating.[64] The growing evidence that vertical integration and PHI have resulted in higher costs and prices supports this view.[65]

To be sure, there are other rationales for vertical integration noted above, as well as other theories to justify vertically-integrated PHI models.[66] Some of our economist colleagues argue that physicians can impose costs on the hospital that they do not have to pay for out of their incomes; such actions raise hospital costs, thereby reducing what buyers would pay for the package (which includes the surgeon's fee). This is a collective (not an individual doctor-by-doctor) problem which physicians cannot control (but perhaps hospitals can) via vertical integration. This is what bundled payment has attempted to address, with mixed results. Other economists argue that vertical integration is not about the rationales discussed above, but rather just an effort to combine upstream into downstream products – that is, physician services (e.g., surgery) and hospital services (e.g.., facilities for surgery and recovery) are more akin to complements. Such a view does not explain why employment is preferred.

Second, was there any preexisting evidence base from industry that vertical integration improved performance? And, if so, in what settings

[64] Robinson, J. C. (1997). Physician-hospital integration and the economic theory of the firm. *Medical Care Research and Review*, 54(1), 3–24.

[65] Dranove, D, and Burns, L. R. (2021). *Big Med: Megaproviders and the High Cost of Healthcare in America*. Chicago, IL: University of Chicago Press, forthcoming.

[66] Post, B., Buchmueller, T., and Ryan, A. (2017). Vertical integration of hospitals and physicians: Economic theory and empirical evidence on spending and quality. *Medical Care Research & Review*, 1–35; Mick, S., and Shay, P. (2016). Accountable care organizations and transaction cost economics. *Medical Care Research and Review*, 73(6), 649–659; Orszag, P, and Rekhi, R. (2020). The economic case for vertical integration in health care. *NEJM Catalyst: Innovations in Care Delivery*, 1(3).

and on what performance dimensions? Evidence from the historical chronicle of industrial firms showed that vertical integration delivered on cost outcomes (via scale and scope economies) but never on quality.[67] That suggests the types of outcomes researchers and executives should have looked for. Moreover, the historical chronicle indicated that industrial firms needed to make enormous investments in three areas to achieve these economies: large production facilities, large distribution and purchasing networks, and managerial expertise. Firm success with vertical integration required not only such investments, but also consolidation of capacity at the different stages along the value chain. Firms that remained federations of previously independent companies without doing the consolidation did not last. Tellingly, the industries that successfully pursued these efforts were capital-intensive; labor-intensive sectors were largely unaffected. Health care providers fall into the latter camp. Not surprisingly, there is thus little evidence of scale and scope economies in provider combinations to warrant vertical integration using lessons from industry as the basis.

Third, despite decades of effort, we still have no consistent definition and understanding of what integration means. This is evident from the multiple typologies and constituent dimensions of integration that (a) have piled up over time and (b) have themselves never been integrated. The chapter's next section turns its attention to this sad, ugly reality.

TYPOLOGIES OF INTEGRATION

At the same time that providers undertook all of these PHI efforts, regulators and researchers were trying to make sense of them all. In the early 1990s, regulators coined two types of integration as antitrust guidance for the IDN vehicles developing during the 1980s and early 1990s (depicted in Figure 6.1).[68] Starting at the same time, researchers developed a succession of integration typologies, multiple dimensions of integration, and empirical investigations to try to link them to important outcomes such as cost and quality.

---

[67] Chandler, A. (1990). *Scale and Scope: The Dynamics of Industrial Capitalism*. Cambridge, MA: Harvard University Press.

[68] Casalino, L. P. (2006). The federal trade commission, clinical integration, and the organization of physician practice. *Journal of Health Politics, Policy, and Law*, 31(3), 569–585.

Both regulators and researchers have centered the bulk of their attention on two main types of integration: (1) financial (also sometimes labeled economic or structural) integration, including physician employment and risk contracting; and (2) clinical integration, including physician use of CMPs (e.g., clinical guidelines, protocols) and other devices to coordinate patient care.[69] Some research teams have also articulated a causal model among these two types, with financial integration driving clinical integration which, in turn, affects cost and quality outcomes. Thus, the simplest way to encapsulate these typologies is the causal model depicted at the start of the chapter.

To be sure, researchers have specified more definitions and elaborate typologies of integration; as a result, the concept of integration and its constituent dimensions have become blurred. No one wants to preside over a disintegrated system. Today, researchers acknowledge there is still no universally accepted definition of health care integration. This makes it nearly impossible to evaluate the effectiveness of the dimensions of integration studied. To spare the reader, the more prominent classification efforts are briefly summarized below, along with the evidence base to support them (if any).

Regulators' Interest in Integration Models

By the early 1990s, regulators acted on their growing concerns about possible price fixing by providers who increasingly formed IDN vehicles – sometimes hospitals bargaining with physicians (the PHOs and hospital-based IPAs in Figure 6.1), sometimes physicians bargaining with other physicians in freestanding IPAs – to negotiate prices with MCOs. In 1993, the Department of Justice (DOJ) and Federal Trade Commission (FTC) issued the joint *Statements of Antitrust Enforcement Policy for the Health Care Areas* which specified a "safety zone" for such joint bargaining. This zone, "financial integration," allowed joint bargaining if the providers shared financial risk (e.g., received capitated payments from, or were subject to withholds by, MCOs) to motivate meeting cost containment goals. In 1996, the DOJ and FTC issued revised guidelines that described new examples of financial integration and developed a second safety zone called "clinical integration:" presence of and investments in organized

---

[69] It is not clear that executives of provider organizations or MCOs have paid as much attention to these dimensions of integration.

processes to control costs and improve quality. These two safety zones are delineated below:

To qualify for the *financial integration* safety zone, the participants in a provider network must share substantial financial risk in providing all the services that are jointly priced to health plans, as a precursor to achieve significant efficiencies. Risk sharing provides incentives for the physicians to cooperate in controlling costs and improving quality by managing the provision of services by network physicians. Examples of risk-sharing included (1) providing services to a health plan at a capitated rate; (2) providing designated services to a health plan for a predetermined percentage of premium or revenue; (3) providing a complex or extended course of treatment that requires the substantial coordination of care by physicians in different specialties offering a complementary mix of services, for a fixed, predetermined payment; and (4) using significant financial incentives for physicians to achieve specified cost-containment goals, such as withholding a substantial compensation with distribution back to physicians based on group performance in meeting the cost-containment goals, or subjecting the network's physicians to subsequent substantial financial rewards or penalties based on group performance in meeting cost and quality targets.

To qualify for the *clinical integration* safety zone, participants need to implement an active and ongoing program to evaluate and modify practice patterns by the network's physician participants and create a high degree of interdependence and cooperation among the physicians to control costs and ensure quality. This program may include: (1) mechanisms to monitor and control utilization of health care services that are designed to control costs and assure quality of care; (2) selection of network physicians who are likely to further these efficiency objectives; (3) significant investment of capital, both monetary and human, in the necessary infrastructure and capability to realize the claimed efficiencies (e.g., care protocols, case management); and (4) development of collective physician efforts to oversee the practice behaviors of individual physicians.

In sum, regulators allowed independent providers to jointly bargain and negotiate prices with MCOs if they could demonstrate they were financially or clinically integrated. Risk-sharing and care protocols were not ends in themselves, but rather means to incentivize providers to control costs and improve quality.[70] Regulators assumed that such integrated arrangements enhanced market efficiency more than they would restrict competition; market efficiency was defined as financial or clinical integration.[71]

---

[70] Casalino, L. (2006). The federal trade commission, clinical integration, and the organization of physician practice. *Journal of Health Politics, Policy, and Law*, 31(3), 569–585.

[71] Page, S. (2004). How physicians' organizations compete: Protectionism and efficiency. *Journal of Health Politics, Policy, and Law*, 29(1), 75–105.

Thus, by the mid-1990s, regulators had specified two major types of integration. The regulators did not view them as a causal model, but rather as alternatives. Thus, their view was:

Provider networks that did not involve the sharing of financial risk could nevertheless avoid antitrust by demonstrating sufficient clinical integration to produce significant efficiencies. Regulators did view them as ultimately contributing to cost and quality outcomes.

Over the next 10 years, antitrust actions taken by these agencies demonstrated that providers had not complied. Instead, providers (1) tended to jointly negotiate nonrisk contracts with MCOs that did not satisfy the first safety zone, and (2) failed to develop any meaningful clinical integration mechanisms, thus falling outside the second safety zone. For example, in a four-year span, the FTC successfully prevailed against a long list of joint bargaining efforts by hospital PHOs and physician group IPAs:

- *FTC v. South Georgia Health Partners* (2003)
- *FTC v. Washington University Physician Network* (2003)
- *FTC v. North Texas Specialty Physicians* (2004)
- *FTC v. Southeastern New Mexico Physicians IPA* (2004)
- *FTC v. Piedmont Health Alliance* (2004)
- *FTC v. Alamogordo Physicians Cooperative* (2004)
- *FTC v. Evanston Northwestern Healthcare Medical Group* (2005)
- *FTC v. San Juan IPA* (2005),
- *FTC v. Partners Health Network* (2005), and
- *FTC v. Health Care Alliance of Laredo* (2006)

The lead author served as the FTC's expert witness in two of these cases and discovered that the components of financial and clinical integration were almost entirely absent. At the same time, other researchers affirmed this absence, noting that most providers "lacked interest" in clinical integration and failed to develop any of the infrastructure needed for financial and clinical integration.[72] They hypothesized several reasons for this lack

[72] Casalino, L. (2006). The federal trade commission, clinical integration, and the organization of physician practice. *Journal of Health Politics, Policy, and Law,* 31(3), 569–585;

of interest and investment, including uncertainty about what constitutes clinical integration, the uncertain benefits of clinical integration and timeline for reaping its benefits, physician skepticism that clinical integration processes are efficacious, and physicians' pursuit of strategies to preserve their incomes and the autonomy of the individual practitioner. Scattered research findings published at this time further attested to this lack of infrastructure inside PHOs and IPAs, the most prominent IDN vehicles developed by hospitals to jointly bargain with their medical staffs.[73]

Since the Antitrust Statements were issued in the 1990s, the FTC has issued multiple advisory opinions that further clarified what clinical integration looks like: in brief, the interaction and interdependence among physicians in their provision of medical care. Any joint venture should thus develop an active, ongoing process to facilitate cooperative activity among physicians – a process in which physicians are actively involved. Clinical integration activities now encompassed actions to:

- form clinical committees to develop and apply clinical practice guidelines (CPGs);
- develop performance benchmarks and physician scorecards as clinical goals;
- engage in quality measurement and management programs;
- develop transitional care programs;
- conduct practice audits to monitor the performance of their peers in using CPGs;
- issue performance reports on a regular basis to physicians;
- make capital investments in computer systems and information training;
- integrate all physicians using a common electronic medical record (EMR);
- exchange clinical information using the EMR to coordinate patient care;
- increase patient referrals among physicians to increase information captured on EMR;

Page, S. (2004). How physicians' organizations compete: Protectionism and efficiency. *Journal of Health Politics, Policy, and Law*, 29(1), 75–105.

[73] Burns, L. R., and Thorpe, D. P. (1997). Physician-hospital organizations: Strategy, structure, and conduct, in R. Conners (Ed.), *Integrating the Practice of Medicine*. Chicago, IL: American Hospital Publishing Inc., 351–371; Bazzoli, G. J., Dynan, L., Burns, L. R. (1999/2000). Capitated contracting of integrated health provider organization. *Inquiry*, 36(4), 426–444; Burns, L. R., Walston, S., Alexander, J. et al. (2001). Just how integrated are integrated delivery systems? Results from a national study. *Health Care Management Review*, 26(1), 20–39.

- develop disease registries, population health programs, and data analytics programs;
- develop tools to risk-stratify patients according to severity-of-illness;
- develop programs to actively manage the highest-risk, highest-cost patients;
- develop quality assurance councils to review physicians' performance;
- participate in physician education programs to improve adherence to CPGs; and
- develop criteria to selectively recruit physicians who can practice cost-effective care.

Nevertheless, providers still did not get the message. More recent antitrust litigation brought by the Attorney General in a western state revealed that hospitals and their physician partners had failed to develop nearly all of these mechanisms.

Researcher Typologies of Vertical Integration

Researchers developed their own schemes ("typologies") to classify the different types of integration they observed. Their approach to clinical integration resembled that developed by regulators. The story was different for financial integration. While regulators focused on payer-provider contracting and the assumption of financial risk, researchers also included the economic linkages in physician-hospital contracting. The latter was easier to study since it relied less on data from MCOs and payer contracts and more on data from hospitals. The physician-hospital linkage approach also addressed the growth in physician employment models (the ISMs in Figure 6.1), while risk contracting was on the wane by the end of the 1990s. Researchers discovered that the ability to pursue financial integration was limited both externally (due to demise of capitation) and internally (reflecting hospitals' failure to develop financial incentives to change physician behavior). This signaled a shift in vertical integration research from HMO to PHI models. As a consequence, financial integration was now sometimes relabeled as economic or structural integration.

For example, two of the authors of this chapter developed a typology that expanded the regulator's framework by articulating three types of integration: noneconomic, economic, and clinical.[74]

---

[74] Burns, L. R., and Muller, R. (2008). Hospital-physician collaboration: Landscape of economic integration and impact on clinical integration. *Milbank Quarterly*, 86(3), 375–434.

Noneconomic integration refers to hospitals' efforts to attract physicians (without paying them) by making their facilities more attractive and accessible, their operations more efficient and convenient, their decision-making processes more participative and responsive, and their staffing better trained. These efforts can take the form of technology acquisitions, hospital branding, process flow improvements, management information systems, physicians' liaisons, referral services, clinical councils, physician leadership development, medical staff development, and additions to the number and skill mix of the nursing staff. Noneconomic integration also includes hospitals' efforts to improve managers' behavioral skills in dealing with physicians and removing the cultural barriers separating them. Noneconomic integration has been pursued by hospitals for decades prior to employment and risk contracting.

Economic integration encompasses hospitals' provision of monetary payments to physicians to provide, manage, and/or improve clinical services and to perform organizational activities. These payments can take the form of professional service agreements (PSAs), medical directorships, stipends, management contracts, gain sharing, and co-management of clinical institutes and centers of excellence. Economic integration can also include joint-venture investments (e.g., in medical office buildings, ambulatory surgery centers, diagnostic imaging centers, service lines, specialty hospitals) and joint-risk reimbursement contracts from payers (e.g., bundled payments, pay-for-performance, capitated risk). Finally, economic integration can cover the aggregation of physicians into the organization, including the formation of group practices, the development of PHO and IPA contracting vehicles, as well as the employment of PCPs and specialists, often based on productivity and quality metrics.

Clinical integration refers to hospitals' structures and systems to coordinate patient care services across people, functions, activities, sites, and time. Common activities of clinical integration are utilization management programs, scheduling and registration systems, information systems that can track utilization by patient and provider, development of care standards, continuous quality improvement programs, clinical service lines, case management systems, population-based community health models, disease and demand management systems, common patient identifiers, clinical practice guidelines, and disease registries.

The researchers concluded that the evidence base for the impact of these types of integration on cost and quality outcomes was sorely lacking. They also concluded that any causal impact of economic integration on clinical integration was also questionable (and could, in fact, be just the opposite).

Health Systems Integration Study (HSIS)

Researchers at Northwestern University and Peat Marwick studied the degree of integration in twelve IDNs (and 58 of their member hospitals) as part of the Health Systems Integration Study (HSIS).[75] HSIS distinguished three dimensions of integration: functional, physician-system, and clinical. The latter two dealt explicitly with PHI.[76]

Functional integration is defined as the coordination of key support activities (e.g., standardization of finance, human resources, planning, marketing) across hospitals in a system. A system is 'integrated' to the extent its hospitals combine and/or share the same support activities (policies, budgets, plans, etc.).

Physician-system integration is the extent to which physicians are economically linked to a system (whether through joint ventures or employment), use its facilities and services, and actively participate in its planning, management, and governance.[77] Rather than financial integration in payer-provider contracting, HSIS studied economic integration in physician-hospital relationships.

Clinical integration encompasses sharing and coordination of clinical services across hospitals in the system, including efforts to reduce duplication. More generally, it refers to hospitals' structures and systems to coordinate patient care services across people, functions, activities, and sites over time.[78]

The HSIS researchers argued that functional integration was the foundation on which their other two types of integration were built. They also argued that clinical integration is the apex of the three, is causally dependent on the development and successful execution of the other two, and is the most important aspect of an IDN, since it entails the coordination of the continuum of care that directly interfaces with the patients.[79] This marked the first articulation of a causal model linking economic integration, clinical integration, and cost and quality outcomes:

Financial Integration → *Clinical Integration* → *Cost and Quality Outcomes*

---

[75] Gillies, R., Shortell, S., Anderson, D. et al. (1993). Conceptualizing and measuring integration: Findings from the health systems integration study. *Hospital and Health Services Administration*, 38(4), 467–489.

[76] Gillies, R., Shortell, S., Anderson, D. et al. (1993). Conceptualizing and measuring integration: Findings from the health systems integration study. *Hospital and Health Services Administration*, 38(4), 467–489; Shortell, S., Gillies, R., Anderson, D. et al. (1996). *Remaking Health Care in America: Building Organized Delivery Systems*. San Francisco: Jossey-Bass; Shortell, S., Gillies, R., Anderson, D. et al. (2000). *Remaking Health Care in America: Building Organized Delivery Systems*. 2nd ed. San Francisco: Jossey-Bass.

[77] It also encompasses homogeneity across hospitals of basic medical staff characteristics (e.g., shared goals, shared practices for hospital-based physicians, a common medical staff development plan, use of common practice guidelines).

[78] Shortell, S., Gillies, R., Anderson, D. et al. (2000). *Remaking Health Care in America: Building Organized Delivery Systems*. 2nd ed. San Francisco: Jossey-Bass, 129.

[79] Shortell, S., Gillies, R., Anderson, D. et al. (1996). *Remaking Health Care in America: Building Organized Delivery Systems*. San Francisco: Jossey-Bass, 42.

However, HSIS researchers uncovered only weak linkages between physicians' economic ties to the hospital and the degree of clinical integration,
as well as weak associations between integration and hospital system
performance.[80] Moreover, they found that clinical integration was the least
developed of the three types of integration, with physician-system linkages
only moderately developed.[81] This should have alerted policy-makers
about "how shaky a foundation" upon which reform efforts were being
built; it should also have alerted health care executives, assuming that
reform rather than profits and growth were their goals.

Of course, this typology was applied to organized delivery systems and
was thus hospital- and system-centric. Physicians were important but were
not part of the planning, and often not explicitly part of the solution. Given
the centrality of physicians in many decisions that drive health care spending, such a focus needed to be supplemented by physician-level focus.

Center for Organized Delivery Systems (CODS)

The need for physician-level analyses was partially addressed by researchers affiliated with the Center for Organized Delivery Systems (CODS). The
CODS study examined clinical integration in 56 medical groups that were
either tightly affiliated (e.g., employed) or loosely affiliated (e.g., contractual
ties) with 15 hospital systems that volunteered for and funded the study. The
resulting heterogeneity of the hospital sample – based on differences in the
levels of economic integration between physicians and hospitals – allowed
the researchers to test a version of the causal model above, assessing the
impact of economic integration using the contrast between employed physicians and loosely-affiliated physicians (e.g., those in PHOs and IPAs).

With regard to clinical integration, the researchers analyzed two usages
of care management practices (CMPs) in the physician groups: care management "deployment" and "comprehensiveness."[82] Deployment was

[80] Gillies, R., Shortell, S., Devers, K. et al. (1994). The Correlates and Consequences of
Clinical Integration in Organized Delivery Systems. Paper presented at the annual
meeting of the Association of Health Services Research, San Diego; Shortell, S., Gillies,
R. and Anderson, D. (1994). The new world of managed care: Creating organized delivery
systems. *Health Affairs*, 13(5), 46–64.
[81] Devers, K., Shortell, S., Gillies, R. et al. (1994). Implementing organized delivery systems:
An integration scorecard. *Health Care Management Review*, 19(3), 7–20.
[82] Shortell, S., Zazzali, J., Burns, L. R. et al. (2001). Implementing evidence-based medicine:
The role of market pressures, compensation incentives, and culture of physician organizations. *Medical Care*, 39(7), 162–178. Physician-System Alignment Supplement.

measured by the product of the number of care management methods used (0–5: guidelines, protocols, case management, disease management, and demand management) and the number of practice settings in which they were used (0–9: e.g., hospital inpatient, emergency room, hospital clinic, freestanding clinic, rehab center, etc.). The maximum score on the CMP deployment index was thus 5 × 9 = 45. Comprehensiveness was measured by summing (a) the percentage of conditions/diseases (out of 19) for which protocols were used, (b) the percentage of quality of care data elements (out of 17) reported to the board, and (c) the percentage of quality of care data elements (out of 13) for which benchmarks existed, and dividing the sum by three.

Univariate statistics revealed a low degree of deployment (mean = 6.33 out of 45) and a moderate level of comprehensiveness (mean = 0.32 out of 1.00). Bivariate statistics revealed that employed and loosely-affiliated physicians exhibited roughly similar levels of alignment (including perceived clinical integration). Multivariate results revealed that CMP deployment and comprehensiveness bore no significant relationship to the group's tenure with the hospital system – suggesting that financial integration may not be important. CMP deployment was not related to the degree to which the physician group used cost, quality, or productivity incentives to influence physician practice behavior, while CMP comprehensiveness was positively related.[83] Overall, evidence for the association of economic and clinical integration was mixed.

University of Minnesota Studies of Hospital-Medical Group Integration

University of Minnesota researchers did not develop a typology, but nevertheless analyzed the causal model. They studied the impact of structure in 267 medical groups in Minnesota on 9 dimensions of group culture: collegiality, information emphasis, quality emphasis, organizational identity, cohesiveness, business emphasis, organizational trust, innovativeness, and autonomy.[84] Group ownership by a hospital or health plan was negatively associated with seven of the nine dimensions; three of these

---

[83] Shortell, S., Zazzali, J., Burns, L. R. et al. (2001). Implementing evidence-based medicine: The role of market pressures, compensation incentives, and culture of physician organizations. *Medical Care*, 39(7), 162–178. Physician-System Alignment Supplement.

[84] Kralewski, J., Dowd, B., Kaissi, A., et al. (2005). Measuring the culture of medical group practices. *Health Care Management Review*, 30(3), 184–193.

were statistically significant (collegiality, organizational identity, and trust). The researchers concluded that external ownership degrades the group's culture, suggesting that financial integration might not contribute to clinical integration.

In another study, they examined similar relationships using a different set of 191 groups in four upper Midwest states.[85] Again, external ownership of the group was significantly and negatively related to four culture dimensions (collegiality, identity, trust, and autonomy), but was positively associated with a quality emphasis.

Finally, they conducted a comprehensive analysis of quality and cost outcomes among 256 medical groups.[86] Hospital ownership was associated with higher costs, avoidable hospitalizations, and inappropriate ED visits. Several dimensions of group culture (quality, collegiality, and participative management) were associated with lower costs. The authors then identified efficient practices that provided the highest quality at the lowest cost. Group efficiency was promoted by physician (rather than hospital) ownership of the group. Finally, in a subset analysis of 52 groups in an employer claims database, they found that physician-owned groups exhibited the lowest rates of inappropriate ED visits and avoidable hospitalizations. Again, economic integration seemed inimical to clinical integration, higher quality care, and lower cost care – i.e., counter to the causal model.

National Study of Physician Organizations (NSPO)

The National Study of Physician Organizations (NSPO) surveyed physician groups and IPAs regarding their use of "care management practices" (CMPs), but not necessarily whether or not they were effective.[87]

---

[85] Curoe, A., Kralewski, J., and Kaissi, A. (2003). Assessing the cultures of medical group practices. *Journal of the American Board of Family Medicine*, 16, 394–398.

[86] Kralewski, J., Dowd, B., and Xu, Y. (2011). Differences in the cost of health care provided by group practices in Minnesota. *Minnesota Medicine*, 94(2), 41–44; Kralewski, J., Dowd, B., and Xu, Y. (2011). "The Organizational Characteristics of Best Medical Group Practices," unpublished manuscript.

[87] NSPO studies include the following. Li, R., Simon, J., Bodenheimer, T. et al. (2004). Organizational factors affecting the adoption of diabetes care management processes in physician organizations. *Diabetes Care*, 27(10), 2312–2316; McMenamin, S., Schmittdiel, J., Halpin, H. et al. (2004). Health promotion in physician organizations: Results from a national study. *American Journal of Preventive Medicine*, 26(4), 259–264; McMenamin, S., Bellows, N., Halpin, H. et al. (2010). Adoption of policies to treat tobacco dependence in US medical groups. *American Journal of Preventive Medicine*, 39(5), 449–456; McMenamin, S., Schauffler, H., Shortell, S. et al. (2003). Support for smoking cessation

The CMPs included practice guidelines, carepaths and protocols, case management, disease management, demand management, patient registries, physician reminders, use of health risk appraisals, patient reminders, practice feedback to physicians, nurse care managers, and deployment of patient-centered medical home components (including use of electronic medical records or EMRs, primary care teams, and electronic data interchange with hospitals and specialists). The NSPO's conceptual model suggested that the presence of "organizational capabilities" (e.g., the provision of hospital resources and hospital employment of physicians) can foster implementation of CMPs – i.e., financial integration can foster clinical integration.[88]

Starting in the early 2000s, the NSPO researchers conducted surveys of medical groups and IPAs in three waves. During the first wave (2000–2001), they analyzed the extent to which a slightly different set of four CMPs (case management, practice guidelines, population disease management, health promotion/disease prevention) were applied to four

interventions in physician organizations: Results from a national survey. *Medical Care*, 41 (12), 1396–1406; Rittenhouse, D., and Robinson, J. (2006). Improving quality in Medicaid: The use of care management processes for chronic illness and preventive care. *Medical Care*, 44(1), 47–54; Rittenhouse, D., Casalino, L., Shortell, S. et al. (2011). Small and medium-size physician practices use few patient-centered medical home processes. *Health Affairs*, 30(8), 1575–1584; Rittenhouse, D., Casalino, L., Gillies, R. et al. (2008). Measuring the medical home infrastructure in large medical groups. *Health Affairs*, 27(5), 1246–1258; Rittenhouse, D., Shortell, S., Gillies, R. et al. (2010). Improving chronic illness care: Findings from a national study of care management processes in large physician practices. *Medical Care Research and Review*, 67(3), 301–320; Rittenhouse, D., and Shortell, S. (2009). The patient-centered medical home: Will it stand the test of health reform? *Journal of the American Medical Association*, 301(19), 2038–2040; Rittenhouse, D., Shortell, S., Gillies, R. et al. (2010). Improving chronic illness care: Findings from a national study of care management practices in large physician practices. *Medical Care Research & Review*, 67(3), 301–320; Robinson, J. Casalino, L., Gillies, R. et al. (2009). Financial incentives, quality improvement programs, and the adoption of clinical information technology. *Medical Care*, 47(4), 411–417; Rundall, T., Shortell, S., Wang, M. et al. (2002). As good as it gets? Chronic care management in nine leading US physician organizations. *British Medical Journal*, 325, 958–961; Schmittdiel, J., Bodenheimer, T., Solomon, N. et al. (2005). The prevalence and use of chronic disease registries in physician organizations: A national survey. *Journal of General Internal Medicine*, 20, 855–858; Schmittdiel, J., McMenamin, S., Halpin, H. et al. (2004). The use of patient and physician reminders for preventive services: Results from a national study of physician organizations. *Preventive Medicine*, 39, 1000–1006; Schmittdiel, J., Shortell, S., Rundall, T. et al. (2006). Effect of primary health care orientation on chronic care management. *Annals of Family Medicine*, 4(2), 117–123.

[88] Rittenhouse, D., Shortell, S., Gillies, R. et al. (2010). Improving chronic illness care: Findings from a national study of care management processes in large physician practices. *Medical Care Research and Review*, 67(3), 301–320: Figure 1.

chronic conditions in nine of the leading physician organizations in the US (e.g., Kaiser Permanente, Mayo Clinic, Cleveland Clinic, etc.).[89] They found a low level of CMP deployment: for each disease, fewer than half of the nine groups used all four care management processes. This observation led the researchers to wonder whether this level of CMP use is "as good as it gets?" In particular, they found that CMP deployment was not significantly tied to either the group's taking risk for hospitalized patients or receipt of bonuses from health plans for quality performance – thus questioning the link between financial and clinical integration in the causal model.[90] The researchers also found that ownership of the group by either a hospital or HMO often exerted a positive impact on CMP presence, although the results were not always statistically significant.

During the NSPO's second wave (2006–2007), researchers found that ownership by a hospital or health plan was associated with overall use of CMPs and various measures of care coordination (EMR, presence of electronic data interchange or EDI with hospital, presence of EDI with specialists, use of registries, and use of nurse case managers).[91] Ownership was not associated, however, with use of primary care teams, patient health reminders, health risk appraisals, patient-centered medical home features, and an index of information technology capabilities. Moreover, ownership was negatively associated with financial performance (profitability). There was some evidence for a linkage between financial and clinical integration, however. A change in the group's receipt of incentive payments from health plans for quality performance was positively tied to an increase in CMP use; overall use of CMPs was also tied to the degree the group took capitated risk for hospitalized patients.[92] Overall, NSPO provided slightly

---

[89] Rundall, T., Shortell, S., Wang, M. et al. (2002). As good as it gets? Chronic care management in nine leading US physician organizations. *British Medical Journal*, 325, 958–961.

[90] Casalino, L., Gillies, R., Shortell, S. et al. (2003). External incentives, information technology, and organized processes to improve health care quality for patients with chronic diseases. *Journal of the American Medical Association*, 289(4), 434–441.

[91] Rittenhouse, D., Shortell, S., Gillies, R. et al. (2010). Improving chronic illness care: Findings from a national study of care management processes in large physician practices. *Medical Care Research and Review*, 67(3), 301–320. Rittenhouse, D., Casalino, L., Gillies, R. et al. (2008). Measuring the medical home infrastructure in large medical groups. *Health Affairs*, 27(5), 1246–1258.

[92] Rittenhouse, D., Shortell, S., Gillies, R. et al. (2010). Improving chronic illness care: Findings from a national study of care management processes in large physician practices. *Medical Care Research and Review*, 67(3), 301–320; Shortell, S., Gillies, R., Siddique, J. et al. (2009). Improving chronic illness care: A longitudinal cohort analysis of large physician organizations. *Medical Care*, 47(9), 932–939.

more encouraging evidence for linkages between financial and clinical integration, but perhaps not so much with profitability.

NSPO researchers also investigated whether economic integration of medical groups (e.g., horizontal and vertical integration – reflected in larger size, multispecialty mix, and hospital ownership) was associated with six domains of integrated care (as perceived by the patient). The latter included: provider knowledge of the patient, staff knowledge of the patient's medical history, specialist knowledge of the patient's medical history, support for self-directed care, support for medication and home health management, and support for test result communication. Hospital ownership of the medical group was not associated with any of these dimensions. Neither was an index of the group's care management processes.[93]

National Survey of Healthcare Organizations and Systems (NSHOS)

Researchers participating in the National Survey of Healthcare Organizations and Systems (NSHOS) operationalized four dimensions of integration that partly resemble dimensions found developed by the HSIS.[94] These include:

- *functional integration* (clinical access to needed patient information, use of information for feedback and quality improvement, sharing of reports among practice physicians, and use of standardized protocols);
- *financial integration* (hospital ownership of physician practice, coordination of administrative activities such as budgeting and planning and financial management across operating units);
- *clinical integration* (coordination of physician practice across sites and disciplines, presence of care managers, post-hospital discharge activities, EMR connectivity between the physician and the hospital); and
- *cultural integration* (e.g., quality and strength of relationships at the physician practice level, including: perceived safety in sharing new ideas, sense of belonging, sense that decisions are made as a group, sense that practice is open to innovations).

[93] Kerrissey, M., Clark, J., Friedberg, M., et al. (2017). Medical group structural integration may not ensure that care is integrated, from the patient's perspective. *Health Affairs*, 36 (5), 885–892.

[94] Colla, C., Yang, W., Mainor, A. J. et al. (2020). Organizational integration, practice capabilities and outcomes in clinically complex Medicare beneficiaries. (Unpublished manuscript). Subsequently published in *Health Services Research* 55(6) Part II, 1085–1097.

The researchers examined the associations among these four dimensions.[95] Financial integration was modestly associated with clinical integration (r = 0.19), but not with functional integration (r = 0.08). Clinical and functional integration were moderately correlated with one another (r = 0.38), as were cultural integration and functional integration (r = 0.31). However, financial integration was negatively correlated with cultural integration (r = −0.28). One measure of financial integration, practice ownership by the hospital, was not associated with participation in Medicare ACOs or most measures of adoption of care delivery processes (e.g., use of evidence-based guidelines, care of complex patients, screening for social needs or clinical conditions).[96] This latter finding suggests that physician employment does not have the intended effect of quality improvement along these dimensions.

There was no overall relationship between the four dimensions of integration and utilization-based health outcomes (e.g., admissions, 30-day readmissions, ED visits, readmissions, and ambulatory care-sensitive admissions) and mortality among Medicare beneficiaries. The dimensions of functional and clinical integration were, however, associated with significantly lower price-adjusted Medicare spending (that accounts for regional variation). Clinical integration was positively associated with several care delivery processes (e.g., use of evidence-based guidelines, use of registries), while financial integration was not. Such findings cast doubt on whether economic and clinical integration impact patient outcomes or cost of care.

Such doubts were strengthened in additional work from the project.[97] The researchers found that practice ownership explained little of the variation in physicians offering nine quality-focused care delivery and

---

[95] Fisher, E., Shortell, S., O'Malley, A. J. et al. (2020). Financial integration's impact on care delivery and payment reforms: A survey of hospitals and physician practices. *Health Affairs*, 39(8), 1302–1311; Colla, C., Yang, W., Mainor, A. J. et al. (2020). Organizational integration, practice capabilities and outcomes in clinically complex Medicare beneficiaries. (Unpublished manuscript). Subsequently published in *Health Services Research*, 55(6) Part II, 1085–1097.

[96] Colla, C., Yang, W., Mainor, A. J. et al. (2020). Organizational integration, practice capabilities and outcomes in clinically complex Medicare beneficiaries. (Unpublished manuscript). Subsequently published in *Health Services Research* 55(6) Part II, 1085–1097.

[97] Fisher, E., Shortell, S., O'Malley, A. J. et al. (2020). Financial integration's impact on care delivery and payment reforms: A survey of hospitals and physician practices. *Health Affairs*, 39(8), 1302–1311.

payment reforms (care of complex patients, participation in quality-focused payment programs, screening for social needs or clinical conditions, use of evidence-based guidelines, use of registries, use of EMR-based decision support, use of quality-focused information management, and patient engagement). Independent practices and organized medical groups typically performed as well or better than hospital-based practices. They came to the "startling conclusion" alluded to at the beginning of this chapter that economic (financial) integration did not impact process measures of quality or coordinated care. In hindsight, that conclusion was neither new nor startling.

Comparative Health System Performance (CHSP) Initiative

The Agency for Healthcare Research and Quality (AHRQ) created the Comparative Health System Performance (CHSP) Initiative to study how IDNs promote evidence-based practices in care delivery. In June 2015, AHRQ awarded 5-year cooperative agreements to three Centers of Excellence at Dartmouth College, the National Bureau of Economic Research, and the RAND Corporation. In late August 2020, several research teams studying PHI presented preliminary findings at the Fifth Annual CHSP Grantee Workshop. Some (but not all) of these findings were subsequently published in December 2020 as a special issue of *Health Services Research*.[98]

One team utilized a pre-post analysis of close surgeon-hospital linkages and found no impact on risk-adjusted mortality.[99] The same team also found that primary care physicians (PCPs) in health systems treating privately-insured patients practiced medicine that was no higher in quality than PCPs outside of health systems, but was higher in cost with higher rates of ambulatory care sensitive admissions.[100] Similar findings regarding quality have been reported in comparisons of integrated versus

---

[98] D. Scanlon and M. Furukawa (Editors). (2020). Comparative health system performance: A special issue of HSR. *Health Services Research*, 55(6), Part II.

[99] Zhou, A., Beaulieu, N., and Cutler, D. (2020). Firm Size, Consolidation, and Surgeon Specialization. Fifth Annual CHSP Grantee Workshop.

[100] Zhou, A., Beaulieu, N., and Cutler, D. (2020). Primary care quality and cost for privately insured patients in and out of US health systems: Evidence from four states. *Health Services Research*, 55(6), Part II, 1098–1106.

nonintegrated physician organizations treating Medicare patients.[101] Such findings did not support the causal model.

A second team studied 59 physician practice sites nested within 24 physician organizations which were members of 17 health systems. They distinguished 5 types of integration, including 2 types of organizational and 2 types of social integration.[102]

- *Functional integration* includes the written policies and protocols for activities that coordinate accountability and decision-making.

- *Structural integration* includes the physical, operational, financial, or legal ties among teams and organizations in a health system. This encompasses ownership of or contractual agreements with noninpatient sites of care; it is thus best thought of as a measure of vertical/virtual integration of the care continuum.

- *Normative integration* involves the sharing of a common culture and normative alignment, the prioritization of patient care integration across units and hospitals within a system, and communication of this vision.

- *Interpersonal integration* includes collaboration, teamwork, and coordination within and across professional groups.

- *Process integration* includes activities that integrate patient care services into a single coordinated process (often termed clinical process integration).

The research team viewed these five types as causally related, with the two dimensions of organizational integration impacting the two types of social integration, which impact clinical process integration – all of which impact patient outcomes.[103] The latter four types of integration resemble many of the integration dimensions studied in the CODS project.

The five integration dimensions were assessed using surveys completed by samples of (mostly nonphysician) clinicians within the practice sites. Regardless of the dimension, the level of care integration was no more consistent within than across health systems.[104] As a result, the researchers

---

[101] Kranz, A., DeYoreo, M., Eshete-Roesler, B. et al. (2020). Health system affiliation of physician organizations and quality of care for Medicare beneficiaries who have high needs. *Health Services Research*, 55(6), Part II, 1118–1128.

[102] Singer et al. (2018). A Comprehensive Theory of Integration. *Medical Care Research and Review*, 77(2), 196–207.

[103] Singer, S., Sinaiko, A., Tietschert, M. et al. (2020). Care integration within and outside health system boundaries: A multi-level study. Fifth Annual CHSP Grantee Workshop.

[104] Singer, S., Sinaiko, A., Tietschert, M. et al. (2020). Care integration within and outside health system boundaries: A multi-level study. Fifth Annual CHSP Grantee Workshop; Singer, S., Sinaiko, A., Tietschert, M. V. et al. (2020). Care integration within and outside health system boundaries. *Health Services Research*, 55(6), 1033–1048.

concluded that "health systems' influence on integration is not observable." In addition, they found that the level of perceived integration deteriorated as one moved from the practice site to the health system and beyond, suggesting that physical proximity is critical. This suggests that all coordination, like health care, is local. Finally, they found little evidence for the relationship between clinical process integration and perceived quality of care (at either the practice or health system level). Only one sub-domain of clinical integration, evidence-based care, was related to perceived outcomes. Overall, the CHSP findings suggest that documenting empirically the effects of PHI may be a thankless and, likely, fruitless task. There may be too much variation in the implementation of economic and clinical integration by health systems to ever discern their effects.[105]

Revisiting the Causal Model Linking Financial and Clinical Integration

The extant literature on the two types of integration casts doubt about their linkage. As noted above, the economic integration dimension of PHI (e.g., physician employment) is more prevalent than the clinical integration dimension (e.g., the prevalence and use of CMPs). Besides CMPs, other elements of clinical integration seem to be underdeveloped as well.[106]

---

[105] Ridgely, M. S. Buttorff, C., Wolf, L. et al. (2020). The importance of understanding and measuring health system structural, functional, and clinical integration. *Health Services Research*, 55(6), Part II, 1049–1061.
Economic variation includes integration efforts undertaken by (1) single hospitals versus multi-hospital systems, (2) systems that include a small versus large number of hospitals, (3) systems with nine different types of physician groupings (e.g., employment, foundation model, IPA, etc.), (4) systems that lack or include post-acute care sites, (5) systems that lack or include their own health plans, (6) systems that lack versus possess the ability to do single-signature risk contracting, and (7) systems that lack versus possess enterprise-wide EMRs. Clinical integration includes the ability or inability to "hardwire" (embed) care integration in EMRs, the presence or absence of standardized, clinical service lines, and the presence or absence of redesigned care delivery models (e.g., team-based care).

[106] Research has shown that financial/productivity incentives have continued to dominate quality incentives in regard to physicians' compensation. Only 20 percent of the physicians surveyed said that quality was included in determining compensation, and only 9 percent stated that it was a very important factor in compensation. Clinical information technology (IT) has also been underdeveloped in physicians' practices and grown more slowly. Even with clinical IT, however, it may not be associated with the use of CMPs. Cf: Reschovsky, J. and Hadley, J. (2007). *Physician Financial Incentives: Use of Quality Incentives Inches Up, but Productivity Still Dominates.* Issue Brief no. 108. Washington, DC.: Center for Studying Health System Change; Rittenhouse, D.,

This was already evident at the beginning of the millennium; two decades later, little has changed except for some new explanations. These include the slower development of clinical information systems, the lack of external incentives from payers to develop such information systems (at least until recently), the lack of financial and staff resources, large start-up and maintenance costs, the disruption to physicians' work flow, and physicians' busy schedules.[107]

Another possible, related reason is that certain types of economic integration (such as the formation of large, multispecialty group practices capable of assuming financial risk) critical to clinical integration have been historically underdeveloped. Single specialty groups, most of which are small in size, have heavily outnumbered multispecialty groups for decades; since the 1970s, the ratio has ranged between 2:1 to 3:1. Over the past decades, the number of large physician groups (100 or more doctors) as a percentage of all medical groups has remained low; indeed, the vast majority of all groups have fewer than 10 practitioners. Researchers reviewed many of the reasons for the shortage of large groups.[108] They include the lack of physicians' cooperation, insufficient capital to grow, lack of physician leadership (paucity of management skills and physicians' reluctance to reward colleagues for administration), failure to manage costs for capitated patients, costs of dealing with regulatory mandates, news about the failures of other groups, and conflicts between primary care and specialist physicians.[109]

Conversely, the number of midsized physician practices ranging from 6 to 50 practitioners has increased.[110] Such practices may be better

Casalino, L., Gillies, R. et al. (2008). Measuring the medical home infrastructure in large medical groups. *Health Affairs*, 27(5), 1246–1258.

[107] Casalino, L., Gillies, R., Shortell, S. et al. (2003). External incentives, information technology, and organized processes to improve health care quality for patients with chronic diseases. *Journal of American Medical Association*, 289(4), 434–441; Rundall, T., Shortell, S., Wang, M. et al. (2002). As good as it gets? Chronic care management in nine leading US physician organizations. *British Medical Journal*, 325, 958–961; Reed, M., and Grossman, J. (2006). *Growing Availability of Clinical Information Technology in Physician Practices*. Data Bulletin no. 31. Washington, DC: Center for Studying Health System Change.

[108] Casalino, L., Devers, K., Lake, T. et al. (2003). Benefits of and barriers to large medical group practice. *Archives of Internal Medicine*, 163(16), 1958–1964.

[109] This all changed within the past 10 years, however, as hospitals built up their ranks of employed physicians. There has been a reported explosion of hospital-affiliated medical groups with more than 500 doctors; however, there is no evidence of better outcomes or lower costs associated with these groups, but rather just rearranged deck chairs.

[110] Liebhaber, A. and Grossman, J. (2007). *Physicians Moving to Mid-Sized, Single Specialty Practices*. Tracking Report no. 18. Washington, DC: Center for Studying Health System Change.

equipped to respond to some economic integration initiatives (e.g., P4P) and clinical integration initiatives. However, the growth in these midsized groups has been confined to single specialty practices; the percentage of physicians in multispecialty practices fell between 1998/1999 (30.9 percent) and 2004/2005 (27.5 percent). Moreover, the growth in group practice may form the basis not only for PHI, but also for new competitors with the hospital in the outpatient market.

A third reason for the weak relationship between economic and clinical integration may be that the 1990s' PHI efforts further depleted the finances of many hospital systems (already weakened by the Balanced Budget Act of 1998) and drained away monies from clinical integration. There is evidence that the greater the investment in integration efforts (e.g., acquisitions of hospitals and physicians, development of health plans), the worse the financial performance of integrated systems.[111] There is also case evidence that hospital systems have poured their strategic investments into acquisitions of new providers (hospitals, physician groups) to expand the size of their systems, leaving the harder work of connecting them all through a common EMR until later.

A final possible reason is that economic integration was not designed primarily to promote clinical integration (let alone quality of care). Indeed, economic and clinical integration efforts may be somewhat orthogonal, hence explaining the lack of a relationship. For example, one hospital executive told us that economic integration was designed to help the hospital pursue its various missions and support the bottom line, while clinical integration was a normative, external expectation to which the hospital must respond.

Summary Assessment of PHI Typologies and Supporting Evidence

The PHI literature is plagued by multiple typologies and dimensions. Not surprisingly, there is no clear and consistent empirical operationalization of many of the concepts surrounding integration and its performance outcomes (e.g., quality measures). There are perhaps too many indicators of economic integration, clinical integration, and quality performance to accumulate any robust evidence base. If that were not enough, the available evidence suggests that some of the major dimensions of integration are not highly and/or positively correlated with one another – begging the question whether "integration" is really integrated. Overall, we still lack documented evidence on whether or to what extent these different types of integration matter, either relative to no integration or to each other. They perhaps are more appropriately characterized as provider reactions to changing external circumstances than steps with "proof of concept" in shaping cost, quality, and health status.

There are other issues as well. These include (1) an empirical focus on a handful of dimensions that are easier to study (e.g., physician employment), (2) a growing and consistent body of evidence that a prevalent type of integration (i.e., physician employment) is associated with higher costs and prices, and (3) little discussion of whether PHI dimensions are causally or conceptually related.

The first and second issues are problematic since empirically-based findings focus on levers that are considered the drivers of physician-hospital alignment and coordination, but which may not produce the desired changes. The second issue is also important since the negative research findings have prompted new rationales for integration that still do not bear up under empirical scrutiny. Some of our more hopeful colleagues consider physician employment and IDNs as a promising approach to improve the performance of the health care system. While they acknowledge that the horizontal and vertical integration strategies pursued by providers in the past have a lackluster track record, they have embraced the rationale offered by providers that such strategic financial investments have been necessary to develop and improve other types of integration that might improve patient care. Thus, while the rise of hospital systems and physician employment may reduce competition, increase prices, and raise health care costs (with no clear quality benefits), these strategies may yet generate meaningful improvements in quality through other means. These other means encompass care delivery innovations and participation in new payment models. Unfortunately, they have found no evidence for this. On the contrary, despite continued consolidation – both horizontally among hospitals and vertically between hospitals and physicians – over the past 30 years, the following problems remain: "Health care costs continue to rise, the quality of care is uneven, and safety remains a serious concern ... Care coordination remains problematic, and the prevalence of burnout among physicians is increasing."[112]

[112] Fisher, E., Shortell, S., O'Malley, A. J. et al. (2020). Financial integration's impact on care delivery and payment reforms: A survey of hospitals and physician practices. *Health Affairs*, 39(8), 1302–1311.

With regard to the third issue, researchers long ago pointed out that the dimensions of integration resembled the three types of quality measures identified by Avedis Donabedian (structure, process, and outcome) in that they were more "loosely-coupled" than we thought.[113] Perhaps what is most troubling about this issue is the lack of a clearly articulated theory or rationale for why these linkages should exist. Researchers and executives have rarely taken the time to explain why employing physicians and/or putting them on salary should be motivating, aligning, or quality-promoting. More often than not, it is assumed that employment, ISM models, and the development of ACOs will reduce costs, promote physician-hospital alignment, and improve quality of care – basically echoing the ideology espoused earlier by Ellwood and Enthoven. As we shall show below, the goals that physicians bring to the PHI table do not closely resemble what executives are looking for in PHI.

WE GOT TROUBLE, RIGHT HERE IN RIVER CITY

Overall, there is substantial evidence that the main dimensions of integration (financial/economic and clinical) have fairly minimal impact on one another and on patient outcomes. Apparently, rearranging the deck chairs of the two parties does not make much of a difference. Efforts to promote integration via PHI face a long list of problems. These include cultural issues of mixing health care's version of oil and water, logistical issues of dealing with a large number of disparate providers, the tendency to dredge up past solutions (that mostly failed) to deal with problems today, the locus of risk-bearing in today's provider organizations, the focus on the wrong targets, the perhaps unrealistic goal of trying to become like Kaiser in an effort to integrate, and the failure to develop mechanisms of "operational integration" that meaningfully and conveniently fit with the work of busy clinicians.

If we are to make progress in PHI, the prior paragraph serves as a long list of mistakes to avoid. As Nassim Taleb noted, we improve our decision-making by eliminating the things that don't work; what remains for consideration are things that have a higher chance of success.[114] We could be even more optimistic and say that after we eliminate the things that don't work, we should define whatever happens with the remainder as a

---

[113] Luft, H. (1981). *Health Maintenance Organizations: Dimensions of Performance*. John Wiley & Sons.

[114] Taleb, N. (2012). *Antifragile: Things That Gain from Disorder*. New York: Random House.

success (no matter how miserable the results are). In discussing these, we hopefully can develop a short list of some things that might work if anything is going to work. Many of the temptations to adopt mistaken strategies can be resisted if decision-makers know the evidence – either that there is none or that what there is suggests ineffectiveness.

Disparate Cultures, Orientations, and Goals

PHI involves two parties – physicians and hospitals – which are different in many ways.[115] These include education, length of training, compensation, and culture. Integrating them is health care's version of mixing oil and water. The different cultures are briefly contrasted in Figure 6.2.

The two parties also come to PHI efforts with very different orientations. These are depicted in Figure 6.3.

Finally, physicians, hospitals, and health systems come to PHI with quite disparate goals (see Figure 6.4). Physicians often espouse clinical goals; only a handful concern care management and coordination. By contrast, hospitals and health systems have pursued economic integration strategies for many reasons, several of them financial. The goals of the three parties are spelled out in the figure below; they are discussed more fully in the Appendix and elsewhere.[116] The italicized goals represent areas of (at least potential) commonality.

Considering just the first two columns, Figure 6.4 suggests some overlap between the goals pursued by hospitals and physicians in economic integration. Both seek to compete more effectively and to raise their revenues in the outpatient market. Both seek to increase physicians' incomes, control, and management over daily clinical activities. Both parties view each other as desirable partners for economic integration, which is partly viewed (perhaps incorrectly) as a way of improving clinical processes and outcomes of care.

However, the figure also reveals the somewhat orthogonal interests of the two parties. Hospitals want to gain leverage over payers and suppliers, to strengthen physicians' loyalty, to minimize physicians' splitting of inpatient volumes, and to correct pathologies in the traditional medical staff, all of which are not usually physician goals. Conversely, physicians

---

[115] British Medical Journal. (2003). Doctors and managers: Bound to differ? *British Medical Journal*, 326, 609–656.

[116] The following section draws heavily on: Burns, L. R., and Muller, R. (2008). Hospital-physician collaboration: Landscape of economic integration and impact on clinical integration. *Milbank Quarterly*, 86(3), 375–434.

Different Cultures in PHI

Physician Culture	Executive Culture
• Doers	• Designers
• 1:1 problem-solving	• 1:N problem-solving
• Reactive	• Proactive
• Immediate response	• Long-term response
• Deciders	• Delegators
• Autonomous	• Collaborators
• Independent	• Participative
• Patient advocate	• Organization advocate
• Professional identity	• Organizational identity
• Independent professional	• Interdependent profession
• Bedside role	• Managerial role

Figure 6.2. Different cultures in PHI

Different Orientations in PHI

	Physicians	Executives
Knowledge	biomedical science	managerial/social science
Patient focus	narrow (1:1)	broad community
Evidence rules	evidence based medicine hard facts	soft qualitative data
Resource view	unlimited	limited and finite
Prior exposure	other doctors	other executives, nurses
Professional Identity	cohesive, tight	less developed, loose

Figure 6.3. Different orientations in PHI

Goals Pursued in PHI

Physician Goals	Hospital Goals	Health System Goals
•*Increase MD incomes*	•*Increase MD incomes*	• Dominate the local market
•*Increase quality of service to patients*	•*Improve care processes & quality*	• Expansion vehicle into new markets
•*Increase access to capital & technology*	•*Share cost of clinical IT with physicians*	• Push out boundary of primary service area
•*Uncertainty over health reform*	•*Prepare for ACOs and Triple Aim*	• Beef up attractiveness to rating agencies
•Low leverage over payers	•Increase leverage over payers	• General desire to grow
•Escape administrative hassles of private practice	•Increase physician loyalty/alignment	• Steal admissions from competitors
•Escape pressures of managed care	•Minimize volume splitting	• Strengthen referral networks
•Exit strategy for group's founding physicians	•Increase hospital revenues & margins	• Control populations for population health
•Increase predictability of case load & income	•Capture outpatient market	
•Increase physician control	•Mitigate competition with physicians	
•Increase career satisfaction & lifestyle	•Develop regional service lines	
	•Create entry barriers for key clinical services	
	•Recruit physicians in specialties with shortages	
	•Address medical staff pathologies	

Figure 6.4. Goals pursued in PHI

seek career and lifestyle goals that involve shifting business risk to the hospital, and may or may not be congruent with the hospital's interest in increasing patient volumes and clinical productivity. According to some analysts, even though physicians may support the hospital's goals, as individuals they may neither share these goals nor feel responsible for achieving them at the expense of their own future income or professional satisfaction.[117] Even if they owned stock in a for-profit hospital, it is still unclear whether the goal alignment would be any greater. If one throws in the health systems that subsume the physicians and hospitals, the diversity among goals becomes even greater. In contrast to the other two parties, system executives explicitly acknowledge that their primary strategy is to "grow" their system – in terms of physicians, hospitals, market share, market dominance, and revenues.

In sum, the (absence of) evidence on effective methods of integration has failed to inform us on potentially discoverable ways to improve how physicians and hospitals pursue mutually held goals; instead, it documents the problems that arise from their conflicting goals. Even some common goals – such as protection from insurer efforts to reduce providers' market power, monopoly profits, and resource costs – are not ones that are well aligned with social objectives (e.g., improve quality and population health). Unless and until the payment system can be restructured to make pursuit of social goals coincide with the joint interests of physicians and hospital

---

[117] Cain Brothers. (2003). *If You're Niched, It Might Be Your Fault.* New York: Cain Brothers.

owners/managers, integration efforts are likely to fail or be counterproductive.

The above discussion also suggests that efforts at "normative integration" in PHI – e.g., shared values, aligned orientations, and similar prioritization of integration – have a steep hill to climb. The divide between physicians and hospitals rests on multiple bases that are baked over decades into their professional training and experience.

Logistical Issues in PHI

Another reason why PHI is so difficult is the sheer number of physicians to integrate. At some hospitals, the medical staff can number well into the high triple digits (or even thousands). Not only are they numerous, but physicians are also segmented by specialty and subspecialty areas, each of which has a differential impact on the hospital's revenues and margins. Those different specialty groups often have conflicting incentives and conflicting underlying cultures. In a multi-hospital system, to which nearly 70 percent of US hospitals belong, the burden of these incompatibilities isn't reduced by economies of scale (to the limited extent they exist). Instead, because individual hospitals and their staffs are often locally tribal, these incompatibilities simply repeat themselves locally or regionally across facilities in the same system.

Not surprisingly, specialty areas that have a bigger revenue and/or profit impact may get more of the hospital's attention and be more a target for any integration efforts; by contrast, psychiatry and pediatrics rarely come up for deliberation. Not only that, but the humans in the high revenue specialties have the natural tendency to overstate their contributions to overall margin, revealing a kind of inattention blindness to the other services and specialties required to keep them in business. The highly specialized cardiac surgeon, whose work is reimbursed at levels supporting considerable margin, naturally thinks their personal skill and reputation are what brings in the patients, and naturally believes that the high margins received are reflections on the unique value delivered. But those margins are far more socially constructed by the vestiges of legacy contracting and far less by an invisible hand linking prices with value. And a considerable part of the cardiac surgeon's patient volume may have required the existence of a deep PCP-cardiologist referral network upstream to feed that volume. After all, no one has a cardiac surgeon like they might have a dentist or a barber. Had those referring networks departed the arrangement, the flow of patients might be substantially reduced. But the financial analysts have a much easier time measuring first-order contributions margins than anything beyond that. The cardiac surgeon can see the receipts and will naturally understate the contributions of others. Like the old nursery rhyme "The House that Jack Built," the cardiac surgeon has fixed the aorta with no one else's help.

Further complicating this picture is that different specialties have a differing mix in their compensation methods and sources, and aggressively compete with one another (e.g., radiology versus cardiology, cardiology versus cardiac surgery, orthopedic surgery versus neurosurgery). Payments from hospitals will likely vary as a percentage of the physician's total compensation across specialties. Because different specialties will have a differing mix of commercial versus Medicare versus Medicaid sources, it may be impossible to discern the impact of any particular payment model.

Finally, the spatial differences among the two parties complicate PHI. Physicians have traditionally been fragmented into small medical practices scattered throughout a geographic area. By contrast, hospitals are organized at a handful of centrally-located sites (and the system headquarters even more so). Getting the parties together is nearly impossible. The situation has not been helped by the growing withdrawal from hospital practice by many community physicians, who have left the inpatient care of their patients to hospitalists situated full-time at the facility.

Dredging Up Past (Failed) Solutions

As noted earlier, PHI has been attempted twice during two epochs (pre-2000 and post-2000). The two epochs share many similarities. The earlier epoch contained IDNs; the latter includes ACOs. Both also include strategic alliances among hospitals and their medical staffs. The former included PHOs, the most popular alliance vehicle of the decade; the latter includes clinically integrated networks (CINs), which are PHOs on a *slightly* larger geographic scale. The two epochs similarly promote a continuum of care, narrow provider networks, physician alignment, population health, and reductions in care and cost variations (which are theorized to represent low-value care). They also commonly share per-capita payment to an entity responsible to provide a range of medical services to a designated population. Finally, both epochs analyze the cost-quality relationship, either in terms of cost effectiveness analysis (1990s) or simultaneous pursuit of a broad array of quality metrics and cost reduction benchmarks (2010s).

Not only are these parallel historical developments, they seem to be achieving the same lackluster performance results in terms of cost containment and quality improvement. Why does history seem to be repeating what was regarded as not satisfactory the first time around? One positive interpretation is that the 1990s' solutions were good ideas but were before their time, lacking the infrastructure and supporting systems to make them work. These supports might include electronic medical records (EMRs), real-time patient information, data analytics, and other innovations. With the development of the latter in the new millennium, payers and providers may be poised to implement the desired changes in a more graceful way with greater effectiveness.

A different (but less kind) interpretation draws on the insight of John Kenneth Galbraith.[118] Galbraith wondered why the lessons from financial crashes were often repeated with nothing learned. He concluded that old ideas get re-spun by newer generations of managers and policymakers every 20 years as the prior generation (who were chastened enough not to repeat them) died off or retired, whereas the new generation believed they had developed an innovative new vision. Some researchers applied Galbraith's insight to state health care reforms taking place in the early 1990s such as MinnesotaCare (1993), which mirrored the effort of the national Clinton plan (Health Security Act) to implement Enthoven's managed competition between rival accountable health plans.[119] MinnesotaCare was designed to solve all three angles of the iron triangle ("contain health care costs and improve access and quality")[120] by encouraging the formation of competing, HMO-like "integrated service networks" which would be reimbursed under a regulated all-payer system. Its design and roll-out were severely limited by relying on health planning mechanisms deployed (unsuccessfully) during the 1970s, including: certificate of need laws (to approve capital expenditures), mandated (standardized) benefits, and central health planning agencies. In the researchers' words:

The most troublesome aspect of Minnesota's health care reform legislation is not the regrettable parts, per se, but the strong indication that our policy makers find it necessary to keep repeating their mistakes ... The lesson of the 1970s health

---

[118] Galbraith, J. K. (1990). *A Short History of Financial Euphoria*. Knoxville, TN: Whittle Books.

[119] Conant, R., Dowd, B., and Christenson, R. (1995). *MinnesotaCare: A Law That Lost its Way*. Center of the American Experiment. Available online at: www.americanexperiment.org/article/minnesotacare-a-law-that-lost-its-way/.

[120] Minnesota Health Care Commission. (1994). *Minnesota Health Reform Master Plan*. Minneapolis, MN: Minnesota Health Care Commission.

planning efforts, repeated in the 1993 Act, is that even if it were technically possible for the government to know enough to reorganize the system efficiently, the government wouldn't be capable of pulling it off.[121]

Which interpretation is correct? The experiences of the 1990s showed some short-lived success by HMOs in lowering cost but little success by IDN and PHI efforts. The primary vehicles for cost containment were lower payment to providers (with perhaps lower real costs) and MCOs saying "no" to patients, who understandably hated them. Spending fell for several years as the privately insured moved (or were moved by their employers) to HMOs and PPOs in the early 1990s, causing a "rate panic" among hospitals. But the rate of growth returned to its historical level, albeit from a modestly smaller base. Efforts to develop narrow networks using HMOs appeared to lower spending without harming quality, but stumbled due to patient and physician protests (i.e., the managed care backlash). Capitation and closed networks never really spread from California to the rest of the country. The new organizational models like IDNs failed to reduce cost or improve quality. Provider efforts to develop a care continuum did not succeed financially, owing to the high expense of network development coupled with relatively low revenues from services provided outside the hospital. The care continuum may also have been an "orphaned concept" lacking any real stakeholder support. For example, when was the last time you as a patient asked for some integrated care from a care continuum, other than having your lab tests or chest x-ray done right after the doctor visit?

All else being equal, such results do not bode well for the 2010s' variants whose goal is to permanently reduce the rate of spending growth closer to GDP growth. While real health expenditures have been rising at about 1 percent above GDP growth for much of the past decade, compared to 2 percent+ in prior decades, they are more a function of economic/cycle factors than any policy/structural reasons. Sluggish growth in GDP has caused health care spending to fall in all Western countries. Managed care also succeeded in the 1990s by cutting utilization of hospitals; it is not clear there is that much more to cut today.

The 1990s effort at transformation using IDNs was largely initiated and implemented by the private sector with the government as a passive observer (that largely resisted calls from physician organizations to

---

[121] Minnesota Health Care Commission. (1994). *Minnesota Health Reform Master Plan.* Minneapolis, MN: Minnesota Health Care Commission.

intrude). This time around, the government is leading the transformation in public programs (especially Medicare) and legitimizing similar changes in the private sector; this government endorsement has served thus far to protect efforts from earlier criticism about care decisions being based on monetary incentives.

However, the major difference between these two epochs is the mantra and ideology of reorganization (and who is leading the charge): the iron triangle versus the triple aim. The iron triangle argued that, faced with constrained resources, societies must make trade-offs among the three goals: increased access, higher quality, and lower cost of care. Such trade-offs were occasioned by new technology that increased quality but also drove up health care costs. By contrast, policymakers in the new millennium have advocated the "triple aim" goals to be pursued at the population level: the patient's experience of care (care), population health (health), and per capita spending on health care (cost). Unlike the iron triangle, triple aim advocates do not view these three goals as irreconcilable but simultaneously possible in the presence of an "integrator" (e.g., ACOs). Moreover, the triple aim views waste and inefficiency rather than technology as both the major driver of cost and (low) quality and as subject to change if only data, incentives, and provider attitudes would cooperate. Successful pursuit of the triple aim by insurers or providers has yet to be empirically demonstrated. CMS built the three aims into the MSSP scorecard as the quality and efficiency performance measures for ACOs. In doing so, the MSSP challenges providers to deliver on all three aims (and perhaps all three angles of the iron triangle) simultaneously, using new models of health care delivery (e.g., PCMHs, care coordination) as the vehicles. To date (as noted earlier), ACO results have been tepid.

Low Level and Wrong Locus of Risk-Bearing

In contrast to physician employment, there has not been a concomitant rise in other types of financial or economic integration. As mentioned above, risk contracting did not spread prior to 2000; the past two decades suggest little has changed. Recent statistics published by Moody's Investor Service show that FFS (e.g., fee schedules) and volume-based and productivity-based payments (e.g., RVUs, DRGs) still dominate hospital reimbursement. By contrast, there is very little capitation and risk-based payment, and thus no movement from volume to value (Figure 6.5).

Evidence issued annually by the Health Care Payment Learning & Action Plan (HCP-LAN) similarly suggests slow movement in the desired

	2014	2015	2016	2017	2018
Reimbursement Methods (% of net patient revenue)					
Traditional Capitation (per member per month) (%)	1.5	1.6	1.5	1.6	1.8
DRG (%)	40.6	41.5	40.8	41.4	41.0
Percent of charges (%)	17.8	17.0	17.0	16.3	16.0
Fee schedule (%)	25.6	27.2	28.4	29.3	29.8
Per diem (%)	2.7	2.5	2.1	2.0	2.0
Risk based (%)	1.6	1.6	1.7	2.0	1.9
Other (%)	5.0	4.6	4.4	4.3	3.9

Figure 6.5. Reimbursement methods (percent of net patient revenue)

direction. Data from 2016 suggested that 43% of insurer payments were based on FFS, 28% were based on FFS linked to quality or value performance metrics (akin to P4P), and 29% were based on APMs with an FFS chassis or population-based payment. By 2018, there was only a slight drop in FFS payments (down to 41%) but little change to APMs (up to 34%).[122]

APMs have not only weakly diffused, but have also exerted mixed impacts on providers. Much of the increase in APMs has come in the form of modest P4P payments (that take the form of fees for "checking the box") which research has shown to (1) serve as (too) weak incentives to alter physician behavior, (2) burden physicians with excessive documentation, and thus (3) distract physicians from spending more time with patients. Other survey evidence also shows limited penetration of APMs among providers, as well as limited impacts on their costs and quality.[123] Payors have generally not been willing to put major amounts of money on the table to pay for quality, perhaps because they know that their downstream customers (employers and consumers) would not be willing to pay even more for the improvements they would get.

Recent evidence suggests that the greater the level of risk-sharing, the lower the level of hospital utilization and spending. However, the relationships were more pronounced in Medicare Advantage plans, which are mainly controlled by insurers, rather than in ACOs.[124]

Physicians not only prefer FFS over any of the APMs promoted by payers and CMS, but also a large percentage are unaware of how much of their compensation is based on APMs. This is partly due to low awareness

---

[122] HCPLAN. (2019). *APM Measurement: Progress of Alternative Payment Models. 2019 Methodology and Results Report*. Mitre Corporation.
[123] Burns, L. R., and Pauly, M. V. (2018). Transformation of the health care industry: Curb your enthusiasm? *Milbank Quarterly*, 96(1), 57–109.
[124] Newhouse, J., Price, M., Hsu, J. et al. (2019). Delivery system performance as financial risk varies. *American Journal of Managed Care*, 25(12), e388–e394.

of their eligibility for shared savings and limited knowledge of which patients are attributed to an ACO. The original intent behind ACOs was to motivate communities of physicians (not individual doctors) and their hospitals to assume responsibility for health care costs in their populations. Physician unfamiliarity with APMs also exists because ACO financial incentives exist at the contract level, not at the individual physician level, and the fact that practice organizations shield physicians from direct risk-based or quality-based compensation.[125]

Most individual physician compensation is still heavily RVU-based. Practice-level financial incentives for lower cost are quite small, are often transformed into nonfinancial incentives (e.g., using performance feedback or selective retention based on quality/efficiency) for individual doctors, or are filtered through decisions on raises and contract renewals. Thus, not only do physicians "seek shelter from the storm" of risk via employment, but hospitals and IDNs assist them in doing so. There may also be inconsistencies between financial and nonfinancial incentives (e.g., RVU productivity vs. cut costs) that deter risk transfer, as well as the desire to avoid (1) drastic income reallocation, (2) operational costs of administering complex physician compensation formulas, and (3) imposition of documentation requirements that foster physician dissatisfaction. For all of these reasons, APMs typically have a negligible effect on physicians' income and perceived risk because they do not directly impact the practicing physician. Moreover, the bulk of ACO physicians are PCPs, rather than specialists (who can serve as the target for where to save money).

A recent report issued by the Center for Healthcare Quality & Payment Reform concludes that the APMs developed by CMS have not produced significant savings or quality improvements.[126] Instead, they have increased spending with no significant impacts on quality, have failed to solve the problems with the current FFS system of payment, and have failed to give providers the flexibility or resources needed to deliver high-value services to their patients. That has not stopped (1) CMMI from trying or (2) other insurers from picking up the same schemes. They may have created billions in revenue for consultants, however, while increasing the documentation burden of physicians. The Report concludes that CMS should develop more targeted APMs that identify specific opportunities for reduced spending and/

[125] Friedberg, M., Chen, P., White, C. et al. (2015). *Effects of Health Care Payment Models on Physician Practice in the United States*. Santa Monica, CA: RAND Corporation.

[126] Miller, H. (2020). *How to Create More Successful Alternative Payment Models in Medicare*. Pittsburgh, PA: Center for Healthcare Quality & Payment Reform.

or improved quality, identify the changes in care delivery needed to do so, and design APMs that surmount current barriers to making the improvements. More tellingly, the Report concludes that a top-down, one-size-fits-all approach to APMs will not work for all types of patients and providers. What may work is a "bottom-up" approach whereby providers develop the APMs appropriate to them and their patients, which CMS then allows them to test and develop with its collaboration – not a top-down, CMS-imposed approach based on universal changes in incentives. How to get those at the bottom to pay attention and do so collectively is a major challenge. Some PCPs would like to take control (as happened historically at Kaiser and other West Coast beachheads, though there were other important differences we discuss below) but divided loyalties of specialists remain a problem.

Focus on the Wrong Targets

PHI efforts have often had the wrong targets in mind. Most efforts have focused on developing integration vehicles between hospitals and their medical staffs – PHO, IPA, ACO, and (more recently) the CIN – so that they can jointly contract with payers. These vehicles constitute "structural" approaches to the task of integration. These are misguided for several reasons. First, as we have learned from the quality literature, structures do not translate into the desired processes. Research shows that most of these vehicles have zero impact on desired processes like physician commitment, loyalty, citizenship, and alignment. Moreover, the only vehicle that seems to have a statistically significant impact – the employment model – exerts a very weak effect.[127] Second, structures are not very motivating or engaging to physicians. Physicians can belong to multiple contracting vehicles at the same time and not be able to distinguish which patients are under payer contracts from which contracting vehicles. Third, the presence of such vehicles basically imposes the burden of alignment on a bureaucratic structure that the physician likely does not understand or interact with, and also imposes a huge time burden of data collection and entry by our most expensive resource. Fourth, it is not clear that payers want to do risk contracts and share their profits with providers. This may be the simplest explanation for the low level of APM penetration.

---

[127] Burns, L. R., Alexander, J., and Andersen, R. Forthcoming. How different governance models may impact physician-hospital alignment. *Health Care Management Review*; Burns, L. R., Alexander, J., Shortell, S. M. et al. (2001). Physician commitment to organized delivery systems. *Medical Care*, 39(7), 19–29. July Supplement.

Some of the only consistent relationships ever noted in the PHI litera-ture concerned the quality of the "interactions" or "relationships" between the two parties. What did these "quality interactions" include in the old days? Physicians enjoyed pervasive involvement in clinically-related hos-pital management issues, access to hospital financial information, strong continuity in physician leadership by full-time practitioners, physician leadership development programs, physician leadership that led efforts to contain costs related to clinical practices and promote a sense of shared economic risk, mutual respect and support between managers and clin-icians, and a long history of working together.[128] Effective interactions also included management attributes: stability in top management, a genuine respect and liking of physicians, a high commitment to honest, open, candid, and frequent communication, a willingness to share decision-making with early and ongoing physician involvement, and the joint ability to manage the pace of change.[129] What subsequent researchers failed to notice or remember is that structural vehicles of economic integration (PHOs, employment) were not essential. Instead, the important ingredi-ents were a combination of managerial, cultural, and leadership elements that are perhaps fostered over time.[130] These elements may be resistant to being changed by organizational or financial restructuring; the degree of cooperation among physicians and their esprit de corps for each other and the hospital may depend on past history and informal relationships resist-ant to change.

All of this suggests that integration is not a noun or a structure, but rather a verb and a process. Perhaps the key to integration is fostering opportunities for collegial interaction *among physicians*, not with hospitals, ACOs, and other bureaucracies. While financial incentives are important, they may not be the key motivator for physicians. The thrust of integration should perhaps switch to peer-level interactions – which is what the FTC has emphasized in a series of advisory opinions regarding clinical integration.

Integration advocates should recognize the infrastructure to manage physicians, currently embodied in the hospital medical staff, is inadequate

---

[128] Prospective Payment Assessment Commission (ProPAC). (1992). *Winners and Losers under the Medicare Program.* Washington, DC.

[129] Shortell, S. (1991). *Effective Hospital-Physician Relationships.* Ann Arbor, MI: Health Administration Press.

[130] Bray, N., Carter, C., Dobson, A. et al. (1994). An examination of winners and losers under Medicare's prospective payment system. *Health Care Management Review,* 19(1), 44–55.

to the task. The medical staff is basically a flat organization structure in which individual practitioners have privileges to manage their own patients autonomously with little oversight from the collective. The *medical staff organization* in many hospitals is a misnomer: it exists only in the Joint Commission's accreditation manual and on a hospital's organization chart (and one that is rarely spelled out!). It is more a collectivity of physicians who share a common geography and a desire to treat patients at that facility. This may have been a weakness of the ACO movement to define the "extended hospital medical staff" as an economic, risk-bearing entity. If the staff had wanted to control their peers and be controlled by each other to a greater extent, they would already have done it.

Some physician researchers suggest that perhaps what is needed is greater attention to peer review and credentialing to sway the behavior of colleagues and increase accountability for desired outcomes.[131] Recent evidence suggests that the social influence of peers within physician networks can promote higher quality of care, lower cost of care, and greater uptake of new high-value therapeutic approaches.[132] This includes not only communication, but also social reinforcement and normative, collegial pressure. Perhaps integration efforts should consider approaches to quality and cost improvement that rely on leveraging physician ties, developing valid and locally relevant performance measures, training in change management and implementation, and developing local clinician leaders. But this is hard, time-consuming work. Erecting contracting vehicles is much easier.

Other physician researchers[133] argue that policy-makers need to more closely consider the perspective of physicians before encouraging provider consolidation and advocating PHI efforts, which have continued since the era of the failed Clinton health plan.[134] While physicians may appreciate the clinical support from PHI strategies such as CMPs and care coordinators, PHI may also diminish physician practice autonomy, patient trust, and patient-centered communications that promote better outcomes for

[131] Pronovost P., and Marsteller, J. (2011). A physician management infrastructure. *Journal of the American Medical Association*, 305(5), 500–501.

[132] Keating, N., O'Malley, J., Onnella, J-P. et al. (2020). Association of physician peer influence with subsequent physician adoption and use of bevacizumab. *JAMA Network Open*, 3(1), e1918586.

[133] Berenson, R. (2017). A physician's perspective on vertical integration. *Health Affairs*, 36 (9), 1585–1590.

[134] Medicare Payment Advisory Commission (MedPAC). (2017). *Report to the Congress: Medicare and the Health Care Delivery System*, Washington, DC: MedPAC.

individual patients. PHI may also erode the physician's commitment to professionalism. Getting physicians to be more thoughtful about the costs as well as the benefits of what they order has so far proved elusive. Note that all of these considerations are speculative, not evidence-based. If progress is to be made with an evidence-based model, effort needs to be made for that hard work as well as for brainstorming or imagination.

The Wrong Target: The Unrealistic Aim to "Be Like Kaiser"

The Kaiser system, in its West Coast locations, has long been held up as the gold standard of integration. It includes and combines a venerable physician group (Kaiser Permanente Medical Groups), a provider system with hospitals and outpatient centers (Kaiser Foundation Hospitals), and an insurance plan (Kaiser Foundation Health Plan); the plan is the primary source of patients (and revenues) for the physicians and hospitals in the system. The physicians are recruited out of residency programs, largely developed within the system, and socialized in the norms of multispecialty practice, with extensive reliance on deeply entrenched ties among primary and specialty physicians.[135] The limited proportion of physicians willing or eager to be in the Kaiser model is thought to be one of the main explanations for that model's anemic diffusion. Kaiser physicians use Kaiser hospitals and clinical settings as the locus of their practices and do not "split" their practices with non-Kaiser settings. The hospitals, in turn, are staffed by Kaiser physicians and professional staff and thus benefit from a cohesive medical group occupying the center of patient care.[136] This large structure is also hard to replicate from the ground up in new settings. By virtue of being self-contained and having the insurance plan serve as the major payer to the physicians and hospitals, Kaiser reduces the normal

---

[135] Crosson, F. (2003). Kaiser Permanente: A propensity for partnership. *British Medical Journal*, 326, 654; Carnoy, J., and Koo, L. (1974). Kaiser Permanente: A model American health maintenance organization. *International Journal of Health Services*, 4(4), 599–615; Strandberg-Larsen, M., Schiøtz, M. L., Silver, J., et al. (2010). Is the Kaiser Permanente model superior in terms of clinical integration? A comparative study of Kaiser Permanente, Northern California and the Danish health care system. *BMC Health Services Research*, 10, 91; McCarthy, D., Mueller, K., and Wrenn, J. (2009). *Kaiser Permanente: Bridging the Quality Divide with Integrated Practice, Group Accountability, and Health Information Technology*. New York: Commonwealth Fund.

[136] Goldsmith, J. (2004). Credibility and creativity: A conversation with Kaiser Permanente's George C. Halvorson. *Health Affairs*, 23(4), 133–142.

tensions and balancing acts found in other care settings.[137] In some of its expansion markets, Kaiser does contract out a lot of specialty care, however.

In the Kaiser system, the physicians are salaried (not capitated). Physicians and hospitals are subject to a budget pegged to estimates of premium revenues and thus have an incentive to stay within the budgeted revenues that the system brings in from sales to employers and government. In this manner, the health plan is the "driving wheel."

All of these structural advantages suggest the premiums that Kaiser charges to employers are as low or lower than what competitive insurers charge in the market. The costs of uninsured patients (e.g., those seen in the ED), costs from the normal cross–subsidy of (lower) Medicaid payments, and costs from investing in new technology are not absent in the Kaiser system, but are likely smaller. Thus, the premiums that Kaiser charges may not need to include as much cost-shifting. However, the growth in Kaiser premiums has not been lower than that of other insurers in the markets in which Kaiser operates – and even premiums (rather than costs) are thought to "shadow" the premiums of competitors rather than undercut them dramatically.

Can the Kaiser model be replicated elsewhere, especially outside the West Coast? Kaiser failed to fully replicate itself when it moved into the Eastern and Central US – with perhaps strong franchises in only a handful of markets (Denver, District of Columbia).[138] The insurance product did not succeed in other markets unfamiliar with the Kaiser brand; the physician and hospital divisions serve as the remnant of expansion. Getting physicians who had not been recruited into and developed within the Kaiser system post-residency, and thus had not learned the Kaiser way, proved difficult; Kaiser's effort to expand into North Carolina was staffed by physicians recruited from the medical staffs of local hospitals. In addition, the Kaiser model and its full array of medical specialties requires (1) a large population base to supply the appropriate number of patients to keep specialists busy and to afford the resultant overhead, as well as (2) a geographic distribution of facilities to meet the patient needs of the employer base with which Kaiser contracts.

This raises the broader issue of how group practices like Kaiser replicate themselves when they attempt to practice in new geographies, and how

---

[137] Burns, L. R. (1999). Polarity management: The key challenge for integrated health systems. *Journal of Healthcare Management*, 44(1), 14–33.

[138] Gitterman, D., Weiner, B., Domino, M. et al. (2003). The rise and fall of a Kaiser Permanente expansion region. *The Milbank Quarterly*, 81(4), 567–601.

much the combination of the insurance product with the provider system is key to the Kaiser success. For example, another well-known group practice, the Cleveland Clinic, has had difficulty in expanding into new geographic markets. The Cleveland Clinic diversified into Florida and experienced more than a decade of financial losses. The Clinic achieved nowhere near the market share that it achieved in its home state. As with Kaiser's efforts in the east, getting local primary care physicians to refer to Cleveland physicians took time and effort; indeed, early on the local medical community was hostile to the Clinic, viewing it as huge competitive threat.[139] Health care professional practice is local. And the special nature of a cohesive practice may not be easily reproduced when the physicians are recruited in an open market rather than developed from within. We have examples of national insurance companies (Anthem), but not national hospital systems (the Hospital Corporation of America is mostly located in the South) and national physician groups. Thus, the Kaiser model is not likely to be replicated elsewhere. The difficulties of achieving integration discussed elsewhere in this paper are the challenge to overcome.

We should recall that the Kaiser model served as the motivator for the 1973 HMO Act and the poster child for Enthoven's model of managed competition promoted during the Clinton health plan era. Years later, Enthoven tried to explain the forces in the late 1990s that torpedoed his model (blaming the managed care backlash by consumers, and employers' unwillingness to offer employees choice among health plans).[140] Other economists were more dubious about the managed competition model – suggesting that such competing Kaiser-like HMO plans would turn into local monopolies and result in less competitive markets.[141] Such had occurred in Minnesota during the 1990s following passage of legislation that encouraged the formation of the ISNs.[142]

Despite more than 50 years of public policy advocacy on behalf of IDN and ISN formation, there is scant evidence either of measurable societal

---

[139] Winslow, R. (1989). Medical clash: Expansion of hospital into new territories draws local staff's ire. *The Wall Street Journal*, August 19, 1.

[140] Enthoven, A. (2005). The US experience with managed care and managed competition. *Conference Series Proceedings*. Boston: Federal Reserve Bank of Boston, 97–117.

[141] Chernew, M. (2005). Comments on Enthoven's 'The US Experience with Managed Care and Managed Competition.' *Conference Series Proceedings*. Boston: Federal Reserve Bank of Boston, 119–125.

[142] Conant, R., Christenson, R., and Dowd, B. (1995). *MinnesotaCare: A Law That Lost its Way.* Center of the American Experiment. Available online at: www.americanexperiment.org/article/minnesotacare-a-law-that-lost-its-way/.

benefits or of any comparative advantage accruing to the providers who form Kaiser-like models. This actually begs the question, what is the evidence base for Kaiser itself? Researchers summarized the results from three, multi-year field investigations of medical groups and found few beneficial impacts of either large group size or multi-specialty mix on cost and quality; indeed, sometimes these group features exerted negative impacts.[143] In a more recent report, the researchers found no evidence of cost or quality benefits in an analysis of 15 risk-bearing IDNs.[144] Indeed, there is little evidence that the three components of Enthoven's model – larger medical groups, multispecialty practice, and receipt of capitated risk payments – had even materialized. According to industry analysts, there may be only a handful of markets where IDNs really compete against one another.[145]

So, what might we conclude from this? Two cautions come to mind. First, we should remember the adage that "all health care is local" and that what flowers in one climate may not bloom in another (the notion of *terroir*).[146] Second, there is no great evidence base for "best practices" and benchmarking of others.[147] Oftentimes, the reputed best practices of others rest on selection bias that needs to be offset by looking at failures as well as successes. The Kaiser system may not be the solution.

Physicians Themselves Aren't Aligned
(and Neither Are the Parts of the Hospitals)

As noted, one of the ostensible strategic advantages of integration relied on presenting a unified bloc for contracting with payers. PHI could be sustained, in part, through the "enemy of my enemy is my friend" rationale

---

[143] Burns, L. R., Goldsmith, J., and Sen, A. (2013). Horizontal and vertical integration of physicians: A Tale of two tails. In *Annual Review of Health Care Management: Revisiting the Evolution of Health Systems Organization. Advances in Health Care Management*, Volume 15. Emerald Group. Online Appendix.

[144] Goldsmith, J., Burns, L. R., Sen, A., and Goldsmith, T. (2015). *Integrated Delivery Networks: In Search of Benefits and Market Effects.* Washington, DC: National Academy of Social Insurance.

[145] Jeff Goldsmith, personal communication. Two markets that stick out are Portland and San Diego.

[146] Goldsmith, J. and Burns, L.R. (2016). Fail To Scale: Why Great Ideas In Health Care Don't Thrive Everywhere. http://healthaffairs.org/blog/2016/09/29/fail-to-scale-why-great-ideas-in-health-care-dont-thrive-everywhere/. September 29, 2016.

[147] Denrell, J. (2005). Selection bias and the perils of benchmarking. *Harvard Business Review*, 114–119.

for alliance – a very fragile connection in geo-politics in the setting of otherwise substantial cultural and ideological differences. But that seeming alignment of physicians and hospitals in negotiation with an external payer doesn't guarantee effective alignment *within* the system. The negotiating bloc might offer the synergistic bargaining power that effectively increases returns to both physicians and the hospital, but that still leaves the question of how to allocate physician returns within a large, diverse physician group with multiple specialties (and maybe sites). The same concerns exist, although perhaps less so, in allocating funds across member facilities within a hospital system.

This situation is more complex within medical staffs than inside other professional firms (e.g., law practices) where partners need to divvy up the money. It is true that when large law firms distribute profits to their lawyers, they must address the challenges that some forms of law are traditionally reimbursed better than others, and some activities of the firm may be seen as loss leaders requiring substantial internal redistribution of those profits. But those differences are tiny compared to what physicians face. Specialty-based differences in conventional reimbursement are vast; referral patterns, clinical interdependencies, and team work across specialties cannot be untangled; and hardened regulatory structures fix some prices but not others. Lawyers in big firms may claim they eat what they kill individually, but in medicine killing is done in packs – and then the packs fight over the food.

The example of the cardiovascular (CV) surgeon illustrates a narrow part of this complexity, but there are simpler examples. A bundled price for a surgical procedure might be acceptable to payers on one side and a PHO on the other. But how much of that revenue goes to the surgeon, how much to the internist who evaluates the patient in advance or may provide the post-operative care, and how much to the anesthesiologist or radiologist? The idea of aligning two stakeholder groups in contracting with the payer seemingly created a single front door for those negotiations. But in doing so, it effectively brought the battles among specialty groups – or at least natural tensions – inside the organization. Social advice often goes the other way: "Take your fight outside." With contemporary physician-hospital integration, the fights play out right in the living room. Tinkering with the compensation formula is considered one of two guaranteed lethal events in managing physician groups; the other is conversion of the billing system.

There is no substantive way to create the effect of integration to outside stakeholders, like payers or patients, without creating substantive integration on the inside, and the kind of alignment required for that integration is hard (and in some cases, like fee splitting, illegal). It may be the central task of IDN leadership. It is hard not just because orthopedists make more money than PCPs, but also because those reimbursement conventions are strongly associated (perhaps causally) with intrinsic views toward money and power, which are expressed in terms of intra-professional envy and jealousy. Much of the theory about integration draws at least implicitly on assumptions that humans are profit seeking and can be motivated that way. The field of behavioral economics somewhat challenges that assumption by arguing that there are other ways to motivate people to do things (and that money alone may not be enough). However, even if effective partnerships between hospitals and physicians are structured through financial arrangements, there is considerable heterogeneity in how much people are motivated by money. However, we are not aware of many hospital systems that have used behavioral economics as their default option.

Imagine a class of medical students who vary in how important money is to their sense of welfare. In choosing among future specialties, they know that the orthopedists can expect to make considerably more money than the PCPs. Those medical students who are more strongly motivated by money will steer themselves away from low paying fields like primary care and toward higher paying fields like orthopedics, regardless of their other preferences. Those less motivated by money won't necessarily avoid the higher paying fields, but are more likely to choose based on other dimensions – for example, how interested they are in the field (e.g., the technologies utilized). The result of these selective pressures is that lower paying specialties are populated by those not primarily motivated by money (otherwise, they would be in other fields). It does not mean that orthopedists are solely motivated by money, but it does mean that if you want to find physicians motivated by money, you are much more likely to find them among a group of orthopedists than a group of pediatricians. However, it is also likely true that high-income physicians may be less motivated by "a few dollars more" and might respond to other "satisfiers."

And that's exactly what we see when the internal negotiations about funds flow don't go well for the orthopedists. If they don't like how much of the pie they get, they pick up and leave. You rarely see groups of pediatricians doing the same thing. Stereotypically, pediatricians aren't as internally organized around the cause of profit as orthopedists are, and they are not as likely to organize themselves into clinical or management alignment with hospitals based on money.[148] There are huge cultural and personality differences among these specialties that make collaboration challenging.

Depending upon its organizational structure and culture, and the metallic composition of the CEO's fist (iron versus aluminum), the health system may not be so monolithic either. On a large scale, a health system created through mergers involving multiple physician groups (again organized around specific geographies) and multiple hospitals must contend with their legacy leadership, boards, and cultures that often overwhelm the potential strategic value of alignment. Even within single hospitals, managers often focus on their narrow budgets without the global vision of the overall organization. Indeed, different parts of the organization are often substitutes for and, thus, competitors with, other parts of the organization. This competition can recapitulate the none-for-all misalignment seen among physicians.

There are subtler examples as well. When expensive new anticoagulants allowed patients with deep venous thrombosis to be discharged sooner, in some institutions the cost increases were seen in pharmacy profit and loss (P&L) statements, but the cost decreases were seen in inpatient P&L statements. Those financial misalignments are probably easier to recognize and realign internally than the misalignments among different physicians – because they are less tied up in ego and self-worth – but they still require effort to be identified and rectified.

There are several of these internal, physician-based fault lines within an IDN that serve as serious headwinds to integration. Moreover, we have known this for a long time. Decades ago, some of our colleagues studied the Allina Health System over time in great detail.[149] Their early case study of Allina highlighted the problems of integrating multiple, formerly independent physician practices into a larger physician organization – particularly since the practices did not really interact with one another. They then highlighted the second-level integration problem of articulating the relationships between physicians in the smaller, employed physician organization with the larger group of affiliated physicians on the medical staff or

---

[148] According to David Asch, "If you move the cheese in front of a group of orthopedists, you can be pretty sure they will all move toward it. If you move the cheese in front of a group of pediatricians, they will scatter in all directions."

[149] Bunderson, J. S., Lofstrom, S., and Van de Ven, A. (1998). *Allina Medical Group: A Division of Allina Health System.* Case study in J. Duncan, P. Ginter, and L. Swayne, *The Strategic Management of Health Care Organizations.* New York: Blackwell Business, 602–619.

organized into contracting vehicles (e.g., PHOs, IPAs) – in particular to differences in compensation and issues of competition. They also highlighted the third-level problems of integrating the physician organization into the larger IDN – particularly since it competed with the hospital division and the health plan division for resources and attention.

A NEW PERSPECTIVE ON INTEGRATION

The above analysis questions the validity of perhaps the main hypothesis underlying PHI: that financial/economic integration will foster clinical integration which, in turn, will foster desired higher quality or lower cost (although it may yield higher revenues and greater market share). Here we suggest the beginnings of a different avenue to investigate.

Don't Expect the Chief Financial Officer to Do the Chief Operating Officer's Job

Despite the plurality of integration typologies, dimensions, and motivations, most models assume that financial alignment will motivate the operational alignment and eventually the clinical and economic outcomes health care organizations seek. That conceptual model overstates the value of money as an incentive, the operational control that central leadership in health care organizations can exert, whether physician behavior can be changed with more monetary rewards, and just how much money the leadership has to reward physicians.

Simply put, the CEO of a health care system does not have the same kind of operational power as the CEO of a firm in financial services, energy, or retail, because the CEO cannot tell the aortic surgeon what to do any more than the CV surgeon can tell the heart lung machine perfusionist nurse what to do. Health care quality depends critically on highly specialized expertise, and that expertise is diffused throughout the organization, diffusing power along with it. That highly specialized expertise is codified and hardened with explicit rules about licensing and credentialing. Deep expertise and narrow licensure in the setting of complex teams means that nearly everyone has a veto, and no one person can ever say 'yes' and move a decision forward alone. The old joke about medical staffs is that a vote of 99-to-1 is a tie.

In that setting, modest financial incentives have much less power than in ordinary firms; bonuses do not matter, even when they are legal. Dangling a financial carrot or threatening a financial stick provides financial motivation, but the key challenge in mission-driven firms like health care systems is rarely about motivation. Most professionals in health care may already be motivated individually to achieve better financial returns and have been socialized by their medical training to aim for better clinical returns. The key challenge is that it's hard to move complex organizations forward operationally, even when you already agree where you want to go.

We should remind ourselves that the goal is not integration, coordination, or collaboration. These are theorized means to the desired ends of cost control and quality improvement. The theory lacks an evidence basis, however, as this chapter (and others in this volume) show. Instead, the means have become the ends – this may be the problem. Even if this assertion is incorrect, the means (integration) are rarely achieved through top-down imposition of organizational controls, performance metrics, and bureaucratic oversight. Research suggests there is a tension between front-line coordination and organizational control from above; unfortunately, the latter is easier. The former rests on a climate of two-way flows of information, continued learning, and positive conflict-resolution at the front line, with helpful coaching from immediate supervisors. The latter relies more on measurements, monitoring, meetings and reports, and oversight, with minimal trust and conflict resolution. Only the former may be associated with organizational performance.[150]

Don't Expect the Chief Operating Officer (or Chief Medical Officer) to Do the Clinician's Job

That may explain why the evidence for the effectiveness of P4P incentives in health care is so weak.[151] What financial arrangements provide is motivation, but if the deficit isn't motivation but one of operational facility, those incentives target the wrong challenge. Paying parents to love their children more is a waste of money and is likely to be an operational distraction from what might actually work – which is to find ways to make it easier for busy parents to do fun things with their kids (and/or provide child care to relieve some of their burden).

---

[150] Gittell, J. (2000). Paradox of coordination and control. *California Management Review*, 42(2), 101–117.

[151] Asch, D. A., Troxel, A., Stewart, W. et al. (2015). Effect of financial incentives to physicians, patients, or both on lipid levels: A randomized clinical trial. *Journal of the American Medical Association*, 314(18), 1926–1935.

Operational efficiency is hard, but it is particularly hard in health care settings. For example, common operational challenges include reducing inpatient length of stay, decreasing hospital readmissions, or improving patient satisfaction – often in response to financial incentives applied at the organizational level. However, these operational goals seen from the perspective of top management are too general for focused implementation across different clinical settings. One size never fits all.[152] Reducing length of stay for patients with congestive heart failure is a completely different clinical challenge than reducing length of stay for patients with emphysema, or for women following uncomplicated obstetrical deliveries. In health care, much of the operational implementation of new programs must occur on the front lines, be led by clinicians, and must be repeated for each clinical context. That isn't as big a problem in health care as it might be in other industries because in health care many of the most educated and empowered individuals are the physicians and are already there, at the front lines, rather than sequestered in corporate offices far from the company's customers.[153] But many of the efficiencies one might expect from integration in other industries aren't available to health care precisely because the clinical context makes so much of a difference. Selling socks is probably more similar to selling ketchup or television sets than caring for patients with heart failure is similar to caring for post-partum women. At the least, the lines of expertise and authority in clinical programs don't allow overlap across clinical domains. Every clinical context is a new project.

This conclusion should not deter efforts to make changes to the clinical workflow. Executives and clinicians ought to take every such opportunity and celebrate every (even small scale) success. This may be a more fruitful way to go than to expect "the big one" from large-scale, top-down, one-size-fits-all change initiatives pushed by the C-suite or CMS. However, making such changes is "pick-and-shovel" work and not just relying on financial incentives; such work is hard and not glorifying. One is unlikely to get the solution from a book or a consultant – and thus may not be easily found anywhere. Hopefully, that is where the evidence helps.

---

[152] Burns, L. R., and Pauly, M. V. (2018). *Detecting BS in Health Care*. Philadelphia, PA: Leonard Davis Institute. Available online at: https://ldi.upenn.edu/brief/detecting-bs-health-care.

[153] Asch, D. A., Terwiesch, C., Mahoney, K. et al. (2014). Insourcing health care innovation. *New England Journal of Medicine*, 370, 1775–1777.

Some Final Comments

After nearly three decades of research, PHI remains wishful thinking and health care's "field of dreams:" just because you build the integration vehicles that bring together all of your favorite stars, you don't get to watch a great game of cost containment or quality improvement. The downsides of vertical integration are now well-documented: higher prices, higher spending, no improvement in quality, and thus no improvement in "value" (quality divided by cost). An objective analysis of the multiple investigations, all chronicled and summarized above, leads to one conclusion: the causal model of PHI does not seem to hold. It is not for lack of trying. Instead, we argue that researchers may have taken a top-down approach, focused on the wrong targets, and ignored the bottom-up perspective of one of the two parties to these arrangements (the physicians). Moreover, researchers have over-emphasized financial incentives and under-emphasized professional satisfiers.

The evidence reviewed in this chapter does not support much of what health care executives and policy-makers have done. Indeed, the positive evidence on what does work – e.g., local efforts led by physicians to customize solutions to their clinical area, efforts by executives to foster collaborative working relationships with physicians – is not well known. It certainly isn't popular news, since it (1) requires a lot of time and hard work and (2) is not amenable to top-down efforts like corporate strategy formulated in the C-suite or legislative proposals. That may partially explain why positive research evidence gets ignored. Executives and policy-makers want to "do something" and then do those things (which do not work). Evidence is not welcome; it is an inconvenient truth.

APPENDIX: GOALS OF PHYSICIANS AND HOSPITALS IN PHI

Hospital Goals

Capture the Outpatient Market. As patient care has gradually shifted to outpatient settings, community hospitals now view ambulatory care as a major growth market. They have entered this market to compete for profitable patient volumes and may pursue economic integration as a defensive strategy to work with medical staff members to maintain a piece of this market. For some institutions, the feeling is that "half a pie is better than none," that joint ventures can at least reduce market erosion. Executives also hope that economic integration may keep physicians (particularly specialists) from directly competing with hospital service lines in the future. Economic integration therefore is as much an option as cooperation. This growth in the outpatient market has naturally attracted other entrants. Hospitals have witnessed a sharp rise in the number of freestanding ambulatory surgery centers (ASCs) and diagnostic imaging sites nationally or in their own markets, often launched by entrepreneurial physicians with the help of outside investors and chains. Hospitals have used economic integration models to respond to this competition, neutralize the threat of niche providers, preempt their market entry, and prevent the loss of the outpatient market share. Hospitals may also use economic integration as an offensive strategy to increase their outpatient volumes by hiring new physicians and expanding into new geographic areas. Hospitals may also hire new specialists to replace aging community practitioners and thus avoid losing current referrals.

Increase Hospitals' Revenues and Margins. Economic integration also helps increase a hospital's service lines, particularly in profitable areas like cardiac care, neurosurgery, oncology, and orthopedics. Such growth can finance new technology, renovations, and new and replacement facilities, as well as subsidize less profitable services. Service line goals may include hospital branding and attracting patients and prominent physicians to the hospital's programs, which in turn can boost primary care and specialist referrals. They can also attract the interest of product vendors (e.g., imaging companies) in developing favorable technology packages, research support, and sponsorship of the hospital as a demonstration site for their equipment.[154]

Increase Hospitals' Leverage over Pricing. Economic integration can help increase a hospital's leverage with its trading partners in the local market. For example, hospitals have traditionally used economic integration to work with physicians and present a united face in negotiations with MCOs. In contrast, hospitals now work with physicians to demonstrate improvements in quality and efficiency that can justify higher MCO reimbursement rates. Similarly, hospitals are working with specialists to

---

[154] Burns, L. R., Cisneros, E., Ferniany, W. et al. (2012). Strategic Alliances Between Buyers and Suppliers: Lessons From the Medical Imaging Industry, in C. Harland, G. Nassimbeni, and E. Schneller (Eds.), *The SAGE Handbook of Strategic Supply Management.* Sage.

standardize vendor and product choices to extract lower prices from manufacturers.

Improve Care Processes and Quality Outcomes. Economic integration may also be used to improve the process and outcomes of patient care. The goal of some hospitals is fully integrating patients' care across specialists and/or the inpatient-outpatient continuum and thus reducing the use of resources and the duplication of services in order to improve outcomes. Such efforts may be designed to enhance not only the quality, but also the "service" aspects of care and thus attract more patients and referrals. Following Shortell and colleagues, economic integration may also be viewed as the best platform for responding to externally driven initiatives in quality improvement, performance reporting, transparency, and patient safety.

Increase Physicians' Loyalty. Hospitals have focused their marketing attention on "splitters," physicians who split their inpatients between two or more hospitals. Indeed, evidence suggests that this is a sizable minority (37.5 percent) of physicians who are reimbursed for inpatient work in the Medicare program.[155] One hospital problem is that several of their high-admitting specialists (e.g., invasive cardiologists, noninvasive cardiologists, surgeons), compared with other specialties, concentrate less of their practice at one hospital. These high-admitting specialists are also some of the most dissatisfied members of the medical staff.[156] Therefore, by targeting splitters for economic integration arrangements, hospitals hope to gain indirectly the loyalty of patients seen by those physicians.

Bolster Physicians' Practices and Incomes. Many hospitals have used economic integration to reinforce the practices of PCPs in their local markets. Such practitioners have seen simultaneously both a decrease in their reimbursement and an increase in their practice's overhead costs, liability insurance, and debt. Employment models have served to stabilize and sometimes increase PCPs' incomes, preventing their practices from folding, and securing the hospital's referral base. Employment can also supplement physicians' less favorable reimbursement with hospitals' more favorable reimbursement.

---

[155] Fisher, E., Staiger, D., Bynum, J. et al. (2007). Creating accountable care organizations: The extended hospital medical staff. *Health Affairs*, 26(1), w44–w57.

[156] Advisory Board. (2005). *The Agile Cardiovascular Enterprise.* Washington, DC: Advisory Board.

Address Pathologies in the Traditional Medical Staff. Economic integration is also used to address many problems in the traditional medical staff organization, such as the growing reluctance of community-based physicians to take call in the hospital's ER.[157] This reluctance is driven by the opportunity cost of time spent away from their office practice, the inconvenience of time spent away from home, the lack of reimbursement for treating indigent patients, the perception of higher malpractice risks in the ER, and the late and unpredictable hours.[158] The use of economic integration can address these issues by compensating physicians and hiring hospitalists. The medical staff, as well, has been beset by specialists' "turf wars" prompted by medical advances. Whereas the traditional battles were over the scheduling of imaging and procedure times, the more recent struggles have been over technologies and procedures adopted by multiple specialties, such as kyphoplasty/vertebroplasty by both orthopedics and interventional radiology. To minimize turf battles, hospitals have tied these competing specialties together in clinical service lines and multispecialty care teams.

Physician alignment. A common mantra among hospital executives since the 1990s has been the need to increase their alignment with physicians. Like integration, physician-hospital alignment is a broad construct with no clear understanding of what alignment means. Some researchers and practitioners commonly refer to alignment as shared purpose, vision, and goals.[159] Others talk about alignment of financial incentives which may foster integration along sociological or clinical dimensions;[160] some refer to all financial ties in PHI as alignment.[161] Still others suggest alignment follows upon both economic (financial) and noneconomic (sociological) integration and, in turn, fosters clinical integration,[162] or

---

[157] O'Malley, A., Draper, D., and Felland, L. (2007). *Hospital Emergency On-Call Coverage: Is There a Doctor in the House?* Issue Brief no. 115. Washington, DC: Center for Studying Health System Change.

[158] Berenson, R., Ginsburg, P. and May, J. (2006). Hospital-physician relations: Cooperation, competition, or separation? *Health Affairs Web Exclusive*, w31–w43.

[159] Swensen, S. and Mohta N. (2018). Why Big Gaps in Organizational Alignment Matter. *NEJM Catalyst Leadership Survey*. Insights report.

[160] Post, B., Buchmueller, T., and Ryan, A. (2017). Vertical integration of hospitals and physicians: Economic theory and empirical evidence on spending and quality. *Medical Care Research & Review*, 1–35.

[161] Vizient. (2017). *Physician Alignment Is a Critical Tool to Enable a Successful Transition to Value-Based Care*. Irving, TX: Vizient.

[162] Trybou, J., Gemma, P., and Annemans, L. (2011). The ties that bind: An integrative framework of physician-hospital alignment. *BMC Health Services Research*, 11, Figure 1.

they discuss alignment as what is needed to get the dual hierarchies in the hospital to collaborate.[163]

A sample of "definitions" of alignment drawn from the PHI literature over time suggests that alignment may concern the following: (1) hospitals working jointly with physicians in pursuit of their mission and objectives, a process that entails both "process" criteria (trust, communication, problem-solving, conflict resolution, involving physicians in management) and "outcome" criteria (ability to develop joint ventures, increase patient volume);[164] (2) the degree to which physicians and organized delivery systems share missions, values, goals, objectives, and strategies, and work to accomplish them;[165] (3) the degree of overlapping goals (both strategic and economic) in dealing with market pressures;[166] (4) close cooperation among the caregivers and managers, as well as the match between hospital strategy, actions, incentives, and resources to promote clinical integration;[167] (5) cooperation, collaboration, trust, and shared interests;[168] (6) psychological attachment and identification with the hospital;[169] and (7) commitment, organizational identification, citizenship behavior, and trust.[170]

---

[163] Wachter, R. (2004). *Physician-Hospital Alignment: The Elusive Ingredient. Commentary on Hospital Quality: Ingredients for Success.* New York: Commonwealth Fund.

[164] Shortell, S. (1991). *Effective Hospital-Physician Relationships.* Ann Arbor, MI.: Health Administration Press, xiii–xv; Bard, M., Conlon, P., Gartner, G. et al. (2008). Physician alignment: Paths to partnership. *Health Progress*, 20–24.

[165] Shortell, S., Alexander, J., Budetti, P. et al. (2001). Physician-system alignment: Introductory overview. *Medical Care*, 39(7), I1–I8. Physician-System Alignment Supplement. See pp. I-2; Bhardwaj, A. (2017). Alignment between physicians and hospital administrators: Historical perspective and future directions. *Hospital Practice*, 45(3), 81–87. See p. 84.

[166] Alexander, J., and D'Aunno, T. (2003). Alternative perspectives on institutional and market relationships in the US health care sector, in S. Mick and M. Wyttenbach (Eds.), *Advances in Health Care Organization Theory.* San Francisco: Jossey Bass, 45–77. See pp. 68–69. Shortell, S., and Rundall, T. (2003). Physician-organization relationships: Social networks and strategic intent, in S. Mick and M. Wyttenbach (Eds.), *Advances in Health Care Organization Theory.* San Francisco: Jossey Bass, 141–173. See p. 156.

[167] Shortell, S., Gillies, R., Anderson, D. et al. (1996). *Remaking Health Care in America: Building Organized Delivery Systems.* San Francisco: Jossey-Bass, 68–69, 170–171.

[168] Trybou, G., and Annemans, L. (2011). The ties that bind: An integrative framework of physician-hospital alignment. *BMC Health Services Research*, 11.

[169] Dukerich, J., Golden, B., and Shortell, S. (2002). Beauty is in the eye of the beholder: The impact of organizational identification, identity, and image on the cooperative behaviors of physicians. *Administrative Science Quarterly*, 47, 507–533.

[170] Dukerich, J., Golden, B., and Shortell, S. (2002). Beauty is in the eye of the beholder: The impact of organizational identification, identity, and image on the cooperative behaviors of physicians. *Administrative Science Quarterly*, 47, 507–533; Shortell, S. (1991). *Effective*

Growth. At the present time, nearly all hospital executives state that their number one aim is to grow their system and market share.[171] This used to occur by acquisitions of other providers in the local market; it has now spread to acquisitions in other parts of the state as well as across state boundaries. Regarding physicians, hospital growth goals require greater productivity (e.g., seeing more patients) and an emphasis on productivity metrics; these may not support goals of quality improvement or clinical integration.

Physicians' Goals

Increase Physicians' Incomes. Physicians' reimbursement is declining and incomes are stagnating. Physicians' average incomes (adjusted for inflation) fell 7 percent from 1995 to 2003, with the biggest decreases for PCPs (10 percent) and surgical specialists (8 percent).[172] More recent data show no significant growth in adjusted earnings for physicians between the periods 1996–2000 and 2006–2010.[173]

Physician incomes have stagnated for several reasons. Possible explanations include managed care growth, Medicaid payment cuts, sluggish Medicare payment growth, or bargaining by insurance companies. Some observers also claim that increases in practice expenses now outpace increases in reimbursement by a ratio of two to one.[174] Taking a long-term view (1951–2010), there has been a steady rise in the overhead costs of multi-specialty practices that is four times the rate of inflation.[175] More recently, physicians' office overhead expenses as a percent of revenues rose from 55 percent in 1991 to 60 percent by 2005,[176] fueled partly by greater

Hospital-Physician Relationships. Ann Arbor, MI: Health Administration Press; Burns, L. R., Alexander, J., Shortell, S. et al. (2001). Physician commitment to organized delivery systems. *Medical Care*, 39(7), 19–129. Physician-System Alignment Supplement.

[171] Cheney, C. (2019). Growth opportunities: How health systems position themselves under pressure. *HealthLeaders*.

[172] Tu, H., and Ginsburg, P. (2006). *Losing Ground: Physician Income, 1995–2003*. Tracking Report no. 15. Washington, DC: Center for Studying Health System Change.

[173] Seabury, S., Jena, A., and Chandra, A. (2012). Trends in the earnings of health care professionals in the United States, 1987–2010. *Journal of the American Medical Association*, 308(20), 2083–2085.

[174] Garman, D. (2007). *Explore Partnerships to Enhance Hospital-Physician Alignment.* Sg2. Available at: www.Sg2.com (accessed January 20, 2008).

[175] Goldsmith, J. (2018). *The Future of Medical Practice: Creating Options for Practicing Physicians to Control Their Professional Destiny.* The Physicians Foundation, Figure 1.1.

[176] Medical Group Management Association (MGMA). (2006). *MGMA Cost Survey Report.* Englewood, CO: MGMA.

legislative, regulatory, and payer demands requiring more office staff. Likewise, the malpractice premiums of some specialists have also risen sharply. Like hospitals, physicians have seen the prices of medical supplies go up each year, without the same benefits of group purchasing or supplier leverage. Finally, evidence shows that younger physicians are carrying higher debt loads from their medical education compared with those of their predecessors.[177]

To alleviate these concerns, physicians have tried to raise their incomes by increasing their patient caseloads, reducing their public-pay patient caseloads, diversifying their services, offering more profitable services, and adding diagnostic testing.[178] Several of these strategies have led physicians to compete with hospitals for outpatient specialty care. Physicians have also sought employment contracts whereby hospitals pay them by RVUs regardless of the patient's insurer.

Increase Access to Capital and Technology. To develop new services and profitable lines of business, physicians need capital to purchase equipment, erect buildings, hire new colleagues, and support overhead costs. Hospitals are obvious sources of this needed capital and technology and are attractive partners for economic integration, given their relatively greater brand in the market and ability to attract patients.

Increase Physicians' Control. Physicians have traditionally maintained control over the content of their work. This control, the principal characteristic of professionals,[179] has eroded in recent decades owing to a host of factors, such as managed care, consolidation, and the greater percentage of patients covered by public payers (with whom physicians have little or no bargaining power). Physicians thus enter into some economic integration arrangements to increase their control over the operation and management of clinical sites of care, such as joint venture centers and hospital service lines.[180] Physicians have been able to wrest some of this control away from hospitals in part because the local

---

[177] Kerr, J. and Brown. J. Costs of a medical education: Comparison with graduate education in law and business. (2006). *Journal of the American College of Radiology*, 3(2), 122–130.

[178] Voluntary Hospitals of America (VHA). (2004). *Physician Hospital Relationships: Forging the New Covenant.* Irving, TX: VHA.

[179] Freidson, E. (1970). *The Profession of Medicine.* New York: Dodd, Mead.

[180] Berenson, R., Ginsburg, P., and May, J. (2006). Hospital-physician relations: Cooperation, competition, or separation? *Health Affairs Web Exclusive*, w31–w43.

hospital is the only organization with which independent physicians can negotiate from a position of strength.[181] Physicians' control is much more motivating than "physicians' alignment," an aspiration of hospitals that strikes clinicians as patronizing.

Increase Physicians' Satisfaction. Prior survey research revealed declining job satisfaction among physicians and falling retention rates in medical groups due to work hours, pressure to increase patient volumes, call schedules, and the search for higher compensation.[182] Newer generations of physicians are reportedly less eager and willing to work the hours that older generations spent in their medical practice. They also are reluctant to accept risks and take call or unassigned patients. At the same time, they embrace employment and want to be compensated at the seventy-fifth percentile of the medical group's income benchmarks.[183] Such attitudes are largely consistent with hospital employment models.

Increase Quality of Service to Patients. Physicians may enter into economic integration arrangements with a host of service and quality objectives, including increasing patients' service, providing high-quality services at a lower cost, and offering more convenience to patients. Physicians may also hope to make hospitals more efficient to benefit their patients, ensure a great hospital for their family and friends, provide a return on their financial stake in the local hospital, and support the hospital's mission and contribution to the community.[184]

Seek Shelter from the Storm. It is no secret that many physicians are risk-averse. This explains why physicians prefer FFS payment over APMs and taking risk. Physicians know how this reimbursement system

[181] Kaufman, N. (2007). Physician and hospital relationships: The prognosis. Paper presented to Physician Strategies Summit, Orlando.

[182] Kennedy, J. and Beeson, S., (2007). Physician Loyalty and Retention: A Strategic Approach, Paper presented to Physician Strategies Summit, Orlando; Sanchez, A. (2007). *Plan Strategically for the New Medical Staff Organization.* Chicago: Sg2. Available at www.Sg2.com (accessed January 20, 2008).

[183] Peters, J. and Dorsey, S. (2007). Next-Generation Models for Physician Employment: The Ultimate Sustainable Market Growth Strategy. Paper presented to Hospital & Physician Relations Executive Summit, Phoenix.

[184] Cohn, K., Allyn, T., Robert Rosenfield, R. et al. (2005). Overview of physician-hospital ventures, *American Journal of Surgery*, 189, 4–10; Epstein, A. (2007). Physician-Hospital Relation Shifts: Organizational Models of Collaboration, Paper presented to the Hospital & Physician Relations executive summit, Phoenix.

works, have thrived under it for decades, and have some control over their incomes. The rise of APMs threatens this. Physicians may thus seek employment from hospitals to escape the uncertainties and payment variations that may be inherent in new payment models. They may also seek employed positions to provide a base to pay off their medical school debt load.

7

Evidence on Provider Payment and Medical Care Management

Ralph Muller and Mark Pauly

INTRODUCTION

One striking feature of the US health system, for people like us who are interested in evidence on how improvements in the way medical care is provided and financed affect its outcomes and costs, is that we have a pluralistic, not to say fragmented, medical care payment system. What is wrong with fragmentation? Think of a restaurant dinner for a large party of people. Usually they would order salads, main dishes, and desserts from a menu, and might be expected to ask the waiter to calculate the part of the check that represents their dishes – they would pay fee for service – and one could describe the pattern as fragmented. However, what if the group wants to divide the check equally? What if wine is cheaper by the large bottle but diners ordering different entrees want different wines, raising the bar tab? What if it is a restaurant where at least some dishes are better shared than on individual plates? Then a more integrated approach to dining and payment may lower cost may be better – at least for many. Many experts judge an arrangement in which health care is divided individually into different courses and ordered and paid a la carte as a system that is fragmented and ultimately costly to administer and inefficient. That is the challenge for payment reform – to move away from itemized "fee for service" (FFS) pricing to combined payment for a set menu or meal plan, and to do so in a way that will do more good than harm.

For the purposes of this book, it may come as a disappointment but no surprise to observe that definitive evidence on the best – or even better – provider payment systems is woefully incomplete.[1] Moreover, the evidence

---

[1] Burns, L. R., and Pauly M. P. (2018). Transformation of the health care industry: Curb your enthusiasm? *The Milbank Quarterly*, 96(1), 57–109.

that exists may be ignored in the design of payment transformation – in which we repeat alternatives known to not work over and over, and ignore things that do work, sometimes because they work too well. After all, a desirable cost reduction for insurers or consumers is a probably undesired revenue or income reduction for providers of care and products.

In this chapter, we first summarize the evidence on the impact, if any, of changes away from FFS provider payment on spending, spending growth, and outcomes or quality. Next, we discuss the patterns of changes in how payment has been made to health providers and health care systems, and whether those changes are consistent with the existence of and conclusions from evidence or if they seem to be determined by other factors. Finally, we develop some of the theoretical constructs that would be needed for an improved payment model, identify the evidence needs to fill out the model, and talk about both expected and ideal futures for provider payment policy.

EVIDENCE ON THE EFFECT OF PAYMENT MODELS ON QUANTITY AND TOTAL SPENDING

Not surprisingly, given our fragmented system, there is considerable variation in the United States in how payments flow to providers depending on the type of insurance plan a person has – or if they have any insurance coverage at all. The variations on which we have the most evidence are not subtle adjustments to get close to the ideal reimbursement level, or fine-tuned measures of quality or outcomes. Instead, they involve major differences in how much additional revenue a provider will get for supplying an additional unit of some medical service, with quality bounded by some metrics and often by standards of professional practice or accreditation.[2]

Let us focus on financial payments for volume first. At one extreme are pure fee-for-service (FFS) payment arrangements (now uncommon in private insurance but still used by original Medicare) in which the plan sets the reimbursement prices for thousands of different services. The provider must decide whether to agree to furnish services at those prices by becoming a participating provider. In many settings, the amount the insurer actually pays the provider is less than the "established" fee because the policy requires patient cost-sharing.

---

[2] Pauly, M. V., Eisenberg, J., Higgins Erder, H. M. et al. (1992). *Paying Physicians: Options for Controlling Cost, Volume, and Intensity of Services.* Chicago, IL: Health Administration Press.

At the other extreme, the provider is capitated at a fixed fee per person per time period – $X per month – regardless of how many services the person actually ends up using. (This is sometimes called "putting the provider at risk," though it is never clear what the risk is – other than the risk of losing more money if providers signed up for a lower payment. More on this below.) In this case, the provider gets zero additional revenue for any service rendered, and may well incur some positive cost, so the addition to net income is either zero or negative. In practice, except for original Medicare, most health plans now use a combination of these approaches – FFS payments at rates agreed to by a more or less limited network of providers, some fixed fees or bundled payments for some subsets of services to some designated populations, and some ad hoc rewards for lower spending or hitting quality goals.[3]

It is also important to note that, in contrast to the old FFS model in which insurer-provider interaction was limited to determining the fee for each procedure, the current FFS model is much more "collectivized" in the sense that the health system and health plan must agree on an overall pattern and level of payment, with much less attention to the additional revenue generated by each and every service and more to the total amount to be transferred for care of the plan's insured population. To go back to our earlier metaphor: it is as if you took a large party to a restaurant where your guests ordered individually, but then you and the restaurant negotiated discounts over the total size of the bill. While some populations (e.g., people with diabetes) and some services (e.g., behavioral health) may be negotiated separately from the total, much more of the focus these days is on the grand total of spending (per member per month) and on performance on a menu of outcomes than on individual services or patients. That the total is negotiated separately from the individual components also makes it much more difficult to identify specific financial incentives to individual providers or specific evidence on the effectiveness of those incentives.

---

[3] Zuvekas, S. H., and Cohen, J. W. (2016). Fee-for-service, while much maligned, remains the dominant payment method for physician visits. *Health Affairs*, 35(3). Available online at: www.healthaffairs.org/doi/10.1377/hlthaff.2015.1291; Berenson, R. A., Delbanco, S. F., Murray, R. et al. (2016). *Payment Methods: How They Work*. Washington, DC: The Urban Institute. Available online at: www.urban.org/sites/default/files/publication/80301/2000776-Payment-Methods-How-They-Work.pdf; Porter, M. E., and Kaplan, R. S. (2016). How to pay for health care. Harvard Business Review (July-August). Available online at: https://hbr.org/2016/07/how-to-pay-for-health-care

Whether or not there is more financial risk to a health system under capitation, bargaining over the bill, or original FFS depends in large part on whether the system is somehow required to furnish costly services if patients unexpectedly become sicker but not be paid explicitly for those services. If not, provider profit is fixed. If so, profit depends on the unpredictable risk of illness in a population (which might not be too unpredictable if the population is large and there is no pandemic, but is still a guess). From the health system's viewpoint, it is the size of its population financed by a particular health plan that determines predictability, even though an insurer with many covered members can also make accurate predictions when they are spread over many providers.

Evidence strongly establishes that provider behavior is different under the two "brute force" extremes of capitation and FFS. The volume and cost of services patients get are lower under capitation than under FFS as long as fee levels are high enough (e.g., at or above current Medicare levels). The relationship of volume under capitation to volume under fee levels as low as typical Medicaid FFS payments is less clear, especially because some providers refuse to treat people with Medicaid coverage, and those who do treat Medicaid patients may perform high volumes of low marginal cost services. The evidence does not strongly establish that the health outcome that follows from providers' decisions under capitation is different for patients than under Medicare FFS. For lower Medicaid fee levels, there is at least the risk of inadequate access. It does appear in a few cases that Medicaid capitation reduces spending to levels even lower than Medicaid FFS.[4]

There are some evaluations of the different payment schemes that use an incorrect conceptual framework. For example, some studies state that FFS is always inferior to capitation or some other method, even in concept – insurers should "pay for value, not volume." The argument is that providers will always do more if they can get more money for it, while capitation will force them to be efficient.[5] However, if fees are not set high,

---

[4] Sparer, M. (2012). *Medicaid Managed Care: Costs, Access, and Quality of Care*. Princeton, NJ: The Robert Wood Johnson Foundation. Available online at: www.rwjf.org/en/library/research/2012/09/medicaid-managed-care.html; Momany E. T., Flach, S. D., and Nelson, F. (2006). A cost analysis of the Iowa Medicaid primary care case management program. *Health Services Research*, 41(4); Hutchinson, A. B, and Foster, E. M. (2003). The effect of Medicaid managed care on mental health care for children: A review of the literature. *Mental Health Services*, 5(1); Kirby, J. B., Machlin, S. R., and Cohen, J. W. (2003). Has the increase in HMO enrollment within the Medicaid population changed the pattern of health service use and expenditures? *Medical Care*, 41(7).

[5] Guterman, S., Davis, K., Schoen, C. et al. (2009). Reforming provider payment: Essential building block for health reform. *The Commonwealth Fund*, March 20. Available online at:

only a limited volume of services will be supplied even under FFS – the implicit cost of work effort plus the explicit practice costs will limit what will be supplied by a provider at any given price. In contrast, a capitated provider group will produce whatever health outcome it achieves in the most efficient way, and might choose an inefficient and poor outcome by incurring as little cost as possible. So the final evaluation of capitation vs. FFE cannot be based on slogans – or on logic alone – but depends on how high incremental fees are set under FFS and how well outcomes and quality can be monitored and enforced under capitation.

PAY FOR VALUE, NOT FOR VOLUME

The mantra for medical payment reform is the title of this subsection. But a visitor from another world might wonder what our problem is. After all, virtually everywhere else in the economy, payment is FFS; supplier revenues rise when more is sold. Whether it is restaurant meals, car tires, or haircuts, very few adults pay capitation – they pay unit prices for services, sometimes divided into very fine detail. Payment based on volume rules the day in a market economy. If instead people paid a fixed amount per person for month for meals, for example, they might fear either overeating or being exposed to unappetizing school cafeteria food – or both. Not only that, "value" in ordinary markets is automatically recognized because goods or services that are better than others command higher prices. This does not happen magically, but rather as a result of supply and demand: Open a restaurant that is better than all others in town, hope to be flooded with calls for reservations, and raise your prices to reflect your greater value.

One thing different about medical care is that insurance that pays its cost often means the customer does not pay more (or much more), even if more or better services are supplied. (Compare this with auto collision insurance which requires you to pay yourself for touchup of an unrelated scratch along with the service that is covered in your estimate.) However, if the medical insurer or payer sets payment at a level at which providers want to supply only what patients need, the issue of paying for volume rather than value can be solved even within an FFS framework, as we will show in more detail.

www.commonwealthfund.org/publications/fund-reports/2009/mar/reforming-provider-payment-essential-building-block-health

So if the problem with excess volume can be solved, what about value? If patients or physicians who advise them can identify suppliers – for example other physicians or specialists – who provide higher benefits, the demand for services from those suppliers would be expected to be higher and the potential for higher prices larger, just as when Chez Pierre becomes the best restaurant in town. In many ways, insurance plans are more like college meal arrangements, which are not known to offer high quality food or service or compete effectively to do so. Hence, insurance can also cause that problem – the premium for higher quality that a supplier can charge can be higher than the value of that higher quality because the insurance, not the patient, is paying for it. Quality (or "gross value") will be too high, but net value (quality minus price paid) may well be too low.

If FFS insurance does not constrain price to an appropriate level, both quantity and quality can be too high for a cost-conscious world unless the "collective" negotiation between health care providers and plans mentioned earlier forbids prices higher than reimbursement (that is, it forbids balance billing) or limits surprise charges by out-of-network providers. So what is the alternative to unconstrained FFS insurance? The most commonly advocated value-based payment systems pay by capitation or bundled payments. This alternative to FFS offers financial incentives for both less quantity and less gross value of care, so it then has to backtrack and add rewards for keeping some dimensions of quality above a lower bound. The fear under value-based payment is that quality and quantity will be too low, not too high – and may be so low that paying higher costs to get more of them makes sense.

Of course, if patients cannot recognize higher quality and insurers do not value it sufficiently, providers may lose money if they provide it. This process in value-based payment of adding sweeteners to offset the bitter may by chance end up at a better place than under FFS that pays higher prices for higher quality (and quantity). Which model is better at balancing quality, access, and cost is an empirical question on which there should be evidence that can be brought to bear.

To sum up: the evidence supports the hypothesis that the volume of services patients get will be smaller at the extreme of capitation payment, where there is no revenue for providers from additional volume, compared to the other extreme of very high payment for additional services. However, there is no definitive evidence on how to titrate additional revenue or prices to hit the target of ideal volume and quality, however defined. As will be discussed later, precise "value-based payment" is still very much a work in progress.

IT IS A MESS IN THEORY, BUT HOW MIGHT IT WORK
IN PRACTICE?

Why is setting payment so complicated, and why is the ideal design still uncertain? We first need to deal with the issue that most insurer payments go to providers who work under several layers of administrative organization that can modify the reward or incentive to the physicians who actually advise on or render service. This topic is discussed in more detail in Chapter 6, but here we consider it from the viewpoint of an hypothesized "manager" of a health system that employs care provider(s). The baseline case is the solo practitioner or small group: Here, what the organization gets paid is what the individual supplier gets. The physician is both the manager and the employee. However, even in small group practices, there may be ways of dividing revenues, cost, or net income among partners that are not precisely related to whatever physician action triggered payment – the group might be paid FFS but divide revenues on an equal-shares basis regardless of variation in services produced. The group might also be paid capitation but divide payments based on volume of services rendered. At the highest level, an organization may both supply care and sell insurance. In that case, it is paid premiums that are capitated, but the health system part can use whatever method it chooses to pay income to providers.

We begin at the top (notionally and historically) by contrasting health plans organized as prepaid groups or systems, most famously the Kaiser Permanente health plans, and compare them with FFS payment of solo or small group practices. (We will turn to hospital and health care systems and their services later.)

The evidence over decades does support the conclusion that, for those professionals who work for Kaiser Permanente and those consumers who choose to use them, the volume of inpatient care is lower than for populations in older-style, private FFS systems, even after controlling for observable characteristics of insureds. Use of primary care and preventive services are higher. However, the growth over time in spending on services is not different for Kaiser-type plans and their FFS counterparts, nor are health and satisfaction outcomes.[6]

---

[6] Pines, J., Selevan, J., McStay, F. et al. (2015). Kaiser Permanente – California: A model for integrated care for the ill and injured. *The Brookings Institution*, May 4. Available online at: www.brookings.edu/wp-content/uploads/2016/07/KaiserFormatted_150504RH-with-image.pdf

Another way to change the marginal price at the system or manager level, short of full capitation, is to set a fixed payment for bundles of services connected with treatment of a particular illness or performance of a particular procedure. Some experiments in bundled payment for joint surgery found modest reductions (2 percent–4 percent) in total cost to Medicare, primarily through lower use of rehabilitation. However, no effects were seen for bundled payments for patients with heart disease over a given period of time. There have also been similar carve-out capitation payments for certain patient populations with specific conditions, such as mental illness. While exploration of these plans continues, the overall pattern is one of a small savings in cost and reduction in services.[7] Of course, changing the overall payment level for, say, a joint rehabilitation bundle might change the volume of joint rehabilitations, whose volume has been growing rapidly.

Thus far, the evidence shows that bundled payment works (when it does work) for patients with well-defined episodes of care that have easily identifiable beginnings and ends. Joint replacement surgery is the classic example. In contrast, bundling for patients with chronic conditions such as heart failure or diabetes (usually as capitated payment per time period for a set of services) seems to be ineffective.[8]

The main effect of bundling when it reduces spending appears to be one that causes physicians to pay more attention to the prices and quantities of referral services, such as rehab. Cost savings from the most economizing bundles are one time and less than five percent, but outcomes are not worse. So bundling is a dominant strategy, though not vastly superior to FFS.

Another model with some potentially attractive features is a mixed model of capitation and FFS. This can take two forms: one is capitation or bundled payment, but with adjustments for the risk of high volumes of services. Rather than the capitated provider having to cover all of the cost of additional services for patients who use more than the average amount of services, the payer will pay something for outpatient care provided by physicians or nurse practitioners.

[7] Navathe, A. S., Liao, J. M., Dykstra, S. E. et al. (2018). Association of hospital participation in a Medicare bundled payment program with volume and case mix of lower extremity joint replacement episodes. *Journal of the American Medical Association*, 320(9), 901–910.

[8] Agarwal, R., Liao, J. M., Gupta, A. et al. (2020). The impact of bundled payment on health care spending, utilization, and quality: A systematic review. *Health Affairs*, 39(1). Available online at: www.healthaffairs.org/doi/abs/10.1377/hlthaff.2019.00784?journalCode=hlthaff

One issue in payment and incentives is that the majority of US hospitals are nonprofit firms, a special legal status. The other is that, except for media advertising, a hospital cannot cause more people to use it and bring in more revenue under FFS – because physicians decide on hospital admissions. Hospitals do, however, engage in community outreach and provide infor-mation to the media about what they do, and so try to increase their volume and revenues in this way. When they are capitated, they can still advertise to sign up more patients – but not to get them to take more services.

The first difference about ownership, between for profit and nonprofit margins, evidence shows to be fairly inconsequential. If the hospital operates in a competitive market, it may choose the same production processes, capital investment, labor demand, and prices as its investor-owned twin for care sold to paying customers. If it has enough market power to make excess revenues in its market, it may then plow those profits back into research, charity or unprofit-able care, higher than market wages for low-skill workers, medical education, or the support of a social or community activity. Nonprofit hospitals seem to have the same production processes, private sector prices, and levels of charity care as for-profit counterparts located in the same types of markets. Nonprofits do seem less willing to leave areas when more people go on Medicaid.

The other difference is that much of the information about the benefit from hospital care and which hospital to use will come from physicians who may not even be employees of the hospital (in the case of smaller community hospitals) or who may be salaried but generally left alone by hospital management. There are anecdotes of physicians soliciting business for hospitals that say they need money, but this seems rare.

What could prompt physicians to create additional demand, revenue, or profits for the hospitals they use?[9] One obvious answer is to make it possible for hospitals to invest in facilities and workers for new service provisions that physicians find attractive. Another is to support agree-ments with large physician specialty practices (for example, orthopedics) for space or franchising in return for patients admitted to the hospital. Whatever the methods, there is little evidence that they are pushed more when reimbursement to the hospital rises or curtailed when it is cut. Capitating the hospital for the full set of medical services provided by the hospital itself or its physicians, in contrast, will incentivize the hospital management to persuade physicians to discourage the use of its facilities

---

[9] Kanter, G. P., and Pauly, M. V. (2019). Coordination of care or conflict of interest? Exempting ACOs from the Stark Law. *The New England Journal of Medicine*, 380, 410–411.

and substitute lower-cost alternatives. What tools hospitals have to redirect such use are unclear, and how effective they will be depends in part on whether they clash with physician incentives (if physicians are still paid by FFS) or are aligned (everyone is capitated).[10]

MEDICARE CAPITATION EFFORTS
IN POPULATION-BASED CARE

The original Medicare insurance plan is the largest remaining insurer in the United States that relies primarily on FFS payment and patient cost-sharing to affect the cost, use, and outcomes of care. However, the Medicare program has used and still uses alternative models to pay private organizations that assume responsibility for the bulk of care for populations of Medicare beneficiaries. Since 1974, Medicare has paid a capitated amount to private Medicare Advantage or Medicare Plus Choice plans largely organized as private health maintenance organizations (HMOs) for those Medicare beneficiaries who actively choose them for the full range of Medicare-covered services. After the passage of the Affordable Care Act, organizations of providers could choose to be designated Medicare Accountable Care Organizations (ACOs) responsible for the care of beneficiaries who used those providers and paid wholly or primarily in ways that put them at financial risk because of either cost levels that are too high or specified outcome metrics that are too low. In each case, the entity receiving payment could contract with or employ hospitals, physicians, and other providers in ways determined by the organization for a range of services, with the only major exception being prescription drug spending for ACO enrollees, which continues as FFS.[11]

What evidence supported the initiation of these programs and their implementation by organizations, and what evidence do we have on their impacts on spending, spending growth, and attractiveness to beneficiaries,

[10] Alexander, D. (2020). How do doctors respond to incentives? Unintended consequences of paying doctors to reduce costs. *Journal of Political Economy*, forthcoming. Available online at: www.journals.uchicago.edu/doi/10.1086/710334

[11] Lowell, K. H. (2018). First annual report: Next generation accountable care organization (NGACO) model evaluation. *NORC at Chicago*, August 27. Available online at: https://innovation.cms.gov/files/reports/nextgenaco-firstannrpt.pdf; Lowell, K. H. (2020). Second evaluation report: Next generation accountable care organization model evaluation. *NORC at Chicago*, January. Available online at: https://innovation.cms.gov/files/reports/nextgenaco-secondevalrpt.pdf

and health outcomes? We first review the case of ACOs and then Medicare Advantage.

The ACO idea was essentially the idea of managed care for a population – very similar to Medicare Advantage but based much more on provider management and control compared to the insurer management and control that characterizes Medicare Advantage. Indeed, ACOs often have internal financial incentives are essentially identical to those facing an HMO, but ACOs are required to pay for care received out of any network of participating providers.

The impetus for ACOs came from yet another attempt to encourage the provider-driven prepaid model embodied in Kaiser Permanente HMOs and similar health plans to expand nationwide (which it had not successfully done), and become available to Medicare beneficiaries in more geographic areas. However, because hospitals and physicians were not eager to bear a full financial risk similar to Kaiser Permanente or any other HMO receiving full payment as a per-member per-time-period capitation fee, ACOs allowed organizations to be paid with less financial risk, especially in their early ("Pioneer") stage. Another reason that ACOs had more exposure to risk than Kaiser Permanente is because the latter sells coverage primarily to employment-based groups, whereas ACOs enroll seniors on an individual basis. The ACO is somewhat protected because individuals become members based not on their choice of health plan (they choose original Medicare FFS) but on where they receive the bulk of their primary physician care. This choice is usually made on some basis other than the individual's perception of their health risk. Moreover, selection of ACOs can be predictable, so it is unpredictable selection that poses a problem.

The attempt to translate models that put organizations with poor patient outcomes or high cost at financial risk has so far not gone well. While there were and continue to be a fair number of provider organizations willing to sign on to the ACO model, many of the best organized systems in the country, such as the Mayo Clinic and Ochsner Health, did not. Most of those organizations that did participate accepted at most only "upside" financial risk (positive rewards for good performance but no penalties). Many entities did not get beyond the stage of a press release and, most importantly, neither significant reductions in spending or its growth nor significant improvements in quality metrics were observed.[12] The hospitals

---

[12] O'Brien, J. (2019). MSSP ACOs do not improve savings or quality, study finds. *Health Leader*, June 17. Available online at: www.healthleadersmedia.com/finance/mssp-acos-do-not-improve-savings-or-quality-study-finds; Markovitz, A. A., Hollingsworth, J. M.,

with bad outcomes and high costs were often those caring for predominantly poor and minority people, and were not able (and perhaps should not be willing) to respond to financial risk by turning around how those patients were cared for.

The Trump administration doubled down on the ACO idea, however, and established a program of "next generation" ACOs. The main difference from previous ACOs was requiring more financial responsibility (two-sided) in return for the potential for greater upside rewards. Included was some reduction in the regulatory restrictions on what ACOs could pay for, allowing them to cover, for example, meals, housing, and transportation if recommended by a physician. The results to date have been similar to those for the Pioneer plans – most cost savings (0.6 percent) were offset by incentive payments, yielding no significant financial gains to Medicare, but with some improvement on quality (hospitalization) metrics. Reduction in spending growth relative to comparators was concentrated in post-acute care spending (e.g., spending on rehabilitation) and home health visits. These changes probably came from differences in care management and not from information technology and provider engagement. This source of savings is similar to that in bundled payment programs that have achieved savings. There has been an uptrend in provider willingness to participate in next generation ACOs.

The Medicare Advantage (MA) program has had a greater impact. More than one-third of Medicare beneficiaries are now in these private plans, often managed by commercial insurers, rather than in either original FFS Medicare or ACOs. The initial impetus for Medicare Advantage plans was an attempt to copy the private sector managed-care revolution with the key feature of capitated payment of an organization that then arranged for care from limited networks of hospitals and physicians.

Research indicates that such entities have lower resource costs than comparable FFS Medicare, but select lower-risk beneficiaries by offering benefits that appeal more to people who are healthy and want to stay healthy – so any net financial gain to the Medicare program as a whole has been minimal.[13] One of the striking features of private commercial Medicare Advantage plans is that they pay as FFS to contracting providers,

Ayanian, J. Z., et al. (2019). Performance in the Medicare shared savings program after accounting for nonrandom exit. *Annals of Internal Medicine.* Available online at: www.acpjournals.org/doi/10.7326/M18-2539

[13] Advisory Board 2017 Medicare Advantage was meant to save taxpayers money – But plans' revenue far exceeds their costs, research suggests. *Advisory Board,* August 9. Available online at: www.advisory.com/daily-briefing/2017/08/09/ma-costs

but at payment rates close to Medicare FFS rates and much lower than they would pay for under-65 beneficiaries. As Medicare FFS has (and continues) to generally limit the increase in its fee levels relative to private insurers, private Medicare Advantages plans have been able to piggyback on Medicare FFS price-controlling efforts, while at the same time using some cost savings to add attractive benefits.

The pattern is that initial efforts were loosely based on evidence of success in achieving lower spending (but no reduction in growth) and good outcomes that have characterized prepaid group practices like Kaiser Permanente for many years – but efforts had little reliance on any detailed randomized controlled trial-type of evidence or academic literature. The commercial insurers administering Medicare Advantage plans have achieved some success even relative to governmentally managed original Medicare. Here again, though, they did not rely on rigorous evidence, but rather on learnings from their private managed-care programs. They also benefitted from their so-far unexplained ability to match the lower fee levels from a public and political price control system for older insured adults in a way that they have not achieved for their private group plans. They also seem to have benefitted from favorable selection of patients.

The evidence does suggest some improvement in cost saving perform-ance and popularity of Medicare Advantage plans relative to original Medicare especially in markets where original Medicare has unusually high costs.[14] In contrast, there has been useful evidence on performance of ACOs in the literature, but that evidence has not shown consistent or substantial effectiveness, much less profitability. It is not known how much this evidence has discouraged providers from participating in ACOs.

BACK TO THE DRAWING BOARD: WHAT GOES ON WITH PROVIDER PAYMENT INCENTIVES IN THEORY, AND WHEN MIGHT THAT MATTER FOR IMPROVEMENT?

The world of health services payment or reimbursement can get very complicated very quickly because of the large number of possible and

---

[14] The Commonwealth Fund. (2016). *Does Medicare Advantage cost less than traditional Medicare?* Available online at: www.commonwealthfund.org/publications/issue-briefs/2016/jan/does-medicare-advantage-cost-less-traditional-medicare; Gold, M., and Casillas, G., (2014). *What Do We Know about Health Care Access and Quality in Medicare Advantage versus the Traditional Medicare Program?* San Francisco: Kaiser Family Foundation. Available online at: www.kff.org/medicare/report/what-do-we-know-about-health-care-access-and-quality-in-medicare-advantage-versus-the-trad itional-medicare-program/

actual ways of paying providers by insurers and sharing the cost with the insured members, and because of variation across providers and patients in how they respond to financial settings. The performance reviewed so far of alternative payment models that are actually used is not very impressive. So it may be useful to go back to basics about incentives, information, and objectives. We begin with a pair of simple though unrealistic models, based on Nicholson et al.,[15] to illustrate what objectives, tools and information insurers need (compared to what they now have) to optimize payment models. We are trying to find the most parsimonious set of needed information that might help plans and consumers who buy them get where they want to go.

Assume there is a population of insured people with identical risk for some illness that can be treated effectively with some medical service but which cannot be prevented. Some insured members are expected to have more severe versions of the illness, which will usually mean they get more benefit from treatment than those with less severe versions; some will not get the illness at all, and so get no benefit from treatment. (They might have benefits from preventive care if it exists.) The insurer knows how many of its population will get different levels of severity and expected benefit from treatment, but not who. The insurer's goal is an arrangement that makes the average net benefit of insured members (health benefits minus premiums and average out-of-pocket payments) as high as it can be, given what it pays for the treatment (and incorporates in the premium). After treatment or illness patients may have different health outcomes but we assume that variation is unpredictable by patient or provider – so the insurer is willing to settle for averages.

We begin by assuming that providers of care maximize their net incomes. However, if net incomes are the same, unaffected by what they do, they will render treatment to those who most need it. Providers also vary in terms of their cost or efficiency in providing the treatment, with some having lower cost than others.

One baseline model might assume, unrealistically, that the insurer knows everything. It knows which patients get sick and how much they will benefit from treatment. It knows the most efficient treatment technology for each provider and how efficient it is, and it knows the value to its insured members for different outcomes. Then the insurance company has an easy problem to solve. It wants to get the treatment to patients whose

[15] Nicholson, S., Pauly, M. V., Wu, A. Y. J. et al. (2008). Getting real performance out of pay-for-performance. *The Milbank Quarterly*, 86(3), 435–457.

benefit from it is greater than the cost to providers to furnish it. This means that the insurer will want to find the ideal quantity of patients treated (call it Q^*) at which the number of patients who get treatment is just equal to the number of providers who have costs lower than the value of patient benefit. (As noted above, the collectivization of current payment models makes exact realization of this goal unrealistic, but it presumably is still the ideal.) At the margin, the value to the least severely ill patient treated equals the cost to the least efficient provider who treats that patient. Every patient who gets a treatment has a benefit greater than the cost to the providers who treat them, and no patients are treated who do not get enough benefit to justify the cost. If the insurer knows all this information, it just issues a rule specifying which patients should be treated and which providers should treat them – and it will also know what the total gain in health will be from this pattern of treatment.[16]

This information-intensive and unrealistic approach is, however, not the only way to get to the ideal number of treated patients in the insured population. If the insurer knows what health outcome the population would attain if care was provided to the right number or fraction of patients, it can just agree to pay some amount if that outcome is attained, and nothing if it is not. That is the theoretically ideal value based capitation or bundled payment for enrollees with this illness. Then, if providers accept the offered payment level, they will do the right thing – provide Q^* units to the patients who benefit the most.

At this level of abstraction, the insurer can either pay based on process, or pay based on outcomes – it gets the same ideal outcome either way. The problem is that both bases for payment are hard and costly to observe; knowing all the details of processes or knowing how to risk-adjust outcomes are major challenges. Such a "central planning" solution based on orders from above, apologists for capitalism have long noted, imposes an unrealistic information burden on planners. Is there a market-based solution, and one that does not require the insurer to be omniscient?

Fortunately, there is. Suppose the insurer knows Q^*, the number of people in its population who have a need for the treatment (call that "demand"), but nothing else about which people require what. It also does not know which providers have which degrees of efficiency and therefore which marginal costs. However, suppose it does know (or can make a reasonable guess) about how much of the service providers are willing to

[16] McGuire, T. G., and Pauly, M. V. (1991). Physician response to fee changes with multiple payers. *Journal of Health Economics*, 10(4), 385–410.

furnish at any reimbursement price the insurer proposes (so it knows "supply"), but nothing else about what providers will do. Then, the insurer just needs to set payment at the dollar amount on the supply schedule at which providers will choose to supply Q* units; as if by an invisible hand, providers concerned about profit will then have an incentive to see that all patients who ought to get the treatment will get the treatment.

The insurer in this model does not need to know which providers are more efficient (since they reveal that by their willingness to supply at lower reimbursement levels) and it does not need to know which patients benefit more since providers treating the patients determine that and will choose to provide care to those who need it. Perfect FFS is perfect, and we need look to no other alternative payment system to improve things.

If insurers can define and measure the service when it is furnished, if they know how many of their insured enrollees should get it, and if they know the provider supply curve for this service, they can set the ideal FFS price P* at which everything works out for the best. There is no incentive for providers to oversupply because doing so would make them lose money – they would get more revenue, but it would not cover their cost. There is no incentive to undersupply because then providers would be losing profits they could have grabbed. Insurance can cover 100 percent of the price since the service is rationed among patients by providers based on need and value.

So why is what actually happens in any country, and especially in the United States, so far from this nirvana? Insurers may not know P* or know the supply curve. Prices under FFS may have wandered so far from P* that it is better to collectivize the payment process described above. Negotiating a total payment for all care with a health system will be simpler than trying to set reimbursement for each service right on the mark. Providers or anyone other than the patient may not know how sick they really are and how much they would value getting better. You can probably think of other flaws. The story of evidence on provider payment can thus be told as one of attempts to generate enough information to approximate this ideal solution.

Of course, the story so far assumes that the payer (insurer or patient) can define the service precisely, specify its quality, and make sure that it is rendered with that level of quality. Sometimes this is possible, but sometimes the quality of care (think of it as the effect on health, although consumers may care about amenities and convenience) is hard to define and assure. If the payer can directly observe quality, it can make payment contingent on supply of that level of quality, and reduce payment if quality is below the contracted level. If it cannot observe or specify quality, the fallback option is to observe the health outcome, and pay based on that. An omniscient payer can do either one,[17] but in reality, outcome quality may be easier to observe than process quality, or vice versa. The ideal payment rule takes all the information (process or outcome) into account but is more responsive to the measure that provides the best combination of accurate observability, correlation with "true" outcomes valued by patients, and resistance to manipulation.

So what messages for payment design (or redesign) can be drawn from this speculative theory? One is that insurers need to know what they want (the Q^*) from health systems and health systems have to know what they want from physicians in advance. They determine this ultimately by seeing what buyers in the market prefer (think different levels of Q^* corresponding to different levels of cost effectiveness and premiums). It helps to know where you want to go.

Having determined that answer (in some fashion), the model says that there should ideally be some additional revenue for systems and payments to physicians who are providing more care than others (you should pay for volume) but to maximize value, you have to get that additional payment right – you should set it at the level that will get you the volume you want. Many believe that current FFS payments in Medicare or commercial insurance provide too much reward for volume – but to reduce them would meet resistance from suppliers. A solution – and this is the main punchline of the model – is a two-part reimbursement scheme – some capitation (or predetermined salary) and some payment for volume or productivity based on the value of that additional volume. This message has already been incorporated into many settings of salaried physicians and some into health plan-health system negotiations. In the latter case, the capitated portion of payment is the collectivized part, but there are adjustments if volumes vary for good reason.

VALUE-BASED PAYMENT IN THEORY AND PRACTICE

The P^* model already discussed is, in many ways, the ultimate value-based payment model even if value based payment advocates have not always

---

[17] Nicholson, S., Pauly, M. V., Polsky, D. et al. (2004). Measuring the effects of work loss on productivity with team production. NBER Working Paper No. w10632. Cambridge, MA: National Bureau of Economic Research. Available online at: https://papers.ssrn.com/sol3/papers.cfm?abstract_id=565843

identified it as such: the price at the optimal quantity represents not only the minimum price that will bring forth that quantity but is also equal to the marginal value of that service. Away from that ideal, a commonsense approach would be to pay higher than the current prices for services you want more of, and lower prices or nothing at all for services you want less of. When you get just enough, stop. So the solution for low-value services – which are thought to be a common source of inefficiency in health care management – is in principle simple: reduce pay for them until their quantity falls to the level at which their value is equal to or greater than their cost.

What are current attempts to move to value-based payment and how do they compare with the P* benchmark? We relied on two surveys of innovative value-based payment schemes to generate a list of examples to summarize, one from the Centers for Medicare and Medicaid Services (CMS) and the other from Boston Consulting Group.[18] The CMS list included the Medicare readmission reduction program we discussed in Chapter 1, and we combined some of the examples of full capitation of health systems (Geisinger Health System, Intermountain Healthcare, Kaiser Permanente) on the Boston Consulting Group list.

(1) *Medicare End-Stage Renal Disease Quality Incentive Initiative.* CMS could reduce payment to an outpatient dialysis facility by up to two percent if it failed to meet national benchmarks, such as dialysis dose. This effort followed several previous CMS efforts to improve quality and lower cost in end-stage renal disease care, but did not rely on evidence that modest reductions in payment would cause facilities to exceed the benchmarks. The most important improvement was a reduction in overtreatment of anemia by use of erythropoietin, the subject of a previous bundled-payment demonstration. Evaluation was by comparison with previous levels of metrics, not by use of a control group of facilities not subject to penalties.[19]

---

[18] CMS.gov (2020). What are the value-based programs? Available online at: www.cms.gov/ Medicare/Quality-Initiatives-Patient-Assessment-Instruments/Value-Based-Programs/ Value-Based-Programs; Horner, B., van Leeuwen, W., Larkin, M. et al. (2019). Paying for value in health care. *Boston Consulting Group*, September 3. Available online at: www.bcg .com/en-us/publications/2019/paying-value-health-care

[19] CMS.gov (2020). Medicare program; end-stage renal disease prospective payment system, payment for renal dialysis services furnished to individuals with acute kidney injury, and end-stage renal disease quality incentive program (CMS-1732-F). Available online at: www.cms.gov/newsroom/fact-sheets/medicare-program-end-stage-renal-disease-pro spective-payment-system-payment-renal-dialysis-services

(2) *Value-Based Payment for Hospitals in Medicare.*[20] The Hospital
     Value Based Purchasing Program is a voluntary program that
     rewards hospitals financially for meeting certain metrics and
     reduces payments by no more than two percent if they fail to do
     so. There does not appear to be any prior evidence of benefits from
     similar programs on which the designers of the intervention relied.
     A study concluded that the program did not improve quality to
     any appreciable extent and did not improve patient engagement;
     evaluators speculated that the financial rewards were too small to
     motivate major changes in behavior, though they provided no
     evidence that such changes would have been effective or would
     have been more costly so that a greater reward was needed.

(3) *Hospital-Acquired Condition Reduction Program.* The evidence in
     support of this program was data that showed that many hospitals
     had above-average rates of conditions judged to be hospital
     acquired. There was little evidence on why some hospitals per-
     formed poorly or could be induced to change management prac-
     tices by financial rewards, though such changes were regarded as
     clinically feasible. The hospitals in the "worst" quartile of the
     distribution of risk-adjusted conditions (measured by a count of
     conditions, not by harm done) could experience a one percent
     revenue reduction penalty. Subsequent evaluations found the pro-
     gram to be ineffective, perhaps due to inadequate risk
     adjustment.[21]

(4) *Oncology Bundled Payment for Medicare Patients.*[22] This program
     included 138 oncology practices and 10 commercial payers. It has
     a per-patient predetermined payment for the duration of a pre-
     specified program of chemotherapy. There has been little prior
     evidence that practices would change behavior to profit from costs
     below the amount of the payment bundle. No significant effect of

[20] American Hospital Association (AHA) n.d. Hospital value-based purchasing. Available
online at: www.aha.org/hospital-value-based-purchasing/home#:~:text=Under%20this%
20program%2C%20Medicare%20rewards,Hospital%20VBP%20is%20budget%20neutral.

[21] Arntson, E., Dimick, J. B., Nuliyalu U. et al. (2019). Changes in hospital-acquired
conditions and mortality associated with the Hospital-Acquired Condition Reduction
Program. *Annals of Surgery* (October 19). Available online at: https://journals.lww.com/
annalsofsurgery/Abstract/9000/Changes_in_Hospital_Acquired_Conditions_and.94840
.aspx

[22] CMS.gov (2021). Oncology care model. Available online at: https://innovation.cms.gov/
innovation-models/oncology-care

the program on spending (within the bundle) was observed and the program was thought to impose a net loss on Medicare so far. A similar radiation oncology bundle program is underway, but no results are yet available.

(5) *Integrated Health Care Association Program.* This organization has engaged a number of delivery systems in California in a variety of value-based payment programs. Their largest is a bundled payment program based on a model of "align, measure, perform." To date, the only finding is that bundled payment implementation increased administrative complexity.

(6) *Capitation of Organized Delivery Systems: Geisinger Health System, Intermountain Healthcare, and Kaiser Permanente.* These systems have had a much longer history of payment for designated population members in the form of global capitation for all services. The organizations themselves integrate hospital and (salaried) physician care. There are few direct financial incentives to physicians or sets of physicians, with Geisinger scrapping a program of financial rewards for what it called ProvenCare bundles. All of these systems rely primarily on physician understanding of and adherence to a culture of controlled peer-reviewed care with selection and training of physicians the primary tool for inculcating culture. This approach has limited the ability of these systems to expand their model outside of the largely monopolistic settings of a dominant health system.[23]

(7) *North Carolina Blue Cross Blue Shield (BCBS) Blue Premier Program.* This program resulted from negotiated agreements with major health systems in North Carolina to meet spending growth and outcome goals. Results from the first year of experience show modest spending savings (four percent) and no significant improvements in health measures. The model was based on Medicare ACO programs, which themselves have failed to show major impacts on spending or quality.[24]

---

[23] Delbanco, S. F. (2014). The payment reform landscape: Capitation with quality. *Health Affairs Blog*, June 6. Available online at: www.healthaffairs.org/do/10.1377/hblog20140606.039442/full/

[24] Rajkumar, R. (2019). Introducing blue premier: Redefining what is possible in health care. *BCBSNC.com*. Available online at: https://blog.bcbsnc.com/2019/01/blue-premier/

A CASE STUDY OF HIGH-LEVEL PAYMENT REFORM – THE
MASSACHUSETTS ALTERNATIVE QUALITY CONTRACT:
WHAT DOES (OR DID) EVIDENCE HAVE TO DO WITH IT?

The most ambitious attempt to change payment of health care systems away from FFS has been the "Alternative Quality Contract" (AQC) implemented by the Massachusetts nonprofit BCBS plan for its HMO customers treated in large group practices and health systems. Massachusetts had and still has one of the highest levels of health care spending per capita in the United States, and claims costs for BCBS customers had been increasing at a rate of 10–15 percent in the years prior to the rollout of the AQC during the Great Recession.[25] The goals of the innovation were to improve quality measures and slow the growth (but not reduce the level) of spending per person.

The contract took the form of specifying a maximum growth in spending (per member) or "population-based global payment" for all services, whether rendered by contracted or noncontracted providers. The payment was based on FFS reimbursements at baseline that were increased by a specified growth rate with quality incentives up to plus or minus 10 percent of the benchmark payment amount.

The core design at the health care system level was thus based on capitation with an amount based on historical reimbursement but with a prespecified growth rate. Health systems participated voluntarily and almost all large systems or groups previously part of the HMO agreed to do so. How capitated amounts and bonuses or penalties were divided among providers within a health system is unclear, although organization-specific.

The evidence in support of the intervention design was the kind of evidence about capitation already discussed in this chapter – that it was associated with lower spending growth as it is phased in, without large negative effects on health indicators and with mixed effects on measures of process of care thought to be clinically relevant to outcomes.[26]

---

[25] Agency for Healthcare Research and Quality (AHRQ) n.d. Blue Cross Blue Shield of Massachusetts alternative quality contract. Available online at: https://ahrq.gov/working forquality/priorities-in-action/bcbsma-alternative-quality-contract.html

[26] Song, Z., Safran, D. G., Landon, B. E. et al. (2020). The 'alternative quality contract' in Massachusetts, based on global budgets, lowered medical spending and improved quality. *Health Affairs (Millwood)*, 31(8), 1885–1894. Available online at: www.ncbi.nlm.nih.gov/pmc/articles/PMC3548447/

The one major difference between AQC and prior capitation agreements was an attempt to protect recipients of capitation from severe financial risk. In prior decades, entities that agreed to accept some level of capitation often found those levels were below their costs and what they could have obtained under FFS models. The reasons are not well understood but appear to be a combination of poor bargaining, regression to the mean, and random incidence of high cost patients. The AQC guarded against financial risk by setting payment at least as much as baseline plus some increase, having "reinsurance" for cases above $100,000 in cost, and offering financially meaningful bonuses for quality improvement.

In the early years, the AQC was associated with improvements in quality measures, but any cost savings were offset by bonus payments; in later years, there were some net financial gains to BCBS. The reduction in spending growth averaged about 2% per year (e.g., from 11% to 9%).[27] During the recession, when national spending growth was driven by price increases, the savings were from lower prices. Since then, the savings relative to trend are in the volume of specialist referrals, tests, and imaging.[28] There is no evidence of slowdown in the diffusion of costly but beneficial new technology, which has been the primary driver of spending growth nationwide. Neither reinsurance nor risk adjustment have been major factors, apparently.

BCBS of Massachusetts is proud of its accomplishment and has extended the program to smaller practices but with more financial risk protection for them. After a decade, no other private insurer has copied the program in any other state. Medicare, California Medicaid and private ACOs have put some similar modest programs in place. In addition, the State of Maryland has modified its unique hospital rate-setting program to incorporate global budgeting features for hospitals.

What role did evidence play in the design and implementation of the AQC, and what generalizable evidence has been generated by it? BCBS of Massachusetts points to the Avalere Health summary of multiple peer-reviewed studies of global budgeting. However, those studies were all done by the Harvard team evaluating the AQC. In addition, Avalere Health turned to "key opinion leaders," not peer-reviewed evidence to support its

---

[27] McWilliams, J. M., Landon, B. E., and Chernow, M. E. (2013). Changes in health care spending and quality for Medicare beneficiaries associated with a commercial ACO contract. *JAMA*, 310(8), 829–838. Available online at: https://jamanetwork.com/journals/jama/fullarticle/1733718

[28] Song, Z., Ji, Y., Safran, D. G. et al. (2019). *New England Journal of Medicine* 381, 252–263. Available online at: www.nejm.org/doi/full/10.1056/NEJMsa1813621

proposal that financial skin in the game is needed to produce meaningful change in provider behavior despite the general prior failure of pay-for-performance models.

The conceptual story about how the AQC is supposed to impact individual physician choice relies on the claim that they are provided with greater "flexibility" to suggest home health care, behavioral health, and the like without evidence that before the change they were deterred from suggesting what they think is the best care. Physicians said they needed an incentive plan that would reward them for not prescribing low value services. Apparently, physicians need incentives "to be thoughtful" about referrals to specialists and tests because otherwise they would do so in a thoughtless fashion.

It appears that there was no evidence for key design features in the AQC. Rather, design was based on the common sense ideas of plan designers and the judgment that providers would accept them or health systems would require them to participate.

WHAT YOU ARE PAID MAY MATTER MORE THAN HOW YOU ARE PAID

The great bulk of the discussion on payment reform has paid attention to what we have just discussed – how revenues the provider gets might vary (or not) with the volumes, quality, and outcomes of care supplied. Equally or more important to a provider is the level of payment. Physicians might be more likely to agree to switch from FFS to capitation if the new capitation rate is set to provide as much revenue as previously under FFS – and physicians will refuse "value-based payment" if what they will get is much less than before.

Not only might the level of payment matter for acceptance or resistance to payment change, but it might also influence what is supplied. The most obvious example is the charge that FFS leads to more volume – except when the fee is set as low as it is in Medicaid and the actual volumes of services meets quality standards. (Of course, if the "services" under FFS are so poorly specified in terms of quality or intensity that a Medicaid mill can always make them cheap enough to be profitable based on volume, nothing can work.) Even capitation can lead to increases in volume if those increases attract new customers to a health system.

So how is the level of payment set – or how should it be set – and what evidence bears on this question? Let us begin first with what happens in practice. There are three different markets into which health systems and physicians sell: privately insured, Medicare, and Medicaid. Each is different.

For private insurance, both payment levels and the form of payment are set, to a greater or lesser extent, by negotiation. Hospitals can and do drop out of or are dropped from provider networks based primarily on the overall level of payment – and not on the nuances of payments linked to indicators of volume, quality, or outcomes. Insurers that want to offer a broad network of providers in an area have to be ready to pay higher prices or payments, and hospital systems try to make themselves indispensable to an insurer, to compel high payments.

The evidence on how to negotiate or what determines the negotiated outcome is weak. We know that hospitals on average charge and often collect higher FFS prices from private insurers than from original Medicare. However, they seem willing to accept much lower prices for private Medicare Advantage patients that are much closer to the original Medicare rates. The reason an insurer would pay a hospital a high price is because it needs the hospital as a supplier for its insured enrollees – so more prestigious hospitals are able to command higher prices. However, the negotiation process must have an upper bound – an insurer willing to pay (and paying) two times the Medicare rate is probably not willing to pay four times the Medicare rate to a particular hospital. The absence of hospital competition is obviously part of the reason for high private prices, but the absence of the option to refuse original Medicare patients is much of the reason why Medicare is able to pay so much less. Compared to some idealized competitive market, we do not know whether private prices are higher than the competitive ideal (because hospitals have monopoly power) or Medicare prices are lower than competitive ideal (because Medicare has monopsony and especially political power).

For physicians, there is a different problem because they can and do decline to provide services to people covered by some insurers. Most still see Medicare FFS patients, though many are refusing to take new patients, and a much larger fraction refuse Medicaid patients because the payments are so low (although primary care physicians took more Medicaid patients when payments temporarily increased under the Affordable Care Act). For patients with Medicaid, the level of payment as well as its form clearly matters a lot right now. However, here as well, the unanswered question is the cost of taking a "money-losing" patient whose insurance pays at a low level. As long as the payment is still above marginal practice cost, the relevant measure is what the doctor could have earned with alternative use of time. For example, taking on a Medicare FFS patient might mean turning down privately insured patients whose insurance pays well. Then physicians might treat Medicare FFS patients only if the private insurers reduce their level of payment. "Creating demand" for private patients (by telling them to "come back in a month for a followup") is possible but with much debate on whether there is scope for it either clinically or ethically.[29] An alternative is the physician having more leisure time, but that may not be so attractive depending on the pace of work.

In all cases there are some obvious truths. Insurers with larger market shares will have more bargaining power. Providers who have larger market shares will have more counterbargaining power. Providers who have alternatives to a given insurer's business will have counterbargaining power. If patients dislike giving up their providers, insurers will have less bargaining power. Beyond these propositions there is a fundamental indeterminacy in theory about where payment will fall and a fundamental instability wherever it is set, along with a fundamental inefficiency as insurers and providers expend real resources (whether on advertising or computer programs) as they jockey for bargaining power. The invisible hand of competition (large numbers of providers facing large numbers of different insurers) can settle these matters but is often unavailable. So it is not surprising that there is little evidence base for bargaining over levels of payment – there cannot be definitive universally applicable evidence. The participants will just have to muddle through.

BEHAVIOR AND EVIDENCE ABOUT THE EFFECTS OF BEHAVIOR IN AN IMPERFECT WORLD

Let us reconsider payment from commercial insurers. The most important point to note is that neither insurers nor providers currently have the knowledge to adjust quantities of specific services according to their reimbursement rates. This means the insurer side has no specific evidence on how providers would respond to changes in the price it pays – it does not really know its supply curve. This imprecision is matched by (and largely caused by) the fact that providers do not know the "cost" or profit margin at a given payment rate for individual services – so cannot make decisions

---

[29] Phelps, C. E. (1986). Induced demand – Can we ever know its extent? *Journal of Health Economics*, 5(4), 355–365. Available online: www.sciencedirect.com/journal/journal-of-health-economics/vol/5/issue/4; Fuchs, V. R. (1986). Physician-induced demand: A parable. *Journal of Health Economics*, 5(4), 367. Available online at: www.sciencedirect.com/journal/journal-of-health-economics/vol/5/issue/4

on what agreements to furnish care or volumes of care would add to profits. Both groups rely on lumping things together and then guessing.

In particular, in the negotiations between health systems and commercial insurers over what is to be paid (however it is paid) for the managed care enrollees, insurers rely on managed care to control the use of specific services. They therefore pay on a "book of business" basis – what they paid in the previous year for services for all members plus or minus a negotiated update factor. Distinctions within that total will be no finer than broad categories, such as maternity or oncology. Likewise, in responding to such offers, health systems will not know the cost (either average or marginal) of providing specific services to their privately insured patients, other than at a very coarse level, such as line of care (again such as maternity, oncology) or perhaps for their hospitals or doctors in specific geographic areas. At most they will rely on evidence and judgment that surgery generally pays more than referring a patient for medical management and use of drugs (which the health system does not profit from). Likewise, the insurers deal with health systems as bundlers of hospitals and physician groups and do not try to find out the cost (however defined) of individual physicians in groups.

For Medicare, providers are required to submit data on costs for hospital care, at least, and hospitals sometimes take this data seriously as measures of their resource use (as well as part of a reporting requirement to CMS). We do have some research evidence based on Medicare cost data that apparently more profitable services are favored by providers – though we do not have a comparison of what would have happened if providers had only private accounting data available. The quality incentive in physician payment embodied in the Medicare Access and CHIP Reauthorization Act (MACRA, the new Medicare FFS model for physician payment, most of which has yet to be fully implemented) did not have prior evidence of effectiveness, so its impact, if any, is uncertain because it is yet to be seen and will be hard to evaluate (with no randomized controlled trial control group).[30]

MANAGEMENT AND PROVIDER BEHAVIOR CHANGE

Managers of systems faced with changed revenue functions can change their bottom lines only if they can bring about changes in behavior of those rendering care in their systems. If a change is judged to be feasible and

---

[30] CMS.gov. (2019). MACRA. Available online at: www.cms.gov/Medicare/Quality-Initiatives-Patient-Assessment-Instruments/Value-Based-Programs/MACRA-MIPS-and-APMs/MACRA-MIPS-and-APMs

beneficial, the natural question to pose is why that change is needed – why has it not already been made? As we have commented at a number of places in the discussion to this point, the explanations usually involve erroneous or incomplete information for physicians and other staff members, or a failure on their part to be thoughtful about benefits and costs of doing things differently.

Some insight may come from reviewing some concrete examples physicians give about why they did not behave appropriately under FFS and could do better under capitation. We were taken with the story about his own practice told by Dr. Daniel Frank, Chief Medical Officer at OptumCare, the capitated arm of UnitedHealthcare, to explain why their program of capitated payments for primary care seemed to produce better outcomes than its FFS counterpart:

> Before joining OptumCare, Dr. Frank was a primary care physician working in Florida. A female patient came in with chest pain, which he suspected was related to anxiety. Because the time allocated for visiting with patients was short, he referred his patient to a cardiologist for screenings, all of which came back normal. It was only after that protracted process he was able to circle back to his initial gut sense that she was dealing with anxiety.[31]

How would this have been different under capitation-based management, and would the difference be an improvement? We obviously do not have all the details, but Dr. Frank was clearly working in some type of system that scheduled time slots for patient visits for primary care. There is nothing in FFS payment that "allots time" for doctor visits; there is no taxi meter. Instead, it is the need to schedule visits and not delay patients that constrains practice scheduling. Presumably the same is true in OptumCare clinics. In principle, solo practice primary care physicians can decide how much time to spend with a patient but even here, smooth running of an office deters taking more time than average.

Had Dr. Frank had more time, would he have done things differently? Would he have sent the patient with chest pain away, telling her his feeling that it was generated by anxiety? That screening tests confirmed his initial suspicion is testimony to his skill as a diagnostician, but it is hard to construe that fact as a critique of FFS. More to the point of our discussion, would a manager of the system (the chief medical officer) have advised

---

[31] UnitedHealth Group. (2020). Physicians provide higher quality care under set monthly payments instead of being paid per service, UnitedHealth Group study shows. *UnitedHealth Group.* Available online at: www.unitedhealthgroup.com/newsroom/2020/uhg-study-shows-higher-quality-care-under-set-monthly-payments-403552.html

physicians to treat patients with chest pain with suspected anxiety differently under FFS than if the payment was capitation? Perhaps the manager might have judgment warped by the potential profitability of more cardiologist visits and imaging services, but that is not in the anecdote and unlikely in real life. The woman would have gotten a short visit and a referral for screening most likely under OptumCare as well; the study of capitated physicians to which this anecdote was attached found those physicians recommended slightly higher rates of screening (for breast and colon cancer) than some FFS comparison groups of physicians.[32]

CONCLUSION

The one conclusion that would get unanimous agreement is that payment reform in the direction of value-based payment has yet to realize its full potential. What is much more controversial is how much potential there is. Opinions on that depend on whether a person believes both that general changes in provider behavior and care management exist that represent more than cosmetic changes and that high-level payments to providers can be used to change them. Refusing to pay for something usually discourages it, and increasing payment to lavish levels usually (though not always) encourages it – but evidence on how to titrate high-level payment to health care organizations in a way that changes the behavior of the people in those organizations is weak. We are still trying find out which end is up.

---

[32] Minemyer, P. (2020). UnitedHealth study: Primary care docs in value-based models achieve better patient outcomes. *Fierce Healthcare*, August 12. Available online at: www .fiercehealthcare.com/practices/unitedhealth-study-primary-care-docs-value-based-models-achieve-better-patient-outcomes

8

Evidence on Ways to Bring about Effective Consumer and Patient Engagement

Kevin Volpp and Mark Pauly

INTRODUCTION

Medical care is a service, which means that its supply depends on the characteristics of the person receiving it as well as the characteristics of the person furnishing it; medical care requires participation by the customer in the process of producing the service. A good comparison is with automobile repair and maintenance services: when you have to bring your car in, you often do not know what is wrong or what it will take to fix it, and even after you pay for preventive care for your brakes or oil you cannot tell if it made a difference in outcomes.

Similarly, it is difficult for consumers to evaluate a drug or service, especially if it does more than provide immediate symptom relief. A service that involves the prospect of improving future outcomes has inherent uncertainty. Buyers are bound to have imperfect information and not have fully accurate knowledge of all relevant facts. They will probably have less information than the suppliers about how things work but better information on what performance goals they have for the future. Consumers who are aware of their lack of knowledge seek advice from experts, and in medical care those experts are typically physicians or nurses. They are or should be aware, however, that future outcomes depend on their behaviors as well as on medical services and medical advice, which sometimes they do not follow, just as they may skip or delay the scheduled maintenance in the automobile owner's manual.

For patients who want to improve their health, the question is what path to follow. Typically, patients as consumers seek advice based on their current health state about the risks and benefits to expect from different medical services, diets, or other health-improving activities. They presumably want to know how much more effective one treatment will be compared to another or no treatment, given their out-of-pocket costs. As with any advice, consumers do not always follow it. Some nonadherence may be rational – patients may have additional information not communicated when advice was first sought, circumstances may change, or patients may have strong preferences towards a less aggressive treatment plan or natural remedies. Some choices may be irrational or behavioral – patients may fail to adhere to advice because they overweight the present compared to the future, because they have preferences that change over time, or because the choices are presented in a way that overwhelms them with so many options that they end up making ill-considered decisions based on emotional factors or the order in which the choices appear.

While we might hope for medical care to be delivered in an 'optimal state' in which the omniscient clinician consistently recommends the best possible course of action taking into account patient preferences and patients follow those recommendations, this often is not the case in reality. As a result, outcomes may be inferior and/or costs higher than if this 'optimal state' were true. This may be true for both consumption of health services and for health behaviors that clinicians may recommend. Recognizing reasons why this 'optimal state' is not attained can be helpful in motivating managerial actions that facilitate a process and outcome closer to the 'optimal state.'

For those interested in engaging patients as part of evidence-based medical management, there are (at least) three issues to consider. One is the evidence that could or should be presented to the patient/consumer. A second is how the evidence is presented to the patient and by whom. A third is evidence on how patients respond to a recommendation or prescription. What most affects patient behavior, and what processes or costs are involved in making that impact? An ancillary but still important issue is the degree to which physician recommendations are or should be based on evidence about patient preferences, goals, and constraints and not just on clinical information.

We have considerable evidence on the relationship between the content of information offered to the patient, the setting, incentives for complying with recommendations, and outcomes. We have much less evidence on what type of evidence, persuasion, summarization, and simplification consumers would choose *a priori*. At present, clinicians sometimes fail to recommend the most appropriate care for their patients, and patients often fail to follow through on their recommendations. Bad advice should not be followed and good advice presented badly will not be followed, but what is the evidence on how to improve both the content of physician advice and patient adherence to it?

If a health system, insurer, or group of physicians uses incentives to encourage provision of services that would otherwise be done less frequently, and the outcome is forecasted to be better or cheaper, will a patient prefer that system to one that failed to use such approaches? Or would they prefer a system that just furnishes more information or more timely information? If there is some cost to "nudging" consumers – a higher premium to cover lower copayments for high-value medications, more payment for more time with your physician, or the cost of a "precommitment device" that helps people follow through on health goals, such as going to the gym or losing weight – will consumers value that? How much do patients want to be "nudged" by their clinician, and would they feel differently about similar interventions implemented by an employer or insurer? In this chapter we explore these questions through a few examples ranging from medication adherence to health behavior more broadly.

We also consider later in the chapter the extent to which patient preferences are taken into account in both the content of provider advice and final patterns of use of care. Sometimes patients and their advocates claim that the preferences of particular patients are often not taken into account by providers or even queried in advance of offering advice. Occasionally the disregard is thought to be systematic, but often it results from providers choosing recommendations appropriate for most patients but not necessarily the patient in front of them. Another quite different approach to patient preferences begins with insurance coverage that exposes patients to the true cost or price of their care with deductibles, and then imagines that the delivery system should respond to the consumer direction that follows from response to such incentives. Here as well providers may not always be able to provide the information that helps patients choose high value care and avoid low value care given preferences the patient may have for low cost and better or more convenient care.

REASONS FOR ADHERENCE AND NONADHERENCE

Since patient-consumers take the time and often pay out of pocket for physician advice, why do they then often fail to follow it? Part of the problem is that patient-consumers may sometimes present with a medical problem not by choice but out of necessity and once they feel better may not fully appreciate the need to continue a medication or other treatment. A physician may not fully understand a patient's preferences about side effects, cost, and the value of health. Even if clinical knowledge is perfect, a physician recommendation may not fit the preferences of a patient given at least a partial mismatch or incomplete information about that patient.

An example of an apparent breakdown in what medical science would recommend and what happens in practice is low medication adherence after a heart attack.

There is strong clinical evidence that medications typically prescribed after a heart attack are effective in preventing future adverse events – this is highly effective secondary prevention. However, more than half of patients do not take or continue to take medications that lower risk – typically statins, aspirin, beta blockers, or other medications such as a blood thinner or ACE-inhibitor in the year following a heart attack.[1] These drugs have each been shown in carefully done clinical trials to be effective in reducing bad outcomes. What is going on?

Any realist who has contemplated our imperfect human nature knows that many people (the observer usually included) do not consistently behave in ways others think to be rational. A challenging mix of forgetting, inattention, personal biases, emotions, and focus on immediate gratification as opposed to benefits that happen at some later point in time combine with relevant information, such as discomfort from or fear of side effects, to produce consumer decisions that are not always in concordance with what physicians think may be in their patients' best interest. In particular, individuals are known to have present-biased preferences, focusing to an extreme on the immediate costs and benefits of their actions and not the downstream risks.

For many behaviors where a patient takes a course that their clinician might not have recommended, such as continuing to smoke, the response we see in clinical practice is an effort to "try harder" and hope that further clinician efforts to admonish or encourage the patient will influence future behavior. One challenge for clinicians is that they often do not know if patients are following their recommendations. Other challenges include that patients may not have understood the advice they were given in the short face-to-face encounter they had with their harried physician. They may not have realized or had explained to them how important it is to take aspirin and statins. They may underweight the benefits to their future

---

[1] Choudhry N. K., Avorn J., Glynn, R. J. et al. (2011). Post-myocardial infarction free RX event and economic evaluation (MI-free) trial. Full coverage for preventive medications after myocardial infarction. *New England Journal of Medicine*, 365(22), 2088–2097. Available online at: https://doi.org/10.1056/NEJMsa1107913. Epub 2011 Nov 14. PMID: 22080794.

health, or they may attach low value to future health as opposed to exerting effort right now to give up something they enjoy, such as not exercising or smoking. The more sophisticated patients may feel that results from randomized trials done in largely white patient populations may not apply to them (and physicians may not have addressed this). These patients may have strong prior beliefs, or (based on past experience) may feel that physician-provided evidence was not a reliable predictor of what they subsequently experienced.

These calculations – or decisions made based on feelings as opposed to any deliberate cognitive process – made by the population of heart attack patients result in a willingness to take medications (expressed in terms of time or money) that may or may not correspond to what demand would be if patients fully understood the likely benefits of the medication. Demand would be expected to vary across patients by, for example, the severity of their heart attack (Acute Myocardial Infarction or AMI) or how well patients feel following the acute event. This "demand" curve plots the distribution of obstacles to adherence that could be overcome by some other approaches, either by presenting information in a different way or altering some other influence on drug use (like cost sharing or convenience).

Note that if a patient understands the health benefit from a medication and the medication is cost effective for that patient at the current drug price (meaning benefits are available at a reasonable cost), patients who have sufficient financial resources will adhere to the drug even without insurance. Benefits for these patients might be a significant reduction in the chance of a heart attack, stroke, or the need to be rehospitalized. Other perfectly informed patients who correctly perceive their benefit to be positive but small might not choose to purchase the drug unless insurance reduces the price. Others may have an inaccurate sense of the risks or benefits or might have negative feelings about taking daily medications and might thereby choose to not take the medication even though it would provide a reduction in risk at a reasonable cost.

Are there reasons why this population of patients would want their clinician, insurer, or employer to pay for interventions that lead them to be more adherent than what they would otherwise choose when left to their own devices? The answer is affirmative, for (at least) two reasons. The first is that on some level, individuals likely would want the risk of a significant illness lowered by others even if they themselves don't take all the actions they could to lower that risk. Secondly, if insurance covers all of the cost of a future adverse health event (revascularization or treatment of subsequent strokes or AMI), the person with such insurance will not benefit directly from the cost savings and likely would therefore prefer to have some upfront portion of the financial savings shared with them up front. This can be described as a "cost offset" whereby an insurance company saves money due to a reduction in future risk and health care costs because a patient adheres to a medication or engages in other activities that lower their health care risk. In such a scenario, economists would argue that cost sharing for a preventive activity should be reduced by at least that amount. Sometimes that amount is greater than the gross cost of the medication, so cost sharing should be negative and the medication should be offered with a copayment less than $0. This can also be thought of as a way to time cost or inattention cost.

There is another, potentially more useful way to look at the cost offset, however. Clearly, it would be desirable from the standpoint of both the consumer and society for the consumer to adhere to a medication if the cost of doing so is less than the cost offset. If some method other than lowering the copayment the consumer pays is more effective at increasing adherence (such as a system that increases convenience), it would make sense to support that intervention. In effect, the cost offset provides the resources to fund initiatives that facilitate getting patients to take their medications or engage in other risk-reducing activities, provided that doing so saves more than the cost of getting them to change behavior.

However, it is important to recognize that a preventive service whose usage creates a cost offset should be considered a special case. As long as the preventive services for a condition provide improvements in health at a reasonable cost – where reasonable is defined as a similar improvement in quality of life for the amount spent for treatments for the condition within the same health insurance plan – then these preventive services, including the extra efforts to support adherence, should be covered by insurance.[2] This general logic has supported the notion of "value-based insurance designs" (VBIDs), a term originally coined by Mark Fendrick, whereby health plans set patient cost sharing based on the value of the treatment being received and not simply as a function of the cost.[3] While such programs are conceptually appealing, lowering cost sharing even to zero

[2] Pryor, K., and Volpp, K. (2018). Deployment of preventive interventions – Time for a paradigm shift. *New England Journal of Medicine*, 378(19), 1761–1763. Available online at: https://doi.org/10.1056/NEJMp1716272. PMID: 29742382.

[3] Chernew, M. E., Rosen, A. B., and Fendrick, A. (2007). Value-based insurance design. *Health Affairs (Millwood)*, 26(2), w195–w203. Available online at: https://doi.org/10.1377/hlthaff.26.2.w195. Epub 2007 Jan 30. PMID: 17264100.

typically has increased adherence to medications by only 3–6 percentage points, so while helpful in improving uptake of evidence-based clinical recommendations, this has not been a panacea.[4]

Suppose we use lower cost sharing or employ other strategies to get people to use cost-effective drugs. Might some still fail to do so because of misinformation, inattention, or some decision bias? For example, let's take the case of people who have strong present-biased preferences. These people may fail to realize links between present and future or intend to change their behavior "later." Let's say hypothetically they view the non-monetary and monetary cost of taking the medication as negative $5 and the benefit of taking the medication as $8 but, since the benefit is in the future, they discount it by 50 percent. Adding −5 plus 0.5*8 = −1, and the rational decision maker would thereby decide not to purchase the medication today. However, in thinking about the future, the decision maker would discount both costs and benefits. In this case, let's assume that both costs and benefits are discounted by 50 percent, since ½ (−5 + 8) = +1.5 and this is greater than zero. In other words, buying the medication next week looks like a logical thing to do if the decision maker discounts the cost one year from now at the same rate as the benefits many years after that. Of course, next week and the week after that, the same calculations will hold true. The decision-maker will be confused about what is cost effective – and so will outside experts.

If people are sophisticated and know their tendency to procrastinate and prefer the outcome that would happen if they took the medication, they may be willing to pay for a program that gets them to do what their future self would have liked them to have done. Examples of this might include pre-committing by signing up for an automatic refill program that sends the medication to them every 90 days – without having to deliberate each time whether it is worth it. Or, they could sign up for a monitoring device that reports their adherence to their spouse or their clinician. On the other hand, people may regard a decision to not be fully adherent as optimal for them (given the information they have). Then they will not prefer a plan that uses different strategies that induce them to do what they "should" – unless they can be offered evidence that people like them who sign on to

---

[4] Choudhry N. K., Avorn J., Glynn, R. J. et al. (2011). Post-myocardial infarction free RX event and economic evaluation (MI-free) trial. Full coverage for preventive medications after myocardial infarction. *New England Journal of Medicine*, 365(22), 2088–2097. Available online at: https://doi.org/10.1056/NEJMsa1107913. Epub 2011 Nov 14. PMID: 22080794.

such a plan actually end up better off. Economists would define this by saying the individual would have additional quality-adjusted life years that more than offset any higher premium.

In the case of drugs after a heart attack, there was a well-designed randomized controlled trial that tested the VBID concept by randomly assigning insured people hospitalized with AMI to zero copayment versus usual coverage (about $12–24 per month) for statins and blood pressure drugs. There was a small but significant difference in adherence – 44 percent with free drugs to 39 percent with cost sharing – but this small difference in adherence had enough of a cost offset that total costs were unchanged – the drugs paid for themselves.[5] This study has led some insurers and employers to lower cost sharing. Of course, most treatments have positive incremental costs even with cost offsets, but this turned out to be an obvious win. A rational insured would not have imposed cost sharing in the first place on treatments that would be expected to pay for themselves for everyone who would use them.

But would this change be advantageous to all workers who had AMIs? Would they choose the insurance that charged $0 for these medications but charged higher premiums or the plan with a lower premium that charged standard copayments? We could imagine that those who would have been adherent with cost sharing would prefer free care. They would have more financial protection, and those enticed to take drugs would have lower expected cost. Still, the 56 percent who would remain nonadherent might be a harder sell – they would be paying a little more for coverage they would not use and might not seem to be convinced of the value of that coverage. However, it is likely that many of them are not aware of the details of what their insurance plan covers given widespread lack of understanding of plan design and the complexity of many health plans.[6] More generally, using cost sharing to bribe patients to be nonadherent to their physicians' prescriptions seems like a dubious idea– unless physicians write many prescriptions for drugs of low or no value.

This example deals with a case where the clinical evidence for a benefit from following physician advice is known by all physicians to be positive and large on average. There are other treatments where a provider consensus on treatment has not been established, what Wennberg has called the

---

[5] Ibid.

[6] Loewenstein, G., Friedman, J. Y., McGill, B. et al. (2013). Consumers' misunderstanding of health insurance. *Journal of Health Economics*, 32(5), 850–862. Available online at: https://doi.org/10.1016/j.jhealeco.2013.04.004. Epub 2013 Jun 26. PMID: 23872676.

"gray area" in treatments, with much more variability in what physicians offer.[7] In this case, patient adherence will (and probably should) be far below 100 percent. Arguably, efforts to improve adherence should focus on the clinical contexts in which the benefit is large and reasonably certain.

NUDGING AND LIBERTARIAN PATERNALISM

In real-world settings, will consumers be willing to pay for the cost of programs that encourage them to do things they "should" do but probably wouldn't do on their own? In some cases, people will pay for precommitment– paying a health club fee in advance knowing you will not be likely to force yourself to use it enough to make your money back is a well-documented phenomenon. But often they will not– voluntary behavioral modification can be a hard sell.

Another approach is for employers or insurers to decide to roll out interventions intended to influence decisions in favor of healthier alternatives without limiting freedom of choice. This approach is called "libertarian paternalism" or alternatively "asymmetric paternalism" by behavioral economists.[8] The idea is to influence the behavior of those who make suboptimal choices and do not have strong preferences without affecting the decisions of those who make informed and deliberate decisions. For example, an employer can have a cafeteria that gives the healthy foods "prime position" in the cafeteria and move vending machines to less convenient locations, or forbid smoking on the employee campus forcing those who want to smoke to take a long walk first. Rather than hiding stairs behind heavy doors and cinderblocks and having gleaming elevator banks in the main lobby, an employer may put beautiful stairs in the main lobby and make the elevators less convenient. Stronger versions of this might include not serving unhealthy foods in the cafeteria at all or banning vending machines altogether (i.e., if you want the unhealthy food you have the choice of bringing it in from home or going to an outside venue to get it). Such approaches may be popular or unpopular depending on the nature

---

[7] Wennberg J., and Gittelsohn, A. (1973). Small area variations in health care delivery. *Science*, 182(4117), 1102–1108.

[8] Thaler, R. H., and Sunstein, C. R. (2008). *Nudge: Improving Decisions about Health, Wealth, and Happiness*. New York: Penguin Books; Brennan, T., Loewenstein, G., and Volpp, K. G. (2007). Asymmetric paternalism to improve health behaviors. *JAMA*, 298 (20), 2415–2417. Available online: https://doi.org/10.1001/jama.298.20.2415. PMID: 18042920.

of the employee population and the social norms that are germane to that population.

Social norms may also evolve in ways that make such approaches more palatable over time. It is now difficult to imagine *not* having a ban on smoking on airlines or in public buildings, given the health costs to nonsmokers of having to breathe in second-hand smoke, but at one time such bans were seen as highly controversial infringements on individual freedom. Healthy food choices in employee cafeterias are likely to be popular in environments where workers are choosing to buy those types of foods at home and less so in environments where the menu does not reflect the existing preferences of the workforce. An interesting question is whether social norms can be positively influenced through the actions of a well-intentioned employer concerned about future health care costs who shapes the environment in which individuals make choices to favor healthier choices. Behavioral economists would refer to this person as the "choice architect."

Many individuals say they want to engage in health-promoting activities that benefit their future selves but have trouble following through. Think of the ubiquitous New Year's resolutions that become challenging for many to adhere to by February or March. Some people precommit to gym memberships, and still do not show up despite a zero user cost. There are many factors that conspire to make it challenging for us to achieve our most favorite version of our future self: limited information, emotional influences, bandwidth considerations, undue influence from fast-food purveyors or other commercial entities who use our behavioral biases against us, present-biased preferences. We are influenced by the environments in which we live, which may or may not favor healthy behaviors. Time-inconsistent preferences are a big challenge: a smoker after being hospitalized with a bad bout of emphysema will swear never to smoke again; the same person withdrawing from nicotine will want nothing more than to have another cigarette right now and start smoking again. "Hot" and "cold" states are an example of this, whereby someone will make one set of choices when under the influence of mind-altering substances or with a delicious (and unhealthy) meal placed right in front of them when hungry, in contrast to the choices the rational future-oriented decision maker would make when sober or satiated.[9] These time-inconsistent preferences

---

[9] Loewenstein, G. (2005). Hot-cold empathy gaps and medical decision making. *Health Psychology*, 24(4S), S49–56. Available online at: https://doi.org/10.1037/0278-6133.24.4 .S49. PMID: 16045419.

have given rise to the notion of internalities – where in contrast to externalities where my actions have implications for others, my short-run actions are suboptimal from my own long-run perspective.[10] In other words, I am not fully taking account of the consequences of my actions on my future self.

Another challenge is that individuals tend to be motivated by actions that produce measurable, tangible benefits to a greater degree than by actions that do not produce tangible progress toward a goal. Factors working against adherence, such as time or monetary costs, are tangible, whereas benefits such as a reduction in long-term risk of an adverse outcome are intangible and often delayed. Poor adherence to treatments for disorders such as hypertension and hyperlipidemia, which show no tangible manifestation (i.e., are usually asymptomatic), are partly explained by this phenomenon.[11]

Let's examine some of the evidence on what has worked in terms of changing behavior to appropriately favor future health and wellbeing. One approach that has not worked is simply providing information about benefits. Lots of studies have documented this. The Centers for Disease Control and Prevention (CDC) for years has relied on providing information to clinicians and patients about the lack of utility in prescribing antibiotics for upper respiratory infections, most of which are caused by viruses and thereby unaffected by antibiotics. Nonetheless, antibiotic prescribing rates have remained stubbornly high and haven't changed much over time.[12] Adding recommended calorie intake per day or per meal to mandated calorie information posted on chain restaurant menus has had limited impact on caloric intake.[13] Providing information about the

[10] Herrnstein, R. J., Loewenstein, G. F., Prelec, D. et al. (1993). Utility maximization and melioration: Internalities in individual choice. *Journal of Behavioral Decision Making*, 6 (3), 149–185. Available online at: https://doi.org/10.1002/bdm.3960060302.

[11] Brennan, T., Loewenstein, G., and Volpp, K. G. (2007). Asymmetric paternalism to improve health behaviors. *JAMA*, 298(20), 2415–2417. Available online: https://doi.org/10.1001/jama.298.20.2415. PMID: 18042920.

[12] Barnett, M. L., and Linder, J. A. (2013). Antibiotic prescribing to adults with sore throat in the United States, 1997–2010. *JAMA Intern Medicine*, 174(1), 138–140. Available online at: https://doi.org/10.1001/jamainternmed.2013.11673; Fairlie, T., Shapiro, D. J., Hersh, A. L. et al. (2012). National trends in visit rates and antibiotic prescribing for adults with acute sinusitis. *The Archives of Internal Medicine*, 172(19), 1513–1514.

[13] Downs, J. S., Wisdom, J., Wansink, B. et al. (2013). Supplementing menu labeling with calorie recommendations to test for facilitation effects. *American Journal of Public Health*, 103(9), 1604–1609. Available online at: https://doi.org/10.2105/AJPH.2013 .301218. Epub 2013 Jul 18. PMID: 23865657; PMCID: PMC3780676.

benefits of exercise does not lead college students to go to the gym more often, but paying them to show up does.[14] Manipulations of the choice environment are probably the easiest way to influence behavior in sustainable ways. The more binding the constraint, the bigger the impact, but this may engender complaints about overreaching paternalism. For example, serving only healthy food in a cafeteria could lead to complaints that this is unfair to those who prefer burgers and fries. Keeping the same menu but putting an attractive salad bar in the prime position in the front of the cafeteria and having the burgers and fries available but relegated to the back corner is less likely to engender a backlash. This is an example of asymmetric paternalism whereby individuals who are prone to making suboptimal choices are helped while not affecting those who make informed and deliberate decisions. This is different from heavy-handed paternalism in that freedom of choice is preserved and focuses on protecting me from the consequences of my own actions as opposed to preventing individuals from adversely affecting others.[15]

There are many such examples of asymmetric paternalistic interventions. Listing healthy alternatives first on a menu (as opposed to in random order) has a significant impact on the proportion of healthy alternatives chosen.[16] Rather than relying on willpower, a depletable resource, schools can ban or make products such as soda and candy less accessible. Not allowing smoking on campus serves as a default of sorts whereby smoking is still possible, but it requires extra effort to go smoke. Providing 90-day instead of 30-day refills and letting people opt out if they prefer 30-day refills would be an example related to medication adherence.

Recent work has highlighted that "cognitive load" often leads to suboptimal decision-making. This is particularly a challenge for people who are grappling with many challenges and/or who have fewer resources to draw on.[17] Patients with multiple chronic diseases can benefit greatly from systems that make it easier for them to stay adherent to treatment. For

[14] Charness, G., and Gneezy, U. (2009). Incentives to exercise. *Econometrica*, 77, 909–931. Available online at: https://doi.org/10.3982/ECTA7416

[15] Loewenstein, G., Brennan, T. A., and Volpp, K. G. (2007). Asymmetric paternalism to improve health behaviors. *JAMA*, 298(20), 2415–2417.

[16] Wisdom, J., Downs, J. S., and Loewenstein, G. (2010). Promoting healthy choices: Information versus convenience. *American Economic Journal: Applied Economics*, 2(2), 164–178. Available online at: https://doi.org/10.1257/app.2.2.164.

[17] Mullainathan, S., and Shafir, E. (2013). *Scarcity: Why Having Too Little Means So Much.* Times Books/Henry Holt and Co.

example, imagine a patient who is on 10–12 medications that all have different refill dates. Keeping track of which is due and when is a complex organizational task. Synchronizing refills whereby all prescriptions are refilled on the same date dramatically simplifies this and results in adherence improving by roughly 10–21 percentage points for less adherent patients.[18] Another example of an approach that can make adherence easier for patients is automatic refills for medications for chronic conditions. Making more salient to patients the convenience of automatic refills through an "enhanced active choice" manipulation doubled the rate at which CVS pharmacy customers enrolled in an automatic refill program.[19]

Health plan choice itself can be a context that is rife with "choice overload" whereby individuals are exposed to far too many choices and that leads to suboptimal decisions. Recent work by Bhargava, Loewenstein, and Sydnor illustrated this at a large US firm in which 61 percent of employees chose plans that were dominated by other health plans, meaning that they chose plans that were more expensive than other plans regardless of how much care the employee required. This resulted in excess spending equivalent to 24 percent of chosen plan premiums. Low-income employees were significantly more likely to choose dominated plans. This finding highlights that, in contrast to a frictionless benchmark model of consumer demand, the complexity of the plan might cause individuals to choose suboptimally due to an inability to accurately evaluate and compare plans.[20] However, in other settings, individuals who choose high deductible health plans are feared to do so in error, while in still other situations they engage in adverse selection in which they select the plans most advantageous to their risk situation.

ENCOURAGING HEALTHY BEHAVIORS THROUGH PRECOMMITMENT STRATEGIES

Underinvestment in activities that promote future wellbeing – when people may fail to realize links between present and future or intend to change behavior "later" – is a common phenomenon. As we described earlier, a

[18] Doshi, J. A., State, J., Lawnicki, V. et al. (2016). A synchronized prescription refill program improved medication adherence. *Health Affairs (Millwood)*, 35(8), 1504–1512.

[19] Keller, P., Harlam, B. A., Loewenstein, G. et al. (2011). Enhanced active choice: A new method to motivate behavior change. *Journal of Consumer Psychology*, 21, 376–383.

[20] Bhargava, S., Loewenstein, G., and Sydnor, J. (2017). Choose to lose: Health plan choices from a menu with dominated option. *The Quarterly Journal of Economics*, 132(3), 1319–1372. Available online at: https://doi.org/10.1093/qje/qjx011

smoker who faces an upfront cost in terms of effort to quit/withdrawal symptoms and health benefits in the future, which are heavily discounted, will often decide repeatedly to quit next week (when both costs and benefits are discounted). Behavioral economists will often describe this battle between the "myopic doer" and the "far-sighted planner" as a battle between the two selves[21] – the same individual will set the alarm to go to the gym early in the morning and then hit the snooze button repeatedly the next morning. This is often described as a self-control problem and various strategies have emerged that individuals have adopted to combat that.

Let's look at a few of these and see what we can infer in terms of demand for "self-control" devices often via "precommitment" whereby individuals are voluntarily constraining their future choices on behalf of their future self. A popular one is buying an annual membership in a health club, whereby a flat monthly fee leads to paying more than if individuals were to pay a per-visit fee. Individuals are presumably doing this to make the cost of going to the gym each time zero and to increase the likelihood they would do so. The seminal work by DellaVigna and Malmendier on this found that gym members who chose contracts with a flat monthly fee of over $70 attended on average 4.3 times per month paying a price per visit of more than $17, even though they could have paid $10 per visit using a 10-visit pass.[22] Interestingly, those consumers who chose a monthly contract were 18 percent more likely to stay enrolled beyond one year than users committing for a year despite higher cancellation fees. This suggests overconfidence in future attendance as well as a desire to be "bound to the mast" by a future contract.

The notion of literally being bound to a mast – and having one's future choices thereby constrained – stems from the story of Ulysses and the Sirens, where Ulysses wanted to hear the beautiful sound of the Sirens' voices but knew that anyone who did would jump into the water and drown. He had his men bind him to the mast and stuff their own ears with wax, and forbade them from following any orders he might give while he was listening to the Sirens on penalty of death. The notion of encouraging "precommitment" has gotten considerable traction from behavioral economic researchers who have seen potential application to health behavior with ideas ranging from simply making an appointment with a friend to go

---

[21] Thaler, R. H., and Shefrin, H. M. (1981). An economic theory of self-control. *The Journal of Political Economy*, 89, 392–406. Available online at: https://doi.org/10.1086/260971.

[22] DellaVigna, S., and Malmendier, U. (2006). Paying not to go to the gym. *American Economic Review*, 96(3), 694–719.

to the gym (since you are less likely to cancel on your friend than simply decide not to go if going by yourself) to financial "deposit contracts" whereby individuals put their own money at risk and forfeit it if they do not follow through.[23] Once an individual (who is sophisticated enough to recognize their own proclivities and wants their future self to have choices constrained) commits funds to such a program via a deposit contract, their motivation is augmented by loss aversion, as individuals experience much greater disutility from losing money than the utility of winning a similar amount of money by a ratio of about 2:1.[24]

What sort of demand do we see for these deposit contracts – and how effective are they for the individuals who chose to participate? A series of studies indicates that uptake rates tend to be low but that individuals who choose to participate are quite successful in achieving their goals. One of the earliest studies of this was by Gine, Karlan, and Zinman among smokers in the Philippines, in which smokers were randomly assigned to be offered an opportunity to put their own money into an account that they could not withdraw from for 6 months.[25] If they tested negative for smoking after 6 months, they would receive the money back (without interest). If unsuccessful in quitting, the money would be donated to charity. In standard economic thinking, it would make no sense for anybody to do this. Nonetheless, 11% of eligible smokers agreed and committed on average roughly 3% of their monthly incomes over 6 months. Among all those *offered* the chance to participate (not just those who chose to participate) biochemically confirmed smoking cessation rates were impressively about 35% higher at 12 months. Among employees of a US health insurance company, an offer to have the opportunity to put one's own money at risk based on future weight loss, with that money either unmatched, matched 1:1, or matched 2:1 by the study, 29% made one or more deposits, but greater matching did not increase participation.[26]

[23] Rogers, T., Milkman, K. L., and Volpp, K. G. (2014). Commitment devices: Using initiatives to change behavior. *JAMA*, 28(311), 2065–2066.
[24] Kahneman, D., and Tversky, A. (1979). Prospect theory: An analysis of decision under risk. *Econometrica*, 47(2), 263–291.
[25] Gine, X., Karlan, D., and Zinman, J. (2010). Put your money where your butt is: A commitment contract for smoking cessation. *American Economic Journal: Applied Economics*, 2(4), 213–235.
[26] Kullgren, J. T., Troxel, A. B., Loewenstein, G. et al. (2016). A randomized controlled trial of employer matching of employees' monetary contributions to deposit contracts to promote weight loss. *American Journal of Health Promotion*, 30(6), 441–451.

To further assess the role of self-funded commitment contracts in improving the long-run effects of an exercise program on behavior, 1000 employees at a Fortune 500 company were offered a one-month financial incentive to attend an onsite exercise facility at $10 per visit for up to 3 visits per week. After completion of this one-month incentive period, half of the group was randomly selected to be offered an opportunity to create a self-funded commitment contract whereby employees would keep the money if they continued to use the gym, but if not money was donated to charity: 12% elected to create a commitment contract. The participation rate among those who had attended the gym at least once was 22%. This resulted in a doubling of gym attendance relative to a control group with roughly a 20% increase in gym attendance even 2–3 years after conclusion of the intervention.[27]

Among smokers employed by CVS offered the opportunity to put $150 of their money in a deposit contract (matched with $650), 13.9% agreed to participate. Quit rates in this group were remarkably high (52%) but given that only 13.9% agreed to participate, the overall quit rate was lower than in another arm of the study that was simply offered a gain-based incentive.[28] Nonetheless, CVS was intrigued by the 52% figure and decided to offer all employees a new program, "700 Good Reasons to Quit," in which employees who deposited $50 were offered a 14:1 match, all of which was then at risk if employees were not successful in quitting smoking.

Various programs have been developed that use nonfinancial incentives to encourage people to "help their future selves." Temptation bundling is a way of combining "wants" and "shoulds" whereby people in essence precommit to, for example, only watching TV or listening to page-turner novels while they exercise. After one study that tested this version of temptation bundling, 64 percent of the college students who participated indicated interest in this incentive: they said they would be willing to pay to have gym-only access to their preferred entertainment, indicating some demand for this commitment device.[29]

[27] Royer, H., Stehr, M. F., and Sydnor, J. R. (2015). Incentives, commitments, and habit formation in exercise: Evidence from a field experiment with workers at a Fortune 500 company. *American Economic Journal: Applied Economics*, 7(3), 51–84.

[28] Halpern, S. D., French, B., Small, D. S. et al. (2015). Randomized trial of four financial-incentive programs for smoking cessation. *New England Journal of Medicine*, 372(22), 210892117. Available online at: https://doi.org/10.1056/NEJMoa1414293.

[29] Milkman, K., Minson, J., and Volpp, K. G. (2013). Holding the hunger games hostage at the gym: An evaluation of temptation bundling. *Management Science*, 60(2), 283–299.

In the market, such devices have yet to get traction in this exact form. Stickk.com is a company founded by Yale professors that uses the concept of voluntary participation in deposit/commitment contracts. Deposited money is forfeited if one does not achieve a goal and is donated to either a charity or "anti-charity" (for example, money from a gun-safety advocate will be donated to the National Rifle Association). The company got some traction for a few years but has yet to emerge as a major force in the market. However, one might think of gym memberships and the payment in advance for a year as a good example of how individuals will often purchase products intended to help their future selves live healthier lives even if it is likely that these programs will be costly on average relative to a "pay as you go" alternative.

TAXES, SUBSIDIES, AND OTHER STRATEGIES TO INFLUENCE HEALTH BEHAVIOR

Taxes on cigarettes are widely credited with being arguably the single most effective approach to changing the incentives for smokers or would-be smokers. Taxes reduce the prevalence of smoking and, perhaps more importantly, deter young people, who have less discretionary income, from starting smoking.[30] There has been an increase over time in popular demand for increased taxes on cigarettes, and due to time-inconsistent preferences, evidence suggests that smokers themselves are actually happier about increases in cigarette taxes because they provide a valuable self-control device.[31] There is starting to be similar evidence that taxes on sugary beverages are reducing demand for sugary beverages, as a recent study showed a 38 percent decrease in sugary beverage consumption with a tax of about 1.5 cents per ounce.[32]

Another approach to influence healthy behavior is to subsidize the purchase of health-promoting goods. In a recent experiment supported

---

[30] Chaloupka, F. J., Yurekli, A., and Fong, G. T. (2012). Tobacco taxes as a tobacco control strategy. *Tobacco Control*, 21(2), 172–180. Available online at: https://doi.org/10.1136/tobaccocontrol-2011-050417. Erratum in: *Tobacco Control*. 2012 (3):329. PMID: 22345242.

[31] Gruber, J., and Mullainathan, S. (2002). Do cigarette taxes make smokers happier? NBER Working Paper No. 8872, April.

[32] Roberto, C. A., Lawman, H. G. LeVasseur, M. T. et al. (2019). Association of a beverage tax on sugar-sweetened and artificially sweetened beverages with changes in beverage prices and sales at chain retailers in a large urban setting. *JAMA*, 321(18), 1799–1810. Available online at: https://doi.org/10.1001/jama.2019.4249. PMID: 32930704.

by Weight Watchers (now WW), employees at two large firms were randomly offered the opportunity to enroll in WW with subsidies of 50%, 80%, or 100%, or a 50% subsidy that would turn into a 100% subsidy if they met prespecified levels of ongoing engagement. After randomizing more than 23,000 employees, the study found that enrollment, as expected, went up with the degree of the subsidy from a low of 3.8% in the 50% subsidy group to 6.2% in the 80% subsidy group to 7.7% in the 100% subsidy group. The surprise was that enrollment was no higher in the 50% group with potential to earn 100% than in the 50% subsidy group, perhaps because individuals did not think they were likely to meet the enrollment goals or because (despite the team's best efforts) the incentive wasn't explained clearly enough for people to understand. It was anticipated that there might be a tradeoff between rates of enrollment and average success since less motivated people (on average) might enroll with higher subsidies. However, ongoing engagement and average weight loss were similar across all groups. In essence, about 90% of individuals had stopped going regularly by 12 months and average weight loss was close to 0 pounds across all groups, highlighting the challenge of helping people to successfully lose weight.[33] More broadly, this randomized trial indicates that higher enrollment will result from greater subsidies, but this will not necessarily translate into greater health improvement.

A variety of other approaches are emerging as potential tools in encouraging patient engagement. Reese et al. created a "social accountability mechanism" whereby patients who had had transplants received electronic pill monitors that recorded daily opening of their prescribed medication that was reported to their transplant physician's team. This resulted in a 33 percentage point increase in recorded adherence.[34] The blood levels of tacrolimus (the immunosuppressant prescribed after the transplant), however, did not fully correspond with the observed increase in adherence, suggesting that some of the large difference in adherence was due to lower adherence in the control group and not higher in the intervention group. While simple reminder systems for medication adherence generally have

[33] John, L. K., Troxel, A. B., Yancy, W. S. Jr et al. (2018). The effect of cost sharing on an employee weight loss program: A randomized trial. *American Journal of Health Promotion*, 32(1), 170–176. Available online at: https://doi.org/10.1177/0890117116671282. Epub 2016 Oct 21. PMID: 29277125.

[34] Reese, P. P., Bloom, R. D., Trofe-Clark, J. et al. (2017). Automated reminders and physician notification to promote immunosuppression adherence among kidney transplant recipients: A randomized trial. *American Journal of Kidney Disease*, 69(3), 400–409. Available online at: https://doi.org/10.1053/j.ajkd.2016.10.017. Epub 2016 Dec 7. PMID: 27940063.

not been effective at increasing adherence,[35] "smart" reminders that are triggered by nonadherence seem to have some impact in improving medication adherence.[36] Another approach with promise is the use of gamification. In the first intervention study done in the Framingham population, a multi-decade longitudinal study of individuals and families to examine risk factors for cardiovascular disease, a team of investigators used behavioral economic principles, such as loss aversion (greater disutility of losing points or status), reference points (starting with a mid-level of status that people would not want to lose), goal gradients (easy to attain goals), and the use of social incentives (desire not to let others down) in creating a family-team approach to increasing exercise. The family team would start out with a moderate amount of 'status' that would be reduced if individual members of each team – chosen at random each day – were not successful at meeting their exercise goals. If family members did meet their exercise goals, they would accrue points and status over time would increase. This approach – with a grand prize for achieving the highest levels of status of a coffee mug – was successful at increasing the percentage of individuals meeting their physical exercise goals from 32 percent of the goal in the control group to 53 percent in the intervention group over 12 weeks and is now being tested in a longer-term US National Institutes of Health-funded trial.[37]

USE OF WELLNESS PROGRAMS AND PERSISTENCE OF BEHAVIORAL CHANGE INTERVENTIONS

The evidence is strong that a number of behavioral approaches can be used to alter consumer or worker behavior to improve health. Financial benefits such as savings in health expenditures are more elusive, more modest when

[35] Choudhry, N. K., Krumme, A. A., Ercole, P. M. et al. (2017). Effect of reminder devices on medication adherence: The remind randomized clinical trial. *JAMA Internal Medicine*, 177(5), 624–631. Available online at: https://doi.org/10.1001/jamainternmed.2016.9627. PMID: 28241271; PMCID: PMC5470369.

[36] Kessler, J. B., Troxel, A. B., Asch, D. A. et al. (2018). Partners and alerts in medication adherence: A randomized clinical trial. *Journal of General Internal Medicine*, 33(9), 1536–1542. Available online at: https://doi.org/10.1007/s11606-018-4389-7. Epub 2018 Mar 15. PMID: 29546659; PMCID: PMC6109000.

[37] Patel, M. S., Benjamin, E. J., Volpp, K. G. et al. (2017). Effect of a game-based intervention designed to enhance social incentives to increase physical activity among families: The be fit randomized clinical trial. *JAMA Internal Medicine*, 177(11), 1586–1593. Available online: https://doi.org/10.1001/jamainternmed.2017.3458. PMID: 28973115; PMCID: PMC5710273.

they occur, and less certain – but usually medical costs are not increased. Have managers of health systems, health insurers, and employers been convinced to use this evidence?

The answer is mixed. Probably the easiest trend to identify has been the use of wellness programs by insurers, employers, or the two entities together. There has been less utilization of such programs by health systems except in situations in which the health system is paid through capitation, meaning that they get a fixed amount of money per patient per year. However, there is not much evidence that such programs have either improved health or lowered spending by enough for these effects to show up in the aggregated data we reviewed in Chapter 2. Indeed, there have been some fierce critics of wellness programs in general, some examples of serious employee resistance, and concerns raised about whether such programs are worth the cost.[38]

These concerns are in stark contrast to earlier work that claimed that on average, wellness programs return $3.27 for every $1 spent.[39] However, one must recognize the potential bias inherent in such evaluations: only a subset of programs are evaluated, those that are successful are probably more likely to be evaluated, and only the most successful will likely have an economic analysis conducted. Many of the wellness programs that are implemented nationally have not been evidence-based and have been marketed in ways that overstate their likely impact, creating a mismatch between expectations and likely performance. It appears that, while there have been programs such as those discussed here that have been effective based on rigorous evidence, the presence in the market of other inferior or poorly supported programs has made managers considering them feel wary. There has been little systematic effort to separate the effective programs from ineffective programs and to assess whether observed savings are due to true improvements relative to a reasonable comparison group as opposed to "regression to the mean" in which observed reductions in cost may simply be due to individuals picked because they were high cost reverting back to something closer to average in a subsequent time period.

---

[38] Lewis, A. (2019). It's time to believe the research: Wellness isn't working. *Employee Benefit News*, May 2. Available online at: www.benefitnews.com/opinion/time-to-believe-why-wellness-isnt-lowering-healthcare-costs.

[39] Baicker, K., Cutler, D., and Song, Z. (2010). Workplace wellness programs can generate savings. *Health Affairs (Millwood)*, 29(2), 304–311. Available online at: https://doi.org/10.1377/hlthaff.2009.0626. Epub 2010 Jan 14. PMID: 20075081.

Beyond confusion about effectiveness and cost effectiveness, there has also been ambiguity about how improving the health of some populations is of value to employers or insurers. Savings on the costs of benefits are more tangible, but returns from improved health may not manifest quickly, and breakthroughs with impressive and consistent returns on investment have been rare. Both employers and insurers would clearly prefer that their populations be healthier, but converting this dimension of quality into higher revenues has been elusive. Employers have expressed concern about poor employee health cutting into profits by increasing sick leave costs and reducing on the job productivity. But the absence of a direct observable link between wellness programs and improvements in worker health and productivity in the near term makes this linkage somewhat tenuous.

There have been a number of large randomized controlled trials that demonstrate roughly a tripling of smoking cessation rates using financial incentives, including those done by our group at large employers, such as General Electric, CVS, and clients of the Vitality Group.[40] In a review of 33 randomized trials, the Cochrane Collaborative, an independent international organization that promotes evidence-based health information, concludes: "The pooled [relative risk] for quitting with incentives at longest follow-up (six months or more) compared with controls was 1.49 (95 percent CI 1.28 to 1.73; 31 RCTs, adjusted N = 20,097). Results were not sensitive to the exclusion of six studies where an incentive for cessation was offered at long-term follow up (result excluding those studies: [relative risk] 1.40, 95 percent CI 1.16 to 1.69; 25 RCTs; adjusted N = 17,058, suggesting the impact of incentives continues for at least some time after incentives cease."[41]

---

[40] Volpp, K. G., Troxel, A. B., Pauly, M. V. et al. (2009). A randomized, controlled trial of financial incentives for smoking cessation. *New England Journal of Medicine*, 360(7), 699–709. Available online at: https://doi.org/10.1056/NEJMsa0806819. PMID: 19213683; Halpern, S. D., French, B., Small, D. S. et al. (2015). Randomized trial of four financial-incentive programs for smoking cessation. *New England Journal of Medicine*, 372(22), 210892117. Available online at: https://doi.org/10.1056/NEJMoa1414293; Halpern, S. D., Harhay, M. O., Saulsgiver, K. et al. (2018). A pragmatic trial of e-cigarettes, incentives, and drugs for smoking cessation. *New England Journal of Medicine*, 378(24), 2302–2310. Available online at: https://doi.org/10.1056/NEJMsa1715757. Epub 2018 May 23. PMID: 29791259.

[41] Notley, C., Gentry, S., Livingstone-Banks, J. et al. (2019). Incentives for smoking cessation. Cochrane Database of Systematic Reviews 7(7), CD004307. Available online at: https://doi .org/10.1002/14651858.CD004307.pub6. PMID: 31313293; PMCID: PMC6635501.

Approximately 44 percent of US employers include either rewards for not smoking or surcharges for smoking as part of benefit designs, with penalties averaging $600 per year.[42] While rewards may seem conceptually more appealing, implementing smoking cessation programs that involve penalties may be seen by the majority of employees who are lifelong nonsmokers or ex-smokers as more palatable.[43] Outside of tobacco, employers generally prefer rewards to penalties, with approximately 56 percent of employers offering rewards averaging $304 for participation in a variety of wellness activities.[44] While the proportion of employers choosing to use incentives and the amounts being used for financial incentives for smoking cessation and wellness activities seem similar, many employers appear to believe that smoking cessation incentives are effective in making smokers cover the higher cost of their coverage. In contrast, wellness incentives are increasingly seen as a perk that employers desire, with a less clear direct relationship to the cost of employee benefits and health outcomes.

PATIENT-CENTERED CARE

Another theme in reviewing the relationship between consumer welfare and demands and providers has challenged the provider-directed model of care. That theme emphasizes the priority of patient or consumer desires and outcomes over what providers think is best. It strongly rejects paternalism as a legitimate organizing principle for the provider-patient relationship, as the preferences of the patient should be heavily weighted in any decisions about diagnosis, treatment, or behavior. Often patient determined choices are made in insured settings where the patient does not pay the cost of a choice at the point of use. In such cases, those choices might well be constrained by insurance plan restrictions. It is an open question whether patient desires or rights should override such limits especially if the patient chose the insurance (pre-committed to restriction) beforehand.

---

[42] Dunning, M. (2015). Employers move to keep profit from going up in smoke. *Business Insurance*. Available online at: www.businessinsurance.com/article/20150628/NEWS03/150629867?template=printart

[43] Volpp, K. G., and Galvin, R. (2014). Reward-based incentives for smoking cessation: How a carrot became a stick. *JAMA*, 311(9), 909–910. Available online at: https://doi.org/10.1001/jama.2014.418. PMID: 24493405; PMCID: PMC6083832.

[44] Willis Towers Watson 23rd Annual Best Practices In Health Care Employer Survey. Available online at: www.willistowerswatson23rdannual.com

Libertarian paternalism, in preserving freedom of choice, could be seen as compatible with this world view, depending on the degree to which the "choice architect" is seen as allowing freedom of choices that reflect the preferences of those being nudged and the degree to which those whose choices are influenced accept that influence.

The guiding principle of asymmetric or libertarian paternalism in this context is that policies and programs should be structured to maximize the likelihood that individuals will engage in behaviors that will promote their own future health. It should be possible to do this in such a way that those who might otherwise engage in unhealthy behaviors will be better off without affecting freedom of choice for those with strong preferences. Increasingly, we are seeing lots of efforts to apply libertarian paternalism in settings ranging from the layout of cafeterias to health plan or provider choice. People's feelings about these efforts may largely depend on the "choice architect:" Is it my doctor who I implicitly trust to help me improve my future wellbeing? Is it my employer? Is it my health plan? What are their motives, and do their motivations line up with what I would want for myself?

Another dimension to consider is how strongly people are being "nudged." Nudges are typically defined as not including strong monetary incentives, so it is important to be clear that strong financial incentives are a more aggressive way of influencing choices than the typical nudge. However, as the costs of health care continue to increase to the extent that employers and health plans think that health behaviors contribute to those costs, we may see an ongoing increase in efforts to both nudge and strongly incentivize people to make healthier choices. The key issues, then, will be whether healthier choices save money on future costs of care and whether the returns from such savings are realized quickly enough to reduce the premium charged to those whose behavior is being changed – and whether they can be induced to see the connection between the two.

Although physicians are obviously concerned about their patients, the emphasis on and movement toward "patient-centered care" (PCC) began with a report from the National Academy of Medicine in 2001.[45] Patient-centered care makes more systematic and routine efforts to gather information on patient goals and preferences for physicians to consider in making recommendations to patients about diagnostic or treatment options. This process provides greater emphasis on patient desires for

---

[45] Institute of Medicine (IOM). (2001). *Crossing the Quality Chasm: A New Health System for the 21st Century*. Washington, DC: National Academy Press.

comfort, peace of mind, and risk taking and does not assume that patients have identical preferences or desires along dimensions of treatment intensity, risk, or uncertainty. The literature does not typically discuss patient budgets, insurance, and tradeoffs between nonmedical spending and medical spending, but in principle should do so since care is not free. Instead, the approach is more promotional, encouraging providers to adopt this model on its own merits. Usually this new approach is made actionable by placing it in a model of coordinated and comprehensive care.

The primary objective of PCC is greater patient estimation of welfare improvement from care, usually measured by some metric of patient satisfaction (though the comparator for such measures is rarely explicit – leading to the question, satisfied compared to what?). A secondary objective is sometimes lower medical spending, but attempts to provide PCC would be rated as improvements even if spending rose as long as the increase was not "too much" relative to improved welfare or satisfaction.

The common-sense version of PCC gathers information on what patients seek by asking them. As might be expected, precisely how to elicit this information in a reliable and replicable way is no small task – as wording and context and even the identify of who should ask the patient (the physician who will provide services, the primary care physician, a nurse or social worker) all matter. The underlying assumption is that, presented with this new information from the patient, the physician furnishing care will speak differently with the patient and make different choices or recommendations compared to what would have happened under usual care. To our knowledge, this hypothesis is usually assumed rather than tested. There are some PCC systems where the quantity and quality of information exchanged is measured as well as patient satisfaction, and also some in which good performance on such metrics is rewarded in some way. There is also some research on the kinds of information patients usually want (or may fail to get under usual care). Here again, whether this information really is desired by patients is often assumed rather than tested, and similarly for the hypothesis that providing it makes a difference in what patients do or what outcomes are achieved.

This low-key version of PCC is a response to criticism made by patients or their advocates about how physicians usually communicate, in particular the lack of attention paid to incorporating patient preferences into a recommended diagnostic or treatment path. This criticism seems to have some *a priori* relevance but, as with other ideas that seem relevant that we discuss in this book, actual evidence on whether they matter, much less improve outcomes, is sparse.

CONCLUSION

Patient behavior can be altered by both standard economic approaches, such as either raising or lowering cost sharing, and through behavioral interventions. There are, however, many ineffective interventions (especially in the wellness program area) and generally limited evidence on the cost effectiveness or the return on investment of plans that do work. The movement towards PCC has highlighted the importance of incorporating patient preferences in diagnosis and treatment decisions, but a big challenge remains in how to best help people help their "future selves," even when their "present selves" engage in behaviors that are likely to reduce their future wellbeing.

A number of the strategies we discuss in this chapter, including nudging people through the use of default options and precommitment devices, can make it easier for people to embark on paths likely to promote their future wellbeing. While there is solid evidence for such approaches in numerous research studies, other than defaults, these approaches typically haven't been used in scaled applications. It is often difficult to get even far-sighted people to sign up for programs that require either constraining future choices, such as through precommitment, or that demand upfront effort or cost. Defaults work well because they change the "path of least resistance," making it easy for people to choose healthier alternatives. Standard economic approaches, such as the use of high-deductible health plans to reduce utilization and VBIDs that lower cost sharing, remain the primary levers through which behavior is being influenced in many settings, though these approaches have the downside of not allowing for individual customization based on differences in health characteristics or preferences. Having patients pay for their care through higher deductibles has produced moderate though one-time reductions in use and spending, but without a verdict on whether those savings are enough to compensate for greater financial risk and the possibility of adverse changes in health. The distinction between patients' avoidance of care that physicians think is clinically effective or cost effective and whether such changes result in significant effects on measures of population health outcomes, a distinction made by the first randomized controlled trial of patient cost sharing, remains important and unresolved.[46]

---

[46] Brook, R. H., Ware J. E. Jr., Rogers, W. H. et al. (1983). Does free care improve adults' health? Results from a randomized controlled trial. *New England Journal of Medicine*, 309 (23), 1426–1434. Available online at: https://pubmed.ncbi.nlm.nih.gov/6355851/;

In the face of uncertainty and imperfect evidence, what should health system managers do? In some situations, altering the choice and incentive framework faced by imperfectly informed consumers or providers can cause them to change their behavior in the direction of greater net benefits. Sometimes as well, this strategy can both lower cost and be more effective than trying to cure their information deficit with yet more timely and urgent information. But will buyers of care and of insurance embrace such programs?

The easiest conceptual case is the so-called "two selves" model, in which consumers know at the start that they will make short-run mistakes in behavior that will lead to long-run outcomes bad enough to offset any gain from less worry about following recommendations or doing things on time. As we discussed earlier in this chapter the "myopic doer" will often make decisions the "far-sighted planner" within each of us would regret. In this case, consumers should be willing to accept libertarian paternalistic interventions that encourage healthy behaviors through nudges or health plans that are designed to get them to do what they should for better health outcomes.

A more difficult but possible case[47] is one in which consumers think they are informed enough and don't want any nudges for beneficial but more costly care or wellness programs. Then an offer of an insurance policy with a higher premium to encourage adherence that consumers do not believe to be important will not be chosen voluntarily. There is little evidence on this case.

The most common examples so far are relatively small scale, but promising experiments fostered by employers, their insurers, or the administrators of self-insured plans, to promote more cost-effective outcomes. The link between actions in these experiments and the more fundamental organizational goals of lowering total compensation cost and attracting and retaining high quality workers is unclear. There can be benefits if care reduces absenteeism or loss of productivity for which workers are

Manning, W. G., Leibowitz, A., Goldberg, G. A. et al. (1984). A controlled trial of the effect of a prepaid group practice on use of services. *New England Journal of Medicine*, 310(23), 1505–1510.

[47] Pauly, M. V., and Blavin, F. E. (2008). Moral hazard in insurance, value-based cost sharing, and the benefits of blissful ignorance. *Journal of Health Economics*, 27(6), 1407–1417; Baicker, K., Mullainathan, S., and Schwartzstein, J. (2015). Behavioral hazard in health insurance. *The Quarterly Journal of Economics*, 130(4), 1623–1668; Pauly, M. V. (2014). Demand for insurance that nudges demand. *Encyclopedia of Health Economics*. A. J. Culyer, ed. San Diego: Elsevier Science: 167–174.

nevertheless paid, but the reward for improving future worker health is less clear. An employer with a successful program in a highly competitive labor market could tout the improved health of workers at that firm compared to other employers in the local labor market and if these health gains could be sufficient to offset lower wages to pay for the program.

In short, a number of promising strategies have emerged to use financial and nonfinancial strategies to influence utilization of health services and health behavior. Aligning these levers in support of the goals of the organization who is paying for the health insurance benefits is important in achieving those goals.

9

The Unmet and Evolving Need
for Evidence-Based Telehealth

Krisda H. Chaiyachati and Bimal Desai[*]

OVERVIEW

Telehealth and telemedicine refer to the exchange of medical information from one location to another using telecommunication technology. Both have the goal of improving how and when people receive care. Telehealth broadly encompasses virtual services that support remote interactions using technology. Telemedicine is specific to the provision of clinical services when providers and patients are not in the same location.[1] In this chapter, we discuss the complexity of generating evidence for telehealth, how to contextualize that evidence, and the current state of the evidence.

The US telehealth revolution has been highly anticipated. Telecommunication technology has improved access to many basic needs in our lives – banking, travel, and commerce. By providing a more convenient, potentially cheaper model of care, telehealth could improve access to health care, particularly for people who live in areas with provider shortages or who cannot afford their local providers. Whether it actually does provide or result in better quality of care or lower cost has been unproven and, therefore, frequently debated by payers, providers, and the people who receive telehealth care – patients.

Prior to 2020, telehealth's use never quite reached the tipping point many anticipated; adoption was underwhelming prior to the novel

[*] **Acknowledgments:** We thank Rachel Werner and Mary Naylor for their comments on an earlier version of this manuscript.
[1] HealthIT.gov. (2019). What is telehealth? How is telehealth different from telemedicine? Available online at: www.healthit.gov/faq/what-telehealth-how-telehealth-different-teleme dicine; The American Academy of Family Physicians. (2020). What's the difference between telemedicine and telehealth? Available online at: www.aafp.org/news/media-center/kits/telemedicine-and-telehealth.html

coronavirus (COVID-19) pandemic, particularly for telemedicine. While telemedicine's annual growth was 50–250% among commercially insured adults, even at its peak less than 7 telemedicine visits occurred per 1000 adults per year.[2] Within Medicare, fewer than 1% of beneficiaries living in rural areas, the only geographic setting where telemedicine reimbursement was available, had used telemedicine.[3] Even among patients of the Veterans Administration where telemedicine was unrestrained by geographic restrictions or traditional insurance arrangements, only 17% of beneficiaries received some form of telemedicine in 2019.[4] Users of direct-to-consumer telemedicine, visits with a physician, or nurse practitioners were more likely to be younger, wealthier, and reside in an urban area with an adequate supply of providers.[5] Populations with the greatest need for care were not using telemedicine at rates thought high enough to have a measurable impact on patients' health.

The possible reasons for telehealth's low use prior to the pandemic were numerous. On the patient ("demand") side, few patients used telemedicine because of likely skepticism over the quality of care or the lack of familiarity with using telecommunication technology.[6] People had limited awareness that telemedicine was available to them, lacked adequate broadband services, or were deterred by out-of-pocket visit costs or co-pays.[7]

On the provider ("supply") side, few health care organizations and providers offered telehealth options. Reimbursement rates were low or nonexistent from payers, private or public. While some states had payment

[2] Barnett, M. L., Ray, K. N., Souza, J. et al. (2018). Trends in telemedicine use in a large commercially insured population, 2005–2017. *JAMA*, 320(20), 2147–2149. Available online at: https://doi.org/10.1001/jama.2018.12354

[3] Mehrotra, A., Jena, A. B., Busch, A. B. (2016). Utilization of telemedicine among rural Medicare beneficiaries. *JAMA*, 315(18), 2015–2016. Available online at: https://doi.org/10.1001/jama.2016.2186.

[4] Veterans Affairs Office of Public and Intergovernmental Affairs. 2019 VA reports significant increase in Veteran use of telehealth services. November 22. Available online at: www.va.gov/opa/pressrel/pressrelease.cfm?id=5365

[5] Jain, T., and Mehrotra, A. (2020). Comparison of direct-to-consumer telemedicine visits with primary care visits. *JAMA Network Open*, 3(12), e2028392. Available online at: https://doi.org/10.1001/jamanetworkopen.2020.28392.

[6] Almathami, H. K. Y., Win, K. T., and Vlahu-Gjorgievska, E. (2020). Barriers and facilitators that influence telemedicine-based, real-time, online consultation at patients' homes: Systematic literature review. *Journal of Medical Internet Research*, 22(2), e16407. Available online at: https://doi.org/10.2196/16407.

[7] Drake, C., Zhang, Y., Chaiyachati, K. H. et al. (2019). The limitations of poor broadband internet access for telemedicine use in rural America: An observational study. *Annals of Internal Medicine*, 171(5), 382–384. Available online at: https://doi.org/10.7326/M19-0283.

parity laws,[8] requiring equivalent payment rates for telemedicine and in-person care for the same types of services, the threat of navigating uncertain reimbursement rules and denied charges remained. Even when reimbursement rules were clear, other telehealth restrictions existed: geographic limitations (e.g., rural patients only), prohibitions against providers caring for out-of-state patients, and an inability to conduct telehealth visits to a patient's home. These unfavorable reimbursement and regulatory rules gave pause to telehealth and telemedicine adoption by providers because the significant startup and upkeep costs were met by an uncertain revenue stream.

Despite telehealth use being low, the desire to improve health care's access challenges and improve the convenience of health care propelled hopes that telehealth would be a viable solution. Concurrently, technology companies have increased their presence in the health care sector, optimistic they can develop inroads into health care's multi-trillion-dollar infrastructure. Reciprocally, the excitement among consumers has grown with companies such as Apple and Fitbit developing popular wearable devices (e.g., smartwatches and wrist bands) and these companies have begun to mass digital health startups as more tech-savvy consumers welcome more tech-enabled health care.

Employers are promoting telehealth options. For example, the majority of large employers in the USA have contracted with direct-to-consumer telemedicine companies such as Teledoc and Amwell to provide on-demand virtual, episode-based care for conditions such as a sore throat or urinary tract infection.[9] These telemedicine options have become standard employee benefits, efforts to attract skilled workers, despite the fact that few employees ultimately use these services.[10] Unsurprisingly, technology companies, such as Amazon, developed telemedicine options for their own employees, likely a strategy before growing their health care footprint to their broader consumer base. Prior to 2020, a casual observer of the technology industry might reasonably feel the telehealth revolution was less a question of when than how.

---

[8] Telehealth Parity Laws. Available online at: https://doi.org/10.1377/hpb20160815.244795.

[9] Claxton, G., Damico, A., Rae, M. et al. (2020). Health benefits in 2020: Premiums in employer-sponsored plans grow 4 percent; employers consider responses to pandemic. *Health Affairs (Millwood)*, 39(11), 2018–2028. Available online at: https://doi.org/10.1377/hlthaff.2020.01569.

[10] Ashwood, J. S., Mehrotra, A., Cowling, D. (2017). Direct-to-consumer telehealth may increase access to care but does not decrease spending. *Health Affairs (Millwood)*, 36(3), 485–491. Available online at: https://doi.org/10.1377/hlthaff.2016.1130.

The world of telehealth undoubtedly and understandably changed in 2020, arguably more so than any other health care sector. The spike in telehealth use paralleled the pandemic rise of COVID-19 globally. In Asian and Pacific countries, telemedicine use expanded by nearly 900 percent by the end of the first quarter of 2020.[11] In the US, rates of telemedicine growth were equally impressive, with 50–300 percent increases in telemedicine visits during the first few months of COVID-19 and practices needing to rapidly transform their in-person practices to primarily provide telemedicine services.[12] Remote monitoring programs for COVID-19 were developed to detect potential exposures, symptoms, and support patients once they were infected.[13] These transitions to telehealth were necessary precautions if communication between patients and providers was to be maintained; they were arrangements to minimize in-person contact for a highly contagious virus, accommodate patients wary of contracting the virus, and care for people with the virus outside and inside of the hospital.

Patient and provider demand for telehealth were reciprocated by more favorable (if sometime temporary) reimbursement and regulatory policies. Under the Department of Health and Human Services' public health emergency declaration, CMS expanded the list of reimbursable telehealth services, the Office of Civil Rights waived HIPAA-related restrictions preventing the use of certain telehealth platforms, the Office of the Inspector General permitted temporary interstate licenses for physicians and nurse practitioners, and parallel changes occurred at the state and professional licensure levels to align with these federal changes. Similarly, commercial insurers followed suit and extended coverage broadly for

---

[11] Kapur, V., and Boulton, A. (2020). Covid-19 accelerates the adoption of telemedicine in Asia-Pacific countries. Bain & Company. Available online at: www.bain.com/insights/covid-19-accelerates-the-adoption-of-telemedicine-in-asia-pacific-countries/

[12] Mehrotra, A., Ray, K., Brockmeyer, D. M. et al. (2020). Rapidly converting to "virtual practices:" Outpatient care in the era of Covid-19. *NEJM Catalyst Innovations in Care Delivery*, 1(2). Available online at:. https://catalyst.nejm.org/doi/abs/10.1056/CAT.20.0091; Fox, B., and Sizemore, O. (2020). Telehealth: Fad or the future. Epic Health Research Network. Available online at: www.ehrn.org/telehealth-fad-or-the-future/

[13] Gordon, W. J., Henderson, D., DeSharone, A. et al. (2020). Remote patient monitoring program for hospital discharged covid-19 patients. *Applied Clinical Informatics*, 11(5), 792 –801. Available online at: https://doi.org/10.1055/s-0040-1721039; Tabacof, L., Kellner, C., Breyman, E. et al. (2020). Remote patient monitoring for home management of coronavirus disease 2019 in New York: A cross-sectional observational study. *Telemedicine and e Health*, October 13. Available online at: https://doi.org/10.1089/tmj.2020.0339; Akinbi, A., and Ojie, E. Tracing or tracking? A preliminary analysis of covid-19 outbreak tracker apps on android and user privacy (Preprint). Available online at: https://doi.org/10.2196/preprints.19662.

telehealth services. These changes, occurring in a matter of weeks, completely flipped how health care was delivered during the pandemic. What remains to be seen is whether some or most of these changes will continue to exist after the pandemic ends.

Telehealth's slow and variable growth past could be blamed on unfavorable reimbursement and regulatory policies. Telehealth's future, more so than ever, hinges on the need for greater evidence of its benefits. Proponents of telehealth continue to hope it will meet the promise of improving health care access for people who reside in provider shortage areas or who have historically experienced inaccessible care. However, rigorous evidence supporting its value is greatly lacking. As the USA transitions out of the pandemic, evidence of its value, positive or negative, will influence whether payers continue to pay for it and providers continue to offer telehealth options. Without more robust evidence, pre-pandemic fears that telehealth may lead to lower quality care or that the care achieved is not worth the costs will resurface and swell unabated, proven or not, and payers and providers will regress to their old ways. Whether patients will begin demanding telehealth after the pandemic is unknown.

We explore the current state of telehealth evidence and opportunities for future evidence generation across four key sections. First, we discuss the complexities of generating and interpreting telehealth evidence by exploring a study of remote monitoring as a case example. Second, we describe important contexts to consider when evaluating telehealth services. Third, we review the current evidence supporting telehealth and gaps in evidence using the Institute of Medicine's six dimensions of quality. Finally, we discuss why evidence might or might not shape telehealth's future.

CASE EXAMPLE: REMOTE CARE MONITORING WITH WEARABLE DEVICES

Interpreting evidence in support of or against the integration of telehealth into care delivery is complex due to how it is delivered and to whom, whether it is complemented by in-person care or not, and the quality of the data generated. We explore these challenges by dissecting recent evidence generated for a remote monitoring application embedded into a digital, wearable device – a watch.

For most people, coming to a health care facility is an infrequent occurrence, and the vast majority of their time is spent away from a health care setting. For episodic care, this may be adequate and appropriate, but for chronic care or for medical conditions where a patient requires a period of increased care intensity, the traditional model of infrequent episodic, in-person visits may be inadequate or burdensome.

With the addition of connected and wearable devices, the hope is that the gap between the patient's home and a clinical care setting can be bridged, and care plans may be executed remotely with better outcomes. The opportunity to monitor and detect clinically significant events at home or outside of traditional health care settings is appealing. As consumer medical devices, smartwatches and related technology may be able to capture the correct number of steps an individual has taken, record heart rates, measure blood pressures, and track blood pulse oximetry.[14]

The potential utility of connected and wearable devices increases for more medically complex patients. As technology improves, these devices may become more accurate, smaller and filter out artifacts ("false positive" signals) while integrated into the patient's personal technology ecosystem. However, whether information gathered by these devices provide patients and providers with actionable information that improves health outcomes remains to be seen. Additionally, whether these devices can be simple enough for the most medically or socially complex patients remains untested.

Today, people can purchase a wrist-worn device – a watch – intended for daily use that can perform an on-demand electrocardiogram (ECG), notify their caregiver of an unexpected fall, measure blood oxygenation, and alert the person when a heart rhythm abnormality is detected. These capabilities represent a staggering amount of technology packed into a small device that can also seamlessly integrate into a larger health technology framework.

Using wearable devices to support clinical monitoring has gained the attention of technology giants such as Apple and Fitbit.[15] In 2017, Apple funded the Apple Heart Study to test whether the optical sensors on their smartwatch could detect irregular pulses, namely atrial fibrillation, a common and dangerous condition.[16] Participants in the study who reported no prior history of atrial fibrillation used a smartphone app

---

[14] Case, M. A., Burwick, H. A., Volpp, K. G. et al. (2015). Accuracy of smartphone applications and wearable devices for tracking physical activity data. *JAMA*, 313(6), 625–626. Available online at: https://doi.org/10.1001/jama.2014.17841.

[15] Fitbit Heart Study Information. Fitbit. Available online at: https://healthsolutions.fitbit.com/heartstudy-info/

[16] Perez, M. V., Mahaffey, K. W., Hedlin, H. et al. (2019). Large-scale assessment of a smartwatch to identify atrial fibrillation. *New England Journal of Medicine*, 381(20), 1909–1917. Available online at: https://doi.org/10.1056/NEJMoa1901183

connected to their smartwatch. If their smartwatch detected atrial fibrillation, a telemedicine visit with an assigned provider was initiated, and patients received an electrocardiography (ECG) patch to measure their heart's rhythm for 7 days. The ECG patch was used to verify and test the accuracy of the smartwatch detected atrial fibrillation.

The study's authors reported two interesting findings. First, among participants who had a smartwatch-detected rhythm consistent with atrial fibrillation, the positive predictive value (i.e., the probability that an alert represents a true-positive notification) for atrial fibrillation was between 0.71 and 0.84. Put another way, 16–29 percent of alarms would represent false positive results. While the accuracy of a device is a necessary first step, the ability to measure does not guarantee clinical efficacy or actionable data. The prevalence of atrial fibrillation varies widely in the general population, with younger patients being at very low risk and patients older than 65 years having risk that increases significantly with age. Consistent with Bayes' Theorem, the accuracy and positive predictive value improves in populations with higher disease prevalence. Testing smartwatches among volunteers or healthier populations, as was done in this study, generates insufficient evidence to "prescribe" a smartwatch to patients with greater concern for atrial fibrillation. And giving smartwatches to the entire population may result in an unacceptably high rate of false positive alarms, which could have both adverse clinical and financial consequences.

Second, over half of participants whose smartwatch sensor alerted them to a concerning heart rhythm contacted a health care provider outside of the study's assigned provider. Circumventing the study's providers highlights the need for integration into existing clinical processes and existing clinical providers. If study participants were going to seek care from their providers anyway, how might wearable devices transmit data in timely and digestible way to a patient's physician without overloading that physician with excess, after-hours work? The burden would be even greater if that information was related to a false positive. Finally, might patient risk-taking behavior be changed if they had reassurance from a device?

With evidence that a smartwatch could detect atrial fibrillation, the Apple Heart Study has generated many more questions. Is it cost-effective compared to the current standard of care? Does it meet the needs of patients? Are physicians prepared to deal with the increase in "digital complaints" raised by home-monitoring devices? Could smartwatches improve health equity by providing a low-cost way to deliver home monitoring, or might they exacerbate disparities between rich and poor or along lines of race and ethnicity because only the privileged can afford these devices? Or would public insurance plans pay for them if they were cost effective? Answering fundamental questions pertaining to safety, effectiveness, patient preferences, access, efficiency, cost, and equity are all fundamentally necessary as we judge telehealth services and determine whether to support wider adoption and use. However, consumer demands for digital devices and telehealth may override this evidence, forcing providers and payers to figure out how to efficiently integrate telehealth into the delivery of care even when the evidence may not support it. Whether the evidence precedes the adoption of telehealth or if adoption precedes the evidence, high quality evidence can inform whether these technological advances are best for the US health care system and the patients we serve.

A PRIMER ON TELEHEALTH DESIGNS AND CONTEXTS

Understanding the design and context of a telehealth service is important before evaluating the evidence (or lack thereof) for it. Four key questions should be asked:

- Is the telehealth service real-time (synchronous vs. asynchronous)?
- Where is the visit occurring (from home vs. in a health care setting)?
- Who are the participants (patient-to-provider vs. provider-to-provider)?
- How is the telehealth service integrated into the care continuum?

Synchronous vs. Asynchronous

Synchronous telehealth consists of real-time exchanges of information outside of traditional office-based visits. Information or data (e.g., voice, images, SMS, and audio) are exchanged within a matter of seconds or minutes, often in a conversational tempo. Asynchronous telehealth, often referred to as "store and forward," occurs when information is stored in a digital location so that the recipient of information can process the data at a subsequent time point. Asynchronous telehealth modalities can be used to transmit images, audio auscultation, video recordings, remote physiologic monitoring, and patient-entered data, such as blood pressure readings or weights. Whether the telehealth encounter is synchronous vs. asynchronous may have substantial impacts on the cost of delivering that care, the cost charged to patients, and the quality of care may vary depending on the clinical condition being treated. Certain skin conditions may be treated more cheaply and with high quality via asynchronous approaches compared with not only in-person appointments, but also synchronous video visits.

From Home vs. Health Care Setting

Telehealth encounters can originate from patients when they are in a variety of physical settings. In a patient's home or a long-term care facility, a physician or nurse practitioner may not be on site. Telehealth can provide access to a provider when there is not one or when mobility to a health care facility is challenging. Yet, even in traditional health care facilities, accessing the right type of provider or specialist may be challenging. In a "hub and spoke" model of telehealth, regional or "spoke" health systems who see patients with urgent or specialized medical needs may act as the originating site for a telehealth visit. The specialist provider is at a remote "hub" site. Historically, the originating site has been limited by regulations and payers, limiting them to health care settings – medical offices, emergency departments, or hospitals. During the COVID-19 pandemic, originating site options have expanded greatly, particularly to patients' homes.

Patient-to-Provider vs. Provider-to-Provider

Understanding who is participating in the telehealth encounter, and who is not, will help further contextualize and conceptualize reasonably expected treatment options and health outcomes. While connecting patients to providers is often the primary consideration when designing telehealth interventions, provider-to-provider telehealth can expand access similar to hub and spoke models for patient-to-provider care. These exchanges can occur synchronously through video or telephone-based conversations or asynchronously through electronic health system conversations. E-consults are an example of asynchronous, consultative, provider-to-provider communications designed to facilitate the clinical management of patients. Often e-consults are used to connect specialists with providers who desire input from greater clinical expertise for clinical conditions, such as managing autoimmune disorders or diagnosing rare conditions.

Care along a Continuum and Utilization

Evaluations of any telehealth service must consider where telehealth exists along the care continuum. Often telehealth evaluations and evidence are cast as telehealth vs. in-person care. These 1-to-1 comparisons may be valid for telehealth services for low clinical complexity, low-acuity services. However, even in these seemingly brief episodes of care, patients may have been referred to a telehealth service by a provider who typically sees patients in person, and a telehealth service may request a patient be evaluated in person. To completely divorce telehealth from the continuum of care is nearly impossible because all care is conceivably longitudinal or, at minimum, may require some followup care.

More commonly in real-world settings, telehealth is complementary. It is part of a sequence of treatment options resulting in a health outcome, desired or not. In-person, conventional care can always happen before a telehealth visit or result from it. While understanding the design of a telehealth program is important – synchronicity, the originating site, and who is participating in the telehealth encounter – the design and delivery have to be put in the proper context along the continuum of care. The observed continuum of care can be planned or unplanned, depending on the providers' plans and the patient's adherence to those plans. For episode-based conditions, such as stroke, the care continuum can be more defined and time-limited (e.g., time from onset to recovery, disability, or death). For chronic conditions, such as diabetes or hypertension, the care continuum is longitudinal and often nonlinear.

Further, the care continuum is dependent on the availability of diagnostic and clinical interventions (e.g., diagnostic imaging, laboratory, and physical examinations), which is variable across care settings and geographic regions. Just as there are interventions offered during an emergency room visit that are impossible or cumbersome in an office visit, there are limits to telehealth's telephone or video modality. While the introduction of telehealth options into this continuum seemingly complicates how and when care is delivered, the choice of where patients choose to seek care and whether patients need to be referred to higher resource venues has always been a central concern for any provider in any health care system.

Successfully integrating telehealth into care will depend on providers' ability to "right size" its use, finding the set of clinical opportunities where telehealth is more sensible than low intensity care (e.g., telephone calls) but the patient does not require an in-person visit. Maximizing telehealth's utility will require an understanding of the patient's needs at that moment, and patient or provider travel and wait time, as well as what the modality is able to offer.

The challenge is a "Goldilocks" problem: a video visit is overkill for a prescription refill, insufficient for the child who requires immunizations,

Rank ordering information richness of ambulatory health care interventions

Figure 9.1. Rank ordering information richness of ambulatory health care interventions

but maybe just right for assessing a variety of low-acuity complaints. Ambulatory health care interventions can be ranked from lowest to highest based on information richness, each with its own combination of resource intensity, therapeutic flexibility, and, therefore, cost. Telehealth interventions (light red) can be inserted within this continuum of options (Figure 9.1). The labor and overhead costs and resource needs required to conduct an in-person visit are very different from evaluating a person's rash on an uploaded photo, for example. Also, given the modality, condition, and patients' desires, each intervention has the ability to satisfy health care quality goals to varying degrees.

The insertion of telehealth comes with startup costs that are not limited to material or technology costs. As when learning any new technology – telephone, email, and patient portal messages – providers and patients of the past and the future must weigh and learn how and when to incorporate these options to achieve outcomes they desire while not being overburdened by them. Patient portal messages and the electronic health record have led to substantial after-hours work, creating more administrative burdens to respond to patients in a timely manner, if not more visits.[17] Similarly, telehealth may increase or double the work for providers, a cost for greater convenience to patients.

Let's use the assessment of a cough using telemedicine as an example. After clinical assessment (given an inability to conduct a physical exam) via video or phone, a provider may ask a patient to be seen in-person to have their pulse oximetry measured, receive a more thorough physical examination, and be referred for an x-ray. Not only is the clinician's time

[17] Bavafa, H., Hitt, L. M., and Terwiesch, C. (2018). The impact of e-visits on visit frequencies and patient health: Evidence from primary care. *Management Science*, 64 (12), 5461–5480. Available online at: https://doi.org/10.1287/mnsc.2017.2900; Bryan, M., Norton, D., Birstler, J. et al. (2020). Resource utilization among portal users who send messages: A retrospective cohort study. *Wisconsin Medical Journal*, 119(1), 26–32. Available online at: www.ncbi.nlm.nih.gov/pubmed/32348068

spent per patient doubled (if not greater), but additional time is also required of administrators and support staff to coordinate two appointments. In these scenarios, telehealth is not only an unnecessary cost, but it may also be an unnecessary gatekeeper, preventing the right form of care from the outset. However, let's say the patient cannot or will not travel to see the physician. In this scenario a telemedicine visit may increase access when the person wouldn't have made the trip otherwise.

Telehealth may be more efficient at moving patients through the care continuum to the right care setting. A 2016 study by Gattu and colleagues demonstrated high inter-rater reliability between in-person and telemedicine evaluation of pediatric respiratory distress, suggesting that for the triage function of determining the "next best step" for clinical care, telemedicine may be adequate for this condition.[18] The implications of this are significant when we consider just how common upper respiratory tract infections, fever, and cough are in pediatrics. It suggests that telemedicine may be appropriate for the initial assessment of respiratory distress in children, with the potential to avoid unnecessary urgent care, emergency department, and inpatient encounters while still providing high-quality, patient-centered, safe, equitable, and effective care. Plainly stated: averting a single avoidable emergency department visit for cough might pay for a number of "triage" telehealth visits for cough in the pediatric population, if that emergency department visit is more avoidable when telehealth is in the health care ecosystem versus not.

Telehealth adds to the challenge patients and providers face navigating the health care ecosystem in search of care at the right time and right place. Some episodes of telehealth care will result in additional care relative to just starting off with an in-person visit. But if telehealth avoids unnecessary visits to high-acuity, high-cost health care settings, we might be more forgiving of these overuse scenarios. Telehealth will result in both overuse and underuse, substituting for some forms of care and complementing existing care approaches. Therefore, contextualizing telehealth evaluations along the greater care continuum is critical. Telehealth should be evaluated *with* other modes of care, not *versus*. Otherwise, comparisons of telehealth versus, say, in-person care in isolation will always miss the bigger picture.

Yet even if we contextualize telehealth within the continuum of care, how we ultimately determine telehealth's value will need to be weighed

[18] Gattu, R., Scollan, J., DeSouza, A. et al. (2016). Telemedicine: A reliable tool to assess the severity of respiratory distress in children. *Hospital Pediatrics*, 6(8), 476–482. Available online at: https://doi.org/10.1542/hpeds.2015-0272.

against the errors that may occur transitioning in and out of in-person care, how patients feel about telehealth, the costs of administering telehealth programs, and whether access improves differentially by race or income. The concerns over telehealth's value would be greatly reduced if patients could get to the right care at the right time with similar or better outcomes in a health care ecosystem with telehealth compared to an ecosystem without it. We don't know the answer to many of these questions because we lack rigorous evidence, and therefore the value of telehealth remains in doubt, guided more often by anecdote and intuition rather than evidence. Knowing these answers would favor more widespread adoption of telehealth.

TELEHEALTH'S EVIDENCE

Telehealth services and new care models that use telehealth should be evaluated like any other aspect of health care delivery and innovation: Does the existence or integration of telehealth into the health care ecosystem provide better value relative to existing forms of care? Value is defined as the benefit from the highest quality care minus the cost. Obtaining the highest value is achieved by maximizing this net benefit.

We explore evidence in six key areas where telehealth may or may not have value and provide context for how the value proposition may evolve as telehealth continues to evolve within our health care ecosystem. We discuss telehealth's evidence within the Institute of Medicine's six domains of health care quality: timeliness and access, efficiency and costs, safety, effectiveness, patient-centeredness, and equity.[19] When assessing the evidence generated from evaluations of telehealth, each of us should weigh these six quality dimensions either in singularity or in combination. Each one of us is a stakeholder in the health care sector, and we will prioritize different quality dimensions when deciding whether to start, support, continue, refine, or end telehealth programs.

Timeliness and Access

Telehealth's potential is built on the promise to improve the timeliness and accessibility of health care in the USA with low additional cost. Telehealth

---

[19] Institute of Medicine (US) Committee on Quality of Health Care in America. (2014). *Crossing the Quality Chasm: A New Health System for the 21st Century.* National Academies Press (US). Available online at: https://doi.org/10.17226/10027.

may be a tool to increase access to care, particularly for populations and communities who face diminished access.[20] More timely, accessible care may be particularly important for rural communities where the supply of providers – primary care and specialty care – are limited, and the number of providers choosing to live and work in rural areas is declining.[21] Yet even urban communities face challenges with accessible care, particularly neighborhoods that are low-income or have a large proportion of racial minorities.[22]

Barriers to access related to challenges of proximity (i.e., long drive times) or wait times (i.e., an inadequate supply of providers) can be theoretically overcome if more care is delivered using telehealth, but the extent to which this can be done in reality is understudied.[23] The evidence is mixed. A prior evaluation of telemedicine for mental health conditions indicated that telemedicine visits represented followup visits rather than substitutes for initial visits.[24] Here, patients who already had regular access to mental health care may have benefited from more frequent visits, not patients who had limited to no access to mental health care at baseline.

In contrast, creative models of care delivery that leverage "eConsults" have shown promise. In many medical specialties, the demand for specialized care overwhelms the limited supply of specialists. Consider the pediatric patient with severe refractory eczema (an inflammatory condition of the skin), just exceeding the common scope of practice of a primary care physician. The patient requests a specialty referral to a pediatric

---

[20] Board on Health Care Services, Institute of Medicine. (2012). *The Role of Telehealth in an Evolving Health Care Environment: Workshop Summary*. National Academies Press. Available online at: https://play.google.com/store/books/details?id=LCxeAgAAQBAJ

[21] McGrail, M. R., Wingrove, P. M., Petterson, S. M. et al. (2017). Mobility of us rural primary care physicians during 2000–2014. *Annals of Family Medicine*, 15(4), 322–328. Available online at: https://doi.org/10.1370/afm.2096.

[22] Brown, E. J., Polsky, D., Barbu, C. M. et al. (2016). Racial disparities in geographic access to primary care in Philadelphia. *Health Affairs(Millwood)*, 35(8), 1374–1381. Available online at: https://doi.org/10.1377/hlthaff.2015.1612.

[23] Horn, B. P., Barragan, G. N., Fore, C. et al. (2016). A cost comparison of travel models and behavioural telemedicine for rural, native American populations in New Mexico. *Journal of Telemedecine and Telecare*, 22(1), 47–55. Available online at: https://doi.org/10.1177/1357633X15587171; Yilmaz, S. K., Horn, B. P., Fore, C. et al. (2019). An economic cost analysis of an expanding, multi-state behavioural telehealth intervention. *Journal of Telemedecine and Telecare*, 25(6), 353–364. Available online at: https://doi.org/10.1177/1357633X18774181.

[24] Mehrotra, A., Huskamp, H. A., Souza, J. et al. (2017). Rapid growth in mental health telemedicine use among rural Medicare beneficiaries, wide variation across states. *Health Affairs(Millwood)*, 36(5), 909–917. Available online at: https://doi.org/10.1377/hlthaff.2016.1461.

dermatologist, the primary care physician agrees to this as the best next step, but the local specialist has a long wait list – months if not a year. The eConsult model allows the primary care physician to photograph the rash and send an electronic request for a second opinion directly to this dermatologist (or some other in a different location who is less busy), complete with appropriate medical details such as an assessment of severity, time course, and the lack of response to prior therapies. Because turnaround time for eConsults may be 24–72 hours, the patient receives a specialist recommendation for therapy in an expedited fashion or, if the case cannot be managed virtually, the specialist has enough clinical insight to triage the patient and arrange an in-person appointment. The value of this clinical evaluation, even remote, can help patients be seen sooner than had the patient called the specialist's office staff for the next available appointment.

In these arrangements in which some costly actions can be avoided, the eConsult can be a more cost-effective option for patients and payers. eConsults can help offload in-person appointments that don't need to occur in-person and helps specialists prioritize patients who need appointments sooner. The access benefits of eConsults has been consistently reported in multiple specialties, adults and pediatrics, including for nephrology,[25] endocrinology,[26] and dermatology.[27]

Particularly for specialty referrals, solutions are long overdue. A 2014 survey suggests there are 19.7 million clinically inappropriate specialty referrals annually.[28] In addition, 63 percent of those patients are rereferred to more appropriate specialists. These patients were estimated to have incurred $1.9 billion in lost wages and additional copays. Telehealth models like the eConsult paradigm have the potential to break this cycle.

However, telehealth's availability does not guarantee improved timeliness or access. For health systems with fixed capacity – when the inflexible

[25] Schettini, P., Shah, K. P., O'Leary, C. P. et al. (2019). Keeping care connected: E-Consultation program improves access to nephrology care. *Journal of Telemedicine and Telecare*, 25(3), 142–150. Available online at: https://doi.org/10.1177/1357633X17748350.

[26] Anderson, D., Porto, A., Koppel, J. et al. (2020). Impact of endocrinology eConsults on access to endocrinology care for Medicaid patients. *Telemedecine and E- Health*, 26(11), 1383–1390. Available online at: https://doi.org/10.1089/tmj.2019.0238.

[27] Seiger, K., Hawryluk, E. B., Kroshinsky, D. et al. (2020). Pediatric dermatology eConsults: Reduced wait times and dermatology office visits. *Pediatric Dermatology*, 37(5), 804–810. Available online at: https://doi.org/10.1111/pde.14187.

[28] Kyruus. (2014). New report reveals 19.7 million misdirected physician referrals in the US each year, November 10. Available online at:. www.kyruus.com/new-report-reveals-19-7-million-misdirected-physician-referrals-u-s-year

limit of time available from providers to meet the demands of care from patients has been met – more visits generated through telehealth may increase the workload for an already strained health system. Offloading this work by hiring additional providers, outsourcing this work elsewhere, or creating efficiencies in care delivery (e.g., automating the intake process or streamlining documentation and billing) will all need to be considered if the access demands of patients overwhelm a health system. The resource demands of telehealth are strongly considered by financial leaders within provider organizations but are missing in the research literature because the costs to administer programs are classically kept hidden to protect industry pricing, are distributed across other programs, or are not well recorded and monitored during the rollout of new programs. Even the most robust studies or clinical trials rarely know or accurately document the costs of starting or maintaining telehealth programs. Yet these pragmatic considerations can greatly impact telehealth outcomes such as access because the financing of these services determines the availability of telehealth offerings. Gains in access for patients can come at a cost, both financial and at the expense of efficiency when delivering care.

Efficiency and Costs

Greater access to more timely care, if achieved by telehealth, may considerably increase the cost of care, especially if care is inefficient. The reason regulatory and payment changes have been slow to create more favorable policies over the past two decades has revolved around one central question: Will the integration of telehealth into the care continuum produce a given set of outcomes for the same, higher, or lower cost relative to in-person care?

Efficiency and costs are complicated to measure because any telehealth visit may substitute for or complement existing forms of care. Take direct-to-consumer oral contraceptives ("telecontraception"), where contraception is prescribed through a website or smartphone app, an alternative to receiving the prescription after a visit to a primary care provider or gynecologist. Telecontraception companies have adhered to nationally accepted guidelines for prescribing, can complete a visit in less than 10 minutes, and a prescription is sent to a local pharmacy or mailed to the patient's home within a week.[29] For patients, the out-of-pocket costs may

---

[29] Jain, T., Schwarz, E. B., and Mehrotra, A. (2019). A study of telecontraception. *New England Journal of Medicine*, 381(13), 1287–1288. Available online at: https://doi.org/10.1056/NEJMc1907545.

range from $0 to $20, but the cost value for patients may be greater if we took into account the time necessary to coordinate a typical in-person visit, time spent traveling to a doctor's office, the cost of gas and parking at the doctor's office, and the time spent traveling to the pharmacy to pick up their medication. In the case of contraception or other forms of cost-effective preventive care (e.g., smoking cessation programs), these tele-health arrangements can have even greater value when one factors in the economics of prevention, like an unwanted pregnancy or smoking cessa-tion leading to lower rates of lung disease or cancer. If a telehealth service can make it simpler, easier, and cheaper for patients to access a prescrip-tion or coordinated preventive care that is known to be high-value, tele-health is a win for us all.

While single or limited-condition telehealth companies have promoted improvements in efficiency and costs, more randomized trials and well controlled studies will be needed. Even if successful, their success may be byproducts of specialization. Direct-to-consumer telemedicine companies that provide primary care or will manage a broad set of low-acuity condi-tions will be challenged to keep costs low and preserve efficiency. The greater the number of conditions treated, the more a telehealth service will need to consider how it can complement and integrate into other existing forms of care. A patient may simply want better access to mammograms. But what happens when that mammogram was already conducted by their usual provider? What happens when that person has a lesion of concern? How would an independent telehealth company efficiently coordinate the patient's followup care and avoid redundant care? For chronic or complex conditions, proving that care can be coordinated efficiently from symptom onset to diagnosis to management will be key. Otherwise, even comple-mentary services run the risk of driving up costs when care is fragmented.

By contrast, even when telehealth is a substitute for existing in-person care, costs and inefficiencies may increase. If the telecontraception com-pany provided a bad service – they didn't take into account a patient's preference to avoid certain side effects or made the process of obtaining a prescription inefficient (e.g., mailing the prescription as opposed to elec-tronically sending the order directly to the pharmacy) – these design flaws would make them lose their appeal to patients and reduce the effectiveness of a telehealth approach. Arguably, these design inefficiencies are unlikely among telehealth startups and companies outside of traditional health care organizations because they depend on obtaining good customer reviews and repeat customers. However, as a greater number of existing, status quo health systems and office-based primary care practices expand their telehealth footprint, if these providers do not feel the same market pressures as startups to provide an efficient service or have the technical know-how, care may be delayed, the patient experience may be interrupted, and developing digital workflows may increase cost.

The convenience of telehealth may increase cost if it induces too much new use – care that would not have occurred otherwise, had telehealth not existed.[30] New use is estimated to occur in anywhere between 15 and 90 percent of all telehealth visits, varying by clinical condition and delivery context.[31] New use may also further exacerbate costs if telehealth visits are more likely to generate in-person followup because telehealth cannot achieve diagnostic maneuvers, such as a physical exam. The problem is that the new use may have low or near zero value. The telehealth visit is then redundant because the patient should have been seen in-person from the start. For payers, one of the biggest fears is that the cost of care may grow significantly if telehealth use and eligibility are not restrained or limited. Because the evidence supporting which conditions should be seen in-person versus telehealth first is lacking, payers have historically used other proxies to limit the inducement of new care, such as geographic restrictions, or only paying for visits originating from a health care facility – hoping that, on balance, these limits discourage more low value than high value use.

However, not all new use or resultant in-person care should be viewed negatively. If new use predominantly consists of visits from patients who faced substantial access barriers before – racial minorities or the poor – then new use with outcome gains due to greater access may be a good thing. Because we don't yet know whether new use is made up by the disadvantaged with pent up demand for care or the well-off seeking unnecessary, additional care, the impact of new use on the value of telehealth remains unknown.

---

[30] Martinez, K. A., Rood, M., Jhangiani, N. et al. (2018). Patterns of use and correlates of patient satisfaction with a large nationwide direct to consumer telemedicine service. *Journal of General Internal Medicine*, 33(10), 1768–1773. Available online at: https://doi.org/10.1007/s11606-018-4621-5.

[31] Ashwood, J. S., Mehrotra, A., Cowling D. et al. (2017). Direct-to-consumer telehealth may increase access to care but does not decrease spending. *Health Affairs(Millwood)*, 36(3), 485–491. Available online at: https://doi.org/10.1377/hlthaff.2016.1130; Nord, G., Rising, K. L., Band, R. A. et al. (2019). On-demand synchronous audio video telemedicine visits are cost effective. *American Journal of Emergency Medicine*, 37(5), 890–894. Available online at: https://doi.org/10.1016/j.ajem.2018.08.017.

Finally, the effects on spending of delivering telehealth are understudied. While telehealth can be delivered from lower-cost facilities (e.g., office spaces instead of clinical spaces equipped with diagnostic instruments and tools), whether these cost savings are offset by the cost of devices and the cost for upkeep (e.g., information technology specialists, cyber security) remains unknown. Moreover, in our experiences, connections between patients and providers still requires support staff. Medical assistants or staff in technology-facing roles remain involved in coordinating, checking-in, and solving the technological challenges faced by patients, irrespective of their digital health literacy. While the perception is that providers and patients are the only two individuals necessary to complete a telehealth visit, this is not true in real world applications and use of telehealth. These ancillary support costs must be weighed when measuring the costs of telehealth.

Safety

While expert derived guidelines for how to provide telehealth safety exist, the overall safety of telehealth remains understudied. The US Agency for Healthcare Quality and Research (AHRQ) has recommended the development and implementation of standardized processes for telehealth, similar to guidelines for in-person visits.[32] Their recommendations include developing guidelines for when a telehealth visit should be escalated to an in-person visit, requirements that providers familiarize themselves with a patient's prior medical records before the visit, teaching providers how to conduct clinical encounters using telemedicine, and creating processes for reviewing near misses and safety events. Additionally, organizations like the American Telemedicine Association (ATA) have compiled guidelines for a variety of telemedicine domains, such as pathology, eye care, stroke care, mental health, diabetes care, and teledermatology.[33] These guidelines are based predominantly in expert opinion, extrapolated from in-person care evidence. There is little to no robust evidence, such as randomized controlled trials, or measurements of the effects of telehealth on safety or of improvements in safety due to implementing recommended guidelines.

[32] Agency for Healthcare Research & Quality: Patient Safety Net. (2020). Telehealth and patient safety during the covid-19 response. Available online at: https://psnet.ahrq.gov/perspective/telehealth-and-patient-safety-during-covid-19-response

[33] American Telemedicine Association n.d. Practice guidelines archive. Available online at: www.americantelemed.org/resource_categories/practice-guidelines/

One major challenge for assessments of telehealth's safety can be attributed to the myriad of ways telehealth has been implemented in real-world practice into the larger continuum of care. Disentangling safety events due to telehealth from the result of care received before or after the telehealth visit is challenging.[34] Usual safety indices for in-person care are less applicable to telehealth evaluations. For example, the classic and easily derived metrics of emergency room visits or hospitalizations from telehealth visits may be tempting. However, telehealth is often used to triage and detect early clinical declines. What may be considered an adverse event for in-person visits may be the purpose of a telehealth visit: detecting clinical deteriorations earlier and expediting care. This gain in detection may be particularly acute if patients would have experienced delays in care without telehealth because their primary care provider or specialists were too busy.

Conversely, telehealth may result in safety concerns if the limitations of pure audio or visual evaluations are not fully appreciated by providers or patients. Providers may miss key clinical signs or symptoms that, had the patient been evaluated in-person, would have guided a different decision-making process. In practice, telehealth connection issues are complicated to troubleshoot. They could represent limitations on either the patient's or provider's side of the connection. Similarly, if patients insist on using telehealth when the clinical situation warrants an in-person evaluation and their provider has been requesting they be seen in-person, delays in care or a missed diagnosis may result in greater harm to the patient. While it would be easy to cast all telehealth as risky in the absence of an in-person evaluation, no or delayed care may be as harmful, if not more. The ability to direct blame for care that has been provided has always been easier to do than when no care has been provided at all. Yet, as discussed previously, providing access to telehealth where in-person provider supplies are greatly limited, such as in rural areas or poor urban neighborhoods, may result in substantial health gains even if telehealth services have higher error rates than traditional face-to-face visits. In these scenarios, the tradeoff of gained access may outweigh the safety risks of telehealth but, admittedly, may be counterbalanced by the ethics of providing less safe care to already marginalized communities. For disadvantaged communities, evaluations of safety are deeply intertwined with access and equity challenges and are inherently complex.

---

[34] Press Ganey. (2020). Four essentials of effective telemedicine, *Press Ganey*. Available online at: www.pressganey.com/blog/the-four-essentials-of-effective-telemedicine

Safety considerations have substantial implications as cyber-liability and malpractice evolves in response to the growth of telehealth. To move forward, rigorous evaluations with well thought-out study designs are necessary to understand the potential patient safety harms and gains when implementing or expanding telehealth services. Improving the safety of care remains an important health care mission. Yet while few rigorous studies exist, we predict providers and patients may move forward with telehealth expansions, cautiously monitoring for untoward or unintended consequences. They may be pressured to move in this direction if competition forces them to expand their telehealth offerings or patients increasingly demand it, creating more safety protocols as experiences with telehealth grows and safety outcomes are captured.

Effectiveness

Telehealth can improve health outcomes. The evidence is strongest for conditions and geographic settings with specialty shortages. Telehealth is particularly beneficial when care is needed but there is no physician to provide care in-person. For example, telehealth can be critical to improving timely evaluations and decisions for patients who develop a stroke – a condition where delays in care can result in permanent disability or death. Lifesaving treatments such as the administration of tissue plasminogen activator to dissolve clots in the brain can be assessed using telestroke carts wheeled urgently into an emergency room or an office-based setting, connecting a patient to a stroke specialist and standardizing the decision-making process. Where stroke specialists are in short supply, telestroke has improved survival rates and the quality of life of those who survive in a number of randomized trials and well-designed observational studies.[35] While robust randomized or quasi-experimental studies are missing, telehealth may also play a key role in caring for older adults in long-term care facilities or nursing homes.[36] In these care settings, providers are lacking, mobilizing a patient for an office-based or

---

[35] Baratloo, A., Rahimpour, L., Abushouk, A. I. et al. (2018). Effects of telestroke on thrombolysis times and outcomes: A meta-analysis. *Prehospital Emergency Care*, 22(4), 472–484. Available online at: https://doi.org/10.1080/10903127.2017.1408728; Kepplinger, J., Barlinn, K., Deckert, S. et al. (2016). Safety and efficacy of thrombolysis in telestroke: A systematic review and meta-analysis. *Neurology*, 87(13), 1344–1351. Available online at: https://doi.org/10.1212/WNL.0000000000003148.

[36] Edirippulige, S.,. Martin-Khan, M., Beattie E. et al. (2013). A systematic review of telemedicine services for residents in long term care facilities. *Journal of Telemedecine and Telecare*, 19(3), 127–132. Available online at: https://doi.org/10.1177/

acute care evaluation can be cumbersome, and unnecessary inpatient admissions can result in worse health outcomes. However, as discussed below, older adults with multiple chronic conditions may have limited ability to maximally use telehealth services. Here, like in so many other examples, telehealth effectiveness will be contingent on factors related to the delivery of care and which patients can access this care.

Additionally, the evidence in favor of telehealth is strong for conditions where a physical exam is not required for an accurate diagnosis or management, such as behavioral health or the care of patients with mental health needs. Examinations are rarely conducted during in-person visits, and patients routinely face barriers to accessible, convenient locations and times with a therapist or psychiatrist. These telehealth modalities may also expand the availability of substance use disorder treatments to rural areas or be more appealing for patients who do not wish to travel long distances for psychotherapy or medication management. While some in-person visits may be necessary to receive specific medications, such as methadone, integrating telehealth into the treatment continuum can have retention rates that are higher or no different than programs without telehealth for substance use disorder patients.[37] The benefits of telehealth may also be extended to other specialties where in-person examinations are not a key component of care, such as the practice of radiology, pathology, and certain situations in dermatology where diagnoses can be made from high resolution images. Many of these specialties have already adopted technical solutions, and concerns over effectiveness may be moot when a provider can easily serve a large geographic region just as well as they can provide their expertise to the providers and patients in their building.

Effectiveness does become more complicated when telehealth is applied to the treatment of acute and chronic medical conditions. New or followup assessments of, say, a murmur or shortness of breath may well be ill-suited for telehealth because critical examination maneuvers, bedside diagnostic tests, and vital signs (e.g., oxygen levels, heart rates, blood pressure) can be more easily and accurately captured in an office because the necessary

1357633X13483256; Seifert, A., Batsis, J. A., and Smith, A. C. (2020).Telemedicine in long-term care facilities during and beyond covid-19: Challenges caused by the digital divide. *Frontiers of Public Health*, 8, 601595. Available online at: https://doi.org/10.3389/fpubh.2020.601595.

[37] Lin, L. A., Casteel, D., Shigekawa, E. et al. (2019). Telemedicine-delivered treatment interventions for substance use disorders: A systematic review. *Journal of Substance Abuse Treatment*, 101, 38–49. Available online at: https://doi.org/10.1016/j.jsat.2019.03.007.

equipment is available and clinical staff have received standardized training. However, telehealth may have an effective role for a number of medical conditions because a large range of clinical conditions require few, if any, of these activities. For example, there is substantial evidence that using telehealth can help medication management and counseling to be effectively integrated into the followup plans for patients.[38] Here, telehealth can perfectly substitute for in-person visits where an exam or in-person biologic data is not collected and, at the same time, complement in-person visits by connecting with patients in-between in-person appointments, motivating adherence or advancing care plans so that in-person appointments can focus on the necessary exam and biologic data collection for managing certain conditions. A number of randomized trials have shown that telehealth-supported management of certain medical conditions can achieve outcomes comparable to in-person alone care, including dementia[39] and diabetes.[40] These results are derived from single center studies or from experimental settings; more and better real-world evidence is needed to increase our confidence in transitioning certain aspects of care to telehealth modalities.

Patient-Centeredness

As providers expand their telehealth offerings and payers consider which services to cover, understanding patients' perspectives on telehealth is important and understudied. Telehealth may overcome parts of in-person

---

[38] Centers for Medicare and Medicaid Services (CMS). (2018). Information on Medicare telehealth. Available online at: www.cms.gov/About-CMS/Agencty-Information/OMH/Downloads/Information-on-Medicare-Telehealth-Report.pdf; Faruque, L. I., Wiebe, N., Ehteshami-Afshar, A. et al. (2017). Effect of telemedicine on glycated hemoglobin in diabetes: A systematic review and meta-analysis of randomized trials. *Canadian Medical Association Journal*, 189(9), E341–E364. Available online at: https://doi.org/10.1503/cmaj.150885.

[39] Spaeder, J., Najjar, S. S., Gerstenblith, G., Gottlied et al. (2006). Rapid titration of carvedilol in patients with congestive heart failure: A randomized trial of automated telemedicine versus frequent outpatient clinic visits. *American Heart Journal*, 151(4), 844.e1–e10. Available online at: https://doi.org/10.1016/j.ahj.2005.06.044

[40] Jiménez-Marrero, S., Yun, S., Cainzos-Achirica, M. et al. (2020). Impact of telemedicine on the clinical outcomes and health care costs of patients with chronic heart failure and mid-range or preserved ejection fraction managed in a multidisciplinary chronic heart failure programme: A sub-analysis of the iCOR randomized trial. *Journal of Telemedecine and Telecare*, 26(1–2), 64–72. Available online at: https://journals.sagepub.com/doi/abs/10.1177/1357633X18796439?casa_token=z8pT_YsMbD8AAAAA:dfDVUGHl7nrw017cBvAysBUubS50X9l0Qnx2lbbvKGSZ0-PaV2Xo-ozokiEcTH–w-ZydOz7cy7P

care viewed as barriers to care with real social costs in terms of quality of life – long travel times, inconvenient appointments, and higher costs. In a study of pediatric, office-based, post-operative visits, patients avoided an average of 70 miles of round trip driving by receiving a telehealth visit while receiving equally efficacious care.[41] For patients, this could represent an entire missed day of work or school and, especially relevant during the COVID-19 pandemic, unnecessary exposure to communicable diseases from other patients. The problem of distance is magnified for highly specialized care needs, where regional experts are often concentrated in metropolitan centers, limiting access for more rural patients. Telehealth can bridge the distance gap, improving access to specialists for patients, giving them options for how they receive care and from whom.

Despite these likely improvements in access and convenience measures, telehealth may not necessarily be patient-centered, and perceptions will vary from person to person. Patients may value face-to-face interactions more, have lower levels of telehealth acceptance, or be less facile with digital health technology.[42] To date, patients who have used telehealth have favorable perceptions of telehealth on par with in-person care.[43] However, these studies represent the perspectives of early adopters willing to use telehealth. As telehealth is increasingly delivered in everyday clinical practice, patients' perceptions of telehealth will evolve. Providers will also adapt, developing and improving techniques used during telehealth visits to engender greater trust and connections with patients, so-called "screen-side" (as opposed to bedside) manner or virtual presence.[44] If that care is efficient – the correct lab or imaging tests are ordered and patients are accurately triaged to in-person care – then patients may be increasingly willing to substitute a telehealth visit for an in-person appointment over

[41] Abel, K., Baldwin, K., Chuo, J. et al. (2018). Can telemedicine replace the first post op visit for knee arthroscopy in adolescents? *Pediatrics* 141(1), 663–663. Available online at: https://doi.org/10.1542/peds.141.1_MeetingAbstract.663.

[42] Saliba-Gustafsson, E. A., Miller-Kuhlmann, R., Kling, S. M. R. et al. (2020). Rapid implementation of video visits in neurology during covid-19: Mixed methods evaluation. *Journal of Medical Internet Research*, 22(12), e24328. Available online at: https://doi.org/10.2196/24328; Slightam, C., Gregory, A. J., Hu, J. et al. (2020). Patient perceptions of video visits using veterans affairs telehealth tablets: Survey study. *Journal of Medical Internet Research*, 22(4), e15682. Available online at: https://doi.org/10.2196/15682.

[43] Press Ganey. (2020). The rapid transition to telemedicine: Insights and early trends. Available online at: www.pressganey.com/resources/white-papers/the-rapid-transition-to-telemedicine-insights-and-early-trends?s=White_Paper-PR

[44] Millstein, J. H., and Chaiyachati, K. H. (2020). Creating virtual presence during a pandemic. *Journal of Patient Experience*, 7(3), 285–286. Available online at: https://doi.org/10.1177/2374373520930447.

time. However, if too many in-person visits result from telehealth visits and telehealth is seen as a barrier to seeing their provider, patients may begin to perceive telehealth as a barrier to the care they need.

Additional considerations for patient-centered care include privacy and language barriers. Privacy can be a concern, not only the protection of digital information, but also the ability to have private conversations from home. When discussing conditions related to substance use disorders or interpersonal violence, how private these conversations may be in a patient's home will need to be evaluated before and during telehealth visits. Not offering in-person options may be a deterrent to seeking care and counter efforts to improve access through a telehealth medium. In addition, patients may require interpreters for multi-lingual telehealth visits. Without technological add-ins whereby interpreters can easily be integrated into the telehealth encounter, patients who are more comfortable with discussing their health needs in a language other than English will be at a significant disadvantage.

Indeed, to achieve patient-centered care, a full understanding of a patient's socio-economic status, preferences for face-to-face visits versus virtual visits, and preferred language will all need to be considered when offering telehealth, especially if the trend is to shift away from face-to-face visits. Otherwise, providers will be alienating patients along the way. Telehealth should be included as a choice among other modes of care delivery, particularly in the beginning, so as not to counter patients' preferences and potentially contribute to health inequities. However, the verdict remains unwritten and evolving. As telehealth offerings expand, technology advances, and patients become more accustomed to health care with telehealth as an option, understanding the patients' perspectives will be critical for improving the patient-centeredness of telehealth.

Equity

Telehealth's impact on equity is understudied. Understanding its impact on equity and adapting the practice and delivery of telehealth will be essential if telehealth is to meet its promise of improving health care access. The basic question for telehealth is to what degree disadvantaged groups find telehealth effective and acceptable. However, fundamental ingredients for disadvantaged groups to benefit from telehealth are already known to be missing from the current health system, and so its growth may result in the digital divide spilling over into unequitable care.

Broadband internet access is lacking in many regions of the country. US counties with the worst broadband access also have the highest rates of chronic disease, including a 25% higher prevalence of obesity and 41% higher prevalence of diabetes.[45] Compounding matters, areas with poor broadband access have worse access to primary care physicians. This double burden of reduced health care access impacts nearly 36 million Americans, or 60% of counties in rural America and 5% of urban counties. The impacts of limited broadband internet access are disproportionately felt by communities with high rates of poverty and communities of color, the result of historic structural inequities and racism.[46] Understanding how to improve broadband access and how better broadband access improves telehealth related outcomes will be important future topics of inquiry. Otherwise, the preexisting "digital divide" will promote health inequities, and if telehealth is to become health care's future, then broadband speed and quality will be a critical social determinant of health. While it may be unrealistic to expect health care systems and providers to alone offset the digital divide, they could become advocates for efforts to do so locally and nationally, along with other groups working to improve equity.

Access to devices and technology may also be critical. How health systems decide to implement telehealth (e.g., requiring a webcam capable device or requiring app-based functionality) is evolving, and how these choices impact groups with limited device access or an inability to afford data plans – cellular or broadband – remains to be seen. If policies or telehealth services require certain devices or certain data plans, communities with high rates of poverty will likely be left out. We believe these choices can be avoided. Leveraging existing technology commonly used by marginalized communities, such as text messaging or audio only encounters, may minimize disparities observed by telehealth interventions, particularly in these early years. If high-tech solutions are the only modality offered or the delivery of care does not account for the economic needs of patients, they can certainly be studied, and evaluations focused on exploring inequalities will need to be conducted.

Just as specificity is important in the discussion related to patient-centeredness above, understanding the specific perspectives and needs of disadvantaged communities is an understudied area of importance. In particular, African American and Latinx communities, who already have a baseline distrust of health care as a whole, have cited concerns about

[45] Federal Communications Commission (FCC). Mapping broadband health in America. Available online at: www.fcc.gov/health/maps

[46] Pew Research Center: Internet & Technology (2019). Internet/broadband fact sheet. Available online at: www.pewresearch.org/internet/fact-sheet/internet-broadband/

telehealth related to confidentiality, privacy, and a greater desire to be physically present with their physician.[47] These perceptions of distrust and marginalization may be easily worsened if telehealth is seen as a barrier to the care they had limited access to before: in-person care. Distrust will be further exacerbated if, perception or fact, wealthier or White patients are less likely to be offered telehealth and more likely to be offered in-person care. Further, if technology cannot accommodate the translation needs of non-English speakers, differential outcomes from telehealth may result from language barriers.

Finally, disparities may occur because different populations may adopt telehealth at differential rates or have different technology-related capabilities. Even seemingly simple technological advances have different rates of use among sociodemographic groups, including race and ethnicity, such as the use of direct appointment scheduling and patient portal options.[48] The observed gaps in adoption may reflect the digital divides described earlier or cultural factors we have yet to understand.[49] If telehealth is the only option but is unaccommodating to different racial, ethnic, and economic groups, telehealth will create the structural disparities we hope to avoid.

Older adults may also be affected by technological advances. For example, while older adults account for nearly 25 percent of physician office visits, nearly 13 million older adults in 2018 would have had trouble accessing telehealth services because they had a limited experience with most forms of technology or had physical barriers, such as hearing or visual impairments.[50] In addition, a disproportionate number of these older adults are already disadvantaged minorities or are poor. While telephone-based telehealth visits may improve access for nearly half of these older adults, a telephone-based solution will be suboptimal care for

[47] George, S., Hamilton, A., and Baker, R. S. (2012). How do low-income urban African Americans and Latinos feel about telemedicine? A diffusion of innovation analysis. *International Journal of Telemedecine and Applications*, 2012, 715194. Available online at: https://doi.org/10.1155/2012/715194.

[48] Ganguli, I., Orav, E. J., Lupo, C. et al. (2020). Patient and visit characteristics associated with use of direct scheduling in primary care practices. *JAMA Network Open*, 3(8), e209637. Available online at: https://doi.org/10.1001/jamanetworkopen.2020.9637.

[49] Eberly, L. A., Kallan, M. J., Julien, H. M. et al. (2020). Patient characteristics associated with telemedicine access for primary and specialty ambulatory care during the covid-19 pandemic. *JAMA Network Open*, 3(12), e2031640. Available online at: https://doi.org/10.1001/jamanetworkopen.2020.31640.

[50] Lam, K., Lu, A. D. Shi, Y. et al. (2020). Assessing telemedicine unreadiness among older adults in the united states during the covid-19 pandemic. *JAMA Internal Medicine*, 180 (10), 1389–1391. Available online at: https://doi.org/10.1001/jamainternmed.2020.2671.

an older population that is more likely to require a visual assessment relative to their younger counterparts. Again, providing patients with choices will be important before constraining them to telehealth integrated options. Choices, particularly in the early stages of scaling up telehealth, will be necessary to avoid disparities in care experienced by disadvantaged populations.

THE COVID-19 "EXPERIMENT" AND TELEHEALTH'S FUTURE

As is the case for so many other facets of health care, the COVID-19 pandemic has altered telehealth's future. Because of the pandemic, the future of more evidence-based telehealth is both unwritten and boundless. As we describe above, telehealth faced a paradox prior to the COVID-19 pandemic. The absence of robust evidence contributed to payers' reluctance to deregulate and pay for telehealth in many markets, delaying widespread implementation and adoption. Conversely, low rates of implementation and adoption hampered efforts to generate needed evidence along the dimensions of timeliness and access, efficiency and costs, safety, effectiveness, patient-centeredness, and equity. The prepandemic telehealth climate was a standoff between payers, providers, and patients because of this circular dependency between evidence and reimbursement.

COVID-19 disrupted the standoff by accelerating telehealth's life cycle, changing how providers deliver care and what patients have come to expect from the health care industry. In April 2020, 90 percent of physicians were offering at least some telehealth visits during the early months of the pandemic.[51] Between March and June of 2020, between 22 and 30 percent of Medicare beneficiaries received telehealth services.[52] If telehealth becomes so popular in certain markets or among certain populations, policymakers, payers, and providers may have little choice but to offer telehealth options after the pandemic. From our vantage point, the question of whether or not telehealth should be reimbursed and offered quickly shifted towards questions of how to make it more effective, to integrate it into the continuum of care, and to advance goals of equity.

---

[51] Reuter, E. (2020). Survey: More than 90% of physicians are treating patients remotely. *Med City News*. Available online at: https://medcitynews.com/2020/05/survey-more-than-90-of-physicians-are-treating-patients-remotely/

[52] Verma, S. (2020). Early impact of CMS expansion of Medicare telehealth during covid-19. *Health Affairs Blog*. Available online at: www.healthaffairs.org/do/10.1377/hblog20200715.454789/full/

The key argument for expansion of telehealth during the pandemic was that it was safer because infections were more likely to occur during in-person visits. In this historic and unconventional context, the argument for telehealth's safety was easily made. As a largely untested model of care was rapidly deployed wholesale under such unusual conditions, the same questions that stymied telehealth's growth were raised, but providers, payers, and patients were forced to accept telehealth, even if temporarily.

Yet while the large-scale expansion of telehealth during the pandemic has increased the sample size and the number of clinical conditions treated using telehealth,[53] the massive adoption of telehealth and the context of the pandemic will limit the identification of adequate controls and generalizability to life after the pandemic. Payment for telehealth flipped from virtually none to all of it guaranteed, on par with in-person care rates. How much did the pandemic skew the way providers delivered care (COVID-19 related or more generally) and the way patients chose where and how to seek care? Many patients were clearly avoiding in-person care, even for conditions as serious and life threatening as strokes.[54] Furthermore, what proportion of provider and patient behaviors will be observed in the immediate period postpandemic and longer term remains to be seen.

Within our own institutions, we have already begun to observe decreases in the use of telehealth, not to prepandemic levels, but leveling off at rates of 20–30 percent of all encounters, varying by specialty and by practice locations. These drop-offs have occurred despite many providers welcoming the addition of telehealth options as a way to improve access for patients, patients being satisfied with their telehealth visit, and providers having improved reimbursement for services, such as telephone-based management, that were not reimbursed before the pandemic. The reason for the substantial decline in telehealth visits is likely a combination of clinical need for in-person visits, patient preferences, and uncertainty around telehealth's financial stability. Throughout the public health emergency period, cost-sharing and reimbursement for telehealth have remained on-par with in-person visits. These fairly consistent

---

[53] Patel, S. Y., Mehrotra, A., Huskamp, H. A. et al. (2021). Variation in telemedicine use and outpatient care during the covid-19 pandemic in the united states. *Health Affairs (Millwood)*, 40(2), 349–358. Available online at: https://doi.org/10.1377/hlthaff.2020.01786.

[54] Kansagra, A. P., Goyal, M. S., Hamilton, S. et al. (2020). Collateral effect of covid-19 on stroke evaluation in the United States. *New England Journal of Medicine*, 383(4), 400–401. Available online at: https://doi.org/10.1056/NEJMc2014816.

arrangements across payers are also the reason predicting the impact of variations or gradations in co-pays or reimbursement after the pandemic will be difficult.

Changes to telehealth payment will be the greatest determinant of telehealth's future. However, to understand telehealth's maximum potential and to answer many of the key questions raised in this chapter, payment models will need to support services after the COVID-19 context. At minimum, if researchers can identify opportunities for identifying natural experiments or quasi-experimental opportunities, answers to critical questions about the cost and value of telehealth may be partially answered. Better yet, if payers can collaborate with health systems to experiment with different payment schema in the hopeful months before the end of the pandemic and for a period of time, ideally 1–2 years after the pandemic, researchers and evaluators may be able to leverage variations in co-payments and reimbursements to better understand telehealth's value. The payers have expressed interests in hearing arguments for improving reimbursements from prepandemic levels but want greater evidence that telehealth has value and providers can minimize wasteful spending. Providers, financially strained by the pandemic, don't want to have these favorable reimbursement rates pulled back because the volume of telehealth visits may be offsetting losses elsewhere due to the pandemic. However, to move towards a telehealth integrated future in health care, both payers and providers will need to each compromise, ideally during an identified transition period, in order to answer questions important for the long-term future of telehealth. Otherwise, we will all be guessing about the correct price point for telehealth services after the pandemic ends.

SUMMARY

A common imagination of health care's future involves a person receiving care from their medical provider in the comfort of their own home, during a time convenient for the person, not the provider. People may have wearable devices integrated into everyday products. Watches, clothes, hats, and glasses could capture people's movement, behavior, and collect important biometrics, such as a person's heart rate, heart rhythm, blood pressure, what they had eaten, and weights could continuously feed into large databases and integrate with a person's medical record to inform the patient and guide their medical providers on how best to improve their health. These databases would be layered with predictive analytics and machine learning tools to further personalize medical and lifestyle advice.

In turn, the health system could deploy digital interventions to the patient, in the form of reminders, prompts for symptom checks and patient-reported outcomes, video check-ins, daily activity goals, educational videos, guided physical therapy sessions, and much more. In 2020, these futuristic imaginations are not far from reality, but the evidence to spur large-scale adoption and payment remains in limbo.

Integrating evaluations of telehealth within the greater continuum of health care also creates new challenges for generating evidence: What is the best way, short of conducting thousands of individual clinical trials for specific health care conditions in a variety of clinical contexts, to demonstrate where it is appropriate to consider telehealth along the continuum of care delivery options? In the pre-COVID environment, in which reimbursement for routine telehealth was unlikely, evidence would be hard to come by, requiring a research study or approved pilot with payers. The pandemic and the resulting explosion of telehealth services has resulted in a telehealth reckoning. But we still need better evidence. Hopefully, we will be entering an incredibly exciting and rapidly evolving time period of better telehealth evidence generation soon; otherwise, the future role of telehealth in the US health care system may be murky.

10

Evidence and the Management of Health Care
for Disadvantaged Populations

Mark Pauly, Ralph Muller, and Mary Naylor[*]

INTRODUCTION

Uneven distribution of income, education, and wealth in the United States combined with racism and class discrimination result in parts of the population having worse health outcomes than others. Such disparities have been the focus of much talk and many serious efforts at documentation, but (as will be shown in this chapter) very little effective action to change them – both because of lack of evidence for change that is effective and lack of implementation of evidence-based changes. Although everyone knows that medical care alone cannot alter all of the disparities in observed health outcomes caused by centuries of discrimination, sometimes it can make a difference. To what extent could evidence about effective programs help health care managers or policymakers take a leadership role in reducing disparities for disadvantaged populations?[1] Is it possible at least to identify actions that would help, and then implement them? The need to convert evidence-based management from an aspiration into reality is especially acute for this problem.

[*] **Acknowledgments:** The authors received helpful comments from Atheendar Venkatarami, Ingrid Nembhard, Risa Lavizzo-Mourey, Marshall Chin, Scott Cook, Andrea Ducas, Mona Shah, and Jacqueline Orr. Brianna Carvalho provided excellent research assistance.

[1] In this chapter we refer both to social and economic disadvantage as a characteristic of population groups. Socially disadvantaged households are those who have been subject to ethnic prejudice or cultural bias because of their identities as members of groups. Economically disadvantaged households are ones with low income or wealth relative to the mean, median, or most common value in a population. Sources: *See* 13 CFR § 124.103 (defining disadvantaged persons as. . .), Cornell Law School Legal Information Institute. Available online at: www.law.cornell.edu/cfr/text/13/124.103; See also, "Disadvantaged populations," in Michalos AC (Ed.). Encyclopedia of Quality of Life and WellBeing Research. Springer, Dordrecht, Netherlands: Springer, 1654–1658.

WHAT GENERAL DECISION RULE FOR HEALTH CARE LEADERS?

The federal Agency for Healthcare Research and Quality appropriately treats disparities as an aspect of quality of care.[2] Quality of care, broadly defined, is any aspect of care that affects health outcomes in a population. Quality is related to disparities in outcomes when it varies systematically across population subgroups defined by race, geography, gender, or socio-economic status; such variation is often inequitable and inefficient. We postulate that managers of health systems and health insurance plans, necessarily constrained by limited resources and seeking sustainable inter-ventions, should, as a rule, seek to deploy those resources to improve quality for different populations in the most effective ways for those populations, adapting to the different circumstances of different groups. The resulting pattern of improvement is likely to be one with larger improvements (and associated commitments of resources) for more disadvantaged populations.

If there is some effective, quality-improving intervention not now being furnished to a particular disadvantaged subpopulation, that should change; that disadvantaged population should get the program and the benefits from the program that will, in some way, more than cover its cost. Similar investments should be made in other effective programs for disadvantaged populations. The set of considerations here should be wide; sometimes individual programs taken alone may not do much, but could combine with other actions to improve the effectiveness of each.[3] A neighborhood health center in a remote or unsafe location may not do much for health unless and until transportation or security are improved enough to make using it accessible and safe for those who use it. Actions might also have economies of scale, where marginal cost is high at first but then falls and makes a program cost effective.[4] There will also be other cases where programs provide some benefits to disadvantaged population but only at

---

[2] Agency for Healthcare Research and Quality (AHRQ). *National Healthcare Quality and Disparities Reports*. Available online at: www.ahrq.gov/research/findings/nhqrdr/index.html

[3] NES. (2019). *NIOSH's Hierarchy of Controls*. Available online at: www.nesglobal.net/nioshs-hierarchy-of-controls/

[4] Bernet, P. M., and Singh, S. (2015). Economies of scale in the production of public health services: An analysis of local health districts in Florida. *American Journal of Public Health*, 205(Suppl 2), S260–S267. Available online at: www.ncbi.nlm.nih.gov/pmc/articles/PMC4355699/

high cost, and those programs should be displaced by ones with more favorable net benefits and similar patterns of equity. So we will be looking in this chapter for evidence on programs that are both targeted and comprehensive and that have effectiveness sufficient for them to make sense to medical care and insurance managers.

But do such programs exist, and if they do, are they practically and financially feasible for managers of health systems and insurers to initiate? Would following an effectiveness-based decision rule point the way for health care managers seeking to reduce disparities, and what presently unavailable evidence would be needed to support actions consistent with that rule? If evidence would matter, what kind of experiments and analysis would help to produce it and incorporate it in decision-making?

VAGUE GOALS AND LITTLE EVIDENCE

In the United States, the health care system is pluralistic, with both public and private financing of insurance and care and largely private organizations or agents supplying care. Perhaps not surprisingly, this system has not made or implemented any definitive societal decision about how much spending, use of care, or health outcomes are appropriate or rightful for all citizens. It does appear that there is loose consensus for some safety net or floor to population-level health outcomes for all Americans, but no agreement on who should decide what it is or pay for it.[5] Similarly, there is a related loose consensus that no race, gender, or wealth subgroup should have health outcomes or access far below the average, but again no agreement on who should take responsibility for correcting divergences across groups.

This imprecise definition of goals and responsibilities is one reason why discussions of disparities tend to be endless but changes few. We will offer some reasons below why programs for minority populations may generally be highly effective relative to those for the rest of the population, though some programs will have only modest effects and so will have low priority. Another reason for reluctance to act is the absence of evidence for large-scale, effective interventions that could change patterns of health outcomes

---

[5] Khullar, D., Song, Z., and Chokshi, D. A. (2018). Safety-net health systems at risk: Who bears the burden of uncompensated care? *Health Affairs Blog.* Available online at: www .healthaffairs.org/do/10.1377/hblog20180503.138516/full/; Stanford Encyclopedia of Philosophy. (2017). *Justice and Access to Health Care.* Available online at: https://plato .stanford.edu/entries/justice-healthcareaccess/

or even use of medical care in ways that would meaningfully reduce disparities; are there things guaranteed to work in a large variety of different settings? Finally, we will show that a major problem for implementation of effective innovations is a mismatch between who might pay for or invest in such innovations and the distribution of benefits from doing so.

Another reason for little effective action is what we have emphasized so far in other chapters in this book: the absence of rigorous evidence on what are and what are not effective programs to appropriately reduce disparities. In this case there is more reason for optimism: there are some innovations that work. We will discuss those interventions, the size of the contribution they can make to reducing disparities and, most importantly, whether managers of health systems and insurance plans are or could be motivated to implement them – and then search for others.

THERE ARE RACIAL AND SOCIAL DISPARITIES

The great bulk of the evidence so far accumulated on health and disadvantaged populations has been directed at finding differences in use of care or health outcomes related to race, ethnicity, gender, or socioeconomic status.[6] Such work is often called disparities research. It has shown that disparities exist in the United States and in all other countries. Both economic disadvantage (low income or wealth) and racism are associated with worse outcomes, and both seem to matter, though the outcome is worse when they are combined. There has been much less effort directed at what, if anything, should change when disparities are discovered. There are many differences in outcomes across individuals and population groups in a society. When does variation call for action?

Part of the answer deals with values and will, and how they might translate into individual or collective action. Does "society," however defined, value reducing differences as a positive step, and if so, how much value does society attach to doing so? When citizens have different levels of these values, as they surely do, how should those values be combined or reconciled? Part of the answer also deals with means. What is the right way

---

[6] Clarke, A. R., Goddu, A. P., Nocon, R. S. et al. (2013). Thirty years of disparities intervention research: What are we doing to close racial and ethnic gaps in health care? *Medical Care*, 51(11). Available online at: www.ncbi.nlm.nih.gov/pmc/articles/PMC3826431/; Chin, M. H., Walters, A. E., Cook, S. C. et al. (2007). Interventions to reduce racial and ethnic disparities in health care. *Medical Care Research and Review*, 64(5 Suppl), 7S–28S. Available online at: https://pubmed.ncbi.nlm.nih.gov/17881624/

to reach a collective decision when people do not agree on values? Majority rule no matter what? Bill of rights? Vote-trading? And the rest of the answer deals with cost. What is the cost of effective measures to improve outcomes, and is that cost per positive step worth the value of each step? If it is, who should pay for it and how can that funding be made to happen? It is evidence on value, effectiveness, and cost we will review, linked to action or inaction of health care and insurance management that might affect disparities.

We describe the categories of disparities in the use of care that have the best evidence and are most often suggested as possible targets of effective action. (As we will see, evidence of effective action is much less common.) In addition to looking at population-wide patterns, we describe three specific examples: overall life expectancy, cardiovascular disease mortality, and maternal and infant mortality.

There is an extensive literature showing that there are significant disparities in measures of health outcomes by race, gender, and socioeconomic status in the United States (as well as in other developed countries, regardless of their health care delivery and financing systems).

SOME CONCLUSIVE EVIDENCE, IN PICTURES

Figure 10.1 shows trend lines for life expectancy at birth by ethnicity.

Figure 10.2 plots the same trends for life expectancy (measured by additional years of life expected) at age 65.

The overall pattern is one of modest reduction in disparities and improvement in health outcomes over the early part of the period but a persistence of differences and little change in disparities over the last part. Disparities in outcomes for the Black population are the largest and most persistent.

Figure 10.3 shows trends for infant mortality since 2004.

Figure 10.4 shows trends in heart disease mortality.

The overall pattern in disparities for selected but important medical conditions is similar to that in the aggregate data. We see some improvement for all ethnicities, but disparities still remain, are most pronounced for Blacks, and are especially large for infant mortality.

Finally, Figure 10.5 shows life expectancy related to income, indicating that disparity is a function of economic status. The impact of having a low income on mortality is especially strong for men.

Hence, the evidence shows there are disparities and that they have not been reduced much in the last decade, despite new effective clinical

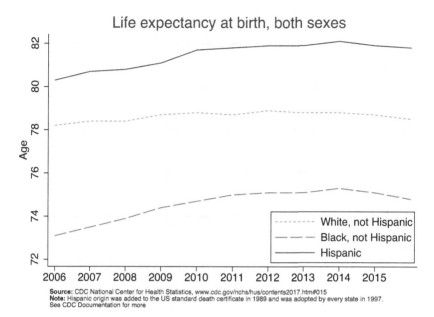

Figure 10.1. Life expectancy at birth, both sexes

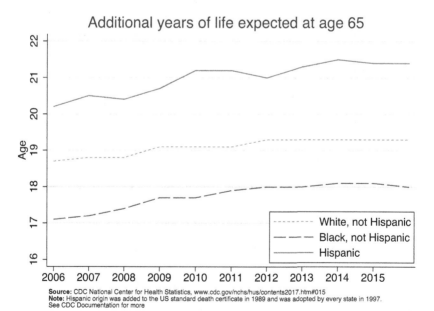

Figure 10.2. Additional years of life expected at age 65

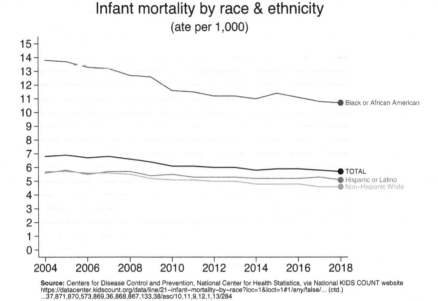

Figure 10.3. Infant mortality by race & ethnicity (rate per 1,000)

treatments and a flood of expressions of concern, philanthropic funding, and government programs. The question we will address is whether evidence-based decisions by managers of health systems or insurance plans have played a role in not only the changes that have occurred, but also in the stubborn persistence of disparities.

What do we conclude about ethnicity-related variations in the quality and rates of use of care in the United States? In the classic 2003 study from the National Academy of Medicine, race and ethnicity-related disparities were identified in access to care and quality of care: "Even at equivalent levels of access to care, racial and ethnic minorities experience a lower quality of medical services and are less likely to receive even routine medical procedures than are white Americans."[7] The types of disparities discussed in the study were most pronounced for cardiovascular care with regard to medication use, revascularization procedures, and asthma care, with inferior monitoring among minority populations. There has been a

[7] Smedley, B. D., Stith, A. Y., and Nelson, A. R. (2003). *Unequal Treatment: Confronting Racial and Ethnic Disparities in Health Care.* Washington, DC: Institute of Medicine (US) Committee on Understanding and Eliminating Racial and Ethnic Disparities in Health Care/National Academies Press.

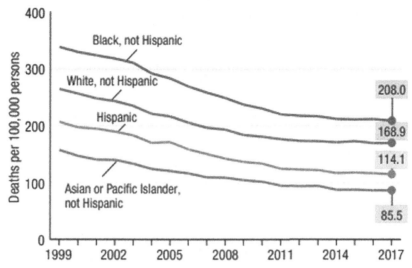

Figure 10.4. Age-adjusted death rates for heart disease, by race and Hispanic origin: 1999–2017

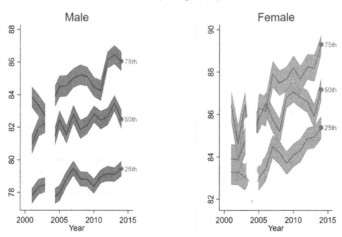

Source: Opportunity Insights Lab (Chetty, et. al.) found at:
https://opportunityinsights.org/data/?geographic_level=104&topic=106&paper_id=0#resource-listing
Note: Value is unadjusted life expectancy; error bars are 1 standard deviation above and below

Figure 10.5. National life expectancy, by income percentile at age 40

modest reduction in some of the indicators of disparities (especially cardiovascular), but a large gap remains.

The conclusion on use of formal care was that "access related factors are the largest contributors to racial and ethnic disparities in cardiovascular care, but disparities in outcomes continue to exist even after controlling for insurance status." While much of the variation in quality is associated with greater use of lower-quality providers by minority groups, differences in clinical care remain even in high-quality health care systems, with insurance differences (Medicaid or no insurance) as partial correlates.

Those conditions that do not show disparities in outcomes tend to be either diseases for which there is no effective treatment or diseases that are severe at onset and have therapeutic indications that are unequivocal and accepted, such as treatment for brain cancer. In cases with more provider or patient discretion, minority populations get shortchanged.

EVIDENCE ON REDUCING DISPARITIES: GENERAL OBSERVATIONS

There is much less evidence on effective interventions to alter these patterns compared to the discussion on their undesirability. In large part this scarcity of evidence on interventions is caused by the lack of evidence on the root causes of disparities – disparities probably reflect some patient decisions (based both on access barriers or misinformation) but largely result from provider choices at the individual patient level. The supply-side choices not explicitly influenced by race are rather based on provider beliefs and value judgments, past experience, ability to communicate with patients, and expectation of payment. Racism, conscious or unconscious, remains a persistent threat that is so far hard to eradicate.

Interventions have tended to focus on patterns of care and the extent to which those patterns adhere to race-blind guidelines. Improving quality in this way has sometimes happened and sometimes reduced disparities as it improved outcomes for patients of all ethnicities – but (as will be shown later in the chapter) sometimes the improvement left measured disparities unchanged or even increased them in outcomes while improving all outcomes in general. However, even for the conditions for which evidence for disparities is strongest and most upsetting, there have been few interventions with evidence of effectiveness, and even fewer that have been implemented at any kind of scale. Disparities remain in care process and outcomes for cardiovascular care, stroke, asthma, and maternal and infant mortality.

VALUE IS SUBJECTIVE – AND A MOVING TARGET

A plausible assumption is that, most of the time, a given treatment will add more to the health of someone or some population that starts out sicker – that the effectiveness of an effective program will vary inversely with the baseline level of health. This relationship is not guaranteed – a program to provide better prenatal care or spread immunizations may have the same health effect on advantaged populations at initial high levels of health as on the disadvantaged, but may still more adversely affect functioning or ability to hold a job for the disadvantaged. A particular treatment may also generally be less effective when given to people near death than people who are sick but expected to survive, so effectiveness is not perfectly correlated with poor health. It will, nevertheless, usually be reasonable to assume that more access to effective care will provide a larger benefit to those who start out with poor access and low use and health – so the additional effectiveness of programs targeted to the disadvantaged will be higher than for those who are not disadvantaged. Programs that affect the disadvantaged are likely to be more cost effective if health improvements are given similar values across groups.

PROGRAMS BIG AND SMALL

Most of the discussion of reducing disparities has had a much stronger emphasis on goals and wishes for interventions than on putting financial and nonfinancial muscle behind evidence-based programs to achieve those goals. The discussion often ends with hopes that participants will figure out what to do about the obvious and troubling patterns of outcomes, but no reassurance or guidance that something can and will be done. Here we go beyond platitudes and wishful thinking to look at incentives explicitly or implicitly present in actual or potential efforts and the results of those incentives.

Research on programs to reduce disparities for disadvantaged populations has concentrated almost entirely on effectiveness, not on cost effectiveness. Some of that research has dealt with "small" interventions at the individual patient-clinician level and some with the "large" structural level (such as broadened insurance coverage or community outreach programs in places where the population is socially vulnerable). We first discuss the latter case.

Studies have largely concentrated on targeted efforts to improve health outcomes of community populations (rather than reduce disparities per se).

That means that any effect on disparities will be related to the composition of the community population and its proportion of disadvantaged people. Programs that have looked at more general interventions for mixed populations (such as fostering insurance coverage for all uninsured) have sometimes found that benefits to vulnerable minorities accompanied benefits to other less vulnerable populations, so that disparities did not fall even though health of the disadvantaged group was improved. Other programs that were limited to disadvantaged communities and not offered to others by definition reduced disparities if they had any effect at all. It is not clear whether health systems can easily implement targeted programs rather than general quality improvement programs. They can use location as a proxy for disadvantage – and that in turn may depend on the neighborhoods in which their facilities are located. Private insurers are even more challenged to target programs to certain populations among their insureds and not others because their contracts offer the same benefits to all insureds.

"Large" interventions with evidence of effectiveness include:

(1)   Use of lay community workers to provide information, encourage screening, and monitor care management and adherence. Such programs appear to have positive effects on outcomes and costs, though not as large as interventions by health professionals, such as nurses or dietitians.[8]

(2)   Housing subsidies or vouchers for higher-quality housing in more advantageous locations. Individual health care systems have tried to deal with housing issues for their disadvantaged patients, especially the homeless, on a one-time basis, hoping that the cost they pay for housing would reduce the high health costs of these populations.

(3)   Attempting to improve the quality of care at sites that care for disadvantaged people by avoiding networks with "tiers of providers who adhere to different (lower) standards of care."[9] There is strong evidence that worse health outcomes for disadvantaged

---

[8]   Viswanathan, M., Kraschnewski, J. L., Nishikawa, B. et al. (2010). Outcomes and costs of community health worker interventions: A systematic review. *Medical Care*, 48(9), 792–808. Available online at: https://pubmed.ncbi.nlm.nih.gov/20706166/

[9]   Smedley, B. D., Stith, A. Y., and Nelson, A. R. (2003). *Unequal Treatment: Confronting Racial and Ethnic Disparities in Health Care*. Washington, DC: Institute of Medicine (US) Committee on Understanding and Eliminating Racial and Ethnic Disparities in Health Care/National Academies Press.

and minority populations happen because they are more likely to use low-quality providers (rather than from their being treated differently within a given provider system). Hence, it seems logical to try to channel them toward higher quality systems. However, there is no evidence that an explicit effort to do so has been successful. Still, the case for better direction is strong. One issue is what to do about health care systems with below average quality; someone has to use them.

(4) Selecting health professionals of the same race or background and emphasizing cultural competency among all providers.[10]

(5) Improving Medicaid payment rates and provider contracts, and assuring that physicians have enough time and resources to provide high-quality care to the disadvantaged – even if that requires more time and cost than for less disadvantaged populations. There is evidence based on variation across states in expansion of Medicaid benefits under the Affordable Care Act that poor people who received such benefits had better outcomes than those who did not. There was an increase in total cost of services – for example, emergency room use rose along with primary care. There is also good evidence that insurance coverage reduced financial stress. For Medicare with uniform coverage, there were still disparities in quality that persist even in the Accountable Care Organization model.[11] Unfortunately, more rigorous studies have yet to consistently show major health benefits (beyond, for example, better treatment for depression), though one study comparing expansion and nonexpansion states did find a 20 percent fall in mortality among low-income people aged 55–64 in expansion states.[12] We discuss how health systems and private health insurers might deal with reducing disparities among those on Medicaid in more detail below.

[10] Alsan, M., Garrick, O., and Graziani, G. (2019). Does diversity matter for health? Experimental evidence from Oakland. *American Economic Review* 109(12), 4071–4111.

[11] Lewis, V. A., Fraze, T., Fisher, E. S. et al. (2017). ACOs serving high proportions of racial and ethnic minorities lag in quality performance. *Health Affairs*, 36(1), 57–66. Available online at: www.healthaffairs.org/doi/10.1377/hlthaff.2016.0626

[12] Miller, S., Johnson, N., and Wherry, L. R. (2021). Medicaid and mortality: New evidence from linked survey and administrative data. NBER Working Paper 26081. Cambridge, MA: National Bureau of Economic Research. Available online at: www.nber.org/system/files/working_papers/w26081/w26081.pdf

(6)   Less fragmented care through patient-centered medical homes. The evidence that these programs improve outcomes or lower cost for the general population is still not strong. Development of a model targeted to underserved populations might be effective but has not yet been shown to be so. Rather than relying on primary care physicians, as discussed in Chapter 5, some effective interventions rely on community health workers and community health centers.[13]

(7)   Federally qualified health centers. The federal government has for decades funded nonprofit health centers in low income communities for the provision of primary and preventive care. Expansion of this network of centers has sometimes been offered as an alternative to expansion of Medicaid. If the alternative scenario would be low income communities with little Medicaid support and no other help, these programs appear to be effective both in providing services and improving health that is worth the cost.[14] Their effect on disparities obviously depends on their location in minority neighborhoods. In principle some expansion of this model could help to reduce disparities, though apparently there has not so far been a targeted effort to do so, although innovations in the FQHC program have been supported by some private health systems and insurers.

Are there programs that delivery systems or health insurers could and should implement that involve these interventions? A necessary condition for doing so would be a determination that a system that was largely constructed to supply medical services to episodic demanders will take responsibility of reducing disparities from racism and low social status for a population. Below we discuss how health systems are being directed toward population-based programs for identified populations.

---

[13]   Kangovi, S., Mitra, N., Grande, D. et al. (2014). Patient-centered community health worker intervention to improve posthospital outcomes: A randomized clinical trial. *JAMA Internal Medicine*, 174(4), 535–543. Available online at: https://jamanetwork .com/journals/jamainternalmedicine/fullarticle/1828743

[14]   O'Connor, E. (2020). No expansion necessary: How Texas can lead the way on Medicaid alternatives. *Texas Public Policy Foundation Policy Perspective*, May. Available online at: https://files.texaspolicy.com/uploads/2020/05/07092736/OConnor-Medicaid-Alternatives.pdf; Poor, J. (2020). State Rep. Wadsworth offers FQHCs as alternative to Medicaid expansion for rural health care, *Yellowhammer.com*. Available online at: https:// yellowhammernews.com/state-rep-wadsworth-offers-fqhcs-as-alternative-to-medicaid-expansion-for-rural-health-care/

Only a few programs to reduce disparities have been subjects of cost-effectiveness analysis. In part, that is because a program has to be shown to affect health to be considered; there is no point in tabulating the cost of something that makes no difference. The other, more challenging, conceptual problem is that the big step is to go from improved individual clinical metrics (such as HbA1c results for people with diabetes) to changes in health outcomes determined by metrics that can be compared across interventions. This is an obstacle even before confronting the issue of attaching monetary values to improvements in survival and quality of life for low-income and disadvantaged people.

The cost of implementing these programs may be higher or lower for health delivery systems than for other organizations (e.g., charities, social services departments of local governments). Given that assumption, existing evidence on costs and benefits should be relevant to determining payment rates to such systems. Here are some examples of programs for which there is evidence of effectiveness and enough basis to conjecture that they are cost effective as well.

SPECIFIC CLINICAL PROGRAMS TO REDUCE DISPARITIES

There are thousands of efforts to improve clinical quality and hence outcomes. Here we review evidence for three different types of efforts that affect health conditions in higher prevalence in minority or disadvantaged communities and that sometimes had disparity reduction as part of their rationale. As for the larger environmental-change programs, the impact on disparities depends in part on whether such programs are also limited to disadvantaged populations or neighborhoods or whether they are made available to everyone.

The three examples are:

(1) Programs to detect and control hypertension (high blood pressure).
(2) Programs to screen apparently healthy people for cancer, especially colon cancer.
(3) Programs to detect and manage diabetes, especially type 2 diabetes related to obesity.

There is an extensive literature on efforts to address each condition in disadvantaged populations. Most articles are more descriptive of interventions and their goals, but those that do report effectiveness almost without exception measure outcomes by clinical process measures – blood pressure, number screened according to guidelines, HbA1c levels. As suggested above, some evaluations are of impacts on disadvantaged populations of programs offered to all groups, while others are targeted at vulnerable populations. A few studies compare impacts on disadvantaged populations with those on the nondisadvantaged or nonminority populations and so can provide information on disparities; most measure the improvement in outcomes only for a targeted disadvantaged population relative to their baseline.

Hypertension control and stroke. Programs to screen for and treat high blood pressure in Black and other minority populations usually involve community intervention (for example, via lay health workers, visits to local businesses) and cultural sensitivity training for health professionals. Most often such programs are grant funded and community based; some programs are initiated and funded by health systems located in predominantly disadvantaged neighborhoods. The results reported are usually positive – in before and after comparisons and sometimes relative to a control group, more patients with hypertension are located and their blood pressure lowered.[15] However, persistence of adherence to programs or program medications is often a problem. We have not found any evidence of lower incidence of stroke or other cardiovascular conditions affected by hypertension from programs targeted at minorities.

Colon cancer screening. There have been many programs intended to increase the rate of use of colonoscopies by the general population over age 50. While outreach programs overall increase the rate of testing, there is little evidence they reduce disparities either in screening or in the incidence of colon cancer.[16]

---

[15] Ferdinand, K. C., Patterson, K. P., Taylor, C. et al. (2012). Community-based approaches to prevention and management of hypertension and cardiovascular disease. *The Journal of Clinical Hypertension*, 14(5), 336–343. Available online at: https://onlinelibrary.wiley .com/doi/full/10.1111/j.1751-7176.2012.00622.x; Ogedegbe, G. O., Boutin-Foster, C., Wells, M. T. et al. (2012). A randomized controlled trial of positive-affect intervention and medication adherence in hypertensive African Americans. *Archives of Internal Medicine*, 172(4), 322–326. Available online at: https://pubmed.ncbi.nlm.nih.gov/ 22269592/

[16] Liu, D., Schuchard, H., Burston, B. et al. (2021). Interventions to reduce health care disparities in cancer screening among minority adults: A systematic review. *Journal of Ethnic and Racial Health Disparities*, 8(1), 107–126. Available online at: https://pubmed .ncbi.nlm.nih.gov/32415578/; Dougherty, M. K., Brenner, A. T., Crockett, S. D. et al. (2018). Evaluation of interventions intended to increase colorectal cancer screening rates in the united states: A systematic review and meta-analysis. *JAMA Internal Medicine*, 178 (12), 1645–1658. Available online at: https://pubmed.ncbi.nlm.nih.gov/30326005/

Diabetes. Diabetes is especially common in minority populations. Dozens of studies show that community-based interventions combined with cultural training for providers are effective in improving indicators of diabetes control. There are few studies of disparities and often they are not reduced by untargeted programs.[17]

TARGETED MODEST PROGRAMS TO REDUCE DISPARITIES

Since 2005, the Robert Wood Johnson Foundation (RWJF) has been funding researchers to initiate and evaluate programs intended to reduce disparities and/or improve the health of minority populations (Black, Hispanic, Native American, immigrants). Their *Finding Answers* report[18] summarizes evaluations of 33 projects. While there was no single output metric (such as additional QALYs), we informally classified those evaluations by whether they reported statistically significant improvements in at least one clinical outcome measure (relative to the control group) or no statistically significant improvement. There were 15 projects with significant positive impacts and 18 without such impacts. It is difficult to generalize across a variety of types of interventions but it appears that financial incentives (to patients or providers) and the use of community health workers characterized effective programs, but education programs and telephone or electronic programs were unlikely to be effective.

The conclusion so far is that some *Finding Answers* programs were effective, but many were not. This is not surprising as many interventions in other industries or in drugs or devices in health care fail to demonstrate efficacy. All but one of the programs measured impact only relative to a control group that did not receive the intervention, not relative to the effect of the program on White people, so little information on reducing disparities within a program is provided. Instead, the projects were targeted at certain minority groups only and not tried with patients of other

---

[17] Golden, S. H., Maruthur, N.,, Mathioudakis, N. et al. (2017). The case for diabetes population health improvement: Evidence-based programming for population outcomes in diabetes. *Current Diabetes Reports*, 17(7), 51. Available online at: www.ncbi.nlm.nih .gov/pmc/articles/PMC5553206/; Peek, M. E., Ferguson, M., Bergeron, N. et al. (2014). Integrated community-healthcare diabetes interventions to reduce disparities. *Current Diabetes Reports*, 14(3), 467. Available online at: www.ncbi.nlm.nih.gov/pmc/articles/ PMC3956046/

[18] Wilson, L. (2013). Finding answers: Disparities research for change. Robert Wood Johnson Foundation. Available online at: www.rwjf.org/en/library/research/2013/10/find ing-answers–disparities-research-for-change.html

ethnicities. In almost all cases, the programs represented efforts to increase the use of care already known to be effective, not to demonstrate new clinical effectiveness.

From the viewpoint of the program leadership, effectiveness depended on two "tracks:"[19]

(1) The presence or development of a culture of equity in the organization in which all workers truly value achievement of equity and

(2) implementation by means of a "roadmap" that tailored the intervention to identify the needs of patients from patients themselves and then met those needs. Identifying the root causes of inequity and then somehow altering or affecting those causes (rather than just treating the symptoms of racism or discrimination) was the long term goal.

As noted in the previous chapter, changing culture in an organization, so that workers work to achieve its goals even without specific orders or incentives, has two requirements: information for workers about those goals and methods, and higher level processes to select and reward workers who are best able to accept and implement the cultural norms. Adapting the path to a goal to the twists and turns of the road to the destination desired by the population is also a daunting task for management. Beyond these general observations, summaries of these and other programs found incentives in the form of pay for performance (to the organization as a whole and actors within it), outreach and integration with the community and community health workers, and incentives and rewards for team based care as most helpful.[20] Sustainability over time or across sites depended on having resources to pay for appropriate staff and finding an equity rationale that would appeal to audiences that would support (politically and financially) the program efforts.

The next logical question we addressed is whether the effective interventions from the demonstrations have spread, while the ineffective ones have been discarded. We explored the dissemination and impact of the 15 programs with positive and significant results by consulting program

[19] Chin, M. H. (2020). Advancing health equity in patient safety: A reckoning, challenge and opportunity. *BMJ Quality and Safety*, 012599. Available online at: https://qualitysafety .bmj.com/content/early/2020/12/29/bmjqs-2020-012599

[20] Chin, M. H., Clarke, A. R.,, Nocon, R. S. et al. (2012). A roadmap and best practices for organizations to reduce racial and ethnic disparities in health care. *Journal of General Internal Medicine*, 27(8), 992–1000. Available online at: www.ncbi.nlm.nih.gov/pmc/ articles/PMC3403142/

websites, sponsoring institution evidence of adoption by that organization, and principal investigator reporting publication of results and further work by the project team on the effective program in other settings. We also performed a general internet search of the subject area and program type in the grant.

In all cases, there was some publication of project results, and in almost all cases that publication was in a peer-reviewed medical journal. Publication in health policy, health management, or health insurance journals of results or project summaries was rare. In almost all cases where there was evidence of implementation and extension of the intervention, the activity occurred at the site of the initial demonstration project if there was a single site. Extension beyond the initial site often occurred as addition of the type of clinical intervention (telephone counseling, online reminders). The core interventions in some programs (use of reminders or outreach) were sometimes undertaken by commercial enterprises, but those commercial programs did not retain a focus on the minority or disadvantaged population. There was some spread to other settings (for example, other Veterans Affairs hospitals),[21] or other countries. However, at present, there is limited uptake of the specific innovations by organizations other than the initial sponsoring entity. Principal investigators who engaged in followup work all did so or planned to do so through additional grant funding. None tried or succeeded in establishing financially sustainable, self-supporting programs.

We examined a similar though smaller list of programs provided by the Commonwealth Foundation. We found much the same pattern: Some programs produced statistically significant reductions in a measure of disparities in some clinical process or outcome metric, but documented dissemination was limited to the sponsoring organization. In a case in which the sponsor was the Blue Cross plan in North Carolina, that did mean dissemination statewide.

Why the apparent lack of general interest in programs shown to work? It does not yet appear to be the case that health systems and insurers are actively monitoring to discover and implement innovations that reduce disparity. Instead it is the originators or innovations or their sponsors that

---

[21] Advancing Health Equity n.d. Incentives to improve quality. Available online at: www .solvingdisparities.org/research/interventions/incentives-improve-quality.; Petersen, L. A., Simpson, K., Pietz, K. et al. (2013). Effects of individual physician-level and practice-level financial incentives on hypertension care: A randomized trial. *JAMA*, September 11. Available online at: . https://jamanetwork.com/journals/jama/fullarticle/17370421

have to put evidence of effectiveness in front of managers. One possible answer, suggested by leaders of the overall effort, is that effectiveness at the demonstration site does not necessarily translate into effectiveness at other sites: effectiveness is context dependent.[22] (By the same logic, some of the programs that failed to show results in the RWJF program might still work in other settings, but the process of retrying promising ideas did not seem to occur.) The other possible reason, less commonly cited, is that a program that has additional costs might have no dedicated or available source of continued revenue to cover those costs. That is, there has to be literal as well as figurative institutional buy-in to support an idea. No entity other than the sponsoring organization volunteered to pay the cost of improved outcomes for disadvantaged populations – at least in the environment that prevailed in the early 2010s.

To sum up: We find that preventive or treatment programs targeted at conditions common among disadvantaged populations are sometimes effective (though not always). (Cost effectiveness is not established with similar rigor.) If those programs are offered to broader populations, they are almost as likely to increase as reduce disparities in outcome measures even as they improve all outcomes. If programs are limited to populations with higher than average proportions of disadvantaged people, they reduce disparities at an aggregated societal level. While the size of the effect on health outcomes (compared to no program) can often be relatively large for people with hypertension, cancer, or diabetes, the impact of any individual program on aggregated health outcomes and disparities in those outcomes is necessarily limited. There is little evidence on "adding up" such programs even among preselected populations, such as those enrolled in a health maintenance organization or accountable care organization, because no efforts to move simultaneously on all or many fronts have been identified.

---

[22] Chin, M. H., Clarke, A. R., Nocon, R. S. et al. (2012). A roadmap and best practices for organizations to reduce racial and ethnic disparities in health care. *Journal of General Internal Medicine*, 27(8), 992–1000. Available online at: www.ncbi.nlm.nih.gov/pmc/articles/PMC3403142/; Kringos, D. S.,, Sunol, R., Wagner, C. et al. (2015). The influence of context on the effectiveness of hospital quality improvement strategies: A review of systematic reviews. *BMC Health Services Research*, 15(277). Available online at: https://bmchealthservres.biomedcentral.com/articles/10.1186/s12913-015-0906-0; Craig, P., Di Ruggiero, E., Frohlch, K. L. et al. (2018). Taking account of context in the population health intervention research process. Ottawa: Canadian Institutes of Health Research-National Institute for Health Research. Available online at: www.ncbi.nlm.nih.gov/books/NBK498650/.

CAN HEALTH CARE SYSTEMS AND INSURERS GAIN FROM USING EFFECTIVE PROGRAMS TO REDUCE DISPARITIES?

The pattern of evidence and behavior described in this chapter is similar to that in some other chapters – while not every effort to solve a problem works, there are some effective interventions with rigorous supporting evidence. But, even so, there is still discouraging news: movement to put those innovations in place by managements has been limited and halting. Our analysis here pushed the usual discussion of program effectiveness further than is common in discussions of disparities by searching for and endorsing innovations that are not only effective, but potentially cost effective, especially if the benefits from improving health are properly valued by others in the community – at more than the disadvantaged population is currently able or willing to pay. So what is the holdup, and what guidance can we get about the best ways of moving forward?

Let us start with the basic logic of decision-making. If an innovation does provide more benefit in total than cost in total, an important implication is that there ought to be a way for agents in society to pay the cost and be each rewarded with greater benefit – *the innovation should be generally beneficial* – all in society can gain from it, not just the disadvantaged or minority part of the population, but also health systems, health insurers, and the taxpayers (of all backgrounds) that provide the bulk of their revenues.

In the simplest case, if a person or an organization makes an investment, they are rewarded with financial benefit that is greater than the cost. The investor need not reap all the benefit – some may be gained by workers in the enterprise or customers who use the product – but enough of the benefit comes back to compensate the investor. If the cost and the benefit would occur in the same time period, the investment would be deterred if the entity that incurs the cost cannot capture enough of the investment. This pedestrian common sense has two applications to investment by health systems or insurers that reduce disparities – if the benefit from incurring cost on behalf of a population's health is lower cost because better health reduces the use of those services, the innovation will be chosen if those lower costs also help the organization. If spending on a program this year lowers the cost of other care for a disadvantaged population by more than the cost, a health insurer collecting a premium or a healthy system being paid capitation will gain. However, if the cost offsets occur somewhere else (to the patient or insurer), the health system will lack proper incentives. Even when total costs increase with an intervention, if health outcomes are improved and there is sufficient positive return to a health system associated with those improvements, there will still be gain for it. In the case in which cost offsets or health improvements occur in future time periods, the return has to be somewhat higher than the cost to compensate for lost interest from alternative uses of the investment, but the same simple principle applies.

This provides a good way to think about when innovations that reduce disparities will or will not be undertaken by health systems or insurers – what it will take to make them impactful and sustainable. Innovations will be easiest to translate into action and sustain in the case in which the benefits from the investment both reduce total cost and happen soon after the cost is incurred – and when the system was responsible for that total cost. If, however, a health system is paid fee for service, it does not benefit financially from lower total cost or use for its population. And if those reduced costs happen not now but in the future, they will have to be greater to account for lost interest on the funding, or the risk that the person will move to another insurer. If total costs rise but health is improved, there needs to be a positive return to the health system or insurer to reflect that benefit, either from the person or those concerned about the person's health.

In this last but important case, what determines and (more importantly) reflects the social value attached to improved health for the disadvantaged? Part of the solution to the challenge of health disparities deals with social values and will, and how they are expressed in collective action. Does "society," however defined, value reducing differences as a positive step and, if so, how much value does society attach to taking the step? One approach would be to assume – and then see if there is support – that all improvements in health have the same value to society regardless of who gains them. This approach is implicit in the UK model of evaluation of innovative drugs and devices where the same monetary value of benefit is usually used regardless of which population will benefit from an innovation. Alternatively, it might be that improvements in health of a given magnitude have higher value when they accrue to the disadvantaged who start from a much lower baseline level of health than the rest of the population. But how are these values to be discovered and used in ways that are feasible and sustainable?

When citizens have different levels of these values, as they surely do, how should those values or goals be incorporated into action? If programs to reduce disparities are to be financed in larger part by the rest of the population, with different levels of concern about the disadvantaged, how are these differences to be resolved? What if "politics" responds to some part of the advantaged population?[23]

Part of the answer also deals with cost. What is the cost of effective measures to improve outcomes, and is the cost per positive step worth the value of each step? It is evidence on value, effectiveness, and cost we will review in the rest of this chapter that is linked to action or inaction of health care management that might affect disparities.

INSURANCE COVERAGE EXPANSION AND DELIVERY SYSTEMS

We have shown that in principle a cost effective intervention that reduces disparities can be implemented in a way in which all parties, not just the disadvantaged, benefit from it. Now we consider the prospects for and challenges of translating this principle into practice.

We begin with the public insurance program, Medicaid. Usually a health system cannot itself affect insurance coverage of disadvantaged people in its target population, but it should have plans for what to do if Medicaid or other similar government programs provide increased coverage for the poor. How can the expansion of coverage be used in the most effective way?

If Medicaid is to continue to be limited in financial resources by the states, are there evidence-based interventions for delivery systems or insurers that are effective enough to make a claim on those resources? On the insurer side, the biggest change in Medicaid is movement of insurance coverage from fee-for-service (at very low fees) to managed care (also at very low per-capita payments). This change has not been shown to reduce cost for a given population[24] but to be a device that states use to slow overall Medicaid spending in periods of budgetary distress.[25] Evidence is lacking that some ways that delivery systems cope with low payment are better than others.

[23] Michener, J. (2020). Race, politics, and the Affordable Care Act. *Journal of Health Politics, Policy, and Law*, 45 (4), 547–566. Available online at: https://doi.org/10.1215/03616878-8255481

[24] Duggan, M., and Hayford, T. (2013). Has the shift to managed care reduced Medicaid expenditures? Evidence from state and local-level mandates. *Journal of Policy Analysis and Management*, 32(3), 505–535. Available online at: https://onlinelibrary.wiley.com/doi/abs/10.1002/pam.21693

[25] Perez, V. (2018). Effect of privatized managed care on public insurance spending and generosity: Evidence from Medicaid. *Health Economics*, 27(3), 557–575. Available online at: https://onlinelibrary.wiley.com/doi/abs/10.1002/hec.3608

CHANGING THE CULTURE OF HEALTH – WHO CAN DO IT?

There seems to be a broad consensus that disparities related to race, and probably those related to social class, are determined by the culture or social environment of where people live and work.[26] That culture is often caused fundamentally by racism or classism, which manifest in poor housing, low-quality schools, high crime, and poor access to transportation. The discouraging implication for health systems or insurers who might want to do something highly effective is that individual programs linked to their usual activities (patient care rendered in more culturally sensitive ways, lower user prices for effective health care) may have only a marginal effect on the problem. They may still be cost effective, but their effectiveness will be modest.

So is there a way for these entities to make an impact on the larger cultural, place-based causes of disparities? Decisionmakers have made two kinds of attempts – the approach of pilot projects for or by individual organizations (or do what you can do and see how it works out) and the approach of organizing cooperation with concerned others (or getting the whole community involved) – where "community" is flexibly defined to include more than just a neighborhood. Do we have evidence on innovations of either type, and their effectiveness and cost effectiveness?

The general answer is: not yet. Some health systems are just now starting efforts to affect the neighborhood health culture by targeting housing as a way of reducing disparities. There have been, one should add, many hospital efforts of the neighborhood-redevelopment type for areas close to hospitals, and perhaps because the value of the hospital's own real estate is depressed by neighborhood blight. But these efforts have not had disparities reduction as the sole focus, as they are can be offered as exemplars of the community benefit a nonprofit hospital is providing to justify its tax-free status. One example of a targeted program is the effort of the Kaiser Permanente health system (and health plan) to use its dedicated "Thriving Communities Fund" to build 41 units of low-income housing with improvements in the economic and social environment in a disadvantaged neighborhood near its Oakland headquarters.[27] (The program is to

---

[26] Robert Wood Johnson Foundation. (2021). Building a Culture of Health. Available online at: www.rwjf.org/en/cultureofhealth.html

[27] Kaiser Permanente. (2019). 3 initiatives to tackle housing insecurity. Available online at: https://about.kaiserpermanente.org/community-health/news/kaiser-permanente-announces-three-initiatives-to-improve-communi

be distinguished from another Kaiser program that paid rent for the formerly homeless but used existing housing.) This is the first such program for Kaiser Permanente and one of the first in the country of this magnitude. However, these efforts are just getting underway, so there is as yet no evidence on effectiveness or even feasibility. Kaiser Permanente partnered with another fund for this effort, and in general it seems that the scale of financing needed for bricks-and-mortar investment in housing as a focus for changing a community's health culture is large. Smaller, more targeted programs to increase the use of effective treatments of hypertension or minimally invasive hysterectomies among their Black members are much more common.[28]

Another instructive demonstration is a program funded by CMS called the "Accountable Health Care Communities" model. Begun in 2016, this legislation allows Medicare or Medicaid to pay entities (often hospitals or health systems) to "systematically identify and address health related social needs" of high using Medicare or Medicaid beneficiaries. The government insurer here pays for services (survey, patient navigation assistance or advice, and ultimately "aligned" efforts to reduce spending on these high cost individuals. The program cannot directly pay for food, housing, or transportation, but it does pay for people to assist beneficiaries in dealing with their needs. A full evaluation of the program is not yet complete, but it has provided rigorous evidence that (relative to a control group) intervention patients can be identified and can be provided with navigation services. That is, it shows that health systems can take action to affect the culture of health for high needs patients if they are paid for it. Interestingly, the greatest impact so far has been on food and diet. Only the Medicare intervention has so far been evaluated REF, providing evidence of a 10 percent decline in ED visits but no evidence of net monetary savings to Medicare. The populations enrolled in the demonstration are about half minority groups, with a larger proportion in Medicaid than in Medicare.

Finally, there have been some investor financed efforts to provide tools to deal with the effects of adverse social determinants of health (though not

---

[28] Greene, J. (2019). Kaiser Permanente reduces racial disparities in who gets minimally invasive hysterectomies. *Kaiser Permanente Spotlight*. Available online at: https://spotlight.kaiserpermanente.org/kaiser-permanente-reduces-racial-disparities-in-hysterectomies/; Bartoleme, R. E. (2016). Population care management and team-based approach to reduce racial disparities among African Americans/Blacks with hypertension. *The Permanente Journal*, 20(1), 53–59. Available online at: www.ncbi.nlm.nih.gov/pmc/articles/PMC4732795/

specifically disparities). New organizations such as CityBlock[29] have made efforts to develop systems to better coordinate social services and to provide evidence of effectiveness. Investors anticipate more public support and funding for such efforts.

CAN PAYMENT BE ENHANCED?

For most health systems, Medicaid patients have low payment rates because states set low reimbursement rates (or in a few cases capitation rates) that are lower than Medicare and much lower than for commercial patients. There is no law requiring Medicaid plans to do this; instead it represents a positive decision by state policymakers to try to pay less than others while not discouraging too many physicians from refusing Medicaid patients entirely and health systems from limiting services. Political decisionmakers at the state level signal with low Medicaid payment rates that they do not value access to care generally, and surely not high-quality care, for this population. Those same authorities will criticize health systems for not overcharging privately insured patients, to cross-subsidize those on Medicaid, and the health systems will be driven to using programs in Medicare or Section 242 waivers to collect what they can. But surely it is obvious that the fundamental problem is that someone in state government for some reason set Medicaid payments too low. There is plenty of evidence[30] that higher provider payments for particular populations call forth more supply, increase provider willingness to treat such patients, and open the doors to higher quality health systems for people in low-income or minority groups.

According to the Medicaid and Children's Health Insurance Program Payment and Access Commission, MACPAC, in 2017, a composite measure of Medicaid hospital payment generosity varied from 50 percent of the national average (New Hampshire) to more than 160 percent (Alaska and District of Columbia). Among the top 10 most generous state Medicaid payments were some more politically conservative states, such as Idaho and South Carolina, possibly reflecting variations across states in the ability or willingness of hospitals to overcharge commercial payers to offset

---

[29] Cityblock. Available online at: www.cityblock.com/

[30] Holgash, K., and Heberlein, M. (2019). Physician acceptance of new Medicaid patients: What matters and what doesn't. *Health Affairs*. Available online at: www.healthaffairs .org/do/10.1377/hblog20190401.678690/full/

Medicaid shortfall. Physician payment rates showed a similar large variation (relative to the average or relative to private payment rates).[31]

There have been lawsuits charging that low payment is discriminatory against minority groups, even though the low payment applies to all on Medicaid. A California lawsuit filed by the Mexican American Legal Defense and Educational Fund in 2017 to take advantage of special provisions in California civil rights law is still working its way through the courts; previous similar cases have been dismissed based on the argument that it is up to the federal government's oversight of Medicaid to enforce and adjudicate questions of the vague provision in the law requiring adequate access to care.[32] Many states will argue loudly that their budgets do not permit them to afford to pay more for Medicaid (although a few do). It is true that overall state tax collections influence Medicaid payment rates to providers (as well as decisions on eligibility). However, states argue this even when tax collections are rising and budgets are in surplus. There is nothing to prevent a state from either raising taxes or diverting spending to help pay more generously for care for individuals who are poor, especially in minority populations. They could do so; they just choose not to.

What if state officials do not take action to reduce disparities? If a state fails to attend to all collective goods, then (as economist Burton Weisbrod has noted) private nonprofit firms such as hospitals may arise to fill the gap.[33] They cannot levy taxes but can rely on contributions to a defined social mission. We have already mentioned the Johnson Foundation Finding Answers program, but is there evidence that local hospitals or insurance plans have other sources of funding for efforts to reduce disparities when governments fail to do so sufficiently? To use other funds, they would use profits that are largely generated by middle class commercially insured patients using certain high-profit margin services to fund programs to reduce disparities.

---

[31] Zuckerman, S., Skopec, L., and Epstein, M. (2017). *Medicaid Physician Fees after the ACA Primary Care Fee Bump.* Washington, DC: Urban Institute. Available online at: www .urban.org/sites/default/files/publication/88836/2001180-medicaid-physician-fees-after-the-aca-primary-care-fee-bump_0.pdf

[32] Mexican American Legal Defense and Educational Fund (MALDEF) (2019). Judge gives green light to civil rights lawsuit affecting 1 in 3 Californians. Available online at: www .maldef.org/2019/06/judge-gives-green-light-to-civil-rights-lawsuit-affecting-1-in-3-cali fornians/

[33] Weisbrod, B. A. (1975). Toward a theory of the voluntary nonprofit sector in a three-sector economy, in E. Phelps, ed., *Altruism, Morality, and Economic Theory.* Russell Sage Foundation: New York. 171–195.

For hospitals that are nonprofit, there is another source of lower cost that might generate resources that could be used to invest in disparity-reduction programs – the lower property and other taxes and advantages associated with their tax exempt status. In principle, the tax exempt hospital should then have lower costs than its hypothetical investor owned twin and could use the potentially increased profits to invest in community benefits. There are state rules and some federal regulations that require reporting and sometimes provision of some benefits in order to retain nonprofit status, as noted above. Usually what qualifies as a community benefit is not very precise, but some states have stricter rules of fractions of revenue to be devoted to charity care of all served by a health system, and a few are more specific about programs for the disadvantaged populations they serve. Here as elsewhere management's challenge is to weigh investment on programs for specific minorities with other programs of community benefit (including research and medical education). However, taxpayers who pay higher taxes when nonprofits pay none (and do not make payments to local governments in lieu of taxes) may reasonably expect that some of those benefits should go effective programs, at least up to the limit of the value of the tax advantages. So far construction of transparent links between tax advantages and such programs have not been established in most states, but the passage of the federal "Social Impact Partnerships for Pay" could provide a vehicle for doing so.[34]

The same approach could be true for health insurance companies. About half of all privately insured people are covered by "Blue" plans that are not investor owned. They might be mutual companies or be chartered under special state regulation, and they usually are not tax exempt – but they do include community benefits in their missions. They could use profits from the sale of insurance to employers, for example, to subsidize programs to reduce disparities. However, these nonprofit insurance plans are usually not offered favorable tax treatment compared to their commercial counterparts.

In both of these cases, however, there are both efficiency and equity challenges. Either high profits by health systems or health insurers have as their mirror image high health insurance premiums, which can discourage some nonpoor people from buying insurance or buying adequate insurance; this is inefficient. (Nonprofit hospitals long argued that they used their tax benefits to keep their charges to private middle class insurers

---

[34] US Department of the Treasury n.d. SIPPRA – pay for results. Available online at: https://home.treasury.gov/services/social-impact-partnerships/sippra-pay-for-results

down).[35] Moreover, the burden of funding disparity-reducing programs as community benefit as the firms discharge their social missions will, for the most part, fall unevenly on their customers. Someone can avoid contributing by getting insurance through a self-insured employer and using a suburban hospital with few disadvantaged patients. Private provision of public goods to make up for political failures almost never works out in an ideal way, but sometimes it is the only game in town (if there is to be a game at all).

Evidence on effectiveness or cost effectiveness cannot by itself produce the change of will and of heart that is needed. It can help if it serves up on a silver platter some highly effective and cost-effective policy options; that may change disparities. Still, some states seem especially unwilling to pay for care improvements for programs targeted at disadvantaged populations, which implies a need for a power shift and/or a change in attitude before pronouncements of concern about disparities turn into action.

The other part of the story deals with the behavior of health systems and private insurers. Evidence does establish that payment levels for hospitals and professional services by private insurers are higher than those for the government programs of Medicare and Medicaid.[36] It also seems fairly clear that the shortfall between private and public payment rates has increased over time. There is "price discrimination" in which sellers of care are generally able to collect higher prices for ostensibly the same services if their buyer is a private insurer or patient than if the care is paid by public plans. There is, however, almost no evidence on why this is or should be so.

There is criticism by Kaplan and O'Neill[37] which correctly notes that some portion of higher private prices will be translated into higher group insurance premiums that receive a tax subsidy. But there is no reason to

---

[35] Nicholson, S., Pauly, M. V., Burns, L. R. et al. (2020). Measuring community benefits provided by for-profit and nonprofit hospitals. *Health Affairs*, 19(6). Available online at: www.healthaffairs.org/doi/10.1377/hlthaff.19.6.168

[36] Chernew, M. E., Hicks, A. L., and Shah, S. A. (2020). Wide state-level variation in commercial health care prices suggests uneven impact of price regulation. *Health Affairs*, 39(5). Available online at: www.healthaffairs.org/doi/abs/10.1377/hlthaff.2019 .01377?journalCode=hlthaff;
Pifer, R. (2020). Paying private insurers Medicare rates would tank hospital revenue by 35%, study finds. *Healthcare Dive*. Available online at: www.healthcaredive.com/news/ paying-private-insurers-medicare-rates-would-tank-hospital-revenue-by-35/577313/

[37] Kaplan, A., and O'Neill, D. (2020). Hospital price discrimination is deepening racial health inequity. *NEJM Catalyst*. Available online at: https://catalyst.nejm.org/doi/full/10 .1056/CAT.20.0593

expect that if this subsidy were curtailed, higher tax collections would channel significantly more resources into Medicaid programs. Moreover, higher private prices should primarily harm the privately insured but not adversely affect those on public programs. Kaplan and O'Neill claim that those higher prices mean that "White patients have better access to quality facilities" than minorities – but fail to note that then they overpay for them.

To sum up: private health systems and insurers can fund disparity reducing programs by charging more to their paying customers – as long as their markets are less competitive. In effect, they impost a private sales tax to pay for a social obligation that government has failed to carry out. The distribution of this tax is itself likely to be unfair, and the higher prices may discourage needed care for the less well insured. So there are some significant downsides to advocating that private firms discharge a costly social responsibility to reduce disparities. If governments still fail in their role, however, this imperfect solution may be the best that can be done – but so far it has not been undertaken in any effective way.

STRATEGIC CHOICE BEYOND PROGRAMS: CONCRETE CHOICES AND THEIR LIMITS

Bad health outcomes are more likely for any population in a given time period if many people in the population are sick or have chronic conditions. This means that a health system that wants to make a major impact on improving health outcomes for disadvantaged populations has two kinds of strategies – "long-run" and "short-run." The long-run strategy is able to reduce the incidence of chronic illness and conditions in the population. Broadly speaking, if effective strategies exist, they almost surely involve primary preventive care, perhaps some secondary preventive care for genetic conditions, and education of patients, including about the use of preventive care. The short-run strategy would help people with chronic conditions manage those conditions, as well as helping people without chronic conditions respond effectively to an acute threat or the onset of a chronic condition. The long-run improvements require a population approach; the short-run approaches are more of a "sick care" strategy that can still be effective even if the long-run approaches fail to prevent the onset of conditions.

Interventions that improve long run health outcomes of disadvantaged populations involve either medical services or other environmental or institutional factors. The latter are more numerous and have stronger evidence of larger-scale impacts. For example, educational interventions in early childhood are sometimes positively related to young adult health. Or urban planning projects may lead to better housing and safer neighborhoods that improve health. Likewise, income transfers such as the earned income tax credit (EITC) correlates with better diet, better prenatal care, and some other correlates of quantity and quality of life. However, unless health systems are very large or have strong local influence, they cannot be expected to play the leading role in such intervention projects. Interventions more specific to the medical services a system does or can provide are smaller scale and more limited in number.

What seems to be most effective here are programs that can target and attract disadvantaged people to receive interventions already known to be clinically effective. There have been successful programs as at Boston Children's Hospital to reduce asthma among children in minority groups.[38] Also, prenatal programs and programs to encourage immunizations and breast and colorectal cancer screening among minority populations, as noted above, seem effective in increasing screening, though impacts on cancer incidence and health outcomes have not been extensively documented. Hospital and physician trade associations (American Hospital Association and American Medical Association) have established offices and both offer and receive grants for programs to reduce disparities, but the programs are in early stages.[39] There are also programs to educate health professionals about disparities, but no evidence that they are effective in changing anything about outcomes or the process of care.[40]

One of the programs for which there is a large amount of rigorous evidence of effectiveness is the Nurse-Family Partnership program.[41] Begun in 1977 in Elmira, New York, under the leadership of Dr. David Olds, this program implements what its name implies: nurses work with

---

[38] Boston Childrens' Hospital n.d. Community Asthma Initiative. Available online at: www.childrenshospital.org/centers-and-services/programs/a-_-e/community-asthma-initiative-program

[39] American Health Association (2020). More than $14 million in research grants awarded for health technology solutions focused on heart and brain health, including special projects related to COVID-19 and CVD. *American Heart Association Newsroom.* Available online at: https://newsroom.heart.org/news/more-than-14-million-in-research-grants-awarded-for-health-technology-solutions-focused-on-heart-and-brain-health-including-special-projects-related-to-covid-19-and-cvd

[40] Dupras, D. M., Wieland, M. L., and, Halvorsen, A. J. (2020). Assessment of training in health disparities in US internal medicine residency programs. *JAMA Network Open,* 3 (8), e2012757. Available online at: https://jamanetwork.com/journals/jamanetworkopen/fullarticle/2769083

[41] Nurse-Family Partnership n.d. The David Olds story. Available online at: www.nursefamilypartnership.org/about/program-history/

low-income pregnant women and their families to improve both maternal and infant health outcomes. Evidence is strong that, among early childhood programs, this strategy causes lower levels of child abuse and neglect and associated private and social costs. In the program, the nurse helps the prospective mother navigate the challenges of pregnancy and infant care up to one year. Mothers are counseled on self-efficacy – cultivating the realization of their potential as mothers – the ecology of the family relationship dealing with family and social situations – and attachment – helping the mother bond to the child through supportive relationships. The nurse counseling is available until the baby is two years old.

Careful research using randomized controlled trials suggests that this program results in participant children obtaining needed pediatric care on time with lower costs for emergency room visits and other types of care, and thriving to a greater extent up to age five. For the cost of the program, money measures of these kinds of benefits show returns up to five times their costs of helping those mothers judged to have higher risks of poor health for themselves or their children (teenagers, unmarried, low income), with returns still in excess of costs even for those who are lower risks.

The program has been implemented in many sites, enrolling more than 200,000 pregnant women over more than 40 years. It has largely been managed by publicly funded neighborhood health centers or state public health departments, but there has been some foundation funding and some participation by hospitals.

The program is not specifically targeted at disparities, but the correlation between risk and race or other measures of social vulnerability means that it serves mainly Black patients in some sites. In particular, the population of young mothers in the Memphis site was overwhelmingly African American.

The evaluation in Memphis was undertaken by Nobel Prize-winning econometrician James Heckman and colleagues.[42] It studied outcomes at several points in the care process and later in the lives of children born to mothers in the program. In Memphis, positive impacts persisted over childhood but were larger and more persistent for boys than girls. Use of hospitals and physician contacts was lower in treatment group children but

---

[42] Heckman, J. J., Holland, M. L., Makino, K. K. et al. (2017). *An analysis of the Memphis nurse-family partnership program.* NBER Working Paper 23610. Cambridge, MA: National Bureau of Economic Research.

the difference was not statistically significant except for lower hospital use by boys at age 10. There were mental health benefits to mothers during pregnancy and greater parental investments in the home environment, but the most important path for improved outcomes was via higher birth-weight for boy babies that was later associated with higher cognitive abilities. For girls, there was an improvement in social and emotional health for girls at age 6.

This evidence might be sufficient to motivate a health system to imple-ment such a program, but there will be some barriers. Most obviously, though the monetary value of benefits to children and parents over 12 years is almost surely enough to offset the direct costs of the program, a health system incurring that cost now will not easily be able to reap those financial benefits in the future. A capitated health system or an insurer may obtain some cost offsets from lower use of care by the child over 12 years. However, the likely turnover of membership in its patient popula-tion will dissipate much of these savings. The improved cognitive abilities later in life are manifested both in better employment opportunities and less crime by boys – but no health care system is paid for that.

The latter day version of the Nurse Family partnership might be the Treasury Department's program created in response to the Social Impact Partnership to Pay for Results Act, implemented in 2019. Although most of the federal grants to local governments under this program went for nonhealth purposes, one did go to the Indiana Nurse Family Partnership program, to fund expansion from its base begun in 2011. This federal government intends this program to fund payments for metrics of success of social programs (and the external evaluations that measure such suc-cess). One funded program to assist pregnant women in South Carolina has been put on hold, but the Indiana program has promised an "evidence-based community health program with over 40 years of evidence showing improvements in the health and lives" of poor first time "pregnant moms." The program appealed to evidence of the high long term return of the type documented by the Memphis initiative; the version in Indiana so far has served 50 percent nonwhite mothers, so is not specifically targeted at racial as opposed to economic disparities. Goodwill of Indiana is the primary nongovernmental sponsor; no health systems or insurers appear to be involved. Evidence on effectiveness is not yet available.[43]

---

[43] Indiana Nurse Family Partnership n.d. About us. Available online at: www .nursefamilypartnership.org/about/

HOW DELIVERY SYSTEMS COULD (AND SOMETIMES DO)
DEVELOP EVIDENCE FROM THEIR DATA TO TARGET WAYS
TO REDUCE DISPARITIES

A large, modern health system will be awash in data on use of medical services by the people it serves. Especially in the era of artificial intelligence and Big Data, is there a way to use this information to diagnose both problems of disparities and potentially effective types of interventions? The answer is yes if two different types of data problems, which are not helped by more numbers that are not the right numbers, can be solved.

One problem is a measure of patient welfare. How can a system measure the impact of disparities on its disadvantaged patients' health? There are clinical data that might indicate health problems, but that information is often incomplete even for people who use the system a lot, and is totally absent for those who stay away. A system could survey patients, but it is hard to get responses that are timely and unbiased. Or it could identify a measure of high resource use that does not itself proxy a good outcome. For example, an inpatient admission is about the most costly thing for a health system.

The other problem is the system probably does not know much about its patients' environments or characteristics outside its walls (unless it makes the effort to find out). It knows patient insurance coverage, age, and gender, but may not know race or ethnicity. It usually does not know their safety, environmental quality, income, family situation, or opportunity for exercise or nutrition. Fortunately, the system does know their postal zip code and that can be linked to neighborhood-level measures of all these characteristics.

Specifically, zip code can be used to locate patients in geographic areas characterized by indicators of social vulnerability, such as racial/ethnic segregation, low average income levels, poor housing or air quality, and even the prevalence of low insurance coverage. Such measures have already been aggregated into something called a social vulnerability index (SVI), which uses measures at the zip code level of average income, housing quality, and the like.[44]

So a health system can link data on SVI to outcomes of its patients. When we used this approach with data from our own health system, we

---

[44] Agency for Toxic Substances and Disease Registry (ATSDR) n.d. What is Social Vulnerability? Available online at: www.atsdr.cdc.gov/placeandhealth/svi/fact_sheet/fact_sheet.html

found, to no one's surprise, that people who lived in neighborhoods with a high SVI had higher rates of hospitalization, controlling for age and sex, than those who lived in areas where few residents were socially vulnerable. Probably that was because our system's patients shared the problems of their neighbors, though it could also come from adverse effects of neighborhood conditions even on those who were otherwise "invulnerable."[45] Not only that, we were able to identify two different pathways by which neighborhood social vulnerability led to hospitalization. It led to a higher prevalence of chronic conditions – people were sicker – and those conditions predicted hospitalizations. But in addition, people were also more likely to be hospitalized after controlling for chronic conditions when they had high SVI. Vulnerability makes sick people sicker. We also found that the impact of SVI differed across clinic sites – some were apparently better able to reduce the impact of high SVI on hospitalization than others. There was also some suggestion that a person from a high SVI area who used a clinic where most of the people were not from such neighborhoods did better than if they used a clinic where almost all patients were from vulnerable backgrounds.

This study used predictive modelling not to predict if something bad would happen, but to target where one might intervene to keep that thing from happening. Obviously, what is missing for making the case for health system action is identifying a specific intervention that can offset the effects of social vulnerability. However, this kind of information on variation across sites on the impact of SVI, if it occurs, may give some clues about where to look for a targeted intervention.

The framework just outlined provides a different rationale for discovering and reacting to findings of disparate outcomes or treatments for people who are disadvantaged, are people of color, or have low income. Differences may serve as map for discovering that opportunities for effective interventions for disadvantaged populations are likely to exist. Low baseline health is not always correlated with greater program effectiveness or higher value of health improvements, but it often is. So let us begin by looking at evidence on disparities to see if it will help us identify potential targets for improvement.

---

[45] Lucarelli, C., Frean, M., Gordon, A. S. et al. (2020). How does cost-sharing impact spending growth and cost-effective treatments? Evidence from deductibles. NBER Working Paper 28155. Cambridge, MA: National Bureau of Economic Research. Available online at: www.nber.org/papers/w28155

Efforts to improve social inequities would be funded by society organized as a government that collects the taxes and makes the expenditures that are determined by its collective choice process to have positive net value. Governments at all levels (federal, state, or local) could design programs with incentives to providers and patients that improve quality metrics.

What can health care systems or private insurers do if there is no additional societal or public funding of rewards to reduce disparities? Health care systems are not owned or managed by the government, and they cannot collect taxes or conscript resources. Other than carrying out programs governments are willing to pay for, are there other social roles or obligations for health care systems to assist disadvantaged people?

The problem for an organization (for-profit or nonprofit) wanting to take on its social responsibility is the absence of even conceptual guidelines about both what it should spend and how it should finance what it spends. To take the latter point first – should it use whatever market power it might have to raise its prices above the competitive level and use the excess to fund programs to reduce disparities? If it does so, should that excess be covered by private insurers, employers who pay for worker insurance, or workers themselves in the form of lower money wages? Should it ask for donations by philanthropists to pay for such programs, the mission statement of many private nonprofit hospitals? Should its stockholders be asked to accept returns below the market average, especially if they are not socially conscious investors?

Financing does provide a way of offering direction about which programs could feasibly be undertaken – those that can be financed. Consider the clearest case of donor or philanthropic financing: A health system should surely undertake all disparity-reducing programs its donors are willing to pay for, although charitable support of patient care has declined since the implementation of Medicaid and Medicare. Governments – in addition to paying directly for care – could provide other payments to encourage care for needy populations. Examples are through a program in Medicare for hospitals with disproportionate shares of low-income or Medicaid patients, or local governments for tax breaks in exchange for community benefits.

There is considerable information imperfection around these programs, so they by no means exhaust the set of cost-effective interventions to reduce disparities; that may be more efficient. But there is no invisible hand that assures this outcome, and the higher prices may discourage use of cost-effective care for those who can and do pay – so nothing is perfect.

The other challenge is when a program incurs large costs initially and returns, either in the form of improved population health or cost reductions, happen in later periods. To get organizations to make these kinds of investments, there has to be a mechanism that links their behavior now to rewards later. Because of customer turnover (changes in insurance coverage, including going from private insurance to Medicare at retirement), a private insurer may have difficulty waiting for a return from investing in a mobile insured that may not come – even if it accrues to society.

CONCLUSION

At this point it appears that "Bold New Visions"[46] for reducing disparities have thus far had limited effect at the structural level and even less effect at the health system or provider level. Some programs that may improve quality for the general population also appear to do so for minority or disadvantaged people – but not necessarily to a greater extent than for middle-class people, and only after many failures. We commented in Chapter 2 that evidence-based improvements in quality or cost in health systems seem not to have added up to major impacts. Disparities may be another example. Though we do not know what the counterfactual would be, the innovations for which there is evidence of cost effectiveness – asthma treatment programs, cancer screening, use of nurse practitioners – do not seem to have resulted in measurable reductions in disparities in any community. Bigger impact strategies are possible – attacks on the epidemics of hypertension and diabetes in Black and Native American populations, effective population-level efforts to reduce obesity – but to our knowledge have not been tried by health systems responsible for large populations of minority or disadvantaged people. The lament that so far there has been an absence of political will, though vague, is common. What is clear is that no public program, no private insurer, accountable care organization, or Medicare Advantage plan, and no hospital or health system donors have yet found or put major resources into achieving the

---

[46] Cooper, L. A., Ortega, A. N., Ammerman, A. S. et al. (2015). Calling for a bold new vision of health disparities intervention research. *American Journal of Public Health*. Available online at: https://ajph.aphapublications.org/doi/10.2105/AJPH.2014.302386

goal of reducing health disparities. Part of the problem is the usual paradox of innovation – without evidence for successful innovation no one will invest, but development of evidence requires investment. The latter task is the essence of research and the plea that more of it is needed is also commonplace but true.

11

Driving Innovation in Health Care

External Evidence, Decision-Making, and Leadership

Flaura Winston and Mark Pauly[*]

LEADERSHIP ARMED WITH EVIDENCE

The bulk of medical care system management in the United States does not ground decisions in use of available, high quality evidence. The previous chapters in this book demonstrate both that there sometimes is a rich scientific foundation in health care organization, delivery, and financing that could, if applied, lead to better outcomes, and that sometimes there is little or no evidence on effectiveness of interventions. However, we also observed that the bulk of health care management in the United States does not ground decisions in evidence, using it if available and taking uncertainty into account if not – instead "magical thinking" is often used to make choices.[1] Ironically, management holds evidence in high esteem for decision-making by clinicians. In this chapter, we explore why management holds itself to a lower standard regarding its organizational, staffing, and planning choices, seeing experience, intuition, and opinions as good-enough evidence for decisions. We explore what needs to happen for this to change.

We begin by demonstrating that evidence-based management is not a simple extension of evidence-based medicine and that the context of health care organizations challenges decision-making. Compared to modern medicine, managers of health systems and insurance plans tend to view every decision as unique and so unable to be assisted by evidence on the results of other similar decisions in other apparently similar circumstances.

[*] **Acknowledgments:** We thank Tim Rawson and Cynthia Bazan of ILN and Natalie Oppenheimer for their invaluable assistance in researching, preparing, writing, and editing this chapter.
[1] Baicker, K., and Chandra, A. (2017). Evidence-based health policy. *New England Journal of Medicine*, 377, 2413–2415. Available online at: www.nejm.org/doi/full/10.1056/ NEJMp1709816

We further demonstrate that even the most innovative organizations rarely use rigorous external evidence in their decision-making. Then, we apply a metaphor, the Valley of Death, to explain the challenges in translating academic research into practical solutions for health care problems.[2] Next, we explore common services used by management to assist with decision-making – consulting, trade conferences and paid subscriptions (for peer institution benchmarking data, industry-relevant problem-solving tips, and industry/government intelligence) – and examine the quality of evidence they use. Finally, we conclude with proposing a new paradigm for health care management research and its dissemination that maintains academic rigor while ensuring relevance and give examples of two efforts that bridge the research-relevance gap.

THINGS ARE NOT EQUAL

David Sackett, a Canadian-American physician and health services researcher, brought about a revolution in the practice of clinical medicine by introducing and promoting the concept of evidence-based medicine as "the conscientious, explicit, and judicious use of current best evidence in making decisions about the care of individual patients."[3] At the time, this was something of a revolt by younger physicians against the textbook assurances based on prominent physician opinion that were part of medical education. The practice of evidence-based medicine means integrating individual clinical expertise with the best available external clinical evidence from systematic research. Key to this concept is a hierarchy in quality of evidence and an understanding that a clinician, tasked with deciding on a treatment plan for a patient, must be skilled in accessing, collecting, and examining the quality of evidence and knowing how to apply it in their decision-making.

---

[2] Coller, B. S., and Califf, R. M. (2009). Traversing the valley of death: A guide to assessing prospects for translational success. *Science Translational Medicine*, 1(10), 10cm9. Available online at: www.ncbi.nlm.nih.gov/pmc/articles/PMC2879158/#R6; Butler, D. (2008). Translational research: Crossing the valley of death. *Nature*, 453, 840–842. Available online at: www.nature.com/news/2008/080611/full/453840a.html; Bornstein, D. (2011). Helping new drugs out of research's "valley of death." *New York Times*. Available online at: https://opinionator.blogs.nytimes.com/2011/05/02/helping-new-drugs-out-of-academias-valley-of-death/; Stanford Innovative Machines Accelerator n.d. What is the valley of death? Available online at: https://ima.stanford.edu/about/what-valley-death

[3] Sackett, D., Rosenberg, W. M. C., Muir Gray, J. A. et al. (1996). Evidence based medicine: What it is and what it isn't. *BMJ*, 12, 71–72.

The complementary model for health management does not exist. Large health care organizations are much more complex: rather than one single decision-maker, these organizations comprise many decision-makers distributed across siloed teams who make a large number of choices about a wide range of things, from patient care issues to what to charge in the parking garage. Executives use staff to help for two tasks: originating novel ideas and deciding to use them. They use internal consensus and various forms of internal know-how and external guidance drawn from best practice, benchmarking with peers, bandwagoning, and expertise and experience from consulting firms to help with both tasks – all to pull together a case for a decision (such as adoption of an innovation). Rather than a rigorous approach for decision-making, discipline is applied to operationalizing the implementation of decisions. However, as we have seen in the previous chapters, health organization leadership makes preventable mistakes by adopting innovations with little chance of success and avoiding those with evidence that might not be popular. For decisions about organizational arrangements, new care programs, or patient management strategies, peer-reviewed literature is rarely consulted, and untested rationales and internal consensus often carry the day. Visceral urges, copying others, or going with what seems reasonable even if untested is much more common – and yet can have serious consequences for patient health, as well as organizations' finances.

Evidence Is in the Eye of the Beholder: What Is Evidence, and How Is Its Quality Determined?

Why does underuse or misuse of evidence happen, and how might organizations move to do better? Is it a matter of the absence of evidence, the cost of generating it, or the unwillingness of leaders to push for evidence-based programs that contradict the experience-based beliefs and vested interests of various stakeholders within the organization? In the previous chapters, we looked at a variety of settings in which these issues are in play.

In writing this chapter, we realized that those involved in health care have a wide-ranging view of what qualifies as evidence and avoiding unpopular programs even if evidence-based. Although most people view evidence as valuable to support claims, assumptions or hypotheses, people disagree about which evidence is valid, reliable, and relevant. Scientists view evidence as systematically collected data that serves to support or refute a scientific theory or hypotheses. Others not as wedded to or knowledgeable about the scientific method might view evidence as information they find that supports a position or recommendation, including opinions and benchmarking of current practice.

The goal of rating the quality of evidence is to provide unbiased and accurate assessments of findings to those charged with making decisions. The higher the quality of evidence, the stronger the support for recommendations based on that evidence. For example, the World Health Organization's (WHO) GRADE process[4] offers four levels of evidence quality. The highest quality is randomized controlled trials (RCTs) (or better yet, systematic studies of multiple randomized trials) and the lowest is observational studies; opinions and consensus statements are also viewed as evidence in their rating system. According to the WHO and other proponents of evidence-based decision-making, key characteristics of high quality evidence include findings demonstrating a large, precise effect size; strong methods and their implementation that are free of bias; and benefits that outweigh the downsides of applying the findings in real-world settings.

VIEWS AND ACTIONS BY HEALTH CARE ADMINISTRATORS REGARDING USE OF EVIDENCE

What, then, influences decision-making by health care administrators, and what role does high quality, rigorous evidence play? In 2019, Dr. Ruiling Guo, Associate Professor of Health care Administration at Idaho State University and Fellow of the Center for Evidence-Based Management (https://cebma.org), applied the theory of planned behavior to understand the factors influencing the use of evidence-based management (EBMgt) in a survey of 154 US health care administrators.[5] She found that administrators largely based decisions on their "personal professional practices," what they had learned from personal experience, and the customs they had acquired. Administrators avoid EBMgt due to their perceptions about the difficulty in using EBMgt and their attitudes about its lack of relevance (most notably the attitude about the absence of strong, available evidence) to solving real-world problems facing them.

[4] Guyatt, G. H., Oxman A. D., Kunz, R. et al. (2008). What is "quality of evidence" and why is it important to clinicians? *BMJ*, 336(7651), 995–998. Available online at: https://doi.org/10.1136/bmj.39490.551019.BE.

[5] Guo, R., Berkshire, S. D., Fulton, L. V. et al. (2019). Predicting intention to use evidence-based management among US healthcare administrators: Application of the theory of planned behavior and structural equation modeling. *International Journal of Healthcare Management*, 12(1), 25–32. Available online at: www.tandfonline.com/doi/abs/10.1080/20479700.2017.1336856

EVIDENCE USE BY HEALTH CARE INNOVATION LEADERS:
A PILOT STUDY

We extended Guo's work to explore the hypothesis that leaders from innovative health care organizations, armed with the ability and skills to access and interpret scientific evidence, might serve as a model for how rigorous scientific evidence might be used in practice. Because there is very little literature on how management decisions in health care organizations are made and none at all on the use of internal or outside evidence, we surveyed seven leaders in health care innovation who are associated with the Innovation Learning Network,[6] a membership-based community that exists to push its members' innovative thinking and decision-making by providing inspiration, enabling knowledge sharing, and connecting a world of *innovation* peers. Members include Kaiser Permanente, the United Kingdom's National Health Service, Mass General Brigham, and the US Department of Veterans Affairs. The bulk of our respondents had senior roles in innovation (such as vice president for innovation or director of innovation) in their organizations. Obviously this is a small and select sample but should represent best practices (or practices by the best) in the industry. Our survey asked them to identify a specific innovation in their organization and then asked them about the role of evidence (and other influences) in the various steps of an innovative process from original idea to evaluation of the outcomes of the final decision. Then we asked if the process followed was typical of what they do. It virtually always was. Here is what they told us.

Where did the initial idea come from? The universal response was from organization staff, and most often from staff dedicated to innovation.

How did the organization make a decision about the innovation? Here again the most important sources were internal evidence from the organization and opinions of key organization leaders based on their judgement and experience. The internal evidence may include internal RCTs. External evidence from the peer-reviewed literature or external RCTs was rarely used for inspiration for innovation or to assist decision-making.

Did you (or do you usually) use outside consultants to help decide on innovations? None of the experts reported using consultants for the sample innovation. However, all but one said they used consultants "sometimes."

When you use consultants, what information do you seek from them? The most common answer here was information on what similar organizations

---

[6] Innovation Learning Network. Available online at: www.iln.org/cpages/home

are doing. Consultants are not typically asked to summarize evidence, rigorous or not, though they do often volunteer anecdotes.

How did you make the decision on whether or not to implement the innovation? Results here were similar to other answers – internal evidence and opinion were the primary tools used.

How do you evaluate the success or effectiveness of the innovation? No respondent reported a formal evaluation. Either expert opinion or low quality evidence were used (e.g., measuring change from before to after implementation, while better than no evidence, is subject to confounding bias – results attributed to the intervention might actually reflect the impact of cooccurring social, economic, cultural, or clinical phenomena).

The overall picture seems to be one in which even the most innovative organizations rely on internal expertise, evidence, and opinion about innovations rather than on external rigorous evidence. When they seek external evidence, for example from consultants, their aim is primarily benchmarking.

Implications for Evidence for Health Care Organizations, Even Innovative Ones

It is clear that even the best-managed health care organizations – the kind that we sampled – do not rely on the kind of evidence-based cost-benefit model advocated by Cass Sunstein or the comparative effectiveness model used by the US Food and Drug Administrates (FDA) to approve or reject drugs and devices.

The full Sunstein/FDA model of requiring RCT evidence before change is made seems impractical and overly restrictive *a priori*. As we have shown, this model itself lacks evidence that it improves health or cost outcomes compared even to current practice, much less to any new approach. The other extreme of largely ignoring rigorous evidence in decision-making, only rarely consulting the research literature and often only when it supports what has already been decided, and relying instead on hunches, following the crowd, and playing the financing and reimbursement angles also seems imperfect. How did we get to this extremist dichotomy: rigor versus relevance?

LEADING IN TWO DIRECTIONS AT ONCE

Management scholars present a Valley of Death between rigor and practical relevance. They describe two extremes for the conduct of research:

"Mode 1" is described as "traditional rigorous research, completely self-referential, and focused only on researchers' questions and answers," while Mode 2 is described as "knowledge production requiring interdisciplinary teamwork among scholars and users, rather than closed end inbreeding research."[7] As might be guessed, these definitions are from critics of Mode 1 who have set it up as a straw person; there is virtually no management research in health care or economic research in the field that is not motivated by some external need or puzzle. However, there are varying degrees of collaboration with users, for reasons such as conflict of interest and user bias toward implemented programs that we have discussed earlier in this book. It seems clear that what is needed is a "Mode 1.5" where the desires of users are internalized by the researcher and the researcher's skepticism and preference for rigor are appreciated by users – the right mixture of mutual respect, arms-length but effective cooperation, and (most important) effectiveness in ultimately producing change that does more good than harm would be ideal. It may be no surprise that at present this model is the least common of the three.

We might distinguish the two paths just outlined as basic and applied evidence development, and it appears that the approach to progress and leadership differs in important ways between the two. When this difference is not taken into account, past studies have found that a "Valley of Death" opens between discoveries in new concepts and evidence that support a new hypothesis and application of those discoveries to meet the needs of large populations.[8] In biomedical science, there have lately been considerable resources devoted to translational research that is supposed to bridge the valley (where evidence for success is not yet available), but for innovations in the management and organization of care, there has so far been even more neglect. What might be done?

At the core, traversing the Valley of Death for management science involves overcoming two key issues that undermine knowledge transfer

---

[7] Huff, A. S. (1999). Presidential address: Changes in organizational knowledge production 2000. *The Academy of Management Review*, 25(2), 288–293. Available online at: www.jstor.org/stable/259014; De Frutos-Belizón, J., Alcázar, F., and Sánchez-Gardey, G. (2019). Reviewing the "valley of death" between management research and management practice. *Management Research Review*, 42(8). Available online at: www.emerald.com/insight/content/doi/10.1108/MRR-02-2018-0096/full/html

[8] See, for example, pages 10 and 54 of Rea, P. A., Pauly, M. V., and Burns, L. R. (2018). *Managing Discovery in the Life Sciences: Harnessing Creativity to Drive Biomedical Innovation*. Cambridge, UK: Cambridge University Press.

and implementation. As described by Debra Shapiro, the Clarice Smith Professor of Management and Organization at the University of Maryland, the issues are "lost before translation" or "lost in translation."[9] Academics and health care administrators live and function in largely separate worlds. Research studies designed in isolation of practitioners may have inherent impracticalities that make implementation not feasible. Further, results presented in forums or with unfamiliar language or terms make even the most relevant discoveries inaccessible to practitioners. The chasm is exacerbated by the lack of incentives for or experience by health care administrators for applying management research and evidence-based decision-making. Therefore, it should not come as a surprise that "knowledge transfer" to management rarely occurs, with a resultant opportunity loss for application of research to solve health care challenges.

How Have Management Scholars Responded to Traversing the Rigor-Relevance Valley of Death?[10]

Since the introduction of EBMgt, there has been much discussion among academics about *how* to bridge the rigor-relevance gap. To our knowledge, none has focused on health care management; however, a 2015 study examined publication practices in academic- and practitioner-oriented journals from 1961 to 2010 and found that management scholars compartmentalize (we assume this applies to health care management scholars). They primarily publish in academic or in management publications, and the few who write in both types of journals limit mentions of theories or scientific methods in their more applied publications. In fact, these more practically oriented publications are rarely grounded in their science and overwhelmingly are written by managers later in their careers.

The articles that address the rigor-relevance gap mostly refer to the need to translate the research results for those in the field and to include practical implementations of the findings. However, while publications increasingly allow (or require) "implications for practice" sections, publications do not require (and few if any include) the presentation of actual application to practice and its evaluation. The irony is that neither the

[9] Shapiro, D. L., Kirkman, B. L., and Courtney, H. G. (2007). Perceived causes and solutions of the translation problem in management research. *Academy of Management Journal*, 50(2), 249–266.

[10] Bullinger, B., Kieser, A., and Schiller-Merkens, S. (2015). Coping with institutional complexity: Responses of management scholars to competing logics in the field of management studies. *Scandinavian Journal of Management*, 31(3), 437–450.

editor nor the reviewers of these scholarly manuscripts, including the section on "implications for practice," are actual managers who are able to evaluate the practicality and relevance of the recommendations.

In contrast, the few scholars who conduct applied research do so with a basic science, theory-driven approach, rarely applying the principles of action-oriented, EBMgt or participatory research. In fact, further irony exists around the discussion of this type of research: it largely occurs in academia with little involvement of practitioners. Further, as these practitioners do not read the scholarly literature, they might not even be aware of this oversight. Therefore, practitioners turn to journals aimed at them (e.g., *Harvard Business Review*), attend conferences where noted management scholars give talks, subscribe to services that claim to distill the evidence, and hire consultants.

HOW ORGANIZATIONS ATTEMPT TO UTILIZE EVIDENCE: CONSULTING, SUBSCRIPTION SERVICES, AND CONFERENCES

In this section, we describe what we know about outside evidence available to organizations and especially the evidence base of advice provided by external consultants. We explore what consultants describe and present as external evidence, little of which reaches even the lower levels of evidence used for clinical decision-making – both based on substance and specificity of recommendations, potentially leading to suboptimal decisions and making it more likely that firms reject rigorous health services research in factor of internal sources. We will argue three propositions:

(1) Currently, decisions based only on consultants' views (to be characterized more below) can lead health care administrators to waste resources and time that could have been better spent on innovations likely to work.

(2) Reliance on this kind of outside advice may also displace the use of plans that are supported by evidence.

(3) Most important, if efforts were made by consultants and/or organizations to generate better evidence for innovation than what so far has been supplied by these external sources, there is a high potential for discovery and subsequent implementation of innovation that will have a beneficial effect on outcomes and spending growth.

Consultants

The Use of Rigorous Evidence by Consultants
We first explore whether and to what extent rigorous evidence (ideally based on RCTs and published in peer-reviewed journals) is used by

consultants. We first examined a number of textbooks used to educate future consultants (e.g., *Flawless Consulting: A Guide to Getting Your Expertise Used* by Block and Nowlan).[11] Most of the material in those textbooks deals with interactions with actual and potential clients – how to acquire them, what to ask them, and how to frame recommendations they will find useful. There is some instruction on how to obtain and treat "the data," but virtually all of that text refers to client-specific data on outcomes, problems, bottlenecks, and production processes more generally. The idea is that the data can help to tell the consultants about the firm and its operations. What then? The consultant is supposed to use the data to identify problems and solutions for the client. That process is not described in detail, but it is not one in which client data are compared to models in the literature or projections of effective solutions are based on the literature. Instead, external information is largely limited to the consultants' knowledge of best practices and how those compare with what the client is doing.

In summary, consultants are not advised to consult rigorous evidence on how to diagnose or treat a client's problem, but instead to rely on client data and interviews combined with the consultant's own judgment and expertise to develop common sense solutions. How is evidence used in practice? Here we consulted (!) some experienced consultants to see what they thought was typical practice.

Evidence on the Outcomes Resulting from Consultant-Informed Decision-Making

Whatever use consultants make of evidence, there is a more fundamental question of whether using consultants as decision aids helps health care administrators make decisions with better outcomes than using alternative measures, such as internal opinion and evidence. Not surprisingly, there has been little investigation about whether consulting makes a difference (or even a good one) compared to its absence. This is largely because the use or nonuse of consultants by health care administrators is not randomly assigned to different settings – those managements choosing to use consultants might be more skilled or, alternatively, facing worse problems than average, so attributing causation is difficult. There have been no RCTs or quasi-experiments, and before and after studies are plagued by

---

[11] Block, P., and Nowlan, J. (2010). *Flawless Consulting: A Guide to Getting Your Expertise Used*, 3rd edition. San Francisco: Pfeiffer.

confounding bias in which apparently positive results might have happened even in the absence of intervention due to other unmeasured cooccurring changes.

Consultants: Some Views and Observations and a Path Forward

In conversation with leading consultants, we learned, not surprisingly, that there was a gap between what they would regard as ideal (or at least good) and what actually happens. To begin with, consultants do not aspire to the quality of evidence required for approval of an innovative drug by the FDA or even by the lower levels of evidence-based clinical care, nor do they seek evidence to establish that, with very high probability, a change will be safe and effective. Instead, tolerance for what will be viewed as ex post bad outcomes is fairly high, not because harms are ignored, but because they're assumed to be inevitable (at some rate) given the resources applied to making the management recommendations (e.g., limits to the research phase, reliance on expert opinion, no or limited pilot testing or evaluation) and the nature of management decisions. The consultant report is used as a guide, rarely as an executable, approved plan that evolves with experience in the field; rather, the corporate sponsor uses the report as an input to finalizing a proposed plan that will likely be modified (cost-cutting, scope reduction, etc.) by leaders, Board members, and colleagues charged with implementation.

Consultants largely seek and rely on the two lowest levels of evidence: case series and expert opinions based on nonsystematic reviews – in other words, know how. They do not seek RCTs of management innovations, both because few exist but also because their clients are skeptical that such results generalize to their specific situations, such as patient populations and behavior, provider actions, costs, and need for timely action. Consultants rarely seek formal evidence that some intervention actually does have similar effects in a wide variety of circumstances; instead they are sympathetic to the view that "it won't work as well here," and try to some extent to modify evidence-based interventions for the particular circumstance a client believes to be important, whether modification is needed or not. They seek to offer the appearance of bespoke tailoring even for off-the-rack programs.

Rather than relying on primary, rigorous literature, a main source of information for consultants is management magazines, such as the *Harvard Business Review* or *Modern Healthcare*, which provide less rigorous summaries, discussions of innovations and their causes, effects, and future prospects. The strongest endorsement for an innovation is that other firms, especially those thought to be leaders, are doing it. How bandwagons traveling in harmful directions are brought to a stop is unclear, since the reinforcing nature of wrongful beliefs can put off evaluation and negative conclusions.

Another way consultants frame the results of the evidence that they present is as so-called best practices. When the list of best practices is more than opinion (relying on some sense of the wisdom of crowds), their evidence to support the superiority of one model or strategy over another is often not rigorous. Our observations of lack of rigor behind best practices concurred with conclusions from research on consultants from a decade earlier by German management professors, Wellstein and Kieser. Interviews with management consultants revealed neither agreement on methods nor on the transferability of best practice recommendations. They concluded that "best practices are mere marketing constructs of management consultants."[12]

When consultants pursue a data-driven approach to best practices, the typical model examines a number of actual practices and then advocates zeroing in on those practices that seem furthest away from average or from some arbitrary outcome standard – rather than on trying to understand the determinants of variation. Homegrown scoring systems involving patient satisfaction are common, as is examination of trends in volume or revenue by service line nationwide. Consultants then try to interpret or project these trends, but not in any formal way.[13] In contrast, the more rigorous evidence-based approach outlined in Chapter 3 would review the research literature on the subject, take account of the rigor of each study, and present the array to the decision-maker without an arbitrary attempt to combine or summarize. This approach requires more management effort and attention – so the final evaluation of using consulting versus using an alternative should itself be evidence-based, as we will discuss later.

There is a distinction between management practices that are common and repeated (where evidence is easy to find and often easy to analyze) and unique decisions (such as on novel policies) where we have targeted our attention. These more challenging innovation decisions have more potential for unintended consequences (because they have not been

---

[12] Wellstein, B., and Kieser, A. (2011). Trading "best practices" – A good practice? *Industrial and Corporate Change*, 20(3), 683–719. Available online at: https://academic.oup.com/icc/article-abstract/20/3/683/676012

[13] Block, P., and Nowlan, J. (2010). *Flawless Consulting: A Guide to Getting Your Expertise Used*, 3rd edition. San Francisco: Pfeiffer.

documented), and it does not appear that consultants are useful for these. Our sample of innovative institutions uses consultants for benchmarking and employs internal teams to evaluate innovation.

More thoughtful consultants have, for obvious reasons, commented on and tried to influence management decision-making processes but often ground their recommendations in their personal experience while rigorously obtained evidence does not play a major part of their toolkit. They also train leaders but do not place much emphasis on how leaders should acquire or judge information, beyond the common sense idea that clear presentations with clear graphics are good for both buyer and seller.

Source of Evidence: Subscription Summaries and Conferences

Beyond consultants, health care administrators and executives turn to subscription services that summarize the field. We explored two of the most common referenced: The Conference Board and The Advisory Board.

The Conference Board
The Conference Board sponsors conferences and provides its own policy notes, mostly on issues of growth of the economy, labor markets, and the federal deficit.[14] Conversations with a leading health care administrator revealed that he uses their advice on evidence about health care innovations, but this information is not widely available: there are no public sources or examples. Summaries of available conferences cover only the opinions of speakers at the conference without sourcing or validating the accuracy of their assertions. For example, the 2019 conference asserted, without citation, that "today's employers realize they have the opportunity to change the climate of fear … through resiliency training and other services." The summary continues by advising employers that "when it comes to wellbeing, address the whole person. Employers know the outcomes of every aspect of an undesirable life and how they [sic] translate to physical wellbeing." In yet another example, summaries speak to the use of technology to control diversity as follows: "Employers face a bigger challenge to get employees to engage. Technology is now playing an important role in connecting with a fragmented team" by "reducing barriers to use of the communications plan and targeting email messages encouraging teamwork and tolerance."

[14] The Conference Board. Available online at: https://conference-board.org/us/

The Committee for Economic Development of the Conference Board did publish a 2015 paper on controlling medical costs, diagnosing the reason for rising cost as "no one has an incentive to provide quality, cost efficient care, and there is no meaningful competition." It thought that "the Obamacare Exchanges are the key to true health care reform; they force competition among insurers and providers to deliver quality of care at the lowest possible cost." This prediction so far has not been fulfilled, perhaps because less than four percent of the population uses the Exchanges.

The Advisory Board

Probably the most highly respected and most evidence-based source of information for consultants and health care administrators has been the work of The Advisory Board (AB)[15] (at least up until its sale and reorganization in 2018). Here we describe the role of evidence in its overall activities and then focus on a specific topic discussed earlier in the book – the way to manage patient transitions from hospital to home.

The published advisories, reviews, and updates from the AB have as their main purpose (and their name implies) providing actionable advice to health care administrators on innovations and trends in health care delivery. Evidence to support recommendations comes from a variety of sources and is often summarized without being comprehensively annotated. Much of the information is on programs undertaken by specific organizations, usually written as anecdotal case examples from AB clients or advisory committees. The bulk of this information is descriptive, outlining the problem to be addressed and the actions taken to deal with it. Often the descriptions are prospective, and when there is evidence of effects, it is of the before-and-after nature, not RCT-based evidence. The AB also surveys its clients and contacts (e.g., 80 hospital systems) to provide benchmarking data. Nonresponse proportion is not provided. These surveys are presented as evidence on what are common trends and what is uncommon (if not reported by respondents).

Sometimes published literature, including but not limited to peer-reviewed articles, is either summarized overall or abstracted. The AB does not do meta-analyses but does summarize them when published summaries are available. Most published studies of management interventions are not themselves RCTs but may have before-and-after or comparison groups. Government data (e.g., Bureau of Labor Statistics data on

[15] Advisory Board. Available online at: www.advisory.com/

physician incomes) or other public data (surveys by provider organizations) is also used, but rarely.

In some situations (e.g., recommendations on immunizations), evidence is graded according to its quality, and when RCTs are not available, the best available quality evidence is used. As a result, recommendations by the AB should be viewed with caution. In fact, the link between the content of advice and specific evidence is often not presented, suggesting hunches/common sense in favor of rigorous grounding.

Case Study: How Strong Is AB Evidence?

There is no study of what difference, if any, AB consulting advice makes to organizations' behavior. It is commonly bought and cited (including by scholarly journals).[16] It is not known whether it is used to shore up support for decisions that would have been taken anyway or whether it sometimes changes the direction of decisions. Compared to no evidence, it seems that this kind of compilation of logic and cases would be helpful, but we do not know what the relevant alternative source of evidence and model of decision-making would be.

Premise: The AB is supposed to provide best practices in consulting and in evidence-based consulting.

In order to examine the quality of AB-recommended best consulting practice, we reviewed how the AB addressed the question of how to manage patients discharged home from hospital as discussed in Chapter 5 by Naylor and Werner.

The AB developed a white paper for its clients (available by subscription only) intended to summarize evidence on ways to improve transitional care. The paper offers advice to hospital health care administrators on steps to take for the best transitional care.

Our evaluation: The discussion is far too broad and the recommendations are not actionable.

The review of the published (some peer-reviewed) literature is weak in being both incomplete and relying on dated work (from 2006). Much of the reviewed literature is case-study material only. It ignores some core components of transitional care, such as the need and methods for risk assessment at intake and how to achieve care continuity. It does not even

---

[16] Sorenson, C., Japinga, M., Cook, H. et al. (2020) Building a better health care system post-covid-19: Steps for reducing low value and wasteful care. *New England Journal of Medicine Catalyst.* Available online at: https://catalyst.nejm.org/doi/full/10.1056/cat.20.0368

classify the components needed for transitional care, let alone provide effectiveness or cost-effectiveness information on them.

The white paper is an assortment of citations with superficial summaries: "abstracts of abstracts." There is no detail on how different models work; a decision-maker need not know all the operational parts of a model but needs either to know enough for credibility or have evidence on effectiveness. Not present are any comments on the relative reliability or rigor of different conclusions or opinions. The paper provides is a well-organized story – but with insufficient support in terms of analysis or evidence to determine if it is true, or how likely it is to be true.

However, the document sounds authoritative and has excellent graphics. It avoids jargon, has understandable writing, and is not technical. As such, it is a first-rate presentation of second-rate data and analysis.

The AB does offer a suite of analyses of major care management innovations (e.g., patient-centered medical homes, transitional care programs). We focus on their information on managing care transitions from hospital to community. Based on our reading, the summary of the peer-reviewed evidence is accurate, though citations to the literature are not complete. The problem is that the evidence, even when rigorous, is usually not conclusive enough to generate advice for what intervention to choose when. Almost all included studies (with some exceptions) compared programs using patient advocates, phone apps, or specially trained nurses (who provided some counseling on discharge and some informational literature with attempted followup phone call) compared to usual care and found improvements, especially in avoiding readmissions. However, there is no conclusive evidence on which intervention is better or more cost effective and how best to implement the interventions. As a result, the advice from the AB is fairly generic (e.g., make some contact with patients, develop a care team of unspecified composition, and have it work well). Finally, many studies cited are not high quality. Individual organizations will believe (perhaps correctly) that their situations are unique and advice cannot be organization-specific. There has not yet been much evidence to support innovations that promote improvements across the board, in a variety of settings (unlike a drug that works equally well for different patients).

Subscription Summaries and Conferences: Some Views, Observations, and a Path Forward

We then wonder what value subscription services provide to decision-makers and how they rely on it. One good outcome is that these summaries introduce concepts and stimulate further investigation by an organization still doing standard practice discharge instructions, and could be used to justify some action (almost any action) a manager had chosen anyway.

What is the problem? For those who want to go further, the underlying research evidence is not accessible to administrators, and these services do not enable that access. As described earlier in this chapter, even if the administrators had access to the original publications, they are not skilled in reviewing evidence. Further, rigorous research is rarely conclusive and more often than not shows what does not work while the administrator needs a path forward to advance on what does work.

Consultants could better bridge this gap (we hope) but do not. They could be held accountable for the rigor of their summaries (by subjecting them to peer review) and for evaluating the robustness of their recommendations (and reporting errata on advice that is not actionable or does not work).

To make advice more useful, the AB will usually offer a checklist for organizations to decide if some innovation "is for them." Some of the checklist contains nostrums, such as whether the organization can implement well and whether it can take a "holistic" view on return on investment – which seems to mean waiting sufficiently long that benefits such as medical staff satisfaction or patient loyalty can be counted as returns along with financial gains. Firm-level RCTs are not advocated, and the possibility or impossibility of specific testing in the organization is often invoked. Common sense, caution, and putting the burden on the organization for execution (with poor execution as a rationale for observed failure) is common.

In this section, we demonstrated that sources of external evidence, when used by leaders to guide health care decision-making, is often weak: operational/benchmarking data, best practice, incomplete and, at times, outdated. As consultants and subscription services will likely remain key sources that inform the decision-making process, these groups should strive to generate more credible evidence, and leaders should be trained in how to evaluate and apply the evidence they receive. However, as evidence might improve the discovery of high potential innovation, the next section demonstrates that a collaborative/action-oriented mindset will be necessary to ensure that these high impact potential innovations will achieve beneficial effect on outcomes and spending growth. For inspiration, we turn to the successful innovation approaches used by technology industries.

LEARNING FROM TECHNOLOGICAL INNOVATION:
ITERATIVE, NOT LINEAR

While many innovation decisions that health system leaders face are idiosyncratic to medicine and nursing, leaders across industries (including health care) face decisions regarding technological innovation. Customer-facing digital technology, as an example, has transformed transportation, shopping and finance where customers have rapid and convenient online access to services. Such innovations have languished in medical care, at least until the necessity of isolation during the novel coronavirus pandemic prompted innovation, as described in the earlier Chapter 9 on telemedicine.[17] Even among highly regulated industries (e.g., finance), issues facing privacy and regulations have been addressed: For over a decade, a debit card can be used to withdraw funds in automatic teller machines around the globe. Therefore, the barrier to digital adoption in health care today is not primarily technical (as robust technology exists), but rather one of culture and decision-making. In this section, we will explore the paradigm of technical innovation adoption and what health care leaders can learn from the action-oriented approach used by technology companies to drive innovation: the discipline of innovation.

As should be obvious, the technological approach is almost always needed, to a greater or lesser extent, to turn new evidence on basic concepts into applications that can scale – and often the key to useful innovation is distinguishing between a curious phenomenon (think Victorian magnetism parlor tricks or the Ether Frolics) and useful modifications (the American electrical grid or painless surgery). It is technological refinement that converts the one into the other. The baseline model employed today, to a considerable extent, picks over evidence that has been generated (often by researchers pursuing their own objectives) to find knowledge nuggets that advance some core theory or a pet technology. The technology development approach, in contrast, actively develops its own evidence with a focus primarily on a need to be filled, rather than a hypothesis to be tested.

One feature essential to technology development is collaboration, formal or informal, both to exchange and develop ideas and to hand off pieces of the development task to the most capable team or expert. Lightbulb

---

[17] Ghafur, S., and Schneider, E. C. (2019). Why are health care organizations slow to adopt patient-facing digital technologies? *Health Affairs Blog.* Available online at: www .healthaffairs.org/do/10.1377/hblog20190301.476734/full/

moments do happen, but even then, the custodian of the insight rarely can see all the way to the end with a useful application. There will be further choices to be made, dead-ends requiring pivots, and failures that end a line of innovation – and technologists realize that no one person will have the vision, knowledge, wisdom, or drive to reach the destination – solving the initial problem or meeting the need.

A key difference in the management of technological innovation versus more traditional management is the goal: solving a problem (e.g., improving access to services) rather than executing on a strategy (e.g., digital transformation). With this action-oriented, goal-directed approach, even if the solution deviates from that originally proposed (or worse, a no-go decision), the improvement or innovation exercise continues. This exercise can be threatening for an academic inventor who has spent a career developing a theoretical foundation and building a solution based on this. When put to the test of the real world, the theory might be inappropriate or flawed or the solution too complex or not acceptable – it takes humility and a willingness to pivot (or abandon a path) to be an innovator. It can also be challenging for a manager who needs a solution yesterday but will need to spend time to create a brand new solution that is not pre-packaged and will require rounds of iteration to optimize the solution to ensure value creation and ability to deliver at scale.

Consider Alexander Fleming's discovery of the mold that makes penicillin. It was literally decades before his overlooked and chance discovery turned into a wonder drug. Fleming himself did not help as he continued to try to use the small amounts of the material he could produce as a topical skin treatment. It required a combination of events for the discovery to become a breakthrough drug: serendipitous rediscovery of Fleming's breakthrough, the case for and resources generated by the need for an antibiotic for troops during World War II, and the discovery by American agricultural biologists that the mold could be grown in quantity in a corn-based liquid. Successful drug development also required the leadership of scientists and health care administrators eager for and pressured to help in the war effort and wanting to further their careers. More recently, consider the decades-long dismissal of mRNA vaccines that now are a highly effective tool against COVID-19.[18] For how many discoveries have we missed their application?

[18] Garde, D., and Saltzman, J. (2020). The story of mRNA: How a once-dismissed idea became a leading technology in the Covid vaccine race. *Statnews*. Available online at: www.statnews.com/2020/11/10/the-story-of-mrna-how-a-once-dismissed-idea-became-a-leading-technology-in-the-covid-vaccine-race

Technology also recognizes two paths to solution-finding that are distinct but not mutually exclusive. As the engineer-decision scientist W. Brian Arthur of the Santa Fe Institute notes, progress involves both totally new insights (the often-mentioned paradigm shift) and technical or technological improvements on ideas already sketched out but not immediately applicable.[19] We benefit both from good new ideas and from making them better – and often there is synergy between the two as the quest to implement turns up puzzles that themselves require new ways of thinking. Herein lies one of the greatest strengths of technology development: continuing to evolve as new subproblems are revealed, which then leads to piecing together solutions through adaptation and invention. As described previously in this chapter, health care leaders often reject peer-reviewed solutions because their situation is unique. Technologists, on the other hand, recognize that all problems have peculiarities; however, they start by looking for commonalities in order to apply proven solutions and reduce the complexity of the problem – and innovate only when necessary.

PROCESSES FOR CROSSING THE VALLEY OF DEATH

As noted above, the technological innovation approach begins with a clearly defined unique need or problem to solve for which there is no available solution. This is not the only necessary condition – there also has to be some idea that novel technologies exist that could meet the need. With a provisional solution in hand, the innovation team then must confront the often more daunting task of crossing the valley from idea to implementation. Every idea is different, and the cast of characters is different. Innovative organization recognize the need for flexibility and do not dictate complex, rigid paths. Rather, they adapt successful frameworks and processes to the problem/context and continue to adapt along the way according to the stage of development.

Successful processes exist to guide the development of discoveries into improvements (Lean, IHI-QI from the Institute of Healthcare Improvement) and innovations (Lean Startup).[20] The models start with

[19] Arthur, W. B. (2009). *The Nature of Technology: What It Is and How It Evolves*. New York: Free Press.

[20] Institute for Healthcare Improvement n.d. About Us. Available online at: www.ihi.org/about/Pages/ScienceofImprovement.aspx; Kenton, W. (2019). Lean Startup. Investopedia. Available online at: www.investopedia.com/terms/l/lean-startup.asp

defining and validating the identified need (empathize and define) in the form of a problem statement: the current state, the future state, the gap that prevents achieving the future state, and the proposed mechanism by which the proposed solution addresses the gap with associated process and outcome metrics. So-called PDSA (Plan-Do-Study-Act) or sprints involve a series of techniques for design and evaluation. At each stage, the evidence base grows as subproblems are identified, addressed, and tested; future investment occurs once predetermined success metrics are achieved. At each stage, the goal is revealing hidden challenges and addressing them by evolving the solution so that when the solution is implemented it provides value.

While it might be clear that this process involves the complementary skillsets of innovators/researchers and administrators/managers (rigorous methodologies and practical experience), what might be less clear is that spanning the valley has risks for both. The manager who is recognized for decisiveness and experience might lose status if they delay action for data (and worse, if the data proven that their intuition was wrong) while the academic who becomes a promoter or ally to promoters might lose credibility and standing in the research community. Academic clinicians who go to industry or become advocates rarely reengage in their academic scholarship, while the management collaborator who gets bitten by the investigation bug and goes on to head a think tank or foundation might find it challenging to get back into the management game. The process is not perfectly symmetrical; there are more examples of researchers who became successful health care administrators than health care administrators who went on to a distinguished research career. It is important to note that these different paths are not mistakes or tragedies for the people involved; the transformations are often good for them and good for society.

EXAMPLES OF SUCCESSFUL BRIDGING PARTNERSHIPS FOR TECHNOLOGICAL INNOVATION

Bridging the Research-Relevance Gap: An Academic-Government-Small Business Partnership

One example of a successful research partnership[21] involves a state, an academic health system, and a small business spinout of research

---

[21] Walshe, E. A., Romer, D., Kandadai, V. et al. (2020). A novel health-transportation partnership paves the road for young driver safety through virtual assessment. *Health Affairs*, 39(10), 1792–1798.

conducted by a university professor/attending physician at the university hospital. Recognizing that crashes are the leading cause of adolescent death, Ohio legislation identified the need to augment on-road driver testing to identify underprepared drivers and allocated funding for a virtual driving assessment. The academic research team recognized that commercialization of their idea was beyond the scope of their academic pursuits, and testing drivers was not in keeping with the usual practice of the health system. A company was spun out, and the academic remained as a scientific advisor, limiting the involvement in day-to-day decisions but remaining committed to guiding the process to cross the Valley of Death. After winning a competitive application process, the partnership formed, including clear roles, work scopes, and plans. Within three years of the establishment of the partnership, a new virtual driving assessment system was integrated into the licensing work flow, a pilot was completed that involved more than 30,000 virtual driving assessments conducted in parallel with on-road testing (as the gold standard for validation), and a database created that linked driving skills assessed virtually with licensing and crash outcomes. The database is used to inform policy for the state as well as provide a source of data for National Institutes of Health-funded research by the professor. All the while, the small business had the opportunity to grow and expand the model within the state (e.g., to driving schools) and to use this foundational research to drive change in other states and settings.

Bridging the Research-Relevance Gap through a Consortium Model: A National Science Foundation Industry/University Center to Advance the Safety of Children

Industry-academic consortia aim to provide the scientific foundation to solve commonly held problems facing an industry. One model established by the National Science Foundation pools membership fees from industry partners to fund a mutually agreed upon portfolio of projects that both builds the scientific foundation to advance the field and grounds the research in its practical application by the inclusion of industry partners as subject matter experts. The scientific integrity of the researchers is preserved by a neutral external evaluator and by a membership agreement that preserves the right to publish.

One such successful consortium,[22] the Center for Child Injury Prevention Studies (CChIPS)[23] – researches children's injuries and promotes application of the results via science-based interventions, policies, and public education toward injury prevention. In more than 15 years of continuous membership and funding by industry, CChIPS has completed over 100 research projects that led to applications ranging from a new severity algorithm used for triage by trauma centers to new safety products to testing protocols. Five key factors underscore the success of CChIPS: (1) in-person meetings and remote interactions in which each party's interests are heard and served and integrity of the science is maintained; (2) an Industrial Advisory Board comprising industry members who serve their companies as connectors – corporate gatekeepers who have earned respect and have influence over decision-makers in their organizations; (3) formalized operating procedures, goals, and target success metrics that are tracked and shared transparently; (4) established policies about how conflicts and challenges to integrity are handled; and (5) expectations for membership, intellectual property sharing, and conflict and disagreement resolution that are memorialized in formal membership agreements.

APPLYING TECHNOLOGICAL INNOVATION LESSONS TO HEALTH CARE MANAGEMENT INNOVATION

Change to drive health care innovation requires shifts by both academics and management that will lead to better models for conducting research that is useful and usable and better models of leadership that seek and know how to use research in decision-making and innovation evaluation. There is much more to gain, translationally, when academics and health care administrators understand the challenges that each faces while also valuing the benefits that each bring to improve problem definition, solution creation, evaluation and decision-making. However, there is little point in health care administrators disparaging a researcher who wants to remain in the ivory tower or researchers berating health care administrators for failing to advance their brilliant ideas. This translational, collaborative work likely involves a special group of people who are drawn to or in a position (for example a time in their career or membership in an

---

[22] Sun, J., and Winston, F. (2019). Forming and maintaining meaningful partnerships between academic scientists and corporations. *Academic Entrepreneurship for Medical and Health Scientists*, 1(1)(Article 3), https://repository.upenn.edu/ace/vol1/iss1/3
[23] https://cchips.research.chop.edu, accessed 2/9/2021.

organization) that values boundary-spanning work. This is why we saw that applied management research is published more often by tenured faculty members than their junior colleagues.

So what paths might be followed to get a better approach and activity toward innovation in the health care system, to do as much good as the innovation can, and to set realistic expectations about the value that the innovation will bring? In order to go further, faster to address complex needs in health care, both leaders and academics need to adapt their processes.

A PATH FORWARD FOR HEALTH CARE LEADERS: MANAGING INNOVATION

As described above, the innovation process is iterative and involves collaboration among multiple disparate experts and stakeholders. What is key is that no one person possesses all of the creativity or insight to guide the solution development path. Rather than positioning herself as the all-knowing executive, the strong innovation leader directs and supports the process: defining the long-term vision (and maintains it as a North Star): the problem to be solved, what success needs to look like, and how one would know when success is achieved (how it can be measured). While the North Star will remain throughout the process, specific project requirements will change as the team learns and identifies new potential opportunities, risks and subproblems along the way that need to be addressed. This action-oriented approach differs from what is more typical in health care – extensive planning followed by execution deviations minimized from the original plan. Rather, the health care innovation leader must keep the team focused on the North Star end goal of solving the stated problem (as tangents likely will emerge) and be comfortable closing an effort if a dead-end is reached or likely. This agile approach, embraced by technology firms, is more akin to systematic research than to project management: key decisions involve testable hypotheses with the burden of proof placed on the innovation team before leaders allow them to advance. As Arthur describes it, "the process repeats until each subproblem resolves itself into one that can be physically dealt with."

A PATH FORWARD FOR ACADEMICS: CONDUCTING RIGOROUS RESEARCH THAT WILL SOLVE PROBLEMS (NOT JUST GET PUBLISHED)

Far too few academic discoveries become implemented innovations (the basic premise of this book) and many blame the Valley of Death on limited investment in technology transfer. However, ineffective technology transfer can result from misconception of the process as a linear, unidirectional hand-off (from academia to industry). As described above, innovation development is, in fact, iterative, bidirectional, and collaborative. It is rare (if not impossible) for a discovery with potential relevance to health care to be implemented without adaptation.

Therefore, for academics who conduct research with the aim of solving problems in health care, we recommend starting the process of knowledge transfer as early as possible so that the research path can, when possible, accommodate and anticipate the issues that health care leaders will face in developing and implementing the solution. Think broadly about the key stakeholders for the research: people on the frontlines (who have real-world insights into refining the problem statement); decision- or policy-makers (who have practical needs regarding outcomes and thresholds on success metrics that need to be met for relevance); and key influencers (who will identify adoption and implementation issues that need to be considered). The key challenge in effective translational research is to remain committed to rigor while incorporating the input of the frontline users, decision-makers, and policyholders in design of the intervention and its evaluation.

Below are steps that academics can take to span the boundaries of the Valley of Death (discovery to application) without sacrificing their rigorous science:

(1) Assemble a team of collaborators who complement the academic's scientific skills with missing expertise in technology transfer, business development, and implementation/translational science. By remaining part of the team, the academic can provide subject matter and scientific advising, but by delegating the translational tasks to other professionals, the academic can continue to pursue their program of research.

(2) Create and nurture partnerships built on mutual respect: The team the researcher would choose must be the team that would have unanimously voted the researcher as a member.

    (i) Recognize that researchers and health care administrators have different languages, motivations, and rewards – and make an effort to understand and respect the other side.

    (ii) Define roles and expectations for team members: For example, recognize the value of managers on the team and leave project management to them. Focus, instead, on serving as the

scientific advisor by sharing expertise, discoveries, and observations that can advance the project. Recognize and value each
member's personal strengths, maintain humility about limitations and clarity about boundaries.

(3) Ensure that the project team works closely with end-users and
decision-makers to guide the process from start to end:

(i) Frontline staff and/or patients: people with the issue or problem who will eventually benefit from the innovation (key
informants for "go-no go" decisions)

(ii) Decision-makers who have resources or budgetary authority
to support adoption and implementation of the solution
(ideally health care leaders who have a vested interest in the
problem's resolution and, therefore, the innovation's success).

(4) Be transparent with the development and evaluation process, but
preserve independence:

(i) Up front, ask what success looks like. What is sufficient
evidence of sufficient magnitude and sufficient generalizability to move toward a decision to adopt or purchase the
solution?

(ii) Once evaluation protocols are set, the team should pursue
data collection and analysis in isolation of those with a vested
interest until the cake is nearly baked (to preserve independence and minimize bias).

(iii) Share results with the interested parties to gain their insights
and interpretation of results and decide if pivots, spin, or
reframing is needed. (They are often needed because research
almost always yields some aspects of results that are unexpected and inconsistent with a single theme.)

(iv) If the results are positive in favor of change, remind partners
of their commitment to implement.

(v) If the results are negative, don't sugar coat them. Pause and
keep the team members from charging ahead anyway without
modification of the ineffective design. Negative results are an
important time to rethink the project and either pivot or stop.

(vi) Failing fast is the key to successful innovation.

This recipe obviously needs to be adapted to fit the environment. At the
core of this model is mutual respect for and interest in the complementary
expertise that each partner brings to the table and a shared long-term goal/
benefit to collaborating. Just as the academic partner should respect the

corporate partner's expertise in commercialization, the corporate partner should respect the unbiased, credible research methods, analysis, and interpretations that are expected of the academic partner. The academic should be free to publish, regardless of the results, because the partners each share in a goal of solving a problem rather than proving a specific solution.

The Final Word: Challenges that Remain to Using Evidence in Health Care and Insurance Decision- Making

As we noted, especially in fields such as health care management, there is no bright line between basic and applied research, or between paradigm-shifting discoveries and improvement on already known evidence. Here, however, we want to offer some advice on how to make and implement evidence-based breakthroughs and how to avoid bandwagons on the way to dead ends.

There are a number of challenges with using rigorous, evidence-based research to lead to implemented changes, so we may as well get them out of the way at the start.

Frequency. Just as with prescription drugs, there are many promising candidates. For health management innovation, they are ideas for new ways to improve the organization and financing of medical care. Just as in the case of drugs, only a few of them work. It follows that the frequency of implementing evidence-based solutions is bound to be disappointingly low. It is hard to come up with more than a handful of such innovations that have been put in place with demonstrated success. Although there surely are some other good ideas that for various reasons are still in progress, it is unlikely that there are many. So, the bar for effective leadership should be low for what we can expect and high for what we criticize.

Causation. The gold standard for rigorous evidence is the RCT, but it may not be available or preferred because it takes too long or it costs too much relative to the expected benefits from increased rigor, or it is politically or ethically unacceptable. Even RCTs, in practice, suffer from doubt about their estimates of the existence and especially the size of any positive effect, in part because of the problems of selection and attrition of participants. There are substitutes for RCTs that use natural variation, applying statistical methods to establish causation. Those methods require exploring the reasons for the observed variation and finding some influences, such as political or administrative choices to lead to some and not others to be exposed to the innovation. However, sometimes finding such natural experiments is impossible. Some doubt always remains about whether the evidence really does show that X causes Y, and to what extent. The decision model in Chapter 3 tells decision-makers what to do in the case of incomplete evidence, and it implies that some may properly decide to defer and others to go ahead with an innovation depending on their prior guesses and the penalty they face from different kinds of mistakes.

This is as far as we can go with evidence. At this point we hope that many decision-makers will implement innovations with strong evidence and do so in a systematic fashion as described above.

Generalizability. Evidence development and most especially RCTs have to take place in a given context or environment, and there is always legitimate concern about whether evidence for effectiveness in that setting applies in a different setting. Usually (and in contrast to an innovative drug) you cannot just put the innovation in a box, mail it to a different and distant place, and have confidence that it will have the same effect away from the Mother Ship. There are some things that can be done to offer greater assurance on the score of generalizability. For individual characteristics such as race, insurance coverage type, or provider culture, you can try to gather observations from diverse populations or buyers and sellers and test if effectiveness varies across subgroups. To investigate the role of the general environment, you can engage in the somewhat unnatural action of trying to replicate the innovation in a place chosen to be very different from the original site. Here again, at some point, decision-makers will have to take a chance that the innovation will play as well in their home town as it did on Broadway.

Financial feasibility and sustainability. Innovations almost always require new additional resources, at least up front. In demonstrations, these resources are part of the cost of the trial and funded by the sponsors of the trial, but such funding cannot be permanent. As already suggested, leadership can lead to implementation if there is a source ready to make implementation possible for programs that yield net benefit. This means paying for quality or improved health outcomes – and not paying more for undesirable outcomes (such as complications or readmissions). It also obviously means that assuming a source of financing for any innovation for which there is evidence of net social benefit may be somewhat unrealistic. There have to be partners who can be sold on the idea – and commit to keep paying for it.

Intellectual property protection. Although the rules for what constitutes a patentable innovation are complex, it is possible that some discoveries for improving care management, especially if linked to devices or software, may be limited to the discretion of a patent holder. Innovations with greater intellectual property protection diffuse less extensively than ones that can be copied without restriction. Although in principle there should always be some possible agreement that would permit diffusion of cost-effective innovations, the transactions costs and delays of negotiation may affect implementation.

Size. There are many innovations that can produce improvements in outcomes or reductions in cost that are significantly different from zero but are, unfortunately, small in magnitude. Small buckets are worthwhile, but are not impressive next to an ocean. This jejune observation does not rule out the chances of gaining by small steps, but it does mean that, to make it to the big time, innovations either need to have rather large effects or somehow be a way of organizing or incentivizing many small steps over the long run. Something that lowers medical spending of middle-income people by 40 percent (such as patient cost-sharing compared to free care) or something that cuts the cardiovascular death rate by XX percent (such as statins) at least gains attention (though it may have other side effects). A program of innovation in a health system that uses small steps but leads to a large increase in market share (because the system is cheaper and better than others in town) can also be a vehicle for adopting an innovation.

With these challenges in mind, what can we say about developing innovations from evidence on changes in payment and organization that can lead to implementation and success? All of the advice already listed for technological innovation and engaging (and tying down) stakeholders before the evidence is collected apply here, as do the cautions about keeping roles distinct. We have already noted the low expectation of success from a given effort for managerial innovations in payment and organization – and stakeholders need to be on board with that. What is probably most important is to create a team of decision-makers who are willing to take a chance on an innovation when there is evidence that it works, and willing to go against the tide when evidence shows that something popular among peers is not working.

12

Concluding Chapter

All Authors

INTRODUCTION

In this book we have provided information on how evidence is used or ignored in decisions about innovations by leaders of health systems and health insurers and by public health policymakers. This "evidence on evidence" – information about the use of evidence on nonclinical interventions – is voluminous, but with many gaps. Sometimes the evidence is encouraging about effective interventions, but often it is discouraging with nothing new found, and it is always suggestive but certainly not conclusive on processes, methods, rules, and policy interventions that might lead to health care improvement from the status quo. We are honest about this ambiguity because this study of evidence revealed the lack of rigor in health care managers' decision-making – but it also revealed some unavoidable costs and delays of seeking perfect evidence. The book, then, is not only a wake-up call, but also a call to action toward a culture of change in how health care and health insurance leadership deal with the science that supports innovation.

We began the discussion in the first three chapters, leading to a goal statement, a postulate, and a caution. We assumed the "improvement" that health care and insurance management strive for has the aspirational goal of improving the quality and outcomes of care, promoting access for as large and as diverse a population as feasible, and controlling health care costs. We postulated that decisions are, on average, likely to lead to better outcomes when they are based on better evidence. But we cautioned that evidence alone might not be sufficient to reach or even make major progress toward the aspirational goals. The Iron Triangle[1] that describes

---

[1] Kissick, W. L. (1994). *Medicine's Dilemmas*. New Haven, CT: Yale University Press.

unavoidable resource constraints – on physical resources financing and willingness to pay, and on managerial time, imagination, incentive responsiveness, and skill – will necessarily leave us short of our goals and perhaps not so far advanced from the starting point. Managers need to see what the real prospects are and not assume them, and they need to see what the real constraints are and not assume them away.

In this chapter, we discuss what the "evidence on evidence" means for two key groups: managers of health delivery systems and health insurers on the one hand, and public policy decisionmakers in government on the other. We provide this information in two parts: (1) the evidence we found on decisions about innovations in health care and insurance management and how that evidence has been used, and (2) whether there is a case for some change in the type, volume, and use of evidence that either policy makers or managers ought to bring about. In our introductory chapter, we noted that Obama Administration policy leader Cass Sunstein strongly advocated that government should make more use of evidence in its decision-making than it currently does. The essays in this book provide conclusions regarding underuse, misuse, or overuse of evidence in decisions on innovations in care management and insurance. For example, Medicare's Hospital Readmission Reduction program may have suffered from underuse of evidence, many models of payment reform misuse evidence on the effects of incentives, and perhaps even the FDA requires waiting too long for evidence of little marginal impact. The essay writers also consider whether there are some changes in public policy that would improve overall cost and health outcomes.

WHAT WE FOUND

Chapter 2 showed that the performance of the US medical care delivery and insurance systems, public and private, has failed to demonstrate desired improvement in cost containment and/or health outcomes. The aspirational goals we all share have not been achieved.

Some aspects of health outcomes and health spending are determined by influences beyond formal medical care and beyond what health systems or health insurers can directly influence. The quality of the environment, the uneven distribution of income and wealth by education, race, and location, and behavioral choices all cause health outcomes to be worse than they would otherwise be. The high wages paid to health professionals and the high profits of suppliers of drugs and devices make spending higher than it would be if wages were suppressed and profits constrained. That said, health care decisionmakers can, hypothetically, put in place changes that do more good than harm in producing cost-effective outcomes if they have rigorous evidence on what those changes are.

However, there may be only a few feasible ways to produce improvement for all while containing cost. But the possibility is worth exploring: Are there innovations supported by good evidence that can achieve both health improvements and cost containment? To summarize our answers to that key question, we split the analysis into two parts: what rigorous evidence exists (or could be found) that impacts decisions on innovations, and what use have managers made of that evidence (or other factors) in deciding on innovations? In the latter category, we include as evidence both a manager's own past experience and instincts or feelings that developed over a career.

What Is Evidence? Where Is There Evidence?

There are no decisions in life that are made with perfect evidence. Indeed, if evidence could be perfect, it might not even be proper to call the action a "decision." However, in the areas of health care management and payment, we found variation in the amount and type of evidence available. The most promising examples of positive evidence were in ways to manage the transitions of patients from hospital to home, and ways to reduce disparities in effective care for disadvantaged populations. At the other extreme, for physician-hospital relationships, use of consultants, and insurer payment of suppliers of medical care, there seems to be a relative paucity of evidence-based innovative ideas in reserve that are ready to go. Between these two poles, there are more promising but as yet unsupported innovations in information technology (specifically telemedicine/telehealth) and patient-provider behavior that may eventually cross the evidence-based threshold – but have not yet.

The Use of Evidence by Managers

Innovations that managers have thus far chosen to implement in care delivery, organizational structure, provider payment, and insurance design have rarely had evidence to support their effectiveness, and worse, many of these innovations have wasted resources. While there have been some successes in innovations in care delivery and payment change (managed care, diagnosis-related group payment), a large number of innovations that have been put in place over the decades were not supported by rigorous evidence of effectiveness for health outcomes or cost effectiveness before being introduced; these innovations also did not generate such evidence after implementation. Sometimes they would then fade away – but not always or not permanently. The long list of so-far failures includes coordinated care, hospital-physician partnerships, patient-centered medical homes, worksite wellness programs, value-based payment to providers for medical conditions and services, and many others. The reasons for investing time and effort in such innovations include surface plausibility, observations that similar providers were implementing the innovation, a sentiment that "something needs to be done," and reliance on anecdotes or observed before-and-after experiences with small sample sizes. There is evidence or suspicion that some innovations may have harmed health (e.g., Medicare Hospital Readmission Reduction Program). Regardless of the reasons, however, the main adverse effect of proceeding without good evidence is the wasting of scarce resources, including skilled worker time that might have produced more benefit, either within or outside the health care and health insurance systems, had decision-makers acted on good evidence.

There is a somewhat shorter list of innovations with rigorous evidence of effectiveness for improved outcomes and cost containment that have often not been put in place. In this book, the best examples are in transitional care and disparities reduction. Usually there is a financial reason that a health system or insurance plan will not implement an innovation with rigorous evidence of effectiveness and cost effectiveness: the system or plan may not be sufficiently reimbursed for the costs or the benefits, especially for improved quality generally or for reduction in disparities. Sometimes the reason for inaction is risk aversion buttressed by concern that any demonstrated effect may not generalize to a potentially different environment, or the absence of foundation, trade association, or executive-level external endorsement of a program.

Implementation of an innovation often proves difficult, especially in settings with insurers. But commonly there is some mismatch between the social benefits from the program and the direct benefits to an individual organization. For example, turnover of membership may discourage an insurer from implementing a cost-effective preventive activity that yields benefits only to the member's next insurer, or a health system may lose profits by reducing hospital readmissions with no reward from the insurer who gains the cost savings. It should in theory always be possible to make a cost-effective intervention mutually beneficial to all parties, but wasted time and administratively costly negotiations and transfers may more than offset the net benefit.

In these cases a redesign of incentives to match payment with benefits and penalties with costs remains the long term goal. In many cases we discussed, health systems incentives could in principle be improved by the use of bundled payment or capitation, but that double edged sword, in penalizing low value uses of resources, also potentially rewards cutbacks in high value but costly services. No one has managed to get the titration right, at least not yet. Insurers, in contrast, are always capitated via a premium, so always have short term incentives to try to manage their costs downwards. But they are impeded by the resistance of providers of care and, longer term, by the simultaneous aversion of insurance buyers to rules which deny them care of value or convenience and to high premiums which happen when there are no rules

For virtually all innovations, there is a gray area in the decision process when the evidence cannot prove an innovation's cost effectiveness with a sufficient high probability to assure success, but it also cannot perform the more difficult task of proving that it is not worthwhile. In the latter case, if the logical argument for the intervention is strong, or if it appeals to intuition – it really does seem like a good idea – health systems and insurers may go ahead. Sometimes they should go ahead, but other times they should wait and either seek or be receptive to new evidence. After the fact, it is hard in individual cases for an external observer to tell whether an organization moved too soon or waited too long – although a batting average on success from a portfolio of innovations can accumulate over time and provide the basis for judging a decision-making process.

WHAT WE WONDER

What reasons are there to explain the pattern just described? Why do managers proceed with innovations when evidence is absent? Are the drivers of their decisions imperfect but persuasive theory (incorrect metaphors, missing side effects)? Pressure to "do something now" coupled with mitigated penalties for mistakes? Overweening pride? When evidence is incomplete, it is trite but true to say that choice is hard. However, some methods or motivations for resolving the uncertainty (and deciding whether or not to wait and seek more evidence) seem suspect from the start, whereas others may be more reasonable ways of coping. Asking consultants for advice, following the crowd, or relying on emotion seem to fall into the suspect category. Examining the logic of the intervention and modelling best and worst cases, conducting pilot studies, learning by doing, or seeking analogous cases may produce better results on average.

Unfortunately, we have to admit that there is very little evidence on the actual effectiveness of different ways of muddling through. There is also little evidence (as opposed to selected anecdotes) about evidence-based interventions that were put in place and found to be effective in slowing spending growth and/or improving outcomes in a perceptible way – either when used in a demonstration or trial or when generalized to the health care system as a whole. It has proven difficult to find many cases of evidence for effective innovations that meet plausible standards of rigor and portability.

Such a record is regrettable but not surprising; in the analogous case of drug discovery, most new ideas promising enough to begin clinical trials fail to show safety and effectiveness sufficient to get US Food and Drug Administration (FDA) approval and make it to market. There is no obvious reason why the failure rate for innovations in health system management or insurance design should be different. In this area, the analog to phase 1 trials is a demonstration project. There does seem to be a difference in expectations – drug candidates are expected to fail much more often than they succeed, whereas demonstration projects are expected to demonstrate success. The Center for Medicare and Medicaid Innovation is a good example of this. With great fanfare, a large number of demonstration projects were launched with very high expectations. We found no evidence of a change in attitude, with more tolerance for or acceptance of failure, in these initiatives to date. Nor did we find evidence for the broader cultural change that would emphasize evidence before initiation, evaluation (after the fact) of whether a change really caused a positive effect or a shift in trend, or direction on seeking information that might lead to improvement.

More fundamentally and tellingly, we do not have evidence that greater use of more rigorous evidence that deters use of unsupported innovations will lead to significant improvements in overall cost containment or care quality. Arguments for the need for greater evidence have the same defect attributed to managerial decision-making. Critics just assume that having rigorous evidence is always a good thing, if not crucial; they assume it will lead to better outcomes than whatever alternative is used in practice – but they offer no proof of this unsupported view, however plausible. Why is there so little recognition of the need for "evidence on evidence"?

Logic would dictate that reliance on rigorous evidence would be associated with improved outcomes; better information in theory should help avoid mistakes. And yet our review of analogous efforts to rely more on evidence in clinical decision-making (evidence-based medicine, Choosing

Wisely) does not demonstrate a gain. We have been stuck in a useless cycle of arguing and recriminating about what is yet to be known.

We did not find a way to determine directly whether managers use evidence in a way consistent with the optimal Bayesian model of Chapter 3, nor did we find that they seek evidence or generate new evidence when and only when its expected benefit is greater than its cost. From the variation we have observed, some managers, health professionals, and insurance marketers and navigators are not doing the right thing, but we cannot say what proportion of organizations are making decisions, or what proportion of decisions are currently being made, in accordance with the evidence. We also cannot say whether too much or too little evidence is being generated and used, given its cost and expected benefit. We cannot come to conclusions because as external observers, we do not know costs in either time or money of applying evidence to adding or removing programs or the probabilities managers use in the Bayesian updating process (if they use that process). We can conclude that evidence is underused in decisions by managers of health delivery and health insurance compared to the FDA model (and may well be underproduced as well). However, we do not know what the right model should be for these decisions (or even if the FDA model, with its delays and bureaucracy, is the right model for decisions about managerial processes and medical products).

While we found and summarize significant material on the use and nonuse of evidence in decision-making, we did not find an evaluation of a model or program for developing and using evidence. More specifically and discouragingly, we did not find evidence that decisionmakers or processes that rely more on rigorous evidence than other managers or processes consistently obtain better outcomes – either because of specific rules requiring evidence or decision-making style. The question therefore remains open – not only with regard to medical care and insurance management, but even with regard to drug approval and clinical medicine.

We did not find evaluations of systematic or programmatic approaches to the development or summary of evidence for use by managers. The Cochrane Collaborative and the Australian model are systematic summarization programs, but clinicians or managers that use them have not been compared to those that do not to see which leads to better outcomes. Further upstream in the process, we did not find evaluations of evidence-generating programs where no evidence previously existed – nor proof that at least in some circumstances, outcomes are better if decision-makers wait for more evidence rather than go ahead with what they have. Here again the question is open – there may be a process, in theory, that improves outcomes by generating needed evidence, but it has yet to be shown.

WHAT SHOULD MANAGERS AND REGULATORS DO? MANY QUESTIONS AND SOME ANSWERS

Do we have the basis for recommending a regulation or suggesting a policy to ensure that innovations that may appear plausible but do not have rigorous support should not be put in place (until they have evidence)? The prototype would be the FDA model. Choosing the lowest-cost treatment option makes sense when cost differences are known with certainty and effective differences in outcomes are so small that not knowing the certainty of this evidence is immaterial. Alternatively, if there is a large enough possibility that the more costly intervention might produce a much improved outcome, we should pursue that option. These rules are obvious for deciding what to do when evidence-based care is unavailable. What about an innovation with an upfront cost that is known to be high but with potential for a large health improvement and/or cost offset? This situation brings us back to the value of information discussion combined with the wish for "lots of luck" for those who go ahead without evidence – as long as they are risking only their own money.

Do we have the basis for recommending a regulation or suggesting a policy that innovations that are supported by rigorous evidence should be put in place and that reimbursement should be changed to support them and managers mandated to use them? Not yet, because we do not have a randomized trial that shows whether and to what extent a decision process bound by such a rule would improve on the status quo. What we can say is that change should be accompanied with the expectation that its impact be monitored (similar to post-marketing surveillance for drugs) and changed if necessary.

Should resources be expended to provide "evidence on evidence" across the spectrum of innovations from new drugs to new insurance arrangements? Can it be shown that using better evidence than what is now used will avoid enough mistakes to offset the cost of obtaining the evidence in terms of real resources and delay? If we are to break out of the current pattern of "fly by the seat of the pants" decision-making combined with Monday morning quarterbacking, the answer is yes. Perhaps an evidence-based health plan could be launched with a specific provision that any savings generated by innovation would be shared with those insured in earlier time periods who paid higher prices – an explicit commitment to share any gains with the insured. This arrangement effectively makes consumers of health care into equity holders – which, incidentally, is the model of mutual insurance. The "Learning Insurance Health Plan" might actually sell.

The idea that innovations could somehow get a "seal of evidence" from external experts as a way to let buyers in a market decide on the value of evidence and of innovations may be a good idea. Such a process might steer innovation away from current patterns and toward other kinds of innovation where the label is more highly valued or more easily generated. Right now, individual consumers, employers who pay for health benefits, or politicians who in principle control government programs do not know which costly innovations have evidence of positive effects; they also do not have evidence on how costly the innovations will turn out to be. An externally generated certification that distinguished the surer things from the wild bets might help these ultimate decisionmakers decide what to do. However, there would also need to be evidence on the effectiveness of even this idea: one stable of experts might do better than another.

So if it is impossible to say whether public policy should compel health systems or insurers to use evidence to a greater extent than current practice, can we explore the potential impact on market share or prices of adopting such a strategy? Would a health system that truly used more evidence and made that practice known be preferred by employers or consumers? Would an insurance plan that used evidence to design its provider reimbursement methods and its coverage/cost-sharing policy to a greater extent than it currently does be able to offer lower premiums, or be more attractive even at higher premiums, than insurers behaving in the customary way? What do we know about the market position of health systems that have adopted evidence-based care, or of insurers that use value-based cost-sharing or provider-payment schemes based on evidence about their effects on costs and quality? The answer so far is that almost nothing is known about how the use, misuse, or nonuse of evidence by health care and health insurance managers contributes to outcomes in terms of cost and quality.

IN SUMMARY

We think that a process of more reliance on evidence by managers in choosing innovations for care delivery or insurance seems like a good idea. Logic suggests that choices made with more high quality evidence (such as randomized trials) rather than less evidence (such as benchmarking) will lead to better outcomes if the additional evidence has little or no cost. Confidence about what to do or which way to go erodes when the cost over time of generating more evidence on real resources is taken into account.

We did not find examples of interventions with high aggregate net benefits supported by evidence being ignored. That is, blockbuster, evidence-based innovations have not been passed over by health system managers. Tautologically, the evidence is less certain on whether innovations with high prospects for large net benefits languished because of lack of evidence, but our review did not find many candidates of this type. Hence, it appears that the main consequence of inadequate evidence is wasting time, effort, and real resources on innovations without proof of effectiveness. The problem is lost money and lost energy, not lost potential quality improvements that would lead to high health gains. There is always hope, but so far the Iron Triangle has meant that prospects for major improvements in care quality, compared to what is currently accomplished by managers, are few. Major cost savings or reductions in spending growth (beyond avoiding waste from chasing poor prospects) may be even harder to achieve.

Still, we do not want to conclude this book with the conventional though true appeal that "more research is needed" on the potential differences in health care outcomes if managers applied more evidence in decision-making than they currently use. To avoid falling into an infinite regress, we need at least to take a stand and say that decision-makers should be transparent about when their decisions are based on evidence (and if so, how much and what kind) and when not (and if so, why not). That information will help users (private and public) of health care and health insurance decide whether they should spend their own or the taxpayers' resources on innovations, and what innovations to choose. Consumers and policymakers should be told when innovations are based on guesswork. This will require a culture change in health care leadership and management in which innovation is seen as a data-driven, systematic process in which leaders make decisions based on the best available evidence, follow their decisions with strong and ongoing evaluations, and seek better evidence when it is lacking. The health care leader of the future will recognize, with humility, that many of their decisions on innovation will fail, but because they anticipated failure, they will be prepared with the evidence needed to inform new innovations that will achieve progress.

Index

Printed in the United States
by Baker & Taylor Publisher Services